THE
BLOOMSBURY
COOKBOOK

Duncan Grant, *The Enraged Cook*, 1912.

THE BLOOMSBURY COOKBOOK

Recipes for Life, Love and Art

Jans Ondaatje Rolls

With 165 illustrations

For my father

page 2: **Detail of the fireplace in Clive Bell's study at Charleston.**
page 5: **Mark Gertler, *Peaches and Green Bottle*, 1931.**

All royalties from sales of *The Bloomsbury Cookbook* will be donated to The Charleston Trust.

First published in the United Kingdom in 2014 by Thames & Hudson Ltd,
181A High Holborn, London WC1V 7QX

This paperback edition published in 2024

The Bloomsbury Cookbook © 2014 and 2024 Thames & Hudson Ltd, London
Text © 2014 Jans Ondaatje Rolls

Designed by Karin Fremer
Illustrated chapter openers designed by Cressida Bell

British Library Cataloguing-in-Publication Data
A catalogue record for this book is available from the British Library

ISBN 978-0-500-29793-3

Printed and bound in China by C&C Offset Printing Co. Ltd

The recipes contained in this book are historical documents and therefore are not as precise as modern recipes, nor have they been professionally tested. Neither the author nor the publishers can assume responsibility for their efficacy, or for the success of the finished dish.

Every possible effort has been made to locate and credit copyright holders of the material reproduced in this book. The author and publisher apologize for any omissions or errors, which can be corrected in future editions.

Be the first to know about our new releases,
exclusive content and author events by visiting
thamesandhudson.com
thamesandhudsonusa.com
thamesandhudson.com.au

CONTENTS

THE CHARLESTON TRUST

It was auspicious that my first meeting with Jans Ondaatje Rolls should have taken place in the kitchen at Charleston, with braids of garlic dangling above our heads, against the backdrop of the plate cupboard luxuriantly decorated with fruit by my grandmother, Vanessa Bell. It is a kitchen that for me holds many memories. Here, as a child, I fought my brother to scrape out Grace Higgens's mixing bowl after she had been cooking her famous 'Grace Cakes', or begged for rock buns. Often, the room was filled with the mouth-watering aroma of sizzling sausages or a roasting leg of mutton. Sam, Grace's battle-scarred tomcat, would be lying in a box beside the Aga. On the other side of the passage lay the dining room where, sometimes, I was permitted to visit my grandparents while they were drinking coffee amid the remains of lunch, laid out on the circular table painted with hoops and swags of grey-green, pink and white. Then 'Nessa', seated in her red Omega cane-backed chair, would give me my favourite treat – a coffee-soaked sugar lump. That was 1960.

Duncan Grant was Charleston's last original occupant, and when he died in 1978 the house itself nearly died as well. Its survival is thanks to the extraordinary efforts of the Charleston Trust, formed in 1980 to acquire, restore and preserve the house, at a point in its history when the building itself was extremely dilapidated, and its wealth of contents was in danger of destruction or dispersal. Under the guidance of Deborah Gage, and with my father, Quentin Bell, as its first Chairman, the Trust raised over £1 million to purchase the house and begin the immensely difficult task of restoration. The structure was consolidated, infestations were combated, and painted surfaces, textiles, furniture and works of art were painstakingly conserved. The garden was restored to its former glory. When the house opened to the public in 1986, the work was praised for being 'one of the most difficult and imaginative feats of restoration current in Britain'.

Twenty-five years later Charleston has become internationally known. Today, despite the more than 30,000 visitors who come to the house each year, Charleston retains a lived-in atmosphere, as if its inhabitants have simply gone out for a walk and will shortly return. Few who visit are immune to Charleston's potent enchantments: its colour, vitality and sense of a vanished world. And yet its future is far from secure. As a trustee of the house, I daily contemplate the fact that we may not have the funds to preserve it for future generations.

Charleston today.

That day in 2009 Jans and I had arranged to meet at Charleston – where else? – to discuss her idea for a book about Bloomsbury food and cookery. No stone seemed to have been left unturned where Bloomsbury was concerned – and yet here, in the kitchen, was an aspect of my ancestry that I had long felt to be under-explored. Five years later, this is the fascinating result: a window onto Bloomsbury via recipes, grocery lists, pantries, kitchens and, above all, dining tables. Jans has written about Bloomsbury food both as a social historian and as a cook, but this very personal meditation on Bloomsbury appetites is also full of humour, insight and unexpected pleasures.

Hugely generous, Jans is donating every penny she earns from this volume to the Charleston Trust. Her book is a treasure trove and a feast – and one that will help, through its sales, to sustain Charleston itself.

Virginia Nicholson
Deputy Chairman of The Charleston Trust

FOREWORD

As a late arrival myself among the chroniclers of the Bloomsbury Group, I know very well how unlikely – indeed, how almost impossible – it is to find anything fresh to say about its members and their celebrated way of life. Bloomsbury is remembered for intellectual and artistic achievement, for sparkling, if malicious, conversation, and for its liberating disregard of social and sexual conventions. Perhaps because of some premature deaths, two of them by suicide, a certain reputation for earnestness and melancholy (what Vita Sackville-West called 'Gloomsbury') has also hung over the group. Laughter and the pleasures of the table are not immediately associated with Bloomsbury, but, as I discovered while researching my biography of Frances Partridge, their gatherings were more often than not hilarious and food and drink were taken seriously and much enjoyed. Now, as I work on a new edition of Dora Carrington's letters, I realize again how important good meals were to her and her circle.

Even so, when I read this marvellous anthology I was amazed. Jans Ondaatje Rolls has indeed found a way to cast new light onto Bloomsbury, not by yet again re-examining their personal or professional lives or analysing their emotions, but by walking into their kitchens and dining rooms, unearthing their cookbooks, trying out their recipes (even the less tempting ones) and, above all, by immersing herself in their writings and paintings. She has followed the scent of cooking through novels, diaries, letters and memoirs, relating every mention of a dish or a meal to a recipe, if not one known to have been available to the writer, then to one of the same period. Her expertise on culinary matters is evident, but it is matched by her knowledge of and sympathy with the characters who devised the dishes and by the glorious drawings and paintings she has gathered to illustrate and complement the text.

So this book is much more than a delightful compendium of Bloomsbury's taste in food. With a light touch and a sympathetic, amused eye, the author provides thumbnail sketches and deft, witty summaries of the people behind the recipes and their complicated relationships. Thus her succinct account of the Ham Spray ménage à trois between Lytton Strachey, Carrington and Ralph Partridge introduces a recipe for Ham Spray Triangles (ham and cod's roe on toast) adapted from the cookbook kept by Ralph's second wife, Frances, until the end of her life. This battered notebook, now expertly conserved in the archives at King's College, Cambridge, has been put to good use by the author,

Vanessa Bell, *Apples*, c. 1916.

in a way that would have amused and pleased its compiler, who herself hardly boiled an egg until the Second World War but thereafter became a keen and accomplished cook.

Above all, however, this book is a happy demonstration of how a gifted writer with a genuine passion for her subject can surprise and inspire. Readers who already know the territory will be richly entertained; those who do not could not receive a better introduction, not just to Bloomsbury's cuisine but also to its curiously enduring fascination. All have many treats in store.

Anne Chisholm

INTRODUCTION

'Theirs was an England largely lost of breakfasts to linger over, "painting lunches", tea at four and dinners to dress for; of fresh vegetables – globe artichokes, new asparagus – sent from country gardens in baskets to town by rail overnight; of pubs serving simple but excellent boiled puddings and steak and kidney pies; and crucially of servants to shop and cook and clean and look after the children.'

Pamela Todd, *Bloomsbury at Home*, 1999

The Bloomsbury Group is familiar to us today as a small, loosely affiliated collection of writers, artists and intellectuals who were dissatisfied with the false values and petty conventions of Victorian male-dominated society. To Bloomsbury members, religion, strict rules of conduct and social duties were not moral imperatives to live by. 'Good' states of mind and the individual's 'truth' and 'happiness' – the watchwords of the Cambridge philosopher G. E. Moore, who helped to inspire the original group at the beginning of the twentieth century – were more appealing and valid ends, which should be pursued and might be achieved. This shared code of ethics unified the group and consolidated its lifelong friendships.

'Lingering breakfasts' and 'painting lunches' were indicative of the civilized way in which the Bloomsbury Group socialized. Conversation was fundamental to their way of life. What better forum, then, for exchanging and developing ideas than the dining table, in a group that included some of the most intelligent and innovative thinkers in the land, such as E. M. Forster, Roger Fry, John Maynard Keynes, Lytton Strachey and Virginia Woolf? They wrote; they painted; they organized exhibitions; they lectured and went about their daily business; but they also made a point of convening regularly to discuss art, literature and philosophy, as well as simply to gossip. They appreciated honest, truthful and intelligent conversation and so spent long hours at the dining table, over fresh, well-prepared dishes, while their servants took care of the needs of their households. As Virginia Woolf explained to the artist Gwen Raverat in 1925:

'Where they [Bloomsbury] seem to me to triumph is in having worked out a view of life which was not by any means corrupt or sinister or merely intellectual; rather ascetic & austere indeed; which still holds, & keeps

Duncan Grant, *The White Jug*, 1914–18.

them dining together, & staying together, after 20 years; & no amount of quarrelling or success, or failure has altered this. Now I do think this rather creditable.'

Despite a profound ignorance of all aspects of food preparation, the members of the Bloomsbury Group were the 'foodies' of their day: enthusiastic about tasty, 'unfussy' dishes and passionate about Côtes de Provence wines and the heady flavours of southern French cuisine, which tied in well with their love of French Post-Impressionism in art. Their servants were sent on cooking courses and provided with the latest 'French-style' cookery books, sometimes with inspired results. Later, after the First World War, Bloomsbury members tried cooking for themselves, and discovered cookery to be to their liking. Helen Anrep, David 'Bunny' Garnett and two or three of the younger members, notably Dora Carrington and Frances Partridge, became excellent cooks. Over 170 original Bloomsbury recipes have been included in *The Bloomsbury Cookbook*.

Here the Bloomsbury story is told in seven broadly chronological chapters, beginning, for example, in the 1890s with 'Before Bloomsbury', focusing on the 1920s with 'An Appetite for Bloomsbury', and finishing up in the very recent past with 'Bloomsbury's Offspring'. Each chapter comprises a series of illuminating narratives, often accompanied by a Bloomsbury quotation, painting, design, sketch or photograph, and most narratives are further enhanced by the inclusion of an appropriate recipe. For example, the narrative for 'Mushrooms with Anchovy Cream' (pp. 37–39) introduces the influence of Moore on the group at the University of Cambridge; and the recipe is taken from *Good Things in England* and is a Cambridge college recipe of the period. Similarly, the narrative for 'Recipe for Bread' (pp. 27–30) describes the unique bond between Vanessa and Virginia Stephen (later known as Vanessa Bell and Virginia Woolf), who were both enthusiastic bread-makers; the recipe is itself taken from the scrapbook of Helen Anrep. All recipes are reprinted as they appeared originally, with grammatical and/or procedural clarifications indicated in square brackets. No attempt has been made to convert units of measurement to modern metric equivalents; for this the reader should consult the conversion table on p. 348.

The Appendix contains many additional recipes sourced from the archives of Bloomsbury's cooks. As for the recipes taken from contemporaneous published sources, it is important to note that recipe books published in the nineteenth century and the early decades of the twentieth century were typically written by the mistress of the house and not by the house cook. These recipes are consequently less precise than would be expected of modern published recipes and should therefore be treated only as guidelines. Although I have tried out most of the recipes in my own kitchen, and made suggestions for the modern cook accordingly, this testing was not systematic and the results cannot be guaranteed. For the reader planning to make any of these dishes for a dinner party or the like, I strongly recommend a dry run beforehand!

Thus, from a stimulating culinary perspective, the Bloomsbury story is revealed. In 'Before Bloomsbury', we visit the unhappy Stephen household at 22 Hyde Park Gate in Kensington, where repressive Victorian conventions, uneasy relationships and personal tragedies determine the future independent attitudes of the Stephen siblings, and where mealtime conversation is stilted, rehearsed and unnatural. We also discover why a new London location – a move to Bloomsbury in 1904 – is crucial to the flourishing of new freedoms and new friendships.

In 'Old Bloomsbury', we meet Leonard Woolf as a young, somewhat rebellious civil servant in Ceylon (and later hear of E. M. Forster working as private secretary for the Maharajah of Dewas in India), taste the piquant flavours of oriental lands, and hear the first murmurings of British colonial unrest. We witness the courtship of Vanessa Stephen and Clive Bell, and of Virginia Stephen and Leonard Woolf, and see how from the outset 'game birds' and 'meals on trays' set the tone for their lifelong communal eating habits. In 1907, Duncan Grant, the talented artist and handsome cousin of Lytton Strachey, enters the Bloomsbury circle and charms his way to their dining-room tables and into their hearts. A few years later, in 1910, a new artistic vision, characterized by bright colours and decorative designs, is introduced by way of Roger Fry, Post-Impressionism and the Omega Workshops that Fry founded in 1913. 'Are you changing with the rest of the world?' Vanessa asks Lytton Strachey – for, indeed, Britain was in the first throes of a revolution. After Virginia's breakdown in 1913 (and, on a cookery course, an ill-fated encounter between her wedding ring and a sticky suet pudding), we understand why a move to the quiet London suburb of Richmond is essential for her well-being, always watched over by her devoted husband, Leonard.

The outbreak of war in 1914 begins 'Bloomsbury in Wartime'. The war catches the group to some extent unawares and precipitates a move out of London, to Wissett Lodge, Asheham House, Charleston and Garsington Manor, where we meet Lady Ottoline Morrell, the artists Dora Carrington (known as 'Carrington') and Mark Gertler, and the writer and food-lover David 'Bunny' Garnett. As conscientious objectors, Bloomsbury's energies are diverted into working on farms and growing fruit, leaving little time for creative expression but enough time for friendships to deepen and triangular love affairs to blossom. In 1917, Carrington and the homosexual Lytton Strachey set up house together at the Mill House in Tidmarsh, not far from Oxford; after the war, Ralph Partridge joins them in a polyamorous ménage. Open relationships suit the Bloomsbury Group's liberal ideology, and although there are jealousies and tensions, not a single friendship founders. Food supplies are limited, but the friends make do with whatever their vegetable gardens and their farmyards are able to provide. Sugar, cheese, butter, margarine and meat are rationed in 1918, but Bloomsbury members continue to meet up for meals and conversation as usual – only now they bring their ration cards. Although chicken is no substitute for turkey, a Bloomsbury Christmas is nonetheless celebrated in 1918 with friends and small gifts. When austerity is finally over and food supplies are replenished, most of the group returns to Bloomsbury, and everyone resumes their pre-war careers.

We now see Leonard and Virginia Woolf purchase their first printing press, and appreciate how typesetting is not only excellent therapy for Virginia, but also the making of their most successful venture together: the Hogarth Press. The Woolfs soon become leading literary publishers and, at Virginia's insistence, they eventually move back to Bloomsbury from Richmond. They also purchase Monk's House in Sussex to be near to Vanessa Bell, who has been living, since 1916, at Charleston with her three children (Julian, Quentin and Angelica), her lover and fellow painter Duncan Grant (Angelica's father), and Duncan's lover Bunny Garnett. Clive Bell visits Charleston at weekends, while John Maynard Keynes (known as 'Maynard') stays for longer periods, sometimes weeks, and writes one of his most important books at Charleston; other Bloomsbury friends pay regular visits too. In 1921, Maynard and the Russian ballerina Lydia Lopokova fall in love, wrecking, when Lydia is present, all semblance of intelligent conversation at the Bloomsbury dining table. But the Keynes–Lopokova marriage proves an exceptionally happy one.

In this period, the 1920s, Bloomsbury is perhaps at its most prodigious, as described in 'An Appetite for Bloomsbury'. John Maynard Keynes is hailed as one of the world's leading economists after predicting that starvation in Germany will be a consequence of the 1919 Treaty of Versailles. Virginia Woolf becomes a Modernist literary phenomenon with her stream-of-consciousness technique – epitomized by the novels *Mrs Dalloway* and *To the Lighthouse* – and also becomes an advocate for feminism with her essay *A Room of One's Own*. In it she states, apropos of the under-nourished women's colleges at Cambridge, 'a good dinner is of great importance to good talk. One cannot think well, love well, sleep well, if one has not dined well.' Lytton Strachey breaks new literary ground in exposé biography with his *Eminent Victorians*, *Queen Victoria* and other books. Roger Fry becomes an esteemed house-hold name in art criticism and design, as do Vanessa Bell and Duncan Grant for their work as modern artists and decorators. The Hogarth Press publishes the most exciting authors of the day, including the Woolfs' friend T. S. Eliot (known to them as 'Tom'). Desmond MacCarthy and Clive Bell become distinguished literary and art critics. The fiercely intellectual (and famously small eater) Saxon Sydney-Turner continues his work at the Treasury. Dora Carrington, who foregoes a brilliant career as an artist to look after Lytton, becomes an excellent cook.

Many of them also travel: Gerald Brenan (a friend of the Tidmarsh ménage) goes to live and write in Spain; Lytton Strachey and many others tour Italy; and virtually everyone goes to enjoy the light and food of Paris and the French Riviera. Travel by the newly available motor car is an especial favourite of the Woolfs. Vanessa Bell and Duncan Grant spend long periods painting in France, and, of course, eating French food. French, Spanish and Italian recipes – not to mention the many Russian recipes provided by Lydia Lopokova – become part of the Bloomsbury way of life, both on the Continent and at home in England, as we discover in 'Bloomsbury and Abroad'. Bloomsbury's travels to Europe introduce them to new vegetables and flavours and a different style of cooking: garlic, avocados, exotic herbs, *daubes* and other novel dishes stimulate their palates and their imaginations. The cooks at Charleston, at Monk's House and in Bloomsbury become competent at providing French cuisine.

The travels, and the exotic eating – often at the choicest London restaurants, such as Boulestin and The Ivy – continue throughout the 1930s. But the clouds are gathering over the fortunes of the group, as chronicled in 'Bloomsbury in Eclipse'. The rise of totalitarian ideologies in Germany, Italy and the Soviet Union are anathema to Bloomsbury's values. Meanwhile, revolution and rebellion escalate in Spain and the Bloomsbury members brace themselves for another international war. There are also deaths in the group: Lytton Strachey in 1932, closely followed by the suicide of Dora Carrington; Roger Fry in 1934; Julian Bell in the Spanish Civil War in 1937; and finally Virginia Woolf, who drowns herself in 1941. Nevertheless, the group continues to celebrate its friendships with good conversation and fine food – right up to the outbreak of the Second World War, culminating in a final summer party at Charleston in August 1939. Then the group itself begins to dissolve; but not its values. These survive post-war through the novels and art of individual members of the group and their offspring, and through their vivid reminiscences, especially the published memoirs and biographies of Leonard Woolf, Bunny Garnett, Frances Partridge, Quentin Bell and Angelica Garnett. In the early twenty-first century, the Bloomsbury Group is even more celebrated than it was in its 1920s heyday.

Between 1904 and 1939, the principal Bloomsbury years, from which most of the recipes in this book are taken, there were profound technological and sociological changes in Britain. The invention of the automobile and the aeroplane not only accelerated the pace of life, but also increased social mobility, cultural diversity and economic productivity. Financial opportunities, particularly for women, improved after the First World War, and for employment women no longer had to rely on their traditional work as domestic servants. Moreover, with the passing of the Equal Franchise Act in 1928, all women in Britain were granted the same political rights as men.

There were changes inside the home as well. The Victorian kitchens of the Bloomsbury members' childhoods – in the Stephen family home at 22 Hyde Park Gate, for example – had been dirty, crowded basement rooms, rarely, if ever, visited by the 'upstairs' inhabitants. 'Who bought the bacon, the butter, the fish? I suspect it was our faithful Mabel. I certainly have no recollection of doing it myself', recalled Frances Partridge in her memoirs. But on the outbreak of war in 1914, all this began to change. With less food about, menus became shorter and less fussy, especially as servants left domestic service to help with the war effort. Widespread use of electricity and plumbing brought the modern kitchen up to speed: age-old coal and wood-burning stoves were replaced by cleaner, easier-to-control gas and electric cookers. Furthermore, by the late 1920s and 30s, electric refrigerators, can-openers and pop-up toasters were beginning to emerge, making food preservation more reliable and food preparation a lot easier. For Bloomsbury members, especially the women, cooking began to become a relaxing recreation. They baked scones and bread, made jams and rustled up simple meals. But a servant or two was still usually on hand to do the shopping, the washing up and any or all of the cooking that was considered uninteresting.

In researching *The Bloomsbury Cookbook*, I perused countless diaries, letters and memoirs searching for references to food – and I was not disappointed. Bloomsbury loved its food, and its members frequently shared their culinary experiences with each other, so finding detailed descriptions of what they ate was not difficult. Sourcing actual recipes was more complicated, however, as none of them had much hands-on experience of cooking before 1915, except for Roger Fry and Bunny Garnett. Fortunately, the recipes of Grace Higgens (née Germany), the cook and housekeeper at Charleston from 1920 to 1971, have been preserved, as have the recipes of Helen Anrep and Frances Partridge, who, by the end of her her long life (she died in 2004 aged 103), discovered the joys of buying 'the bacon, the butter, the fish', herself. Other primary sources include the recipes published by Lydia Lopokova in a London newspaper in 1927, and those Bunny included in his letters to his friend Sylvia Townsend Warner. Angelica Garnett and Bunny's recipes have also been preserved and appear in a small notebook that Angelica began soon after her marriage in 1942. Not all recipes relate to Bloomsbury directly. Many have been sourced from contemporaneous cookbooks and some are my own Bloomsbury-inspired creations.

Over the past four years, I have occupied a world that was not my own, and made friends with artists, writers and intellectuals who died, in most cases, before I was born. In my desire to become more intimate with the Bloomsbury Group, I went to their houses, occupied their rooms, sat at their tables, prepared and tasted their food and read between the pages of their reminiscences to try to feel for myself what it would have been like to have been there at the time. Although this was not possible by any stretch of the imagination, I believe I did achieve an empathy of sorts. I came to understand that Bloomsbury is not merely a district of London once occupied by a group of talented, unconventional and progressively minded friends. It is a living ideology: a belief in the freedom of the individual; a belief in love, truth, hard work and dedication. That is why all the royalties from the sale of this book will go to the Charleston Trust, a non-profit charity 'dedicated to the preservation of the house of the Bloomsbury artists, for the benefit of the public'. For me, Charleston is where the Bloomsbury pulse is strongest, where talent and energy still abound, and where one is reminded at every turn that many of the freedoms we enjoy today exist because of the exceptional vision, self-confidence and determination of the Bloomsbury Group.

Jans Ondaatje Rolls

BIOGRAPHICAL NOTES
ON BLOOMSBURY

Helen Anrep (née Maitland), b. 1885, d. 1965. Wife of Boris Anrep and lover of Roger Fry. She kept a record of her recipes.

Clive Bell (m. Vanessa Stephen), b. 1881, d. 1964. An art critic, he collaborated with Roger Fry on Post-Impressionist exhibitions.

Julian Bell, b. 1908, d. 1937. Elder son of Clive and Vanessa Bell. A promising writer, he died in the Spanish Civil War while working as an ambulance driver for the anti-Fascist side.

Quentin Bell (m. Anne Olivier Popham), b. 1910, d. 1996. Younger son of Clive and Vanessa Bell. Potter, art historian and writer, he chronicled the history of the Bloomsbury Group and wrote a biography of Virginia Woolf.

Vanessa Bell (née Stephen), b. 1879, d. 1961. Artist, designer and 'matriarch' of Bloomsbury, she settled with her children at Charleston in 1916–18. Thereafter it was a holiday home, but from 1939 it again became the main family residence.

Gerald Brenan, b. 1894, d. 1987. Writer who lived in Spain for many years. He fell in love with Dora Carrington, who was married to his friend Ralph Partridge.

Dora Carrington (m. Ralph Partridge), b. 1893, d. 1932. Known to her friends as 'Carrington'. Artist. She fell in love with Lytton Strachey and committed suicide shortly after his death.

T. S. (Thomas Stearns) Eliot, b. 1888, d. 1965. Known to his friends as 'Tom'. American-born poet, essayist and playwright. Close friend of Leonard and Virginia Woolf.

E. M. (Edward Morgan) Forster, b. 1879, d. 1970. Known to his friends as 'Morgan'. Writer, lived for some time in India. Close friend of Lytton Strachey and of Leonard and Virginia Woolf.

Roger Fry, b. 1866, d. 1934. Artist, designer, art critic and lecturer. He brought Post-Impressionism (his term) to England in 1910, and founded the Omega Workshops in 1913.

Angelica Garnett (née Bell), b. 1918, d. 2012. Daughter of Duncan Grant and Vanessa Bell. An artist and writer.

David ('Bunny') Garnett (m. 1. Rachel Marshall; 2. Angelica Bell), b. 1892, d. 1981. Writer, publisher and gourmet. Lover of Duncan Grant, with whom he cohabited along with Vanessa Bell and her children at Wissett Lodge and Charleston during the First World War.

Mark Gertler, b. 1891, d. 1939. Artist born to working-class Polish Jewish immigrants. He fell obsessively in love with Dora Carrington.

Duncan Grant, b. 1885, d. 1978. Artist and designer. His charm won the hearts of many in Bloomsbury, especially Vanessa Bell, with whom he had a child, Angelica, in 1918.

Grace Higgens (née Germany), b. 1903, d. 1983. Housekeeper and cook at Charleston. She kept a record of her recipes.

John Maynard Keynes (m. Lydia Lopokova), b. 1883, d. 1946. Known to his friends as 'Maynard'. A brilliant economic theorist, he worked at the Treasury and wrote *The Economic Consequences of the Peace*, in reaction to the punitive measures imposed on Germany at the end of the First World War. He also set up the Arts Council of Great Britain and was its first chairman.

Lydia Keynes (née Lopokova), b. 1892, d. 1981. Russian ballerina who came to London with Sergei Diaghilev's Ballets Russes. She married John Maynard Keynes in 1925.

Desmond MacCarthy (m. Mary MacCarthy), b. 1877, d. 1952. Literary critic and eloquent conversationalist. He was the English PEN Centre President from 1945 to 1950.

Mary ('Molly') MacCarthy (née Warre-Cornish), b. 1882, d. 1953. Writer. The first to use the term 'Bloomsbury' to refer to her friends living in the Bloomsbury district of London, she was a moving spirit in the start of the Memoir Club in 1920.

Ottoline Morrell (née Cavendish-Bentinck), b. 1873, d. 1938. Society hostess and patron of the arts, who lived for a while at Garsington Manor. She married the politician Philip Morrell and had affairs with Bertrand Russell, Henry Lamb, Augustus John, Dorothy Bussy and Roger Fry.

Frances Partridge (née Marshall), b. 1900, d. 2004. Diarist. She married Ralph Partridge and had one son, Burgo, who married David and Angelica Garnett's daughter, Henrietta. She kept a record of her recipes.

Ralph (Rex) Partridge (m. 1. Dora Carrington; 2. Frances Marshall), b. 1894, d. 1960. An army officer in the First World War, thereafter a pacifist, he later changed his name from Rex to Ralph and cohabited with Lytton Strachey and Dora Carrington. He also worked briefly at the Hogarth Press.

Vita Sackville-West (m. Harold Nicolson), b. 1892, d. 1962. Writer, aristocrat, gardener and lover of Virginia Woolf.

Adrian Stephen (m. Karin Costelloe), b. 1883, d. 1948. Younger brother of Vanessa, Thoby and Virginia. He and his wife, Karin, were analysed by Sigmund Freud, and later practised as psychoanalysts themselves.

Thoby Stephen, b. 1880, d. 1906. Brother of Vanessa Bell and Virginia Woolf. He introduced his Cambridge friends to his sisters and was the catalyst in the formation of the Bloomsbury Group. He died of typhoid.

Lytton Strachey, b. 1880, d. 1932. Writer celebrated for his biographies. A well-known homosexual for most of his life, he lived with Dora Carrington and Ralph Partridge in a love triangle at the Mill House, Tidmarsh, and later at Ham Spray House.

Saxon Sydney-Turner, b. 1880, d. 1962. An intellectual and a civil servant, he worked at the Treasury. He was in love with Barbara Bagenal (née Hiles).

Leonard Woolf (m. Virginia Stephen), b. 1880, d. 1969. Began his professional life in 1904 as a civil servant in Ceylon, but returned to London in 1911. A Labour Party activist, writer, literary editor and publisher, he founded the Hogarth Press with his wife, Virginia.

Virginia Woolf (née Stephen), b. 1882, d. 1941. Writer, celebrated for her novels, essays, letters and diary. She suffered from lifelong mental illness and was looked after by her husband, Leonard, following their marriage in 1912, but eventually took her own life.

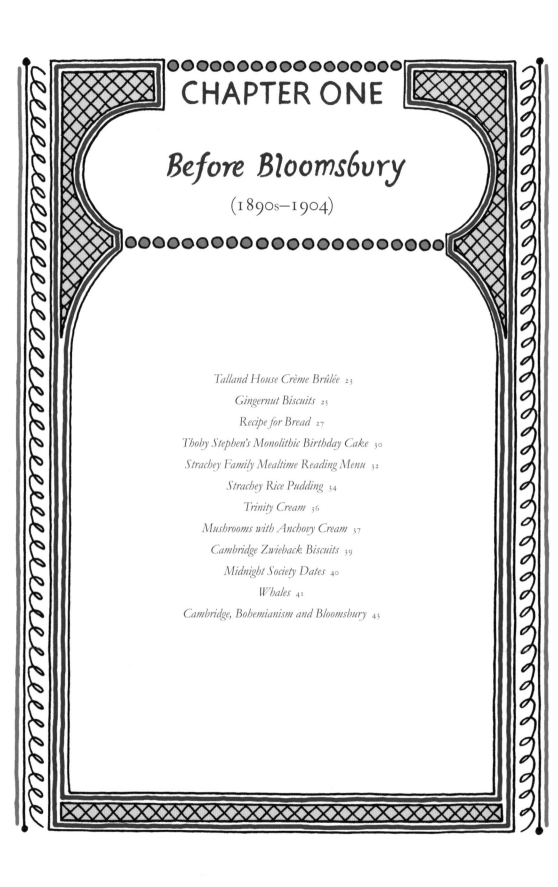

CHAPTER ONE

Before Bloomsbury

(1890s–1904)

Sophia Farrell, the Stephen family cook, 1890. 'Sophie' joined the Stephens in 1886 and remained working for various members of the family until she retired from service in 1931. From the Monk's House photograph album.

Talland House Crème Brûlée

'The kitchen, Sophie's kitchen, for she was dominant over all the other "denizens of the kitchen", as we called them in the *Hyde Park Gate News*,* was directly beneath our night nursery. At dinner time we would let down a basket on a string, and dangle it over the kitchen window. If she were in a good temper, the basket would be drawn in, laden with something from the grown-ups' dinner and pushed swaying out again. If she was "in one of her tempers", the basket was sharply jerked, the string cut, and we [were] left holding the dangling string. I can remember the sensation of the heavy basket, and of the light string.'

Virginia Woolf recalling her childhood holidays in Cornwall,
'A Sketch of the Past', 1939

* *The Stephen family newspaper, 1891–99.*

Julia Stephen with Virginia Stephen, 1884, photographed by Henry H. H. Cameron. From Leslie Stephen's photograph album.

Of all the places that the young Virginia Stephen inhabited or visited, the happiest for her was Talland House in Cornwall. The Victorian villa, set in an acre of land overlooking Porthminster Beach on the edge of St Ives, was an idyllic retreat, perfect for a London-born child usually restricted to the confines of a dirty city and a formal urban atmosphere. In Cornwall she was young and carefree, enthusiastic and happy. There she spent many a blissful hour with her sister, Vanessa, and brothers, Thoby and Adrian, exploring the local beaches and playing cricket on the family's tennis lawn. '[I]n retrospect nothing that we had as children made as much difference, was quite so important to us, as our summer in Cornwall', she recalled in 'A Sketch of the Past' in 1939. '[T]o hear the waves breaking that first night behind the yellow blind; to dig in the sand; to go sailing in a fishing boat; to scrabble over the rocks and see the red and yellow anemones flourishing their antennae; or stuck like blobs of jelly to the rock; to find a small fish flapping in a pool; to pick up cowries; to look over the grammar in the dining room and see the lights changing on the bay; the leaves of the escallonia grey or bright green…; to smell all the fishy smells in the steep little streets; and see the innumerable cats with their fishbones in their mouths…; every day to have a great dish of Cornish cream skinned with a yellow skin; and plenty of brown sugar to eat with blackber-ries … I could fill pages [remembering] one thing after another.'

But when Virginia was thirteen, in 1895, Julia Stephen, her much adored mother, died suddenly** and the Stephens stopped going to Cornwall. Virginia's charmed world was brought to an abrupt end. Those long summer days by the sea were revisited, reborn and retold in the stories of a woman who, as a young girl, had wondered at the flashing yellow eye of a lighthouse and smiled incredulously as she hauled up goodies in a basket tied to the end of a long piece of string. Virginia Woolf's novels *The Voyage Out*, *To the Lighthouse* and *The Waves* were all inspired by memories of her Cornish childhood holidays at Talland House.

Nellie Boxall, the Woolfs' cook from 1916, noted that Virginia's 'favour-ite pudding was crème brûlée'. This is Frances Partridge's recipe. It is excellent, especially if made with the silky yellow cream that comes from the south-west of England.

1 PT CREAM • 4 EGG YOLKS • CASTER SUGAR

Beat the yolks. Boil cream for a very short time, then pour on yolks. Put in dish it is to be served in & let it get quite cold. Sprinkle thickly with caster sugar & brown under grill. (It should make pale brown ice, ⅛ inch thick.) Cool again. [Serves 5.]

Gingernut Biscuits

'I remember one evening as we were jumping about naked, she and I in the bathroom. She suddenly asked me which I liked best: my father or mother. Such a question seemed to me rather terrible. Surely one ought not to ask it. However, being asked, one had to reply and I found I had little doubt as to my answer. "Mother," I said and she went on to explain why she, on the whole, preferred Father. I don't think, however, her pref-erence was quite as sure and simple as mine. She had considered both

** *Julia Prinsep Stephen (née Jackson) died aged forty-nine of heart failure resulting from rheumatic fever. She and Sir Leslie Stephen married in 1878 and had four children: Vanessa (b. 1879), Thoby (b. 1880), Virginia (b. 1882) and Adrian (b. 1883). Both Julia and Leslie were widowed, with children from previous marriages. Julia's children by Herbert Duck-worth were: George (b. 1868), Stella (b. 1869) and Gerald (b. 1870); Leslie's child by Harriet Marian (Thackeray), Laura (b. 1870), had some of form of developmental disability and was institutionalized in 1891.*

Leslie Stephen photographed by Julia Margaret Cameron,
late 1860s. From Leslie Stephen's photograph album.

critically and had more or less analysed her feelings for them, which I, at
any rate consciously, had never attempted. This seemed to begin an age of
much freer speech between us. If one could criticize one's parents, what
or whom could one not criticize? Dimly, some freedom of thought and
speech seemed born, created by her question.'

Vanessa Bell, remembering her childhood with her sister, Virginia,
'Portrait of Virginia Woolf', BBC interview, 1956

In her essay 'A Sketch of the Past', Virginia Woolf explains how she was haunted
and obsessed by the presence of her mother for thirty years after her death: 'I could
hear her voice, see her, imagine what she would do or say as I went about my day's
doings. She was one of the invisible presences who after all play so important a
part in every life.' But Virginia's relationship with her father, Sir Leslie Stephen,
who died when she was twenty-two, was much more fraught. When the loving and
much relied upon Julia Stephen died, Leslie became emotionally dependent on his
children, demanding sympathy from them, and also grew verbally abusive. Vanessa
and Virginia, who were still living under the same roof as their father (their brothers had been sent away to school), bore the brunt of his outbursts. They loved and
respected him (he was an eminent editor and biographer and Virginia shared his
love of books), but they were also angry at him and afraid of him. Moreover, they
were powerless and unable to do anything about their unhappy situation.

Mrs Ramsay, a central character in Virginia's novel *To the Lighthouse*, is the kind and tolerant mother, wife, friend and protector who, like Julia Stephen, still exerts an influence over all those who relied on her while she was alive. Ten years after her death, Mrs Ramsay's husband tries to effect a reconciliation with his children, who despise him for being selfish, sarcastic, stern and unemotional – all things that their mother was not. But when Mr Ramsay offers a gingernut to his daughter and praises his son, all is, quite miraculously, forgiven: 'She should not waste it. He said it so wisely, as if he knew so well all the things that happened in the world, that she put it back at once, and then he gave her, from his own parcel, a gingerbread nut, as if he were a great Spanish gentleman, she thought, handing a flower to a lady at a window (so courteous his manner was). But he was shabby, and simple, eating bread and cheese; and yet he was leading them on a great expedition where, for all she knew, they would be drowned.'

In writing the novel, Virginia exorcized the memory of her parents: 'just as I rubbed out a good deal of the force of my mother's memory by writing about her in *To the Lighthouse,* so I rubbed out much of his memory there too.'

This recipe for gingernut biscuits is from Virginia's niece Angelica Garnett.

2 OZ SELF-RAISING FLOUR • PINCH OF SALT • 3 TSP SUGAR
¼ TSP BICARBONATE OF SODA • 1 TSP GROUND GINGER
1 OZ LARD OR MARGARINE • 1 TBS GOLDEN SYRUP

Sieve flour, ginger, salt, soda together. Rub in fat & sugar. Add golden syrup warmed & mix into a soft but not sticky dough. Form into balls and space out evenly on baking sheet. Bake at 350°F for 10 mins. [Makes 6 biscuits.]

Recipe for Bread

'My Billy*, Thank you very much for the loaf. Your example has fired me, and I made 9 loaves on Saturday which were quite successful. I find that Trissie [Vanessa's cook] once took a prize for bread-making, so she knows all about it and could easily do it herself, only she has so much else to do. So I expect I shall make it twice a week at any rate.'

Vanessa Bell to Virginia Woolf, 23 July 1917

The bond between Vanessa and Virginia was unique – far stronger and deeper than any normal sibling relationship. As children, they were natural rivals, and competed for the affection of their brother Thoby, whom they both adored. There

* *'Billy' was Vanessa's nickname for Virginia.*

were times when Virginia would taunt Vanessa, aptly dubbing her 'the Saint', and Vanessa would retaliate, making Virginia turn 'purple with rage'. Competitive, ambitious and talented, they staked out their respective territories early: Vanessa, it was agreed, would be the painter; Virginia the writer. Their rivalry could easily have turned bitter had there not been a series of dramatic events that drew them closer, in particular the sudden death of their mother and that of their beloved half-sister, Stella Duckworth, two years later.

When, in 1897, the eighteen-year-old Vanessa took over the running of the Stephen household at 22 Hyde Park Gate following Stella's death, she was thrust into the unenviable position of having to extract the weekly housekeeping cheque from her elderly father. His tyrannical fits of verbal abuse, as well as the lecherous solicitations of her half-brother George Duckworth, left Vanessa in a seething state of helpless resentment and unfathomable despair. Later, George's attentions shifted to Virginia, who recalled: 'Nessa and I formed together a very close conspiracy. In that world of many men, coming and going, we formed our private nucleus.'

The Stephen sisters were isolated emotional volcanoes, who found themselves cornered in a petty and repressive male-dominated society. Their solidarity, based on a shared perspective, autonomous vision and determination to live liberated lives, was fuelled to some extent by their sibling rivalry. This combination of solidarity and rivalry helped to fire a social revolution, which eventually brought about sexual and intellectual freedom for women in public and, on the home front, ensured an abundance of freshly baked bread!

This is Helen Anrep's recipe for bread, taken from a newspaper clipping in her recipe book. Helen did not become part of the Bloomsbury circle until 1924, but she could empathize with the sisters' solidarity and their determination to become autonomous individuals. In 1926, she left her husband, the Russian artist Boris Anrep, because she was unhappy at having to share her marital home with his mistress.

Suggested ingredients
4 TSP QUICK YEAST • 2 LB WHITE BREAD FLOUR • 2 TSP SUGAR
2–3 PT WATER • 4 TSP SALT

[O]ne two-cent cake of compressed yeast will raise flour enough for four medium sized loaves of bread. Crumble the yeast into a bowl, being very careful not to handle it too much. Sprinkle on it two teaspoons of sugar and pour over it a pint of lukewarm water. In the course of ten minutes the yeast will have risen to the top. Then stir it until it is dissolved. Make a hole in the centre of the flour and pour in the yeast. Stir it with the flour until it is a thick batter.

Sprinkle salt around the edges where the flour is heaped up, taking care to keep the salt away from the sponge, as it is apt to give it a slightly bitter taste. Set the pan in a warm place. The most important thing is to keep it free from

Young Virginia and Vanessa (with bat) playing cricket, St Ives, 1893–94. From the Monk's House photograph album.

draughts. A draught of cold air from an open door or window has spoiled many a batch of bread. If the temperature of the kitchen is warm and even, say 70 degrees farenheit, the bread will be nicer if it is raised away from the fire; otherwise it should be kept moderately warm. In an hour the sponge will be light and feathery. Knead the bread with slightly warm water. Never use entirely cold water, but always have it warmer in winter than in summer. Good kneading is essential to good bread. If the dough is kept in the right temperature, free from draughts, it will have raised again in from two and a half to three hours; then it should be moulded into loaves when it should be again well kneaded, so as to get all the air out of it and put into the pans. After standing for another hour, it will be ready for the oven. From 40 minutes to an hour will bake it, according to the size of the loaves and the heat of the oven. [Preheat the oven to 500°F (260°C). Place in the oven and immediately reduce the temperature to 350°F (180°C). Bake for about 45 minutes, until the loaves are golden brown.]

Thoby Stephen's Monolithic Birthday Cake

'Mr Thoby Stephen's [twelfth] birthday was on last Thursday. It was of course raining all day except during 2 or 3 hours in the evening. Mrs Stephen gave Mr Thoby a very handsome box to contain his butterflies and moths. Mr Gerald Duckworth always gives him a splendid display of fireworks in the evening. Mrs Hunt accompanied by her little family and those who are staying with her came up early in the afternoon and played games until tea-time. They played the exciting game of 'Cat and Mouse' and even Mr Headlam was made to join. He caused great amusement by sitting down in a chair when he was mouse and allowing Miss Stillman who was cat to run round and round after him thinking that the juveniles were laughing at her for not catching him. Mrs Stephen tried to guide her towards him but she seemed to have an instinct which would not let her touch him. Uproarious laughter continued during the whole scene. Thus passed the afternoon. Tea was soon announced and the whole party trooped merrily into the dining-room. Near the end of the tea Mr Thoby Stephen cut his cake but in such big slices that Mrs Stephen thought it advisable to take the knife. Mrs Stillman got up some charades after tea which were most amusing and were heartily applauded especially the scene where Mr Gerald Duckworth poked Mr Hills with a javelin. Already the cries of the children upon the lawn were making themselves heard when the charades ended. The children were super-exuberant and were kept back with great difficulty and Mrs Stephen was made rightly indignant by the bigger and elder children pushing back the smaller ones, so that they could not see the fireworks. Miniature balloons went up first and they were pronounced a success as only the first one burnt and the others actually went right out of sight! The rest of the fireworks went off "rippingly" but the garden next day was a scene of ruin and destruction. The gate was entirely broken off its hinges but that was not so very wonderful as it had never been extra-ordinary for it's [*sic*] strength.'

Virginia Stephen, aged ten, *Hyde Park Gate News*, 12 September 1892

As children, Vanessa and Virginia were devoted to Thoby. He was clever, fun, good-looking and adventurous, and the two sisters vied with each other for his affection. Later, at Cambridge, Thoby's friends delighted in his charm, his allure and his good-natured sense of humour. Everything about him, from the way he spoke to the way he laughed – and even the way he sliced a cake – was said to be 'monolithic' by his friend Leonard Woolf. In his autobiography, Leonard wrote of Thoby: 'In his monolithic character, his monolithic common sense, his monumental judgments he continually reminded one of Dr Johnson, but a Samuel Johnson who had shed his neuroticism, his irritability, his fears. He had a perfect "natural" style of writing, flexible, lucid, but rather formal, old-fashioned, almost Johnsonian or at any rate eighteenth century. And there was a streak of the same natural style in his talk. Any wild statement, speculative judgment or Stracheyan exaggeration would be met with a "Nonsense, my good fellow" from Thoby, and then a sentence of profound, but humorous, common sense, and a delighted chuckle.'

This monolithic Marble Cake is from Mrs Beeton's *The Book of Household Management*, published in 1895. It is so good you may wish to cut large slices.

White part

2 TEACUPS FLOUR • 1½ CUP SUGAR

½ CUP BUTTER • ½ CUP MILK • 4 EGGS (WHITES ONLY)

½ TSP CREAM OF TARTAR • ¼ TSP SODA

SPICE, TO TASTE

Dark part

2½ CUPS FLOUR • ½ CUP BUTTER • 1 CUP SUGAR

½ CUP TREACLE • ½ CUP MILK • 4 YOLKS OF EGGS AND WHITE OF ONE

½ TSP SODA • ½ TSP CREAM OF TARTAR

CLOVES, CINNAMON, MACE

Mix these separately, and drop into the baking-pan by tablespoonfuls alternately. Bake 2 hours [1 hour 20 minutes at 160°C in one large cake tin]; this makes two loaves, and is very nice. Sufficient for 2 cakes.

Icing
1 TEACUP WHITE SUGAR • 1 EGG (WHITE ONLY)

Put to the cup of sugar water enough to dissolve it, set it on the fire and let it boil till it will 'hair'; beat the white of the egg to a stiff froth; pour the heated sugar on the egg and stir briskly until cool enough to stay on the cake. It should not be put on till the cake is nearly or quite cold. This will frost only the top of the loaves. [Serves 12–16.]

Strachey Family Mealtime Reading Menu

'My first dinner with the [Strachey] family was a rather upsetting experience. The number of sons and daughters was almost beyond computation, and all the children were to my unpracticed eyes exactly alike except in the somewhat superficial point that some were male and some were female. The family were not all assembled when I arrived, but dropped in one by one at intervals of twenty minutes. (One of them, I afterwards discovered, was Lytton.) I had to look round the room carefully to make sure that it was a new one that had appeared and not merely one of the previous ones that had changed his or her place. Towards the end of the evening I began to doubt my sanity, but kind friends afterwards assured me that things had really been as they seemed.'

Bertrand Russell*, *Autobiography*, 1967–69.

If the Stephens were extraordinary, so too were the Stracheys, and it was the coming together of these two families that laid the foundations for the formation of the Bloomsbury Group.

Lytton and his younger brother James, although most relevant to our story, were not the only members of the Strachey family to grace the tables of Bloomsbury. Indeed, there were ten others, including both parents, whose influence was keenly felt, especially after Sir Richard and Lady Jane Strachey (née Grant) moved house from Lancaster Gate to 51 Gordon Square, Bloomsbury, in 1920. The Strachey family name, synonymous with British colonial rule in nineteenth-century India,

* *Bertrand Russell and Lady Strachey were fellow members of a committee to secure votes for women. In 1907 Bertrand stood as the Labour candidate for Wimbledon, on a campaign platform of support for Women's Suffrage, but was not elected.*

The Strachey family – Sir Richard and Lady Strachey, and their five daughters and five sons – 'at prayer', photographed by Greystone Bird, *c.* 1893. The Stracheys' enthusiasm for open, honest conversation became one of the main tenets of the Bloomsbury Group's philosophy.

defies the family's liberal attitude to modern social issues, such as feminism and sexual freedom. A peculiar 'inelasticity' (observed by David 'Bunny' Garnett) was shared by all the Stracheys and discernible in the small details of their daily lives.

Bunny noted the family's 'rigid adherence to certain limitations which they imposed upon themselves' and added that, 'To know Stracheys well, one has to be ready to accept the atmosphere in which they live.' Leonard Woolf wrote of them in his autobiography: 'The level of intelligence in each son and daughter and in the father and mother was incredibly, fantastically high. They were all, like their mother, passionately intellectual, most of them with very quick minds and lively imaginations…. Their chief recreation was conversation and they adored conversational speculation which usually led to argument … over the dinner-table, as almost always happened, the roar and rumble, the shrill shrieks, the bursts of laughter, the sound and fury of excitement were deafening and to an unprepared stranger paralysing.'

And so, with one bespectacled eye focused on their family's distinguished history and the other (also bespectacled) voraciously ingesting Gibbon, Plato and Racine, the ambiance at the Strachey dining table was one of heady self-absorption and passionate erudition. Banter was fast and furious, and daunting for the unsuspecting visitor. Absolute truth, honesty and freedom of expression were the family's only rules of conversation and provided their basic code of conduct. Bloomsbury members not only accepted the Stracheys' moral code and the highly intellectual atmosphere in which they ate, slept and breathed, but also appropriated it, exalted in it, and made it the group's very own.

This is a typical Strachey mealtime 'menu'.

Jean Racine:

Phèdre *Andromaque*

Bérénice *Iphigénie*

Plato:

The Republic *The Apology*

Symposium *Phaedo*

Euthyphro

Edward Gibbon:

The History of the Decline and Fall of the Roman Empire, vol. 1

The History of the Decline and Fall of the Roman Empire, vol. 2.

Strachey Rice Pudding

'For much of his life he was ill – there were times when he was muffled in shawls and drank his Horlick's malted milk at stated intervals. Then he would suddenly revive, go to parties, seek adventures and climb hills. To be with him then was a delight and an education.'

David Garnett on Lytton Strachey, *Great Friends*, 1979

From the age of eight Lytton Strachey suffered from a series of mysterious ailments. He had a hearty appetite, but he was fragile and pale and much too thin for his elongated frame. Special diets made little difference to his health, and the regimen of raw meat, porridge and port he was prescribed was eventually dropped. As an adult, Lytton continued to eat the easily digestible foods that he enjoyed as a boy – rice pudding, milk and rusks – and so, oddly, did the rest of his large family. 'Here comes a glass of milk for me, and a couple of rusks. I believe I am perfectly happy,' he wrote in 1907.

'Every Strachey absolutely insisted on eating rice pudding at least once a day,' recalled Frances Partridge, 'so that the meals struck me as having a curiously nursery flavour.' Just as their extraordinary height, slim frames, intelligence, bespeckled faces and squeaky voices were distinctive Strachey traits, so too was

Lytton Strachey, 1911–12. According to Frances Partridge, the entire Strachey family insisted on eating rice pudding at least once a day.

their curious consumption of this creamy rice pudding. This is another classic recipe from *Mrs Beeton's Book of Household Management,* published in 1895.

¼ LB [PUDDING OR ARBORIO] RICE • 1½ PT NEW MILK
2 OZ NEW BUTTER• 4 EGGS • ½ SALTSPOONFUL OF SALT
4 LARGE TBS MOIST SUGAR, FLAVOURING TO TASTE

Stew the rice very gently in the above proportion of new milk, and when it is tender, pour it into a basin; stir in the butter, and let it stand to cool; then beat the eggs, add these to the rice with the sugar, salt, and any flavouring that may be approved, such as nutmeg, powdered cinnamon, grated lemon-peel, essence of bitter almonds, or vanilla. When all is well stirred, put the pudding into a buttered basin, tie it down with a cloth, plunge it into boiling water, and boil for 1¼ hour. Sufficient for 5 or 6 persons.

Trinity Cream

'The real enchantment of Cambridge is of the intimate kind; an enchantment lingering in the nooks and corners, coming upon one gradually down the narrow streets, and ripening year by year. The little river and its lawns and willows, the old trees in the old gardens, the obscure bowling-greens, the crooked lanes with their glimpses of cornices and turrets, the low dark opening out on to sunny grass – in these, and in things like these, dwells the fascination of Cambridge.'

Lytton Strachey, 'Cambridge', 1907

above left: **Trinity College, Cambridge, coat of arms;** *above right:* **burnt into the top of a crème brûlée.**

It was at the University of Cambridge, where he was an undergraduate from 1899 to 1903, that Lytton Strachey, nicknamed 'the Strache' by his friends, first discovered true happiness. He became part of a close-knit group of scholars and intellectuals who shared his enthusiasm for learning and discussion and who were equally open-minded and liberally disposed. He was a member of two exclusive discussion groups, the Cambridge Conversazione Society ('Apostles') and the Midnight Society, to which most of his friends (Leonard Woolf, Saxon Sydney-Turner, E. M. Forster, John Maynard Keynes, Desmond MacCarthy, Clive Bell and Thoby Stephen) had also been elected.* Maynard later wrote of this time: 'If, therefore, I altogether ignore our merits – our charm, our intelligence, our unworldliness, our affection – I can see us as water-spiders, gracefully skimming, as light and reasonable as air, the surface of the stream without any contact at all with the eddies and currents underneath.'

Lytton's rooms at Trinity College were at 'Mutton-Hole Corner', Staircase K, around the corner from those of Leonard ('the Rabbi') and Saxon ('His Majesty'). He ate most of his meals in the College dining hall, but in May 1901 he took to supplementing his diet with chocolate to help him through examinations, his first History Tripos. 'I am calm and with the aid of chocolate will I hope weather it,' he wrote to his mother. Although totally inexperienced in the preparation of food, he managed, just, to make some soup for Desmond from tabloids (stock cubes). On Saturdays, he ate 'whales', that is, sardines on toast: the traditional snack served at Conversazione meetings. Before Midnight Society meetings, he joined Clive for a 'whisky or punch and one of those gloomy beef-steak pies which it was the fashion to order for Sunday lunch'.

One dish that Lytton is certain to have enjoyed at Trinity was crème brûlée, the creamy pudding adored by Virginia Woolf as a child. It was introduced to Trinity College in 1879. After one of the cooks burnt the college's coat of arms onto the top layer of caramel, the dish was thereafter known as 'Cambridge Burnt Cream' or 'Trinity Cream'. It is still on the Trinity College menu today.

Mushrooms with Anchovy Cream

'George Moore was a great man, the only great man whom I have ever met or known in the world of ordinary, real life. There was in him an element which can, I think, be accurately called greatness, a combination

---

* *Clive Bell and Thoby Stephen were not members of the Conversazione Society but were members of the Midnight Society. Desmond MacCarthy and Bertrand Russell were responsible for proposing Lytton Strachey for membership to the Apostles.*

of mind and character and behaviour, of thought and feeling which made him qualitatively different from anyone else I have ever known.'

Leonard Woolf, *Sowing*, 1962

The individuals within the Bloomsbury Group were born into a Victorian world of tradition where one was duty-bound to fulfil the expectations of one's position within society. The social hierarchy, its rules of conduct and its conventions were the outward expressions of a strict code of morality. 'God's in His heaven – All's right with the world!' wrote the poet Robert Browning in 1841. But for some individuals at the end of the Victorian era, especially those who were not religious, these conceptions of duty, social utilitarianism and morality were deeply unsatisfactory. A new ideology was beginning to surface, in which 'personal affections and aesthetic enjoyments include *all* the greatest, and *by far* the greatest, goods we can imagine', wrote the Cambridge philosopher G. E. Moore in *Principia Ethica* in 1903. 'Good' states of mind and an individual's ethical pursuit of truth and happiness were given prime importance by Moore, and these ideas would prove fundamental to the Bloomsbury Group.

This delicious savoury from *Good Things in England* is a Cambridge college recipe, *c.* 1900. It will, without fail, put one into a good state of mind – if not a great one!

From left to right: Oliver Strachey, G. E. Moore and John Maynard Keynes, 1914. Moore's *Principia Ethica* had a profound influence on the moral philosophies developed at the University of Cambridge in the early years of the twentieth century.

ROUNDS OF BREAD ABOUT 2 IN. ACROSS • MUSHROOMS
9–10 ANCHOVIES • 1 OR 2 TBS CREAM • PEPPER • SALT

1. Cut some rounds of bread about ¼ inch thick and 2 inches in diameter. 2. Fry them a golden brown. 3. Broil some mushrooms and put one on each piece of fried bread. 4. Wash 9 or 10 anchovies. 5. Chop them. 6. Rub them through a sieve. 7. Whip the cream. 8. Mix the anchovies with it, season with a little pepper and salt. 9. Just before sending to table put a piece of this mixture about the size of a walnut on each mushroom and serve.

Cambridge Zwieback Biscuits

'The fire was dancing, and the shadow of Ansell, who stood close up to it, seemed to dominate the little room. He was still talking, or rather jerking, and he was still lighting matches and dropping their ends upon the carpet. Now and then he would make a motion with his feet as if he were running quickly backward upstairs, and would tread on the edge of the fender, so that the fire-irons went flying and the buttered-bun dishes crashed against each other in the hearth. The other philosophers were crouched in odd shapes on the sofa and table and chairs, and one, who was a little bored, had crawled to the piano and was timidly trying the "Prelude to Rhinegold" with his knee upon the soft pedal. The air was heavy with good tobacco-smoke and the pleasant warmth of tea, and as Rickie became more sleepy the events of the day seemed to float one by one before his acquiescent eyes. In the morning he had read Theocritus, whom he believed to be the greatest of Greek poets; he had lunched with a merry don and had tasted Zwieback biscuits; then he had walked with people he liked, and had walked just long enough; and now his room was full of other people whom he liked, and when they left he would go and have supper with Ansell, whom he liked as well as anyone. A year ago he had known none of these joys. He had crept cold and friendless and ignorant out of a great public school, preparing for a silent and solitary journey, and praying as a highest favour that he might be left alone. Cambridge had not answered his prayer. She had taken and soothed him, and warmed him, and had laughed at him a little, saying that he must not be so tragic yet awhile, for his boyhood had been but a dusty corridor that led to the spacious halls of youth. In one year he had made many friends and learnt much, and he might learn even more if he could but concentrate his attention on that cow.'

E. M. Forster, *The Longest Journey*, 1907

E. M. Forster cut a lonely figure before he went up to Cambridge in 1897. He had been an unhappy day boy at Tonbridge School where he had few friends and despaired increasingly of the pretentious values of English middle-class suburbia. At Cambridge, however, he made friends and was selected for membership in the secret discussion society known as the Apostles. Here, with the security of companionship – among Morgan's close friends were Lytton Strachey and Leonard Woolf – the stimulation of intelligent conversation, and the liberating ideas of G. E. Moore's *Principia Ethica*, Morgan found a place in which he could belong and where he could develop his moral convictions. In his second novel, *The Longest Journey*, published in 1907, he reflected upon the nurturing virtues of Cambridge, including the detail of the Zwieback biscuits offered to Rickie, the protagonist, by 'a merry don'. Zwieback biscuits are thin, crisp, double-baked rusks often fed to teething children.

These rusks from *Cambridge Cuisine* are easy and quick to make.

8 OZ SELF-RAISING FLOUR • 4 OZ LARD • 1 LARGE EGG

1 TBS MILK

Sift the flour and rub in the lard, using a knife, mix into a firm dough with the beaten egg and milk. Turn on to a floured board and roll out to ½" thickness. Cut into rounds with a 2" diameter cutter. Place on a floured baking tin and bake in a hot oven for 12 mins or until well risen. Remove from oven, split each round into pieces and return to oven for 8–10 mins until a golden brown. Butter each rusk for tea or serve with cheese instead of biscuits. Gas regulo mark 7 [220°C]. [Makes 30.]

Midnight Society Dates

'There was a sofa, chairs, a square table, and the window being open, one could see how they sat – legs issuing here, one there crumpled in a corner of the sofa; and, presumably, for you could not see him, somebody stood by the fender, talking. Anyhow, Jacob, who sat astride a chair and ate dates from a long box, burst out laughing. The answer came from the sofa corner; for his pipe was held in the air, then replaced. Jacob wheeled round. He had something to say to *that*, though the sturdy red-haired boy at the table seemed to deny it, wagging his head slowly from side to side; and then, taking out his penknife, he dug the point of it again and again into a knot in the table, as if affirming that the voice from the fender spoke the truth – which Jacob could not deny. Possibly, when he had done arranging the date-stones, he might find something to say to it – indeed his lips opened – only then there broke out a roar of laughter.'

Virginia Woolf, *Jacob's Room*, 1922

In their second term at Trinity College, at the beginning of 1900, Clive Bell, Lytton Strachey, Saxon Sydney-Turner, Leonard Woolf and A. J. Robertson established a small reading group called the Midnight Society. It met in Clive's rooms at midnight every Saturday to read and discuss English poetry and plays.

A further member of the society was Thoby Stephen, who then introduced his friends to his two sisters, Virginia and Vanessa: the future Mrs Leonard Woolf and Mrs Clive Bell. Thus this intimate group of intellectuals formed the basis, Clive claimed, of what was later to become the Bloomsbury Group.

Undoubtedly, the novel *Jacob's Room*, published long after the group came into being, was Virginia's eulogy for her beloved brother Thoby, who died of typhoid fever at the age of only twenty-six in 1906. It includes what is obviously a reference to the Midnight Society and its members' appetite for the delicious sweet fruit of the date palm.

Whales

At Cambridge, the Conversazione Society met each Saturday night at half past eight for open, honest, often witty discussion of a paper that a 'brother' had prepared for the occasion. They drank coffee, ate 'whales' (anchovies or sardines on toast) and spoke in absolute confidentiality. The bond between the Apostles was strong and most members remained close friends for the rest of their lives. Most of the men in the Bloomsbury Group had been Apostles.

Every June, the Conversazione Society held a dinner for all Apostles and Angels (graduate Apostles). Clever speeches, delicious food, bottles of wine and intelligent conversation were savoured and digested at an exclusive venue. In 1922 Leonard Woolf made the after-dinner speech at the Connaught Rooms. 'I spoke whales,' he recorded in his diary on 15 June.

This is an unpublished recipe for Sardine Savoury by Frances Partridge.

1 OR 2 TINS OF SARDINES • [BUTTER] • [SALT AND PEPPER]

Carefully remove skin & bones & put through electric mixer. Add some quantity of butter (or butter & cream) & a little salt & pepper & mix into a smooth paste. Serve on fried bread. [Serves 4.]

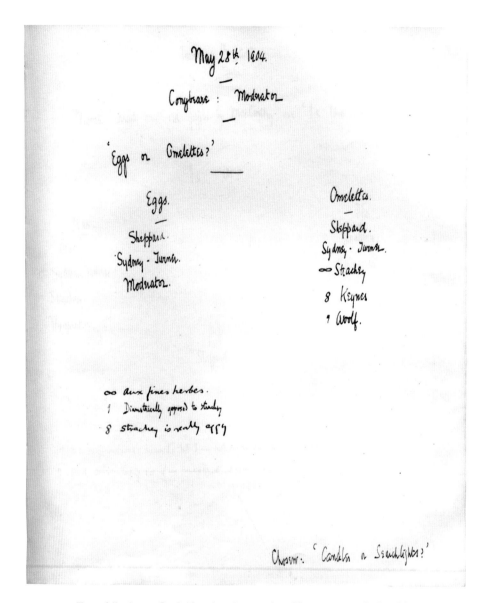

May 28th 1904.

Conybeare : Moderator

'Eggs or Omelettes?'

Eggs.

Sheppard.
Sydney - Turner.
Moderator.

Omelettes.

Sheppard.
Sydney - Turner.
∞ Strachey
8 Keynes
9 Woolf.

∞ aux fines herbes.
9 Diametrically opposed to strachey
8 strachey is really 9[5]9

Chosen: 'Candles or Searchlights?'

Votes following a Cambridge Apostles meeting, May 1904, mentioning John Maynard Keynes, Lytton Strachey, Saxon Sydney-Turner and Leonard Woolf, among other members. Discussion at Conversazione meetings was animated and amusing. Most Apostles, according to Society votes, preferred omelettes to eggs, with Lytton (whom Maynard thought 'really eggy') preferring his omelettes aux fines herbes.

Cambridge, Bohemianism and Bloomsbury

'We were full of experiments and reforms. We were going to do without
table napkins, we were to have Bromo* instead; we were going to paint; to
write; to have coffee after dinner instead of tea at nine o'clock. Everything
was going to be new; everything was going to be different. Everything was
on trial.'

Virginia Woolf, on moving to Bloomsbury in 1904, quoted in *Moments of Being*

Thoby Stephen first introduced his sisters to his Cambridge friends at the Trinity
College May Ball in 1900. Clive Bell and Leonard Woolf were immediately smitten.
Leonard later recalled: 'I first saw them one summer afternoon in Thoby's rooms;
in white dresses and large hats, with parasols in their hands, their beauty literally
took one's breath away, for suddenly seeing them one stopped astonished, and
everything, including one's breathing for one second, also stopped as it does when
in a picture gallery you suddenly come face to face with a great Rembrandt or
Velasquez…. They were at that time, at least upon the surface, the most Victorian
of Victorian young ladies'.

The moral issues and liberal philosophies discussed by the young Cambridge
graduates at the turn of the century married well with the budding bohemian ide-
ologies of the Stephen sisters. Both disparaged the conventions and attitudes of
Victorian society, and both were equally determined to live according to a new
code of ethics. But the transmutation of Cambridge and 'bohemianism' into the
Bloomsbury Group did not properly occur until 1904, after the death of Sir Leslie
Stephen and the subsequent move of the Stephen children from Kensington to
Bloomsbury. Now, liberated from their father and the oppressive, conventional
Kensington world in which they had lived, the Stephen sisters sought fresh stim-
ulation from like-minded, free-thinking individuals. In February 1905, Thoby
invited his Cambridge friends to Bloomsbury, intelligentsia met bohemia and,
discovering their tastes to be complementary, they converged.

* *Bromo, a Victorian bathroom paper containing 'disinfectants and curatives', was a revolutionary, durable, deodorized
paper, hailed as a preventative to 'the piles' – then quite a common complaint.*

CHAPTER TWO

Old Bloomsbury

(1904–14)

Vanessa Bell, *Apples: 46 Gordon Square*, *c.* 1909–10. Vanessa painted this work from the first-floor drawing room of her house in Bloomsbury.

Apples: 46 Gordon Square

'46 Gordon Square could never have meant what it did had not 22 Hyde Park Gate preceded it.'

Virginia Woolf, 'Old Bloomsbury',
essay for the Memoir Club*, early 1920s

Sir Leslie Stephen died in February 1904 at 22 Hyde Park Gate, Kensington. In October, his children – Vanessa, Virginia and their two brothers, Thoby and Adrian – moved to 46 Gordon Square, Bloomsbury. Bloomsbury was not so smart an address as Kensington, but the new house on the east side of the Square was close to the Slade School of Fine Art and the British Museum, and far enough away from the unhappy house of their birth that had seen the deaths of their mother, half-sister and father. Together the Stephen children were determined to make a fresh start and to shrug off the Victorian conventions, repressions and nightmares they had endured for two decades while living in Kensington. 46 Gordon Square liberated not only the Stephens from their gloomy past, but it also liberated their Cambridge friends, and for thirty years it would remain one of the main focal points of all Bloomsbury activity.

This is my own recipe for apple squares, inspired by Vanessa Bell's *Apples: 46 Gordon Square*, which was painted early in her artistic career. These squares are sweet and liberating – delicious with coffee, or whenever one needs a break from the petty and the mundane.

3 CUPS PLAIN WHITE FLOUR • 4 TBS CASTER SUGAR
240 G BUTTER • 4 EGGS • 410 G SOFT BROWN SUGAR
120 G MELTED BUTTER • 80 G DRIED APPLES, DICED
2 TBS LEMON JUICE • 1 TSP VANILLA • 2 TSP FLOUR

Preheat oven to 180°C. Combine the first three ingredients until mixture resembles breadcrumbs. Press into two buttered oblong baking dishes and bake for approximately 13 minutes on the centre shelf of the oven.

Meanwhile, beat the eggs and sugar together. Stir in the butter, apples, lemon juice, vanilla and flour. Pour into the base and bake for 20–25 minutes until golden brown. Cool and cut into squares. Makes 46.

* *The Memoir Club was formed in 1920. There were thirteen original members: Desmond and Molly MacCarthy, Clive and Vanessa Bell, Leonard and Virginia Woolf, Saxon Sydney-Turner, John Maynard Keynes, the diplomat Sydney Waterlow, Morgan Forster, Lytton Strachey, Roger Fry and Duncan Grant. At meetings (held with variable frequency) a member read aloud from a biographical paper he or she had written.*

Thoby's Cocoa and Biscuits

'It seemed to him a good plan to be at home one evening a week and though I do not think it had at first occurred to him to include his sisters in the arrangement, still there they were. So it happened that one or two of these friends began to drift in on Thursday evenings after dinner. The entertainment was frugal. I believe there was generally some whisky to be had, but most of us were content with cocoa and biscuits. In fact, as everyone had had something to eat and perhaps to drink at about eight o'clock, it did not seem to occur to them to want more at nine or at any time between then and midnight. Then, perhaps, exhausted by conversation, serious or frivolous, they welcomed some nourishment. It was one of the things which made entertaining cheap in those days.'

Vanessa Bell, 'Notes on Bloomsbury',
essay for the Memoir Club, 1951

In London, Thoby Stephen set out to rekindle the intellectual spark that he had enjoyed at Cambridge, inviting his Cambridge friends around to 46 Gordon Square for an evening of stimulating discussion. In February 1905, Clive Bell, Saxon Sydney-Turner, Desmond MacCarthy, John Maynard Keynes and Lytton Strachey attended (Leonard Woolf had left for Ceylon in late 1904) and, with Vanessa and Virginia Stephen, the friends discussed everything from 'good' states of mind and individual 'truth and happiness' to art, beauty and sex. They were uncommonly truthful and it was not long before they all became uncommonly close. According to Vanessa: 'When it is said that we did not hesitate to talk of anything, it must be understood that this was literally true. If you could say what you like about art, sex or religion, you could also talk freely and very likely dully about the ordinary doings of daily life. There was very little self-consciousness, I think, in those early gatherings, but life was exciting, terrible and amusing and we had to explore it, thankful that one could do so freely.' Here was the beginning of 'Old Bloomsbury', as Leonard would later dub this period in his autobiography.

Nourishment at Thoby's Thursday evenings was light, and if someone was hungry or wanted a drink, cocoa and biscuits were available from the sideboard. Dame Janet Vaughan (an eminent haematologist and distant cousin of the Stephen family) once noted that Bloomsbury was 'very addicted to cocoa'. Roger Fry, who became part of the group in 1910, was a direct descendant of the J. S. Fry chocolate dynasty. This cocoa recipe has therefore been selected from an early *Fry's Chocolate Recipes* booklet. The recipe for biscuits is from a clipping in Helen Anrep's scrapbook.

Fry's Chocolate Recipes

CHOCOLATE BLANCMANGE

| ½ teacup of cornflour | 1 pint of milk |
| ¼ teacup Fry's Breakfast Cocoa | Sugar to taste |

Well mix cornflour and cocoa, then with a little milk work into a smooth paste. Heat the remainder of the milk, adding sugar to taste. Stir milk and cornflour mixture together. Return to saucepan and boil gently for 10 minutes, stirring all the time. Pour into a wet mould and serve when cold.

CHOCOLATE BLANC-MANGE, CHOCOLATE FRUIT TARTS

CHOCOLATE FRUIT TARTS

| 3 level teaspoons baking powder | ¼ teaspoon cinnamon | 1 teaspoon vanilla | ¼ teaspoon salt | 3 tablespoons Fry's Breakfast Cocoa |
| ¾ cup butter | 1 cup sugar | 2 eggs | 1½ cups flour | ½ cup milk |

Cream butter, add sugar gradually. Add egg yolks thoroughly beaten. Mix and sift dry ingredients three times. Add alternately with milk, add vanilla. Fold in egg whites beaten until stiff and dry. Turn into greased and floured patty pans, and bake 30 minutes in a moderate oven. Cool, scoop out centre, fill with date filling and cover with whipped cream or meringue glace.

HOW TO MAKE A CUP OF PERFECT COCOA

YOU can make an excellent cup of cocoa quickly and economically by using half to one teaspoonful of FRY'S BREAKFAST COCOA. Add an equal quantity of sugar to the cup and mix with boiling water to a smooth paste. Then fill up with boiling water stirring all the time ; add your milk and more sugar if required, when you will have one of the tastiest and most sustaining food beverages.

But if you prefer a richer drinking chocolate, take a heaped teaspoonful of cocoa with an equal quantity of sugar to each breakfast cup. Mix this into a smooth paste and pour on boiling milk and water, or better still boiling milk alone. It should now be boiled again for a minute and whisked briskly just before serving. By doing this the fullest qualities of the cocoa are brought out

DRINKING COCOA

If your oven is too hot the temperature can be reduced by placing a basin of cold water in it

J S FRY & SONS LTD BRISTOL & SOMERDALE

above: Instructions for making cocoa, from the back page of the J. S. Fry & Sons catalogue, *c.* 1920s/30s. Roger Fry's great-great-grandfather Joseph Fry founded the chocolate dynasty in 1761. *opposite:* Roger Fry, *Still Life with a Biscuit Tin and Pots,* 1918. Apart from witty conversation, the only sustenance on offer at Thoby Stephen's Thursday evening gatherings was cocoa and biscuits.

Cocoa

You can make an excellent cup of cocoa quickly and economically by using half to one teaspoonful of Fry's Breakfast Cocoa. Add an equal quantity of sugar to the cup and mix with boiling water stirring all the time; add your milk and more sugar if required, when you will have one of the tastiest and most sustaining food beverages.

But if you prefer a richer drinking chocolate, take a heaped teaspoonful of cocoa with an equal quantity of sugar to each breakfast cup. Mix this into a smooth paste and pour on boiling milk and water, or better still boiling milk alone. It should now be boiled again for a minute and whisked briskly just before serving. By doing this the fullest qualities of the cocoa are brought out.

Biscuits

1 CUP BUTTER • 2 CUPS SUGAR • 3 EGGS • 2 TSP BAKING POWDER
2 TSP BOILING WATER • [3–4 CUPS] FLOUR

One cup of butter, two cups of sugar, three eggs, two teaspoons each of baking powder and boiling water, and flour enough to knead as soft as can be rolled out. [Turn onto lightly floured work surface and knead until soft. Roll out and cut into biscuit-sized portions. Bake at 200°C for about 15 minutes, or until brown. Makes 4 dozen.]

Vanessa's Loving Cup

At the same time that Thoby Stephen was hosting his 'Thursday evenings' at 46 Gordon Square in 1905–6, Vanessa began an artists' discussion group: the Friday Club. Friends, family and students from the Royal Academy schools and the Slade School were invited to attend meetings and share ideas. The Friday Club held lectures – Clive Bell was one of the guest speakers – and exhibitions. Out of their shared love for Thoby and their mutual interest in art, Clive and Vanessa forged a unique friendship.

In 1905 Clive asked Vanessa to marry him, but she declined, preferring to retain her independence. The following year he asked her again, and again she declined. When Thoby died from typhoid fever in November 1906, however, Vanessa changed her mind and accepted Clive's proposal. In marrying one of her brother's closest friends, Vanessa could both bridge her loss and achieve the continuity and stability she needed to keep her 'Bloomsbury' world together. They were married at St Pancras Registry Office on 7 February 1907.

This celebratory cup is from Mrs Beeton's *All About Cookery* (1909).

1 BOTTLE CHAMPAGNE • ½ BOTTLE MADEIRA • ¼ PT FRENCH BRANDY
1 ½ PT WATER • ½ LB LOAF SUGAR • 2 LEMONS
A FEW LEAVES OF [FRESH LEMON-] BALM
2 OR 3 SPRIGS BORAGE

Rub the peel off one lemon with some lumps of sugar, then remove every particle of pith, also the rind and pith of the other lemon, and slice them thinly. Put the balm, borage, the sliced lemons and all the sugar into a jug, add the water, Madeira and brandy, cover, surround with ice, and let the mixture remain thus for about one hour. Also surround the champagne with ice, and add it to the rest of the ingredients when ready.

Freedom Pie

'[Our] freedom was, I believe, largely owing to Lytton Strachey.… His great honesty of mind and remorseless poking fun at any sham forced others to be honest too and showed a world in which one need no longer be afraid of saying what one thought, surely the first step to anything that could be of interest or value.'

Vanessa Bell, 'Notes on Bloomsbury', 1951

Vanessa Bell, *Window, Still Life*, c. 1912–13.

Duncan Grant, *Bathers by the Pond*, *c.* 1920–21. Duncan, Lytton Strachey and John Maynard Keynes were known and accepted as homosexuals among their friends. Male homosexuality, however, was not legalized in England until 1967.

Lytton Strachey first freed himself and then his friends from the restrictive conventions of Victorian England. In 1907 he began calling them by their Christian names. Later that year he pushed the boundaries even further when he asked aloud if a stain on the recently married Vanessa Bell's dress was semen. Virginia Stephen recalled: 'With that one word all barriers of reticence and reserve went down. A flood of the sacred fluid seemed to overwhelm us. Sex permeated our conversation. The word bugger was never far from our lips. We discussed copulation with the same excitement and openness that we had discussed the nature of good.' There was now virtually nothing Bloomsbury would not say or do among themselves; they had been liberated.

The original title of this recipe from Florence White's *Good Things in England* was Fig or Fag Pie – a reference to the British public school system, in which young boys were required to perform menial tasks for the senior pupils. This form of subjugation (which often involved bullying) was an endemic part of boarding school life before 1950, and certainly a practice that the male members of Bloomsbury would have experienced in their youth. This recipe has been renamed with a view to celebrating all kinds of new freedoms.

SHORT PASTRY • ½ LB FIGS • WATER AND CORNFLOUR
½ TSP MIXED SPICE • A FEW CURRANTS • I DSP TREACLE

1. Line a [9 in. (23 cm)] piedish, or plate, with short pastry. 2. Put the figs in a saucepan with just enough water to cover them. 3. Stew until tender. 4. Thicken

the liquid with cornflour. 5. Add the spice, currants and treacle. 6. Mix well, put into the piecrust and bake a nice brown. N.B. – If wished, the mixture may be covered with pastry, and a covered pie be made. [Serves 6–8.]

Raie au Beurre Noir

"'You must go out into the world' my inner voice said – "to learn all that there is to know and be seen in the world of painting. The Impressionists you must see and learn from and then there are other things going on at this very moment of which you know nothing.'"

Duncan Grant's vision of his future in 1902, aged seventeen,
from his unpublished 'Paris Memoir'

Duncan Grant, *Self-Portrait in a Turban, c.* 1909. Duncan was so delightfully witty and entertaining that it was hard not to succumb to his irresistible charm.

As a young boy growing up in colonial India, Duncan Grant liked to design wedding dresses. At an English preparatory school in Rugby, his talent for drawing was duly praised, and at St Paul's School in London, it was quite clear that Duncan's vocation lay not with the British army as his parents had wished, but with the British avant-garde. Encouraged by his aunt Lady Strachey, and on the advice of his mentor, the artist Simon Bussy, Duncan dedicated himself to learning his craft and following his vision.

At the age of twenty-one Duncan went to Paris to study art. His approach was single-minded and comprehensive. Although he devoted most of his waking hours to developing his artistic skills, he found some time to enjoy the mouth-watering flavours of classical French cuisine. But most of his meals were simple and inexpensive. According to his biographer, Frances Spalding, he enjoyed a brioche and coffee in the morning, a simple lunch with his fellow students and, in the evening, perhaps a bowl of vichyssoise or *raie au beurre noir*. Duncan's time in Paris, in 1906–7, was productive, but it was also lonely. One evening, after dining out with Vanessa and Clive Bell and Virginia and Adrian Stephen in Paris, he wrote to his cousin Lytton Strachey: 'I seem to like them all so much, after these frogs and people.'

This French skate recipe from *2,000 Favourite French Recipes*, by Auguste Escoffier, a celebrated chef of the period, is absolutely superb.

Suggested ingredients

2 SMALL FISH SKATE WINGS, DE-BONED AND TRIMMED • SALT • VINEGAR
BLACK BUTTER (RECIPE BELOW) • A PINCH OF PARSLEY

If it [the skate] has not been cleaned, brush, wash and cut it up. Cook in salted water, allowing ½ oz. salt and ¼ pint vinegar per 2 pints of water. When cooked, drain, remove the skin and place on the serving dish, cover with black butter to which is added a pinch of coarsely chopped parsley. Heat 2–3 tablespoons good vinegar in the pan which was used for the black butter, and pour it over the skate.

Black butter

Cook the butter until it is a good brown colour and begins to smoke, then add 1 tablespoon well washed and dried parsley leaves. [Serves 2.]

Studio Omelette

'Duncan was still creating "havoc" when Clive decided he had gone too far. I was never sure what the nature of his crime might have been but I think he may have opened letters addressed to other people. At all events

Vanessa Bell, *Interior with Duncan Grant*, 1934. By the age of seventeen Duncan knew that he was more suited to life as an artist than as an army officer in British East India.

Clive decided that Duncan should have a good scolding. The only question was how should this be managed? He hit upon the idea of inviting him to dinner so that he and the accused should be tête-à-tête. Accordingly they went to some agreeable restaurant in Charlotte Street. They dined very well. Duncan, who had been forewarned of what was to come, waited for the thunderbolt to fall. The soup came; the entrée came; then the cheese, then some fruit, but no thunder. They had coffees and then a *pousse-café*: still no sign of trouble. Another glass, and Clive began to talk about the sacred nature of correspondence. He seemed to be about to come to the point, but somehow – it had been such a pleasant evening it seemed a shame to spoil it – better to order a third glass of brandy and then, coherent thought difficult, they wandered into the open air. "Just time to catch my tram," said Duncan. "Clive, would you lend me a penny?"'

Quentin Bell, *Elders and Betters*, 1995

Duncan Grant was one of Bloomsbury's most loveable individuals. He was 'the most entertaining companion I have ever known,' recalled David 'Bunny' Garnett; 'his lively mind never struck upon the obvious, and his sensibility made him acutely responsive to the mood of his companion.' Duncan was the youngest member of 'Old Bloomsbury' (Adrian Stephen, who was closest in age, was two years older), and he was good-looking, charming and cheerful: everybody's favourite paramour. In 1907 Duncan was introduced to Clive Bell and the Stephens through his cousin Lytton Strachey and it did not take long for them and the rest of the Bloomsbury circle to embrace his friendship wholeheartedly. Claude Summers, author of *The Gay & Lesbian Literary Heritage*, noted that Bloomsbury has been defined 'as a congeries of men and women in love with Grant', and it is true that Duncan had affairs with Lytton, John Maynard Keynes, Adrian, Bunny and Vanessa Bell. But to define the Bloomsbury Group simply as Duncan's innamorati is inaccurate, for he had many affairs outside of Bloomsbury as well.

Duncan was penniless, but somehow this never mattered to him or to his friends. Vanessa recalled: '[He] seemed unaware of the fact. If he wanted to go from one place to another he would borrow the exact sum, twopence halfpenny perhaps, which any of us could afford. If he wanted a meal he appeared, and contributions from each plate were willingly made. So he solved the problem of living on air with satisfaction to everyone'.

Occasionally he invited a friend to his Upper Baker Street studio for dinner and conversation. 'He made me an omelette in a frying pan over the fire, and we ate it on the bare wooden table with bread and cheese and beer,' Lytton wrote to Maynard in 1907. 'After that we drew our kitchen chairs up to the fire, and smoked cigarettes and talked.' Less than a year later, Maynard, too, found himself sitting by the fire in Duncan's studio, savouring Duncan's latest accomplishment.

This is one of Diana Higgens's* recipes from *Grace at Charleston*.

Suggested ingredients, for two
2–3 TBS BUTTER • 4 STRIPS BACON • 1 CUP COLD, DICED POTATOES
3 EGGS • 6 SPOONFULS GRATED CHEESE

Fry together in a little butter, bacon and cold boiled potatoes, cut into small slices or diced. Then beat up the number of eggs required for an omelette. Calculate one (or one egg and a half for each person). Into the beaten eggs stir two or three spoonfuls of grated cheese.

Add more butter to the pan and when it is sizzling hot, pour the cheese and egg mixture over the bacon and the potato dice already in the pan. Cook well until brown one side and then turn the omelette and cook lightly on the other side. This makes an omelette that looks like a very thick pancake. Do not over cook – it must be both moist and brittle. Serve flat.

Clive's Chocolate Layer Cake

Clive and Vanessa Bell's marital bliss lasted only a few short years and from 1914 it was over in all but name. Soon after the children arrived – Julian in 1908 and Quentin in 1910 – their passion for each other subsided, and they took other lovers. When Vanessa became pregnant with Duncan Grant's baby (Angelica), Clive assumed full responsibility for the child. Although this was ostensibly living a lie, Clive and Vanessa saw it as a practical and socially acceptable way of honouring the truth; that is, Vanessa and Duncan's love for one another. Furthermore, they saw no point in ruining a good 'working' marriage when there was nothing wrong with their friendship.

After the First World War, Vanessa and Clive moved back to Gordon Square (Vanessa had been riding out the war at Charleston and Clive at Garsington), and everyone saw everyone else much as they had before, although now Vanessa moved into 50 Gordon Square and Clive moved back to No. 46 (where he had kept rooms throughout the war and John Maynard Keynes was his landlord). They shared the same kitchen staff and took their meals together (at No. 50); and so communal had Bloomsbury's living become that even the servants, or 'the click', as they were known, were in and out of each other's kitchens on a regular

---

* *Diana Higgens compiled a book of her mother-in-law's recipes:* Grace at Charleston *(1994). Grace Higgens was Vanessa Bell's housekeeper and cook; she entered the Bloomsbury story in 1920.*

Vanessa Bell, *Clive Bell and Family,* **1924. When Vanessa became pregnant with Duncan Grant's child (Angelica), Clive assumed full parental responsibility.**

basis (almost as frequently as their masters and mistresses were in and out of the bedrooms above the kitchens).

Clive had many virtues, despite his philandering. The painter Dorothy Brett recalled: 'Clive Bell and Aldous Huxley were working as conscientious objectors. Curiously enough Clive Bell was immensely popular with the farm hands and farmers. He was jolly, never did a lick of work, but kept them laughing and gave birthday cakes to their wives and children.' According to Lytton Strachey, writing of Clive in 1905, 'His character has several layers, but it is difficult to say which is the fond. There is the country gentleman layer, which makes him retire into the depths of Wiltshire to shoot partridges. There is the Paris decadent layer, which takes him to the quartier latin where he discusses painting and vice with American artists and French models. There is the eighteenth-century layer, which adores Thoby Stephen. There is the layer of innocence, which adores Thoby's sister. There is the layer of prostitution, which shows itself in an amazing head of crimped straw-coloured hair. And there is the layer of stupidity, which runs transversely through all the other layers.'

In 1902, when Clive first visited the Stephens, he brought them some partridges. Later, when he would stay at Garsington, Ham Spray and Charleston, he would arrive with small gifts, sometimes chocolates, a brace of birds, or magazines. Whatever the occasion, he was always unselfish and considerate. This layer cake from *Fry's Chocolate Recipes* would suit not only his multifaceted personality, but also his gargantuan appetite for chocolate.

⅓ CUP BUTTER • 1 ½ TSP BAKING POWDER

1 CUP LIGHT BROWN SUGAR • ½ TSP SODA

2 EGGS • ½ TSP SALT • ½ CUP SOUR MILK

⅛ TSP CINNAMON • 1 TSP VANILLA

3 TBS FRY'S BREAKFAST COCOA • 2 ¼ CUPS FLOUR

Grease and flour [21.5 cm (8½-in.)] tin; mix, and sift dry ingredients, flour, baking powder, soda, salt, cinnamon and cocoa. Cream butter, add sugar gradually.

Roger Fry, *Still Life with Chocolate Cake*, c. 1912. Clive Bell had a gargantuan appetite for life, which helps to explain his multi-layered personality.

Separate eggs, beat yolks until thick and lemon-coloured, add to butter and sugar and beat vigorously. Add dry ingredients alternately with milk and flavouring. Beat egg whites until stiff and dry. Fold in, turn into greased and floured cake tins. Bake in moderate oven for thirty-five to forty minutes. [Once cool, cut into layers.] Spread [a] cocoa cream filling between layers and cover top with cocoa or a boiled frosting. [Serves 8.]

Drinks from the Sideboard

'There was little to eat or drink. In those days [*c.* 1910] drink wasn't considered necessary. There was always coffee to start with and on the sideboard a whisky and soda for those who liked the later drink before going away … and buns perhaps to eat. But nothing very much. Nobody seemed to expect very much in those days. Wouldn't have done at all now.'

Duncan Grant, BBC interview for *Omnibus* programme, 1970

Duncan Grant, *Study for a Still Life of Bottles and Books*, 1930s. From 1908 Bloomsbury's Thursday-evening gatherings were held at 29 Fitzroy Square, the home of Virginia and Adrian Stephen.

In 1907, following the marriage of Clive and Vanessa, Adrian and Virginia Stephen moved from 46 Gordon Square to 29 Fitzroy Square, not very far away from Gordon Square. There they resurrected Thoby Stephen's 'Thursday evenings' once they had settled into their new house. In 1909, Adrian noted in his diary: 'We dined alone together and after dinner waited a long time before anybody appeared. Saxon [Sydney-Turner] as usual came in first but was quickly followed by [Harry] Norton [Strachey's sponsor, fellow Apostle and friend] and he by James and Lytton Strachey. We were very silent at first'.

Ottoline's Plum Pudding

'One Thursday, early in 1915, I had dinner at Lady Ottoline Morrell's. I sat next to Frieda [Lawrence] and enjoyed talking to her. Lawrence was sitting next to Forster, and they were deep in conversation. Duncan Grant was there, and so were two girls from the Slade School of Art: Barbara Hiles (later Bagenal) and [Dora] Carrington. During the inspirational dancing afterwards I received a violent blow in the eye from the top of Barbara's head and had a black, partially closed eye in the days which followed.'

David Garnett, *Great Friends*, 1979

In 1909 Virginia Stephen wrote to her friend Madge Vaughan,* 'We have just got to know a wonderful Lady Ottoline Morrell, who has the head of a Medusa; but she is very simple and innocent in spite of it, and worships the arts.' Indeed, Ottoline Morrell merits a whole chapter in any history of Bloomsbury, as a hostess, friend, lover and benefactress, who revered the arts and was extremely generous with her patronage, although her religious beliefs set her apart from her Bloomsbury friends. Her physical appearance was singular. She was six feet tall, with legs that appeared to reach as high as her long aristocratic neck. Her jaw was odd and angular, her eyes vaguely purple, and her hair a dazzling nest of copper tresses. Her clothes were flamboyant, like plumage: bright colours with vivid oranges and pinks, chiffon trousers, audacious blouses, outrageous shoes and feathered hats. The overall effect was that of a surreal work of art.

As a hostess, Ottoline (who married the Liberal MP Philip Morrell) was imaginative and brilliant. She collected the 'plums' of society and mixed them up: bohemians, critics, writers and politicians. She diligently arranged them around her long oak dining table and encouraged them to intermingle at her

* Madge Vaughan, Dame Janet Vaughan's mother, was a childhood friend of Virginia Stephen.

Vanessa Bell, *Still Life of Plums*, *c.* 1945. Ottoline Morrell collected the 'plums' of society and invited them all – politicians, artists and writers alike – to her dinner parties.

Thursday-evening parties in Bedford Square.** Home entertaining was her *métier*, 'plum' pudding her *pièce de résistance*.

Leonard Woolf noted that Ottoline's entertaining methodology 'existed in four forms: you might be invited to a lunch, a tea, a dinner, or to an evening party after dinner, and the last might be very large or fairly small. At all of them the pudding would certainly contain plums, distinguished or very distinguished persons, and the point of the pudding was, it seemed to me, not so much in the eating as in the plums – the bigger the better. In the pudding of society I am not too fond of plums.'

The atmosphere at Ottoline's parties was dynamic and scintillating, excited and exalted. Aesthetes bantered with intellectuals, and everyone, recalled Barbara Bagenal, 'danced madly together'. Bloomsbury had never seen anything like it.

This is Helen Anrep's recipe for Batter and Fruit Pudding, adapted for plums.

*** Ottoline and Philip Morrell moved to 44 Bedford Square in 1906. 'Thursday evenings' were held there from 1907.*

Duncan Grant, *Ottoline Morrell*, 1913. Ottoline became firm friends with Vanessa Bell and Virginia Stephen after having tea with them at Fitzroy Square in December 1908.

Suggested ingredients

1 LB PLUMS • SUGAR • 1 EGG • 6 OZ FLOUR • 1 BREAKFAST CUP MILK

½ TSP BAKING POWDER

Chop up one pound of apples (gooseberries, plums, or any other fruit will do) and put them in a greased pudding basin and sprinkle [plenty of] sugar over them; now make a batter of one egg, six ounces flour and one breakfast-cupful of milk; one half a teaspoon of baking powder must be added to the flour; when the batter is smooth, press it over the fruit and steam gently for one hour; care must be taken that the water remains boiling and does not evaporate too much. [Serves 6.]

Peppard Bones

'She had a small house at Peppard in the Chilterns, where she spent the month of July [1911]. I stayed at Ipsden, six miles from Peppard, and bicycled over every day, arriving about noon, and leaving about midnight. The summer was extraordinarily hot, reaching on one occasion 97°[F] in the shade. We used to take our lunch out into the beech-woods, and come home to late tea. That month was one of great happiness.'

Bertrand Russell, *Autobiography*, 1967–69

Ottoline and Philip Morrell acquired Peppard Cottage shortly after Philip won the Liberal parliamentary seat for Henley-on-Thames in 1906. They entertained frequently: regular guests included Roger Fry, the artist Henry Lamb, Bertrand Russell, Lytton Strachey, Desmond MacCarthy, Vanessa and Clive Bell, Virginia Stephen, and Helen and Boris Anrep.*

Once, when the bohemian painter Augustus John's two young sons came to stay, Ottoline recalled: 'Fearing that they would arrive with only a cotton overall each I went and brought them an outfit of clothes. We found it difficult to get them to eat, and when we asked them what they were accustomed to eat at home, they only answered in a deep voice, "Bones."'

This frugal soup recipe from a First World War cookery book will satisfy unpretentious bohemian tastes, and maybe even hunger. It can be prepared with simple ingredients, such as bones (rabbit and pigeon are fine), seasonal vegetables, pepper, salt and water. A dash of sherry will enhance the flavour, and will render the soup even more palatable.

---

* *Ottoline Morrell had affairs with Henry Lamb (in 1910–11) and with Bertrand Russell (in 1911–16).*

Simon Bussy, *Lady Ottoline Morrell, c.* 1920. Ottoline and her husband, the Liberal MP Philip Morrell, agreed to have an open marriage after Philip's first illegitimate child was born in 1904. Some of Ottoline's lovers (Bertrand Russell, Augustus John and Roger Fry) were regular guests at Peppard, a cottage she and her husband owned from 1907 to 1911.

2D. [1–2 KG] WORTH OF BONES, CHOPPED SMALL • 2 OZ DRIPPING
2 LARGE ONIONS, PEELED AND CUT INTO SLICES
2 CARROTS, SCRAPED AND SLICED • 1 TURNIP, PEELED AND SLICED
½ PT SPLIT PEAS OR LENTILS • 1 TSP MIXED HERBS
SALT AND PEPPER TO TASTE

Put the bones and dripping into a saucepan, and fry a little over the fire to brown slightly, then add 2 quarts of cold water and bring slowly to the boil. Skim, and add the vegetables and peas or lentils (previously soaked). Stir till it boils, then simmer for 2 hours longer.

Remove the bones, add the herbs, and season to taste, then serve. The bones may be used a second time with fresh vegetables. [Serves 6.]

Bunga Bunga

'I hadnt realized till that moment how tired I was – what a strain it had been … how glad I was that it was over. I hadnt realized either how ravenous I was. My lips were parched. I could taste the paint on them. My dress was heavy. My wig made my head hot. Oh if we could only take our things off and have a meal! But that was impossible. It was then I suppose about five in the afternoon. There was no restaurant car in the train until we reached was it Swindon? We had to wait for two hours before we had anything to eat or drink. So there we lay, dazed hungry, but in a state of such relief that it was safely over. All the princes I think fell fast asleep.

'At last the train pulled up. And there a dining car was attached; and Cole went off to arrange about a meal. He had to arrange that it was served in our compartment; for if we ate in public the public would of course see that our dye melted as we drank. A table was procured; the waiters laid the table. But then, to my horror, Cole who persisted in keeping up the farce till the last moment, told the waiters that it was quite out of the question for them to serve dinner unless they wore white gloves. He said it would outrage the Emperor's feelings – to take a plate from a man whose hands were bare. There was the soup, steaming in the plates, but we weren't allowed to eat it until those wretched men had dashed out into the town and bought white gloves; and I believe the whole of that train was kept waiting several minutes while they ran to a shop to get them. That shows you what a very serious business a hoax was to Horace Cole.'

Virginia Woolf, '*Dreadnought* Hoax Talk', 1940

In 1910, Cambridge friends Horace Cole, Guy Ridley, Anthony Buxton and Adrian Stephen, together with Adrian's sister Virginia and Duncan Grant, dressed up as members of the Abyssinian Royal Party and tricked the Royal British Navy into giving them a tour of their flagship, the battleship HMS *Dreadnought*. This hoax, organized by Cole and intentionally leaked to the press, was for many years afterwards a source of frightful embarrassment to the British Navy.

The 'Abyssinians' travelled in a VIP railway carriage from London's Paddington station to Weymouth, Dorset, where they were met with ceremonial red carpet, guard of honour and (because the Royal Navy reception party did not know Abyssinia's) Zanzibar's national anthem. They were greeted by Admiral William May and Flag Commander William Fisher (Adrian and Virginia's first cousin – he failed to recognize them!), who personally escorted the royal party to the pier for a formal inspection of the battleship. 'Bunga. Bunga,' the royal princes exclaimed when shown the men's quarters, the ship's sophisticated navigation equipment and the officers' bathroom.

Food was offered, but politely declined. 'As one might have expected the officers were almost too hospitable, and pressed us hard to eat and drink, but I was too afraid of the effect on our make-up,' wrote Adrian, the supposed royal interpreter, in *The Dreadnought Hoax*. 'I excused us on the grounds that the religious beliefs of Abyssinia made it impossible for the Royal family to touch food unless it was prepared in quite special ways. The feeding problem was easily dealt with, but a worse moment was when I saw that Duncan's moustache was beginning to peel off. A slight breeze had got up, and a little rain began to fall'. And so with one final 'Bunga. Bunga,' a bow and a naval salute, they were ushered back to the station and helped aboard their first-class carriage.

Five years later, on 18 March 1915, HMS *Dreadnought* rammed and sank a German submarine. The British Navy received a telegram of congratulation: 'Bunga. Bunga.'

The 'Abyssinian Royal Party'. From left to right: Virginia Stephen (prince), Duncan Grant (prince), Adrian Stephen (royal interpreter), Anthony Buxton (emperor), Guy Ridley (prince), Horace Cole (Foreign Office official). Duncan, Virginia and Adrian were among the hoaxers who duped the Royal Navy into giving the 'Abyssinian Royal Party' a tour of its flagship the HMS *Dreadnought* on 7 February 1910.

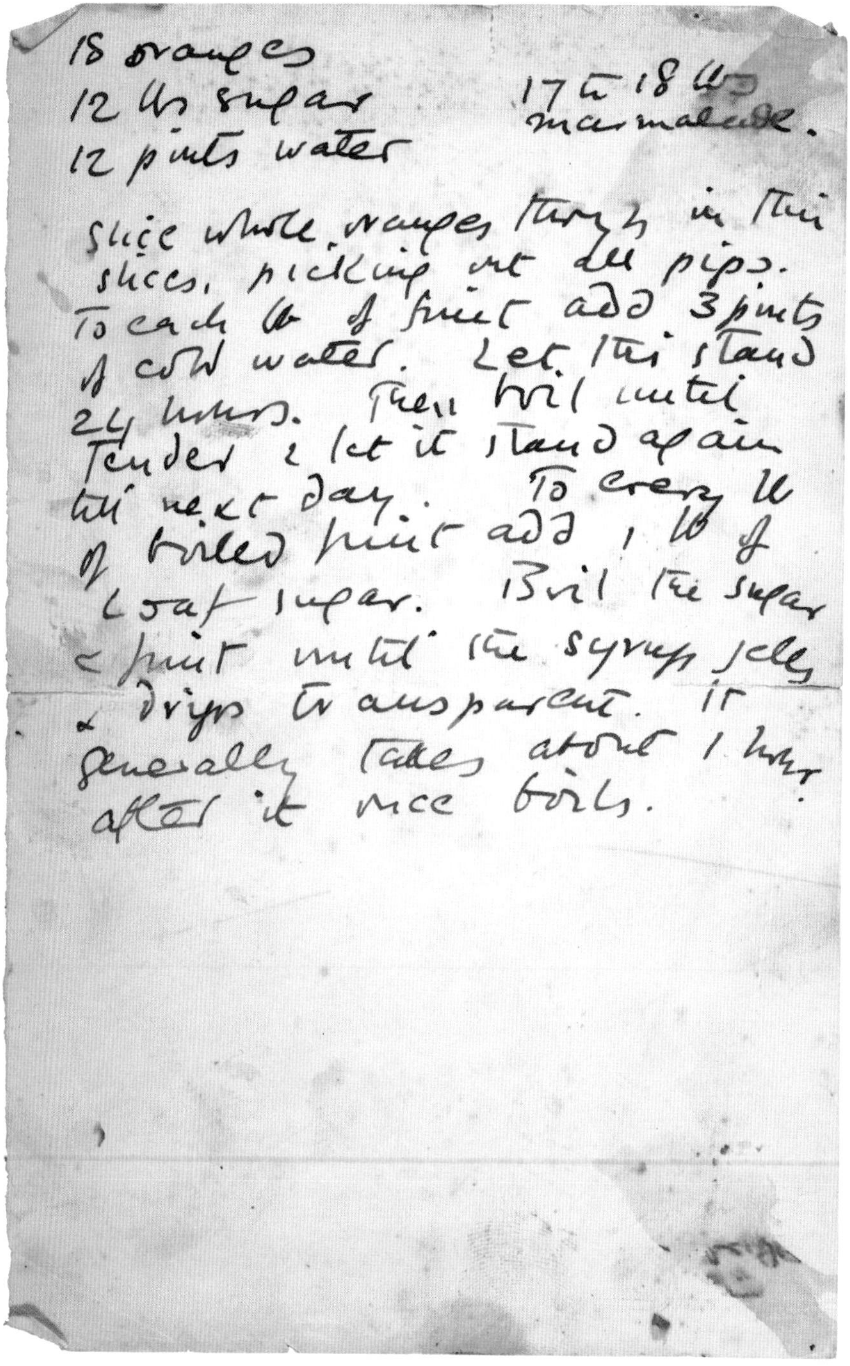

18 oranges
12 lbs sugar
12 pints water

17 to 18 lbs
marmalade.

Slice whole oranges thinly in thin
slices, picking out all pips.
To each lb of fruit add 3 pints
of cold water. Let this stand
24 hours. Then boil until
Tender & let it stand again
till next day. To every lb
of boiled fruit add 1 lb of
Loaf sugar. Boil the sugar
& fruit until the syrup jelly
& drips transparent. It
generally takes about 1 hour
after it nice boils.

Vanessa Bell's handwritten recipe for marmalade, unknown date.

Recipe for Marmalade

'Add to these gifts, which were as one may say open to the public, those
with which in private he [Roger] charmed his friends, a playful intellect for
instance, free fancy and a sense of fun, along with taste in food and wine,
and you have beside a great critic a rare companion.'

Clive Bell on Roger Fry, *Old Friends*, 1956

Roger Fry became part of Bloomsbury in 1910. He was a captivating lecturer,
influential critic and talented artist. He introduced Post-Impressionism to Britain,
formed the Grafton Group (an artists' exhibition society), founded the Omega
Workshops (an innovative domestic design collective) and liberated an entire generation of young British artists from the shackles of Victorianism.

But Roger's friends also saw another side of his personality, when he was
at ease – reading, playing chess or thinking aloud. These were the times when his
absurd gullibility surfaced and his misapplication of scientific reasoning revealed
itself. Often he made far-fetched assertions: that one day the planet would be
governed by birds, for instance; or that an irregularity in the tides signalled that a
'dark star' must have entered the solar system and would shortly collide with the
Earth. Sometimes the deductions of his logic baffled even himself.

Roger's voracious appetite for life had a catalytic effect on pre-war
Bloomsbury. His dynamism, integrity, experience and confidence made him,
Virginia Woolf noted, 'the flesh and blood' of the group, inspiring its members
with a fresh new intellectual and artistic vision. He was especially close to Vanessa
Bell, and although Vanessa's romantic love for Roger eventually waned, their
friendship and mutual creative interests continued. When Vanessa received a box
of oranges and lemons from her new lover Duncan Grant in 1914 (see pp. 82–84),
both she and Roger painted them. Vanessa, Roger and Duncan frequently worked
together, often sharing the same subject matter.

This is Vanessa's recipe for marmalade. To honour Roger's rare gift for
companionship, why not make this preserve of oranges and share it with friends.
It is delicious and plentiful – more than enough to go around.

18 ORANGES • 12 LBS SUGAR • 12 PTS WATER

Slice whole oranges through in thin slices, picking out the pips. To each lb of
fruit add 3 pints of cold water. Let this stand 24 hours. Then boil until Tender &
let it stand again till next day. To every lb of boiled fruit add 1 lb of loaf sugar.
Boil the sugar and fruit until the syrup jells & dries transparent. It generally
takes about an hour after it twice boils. [Makes 17–18 lb.]

Édouard Manet, *A Bar at the Folies-Bergères*, 1881–82. In 1910 Roger Fry included this painting in his exhibition 'Manet and the Post-Impressionists'.

Post-Impressionist Paris Feast

In the autumn of 1910, Roger Fry and Desmond MacCarthy went to Paris to collect art for Roger's forthcoming exhibition at the Grafton Galleries in London. 'I enjoyed choosing the pictures (which will by the bye quite give you the most tremendous shocks). We got about 50,' Desmond wrote to his wife, Molly, from Paris. On this trip Roger and Desmond aquired works by artists who were then little-known in Britain, including Paul Cézanne, André Derain, Paul Gauguin, Henri Matisse, Pablo Picasso, Georges Seurat, Paul Signac, Vincent Van Gogh and Maurice de Vlaminck. These artists' techniques and ideologies differed radically from those of their predecessors, the Impressionists, and further still from those of their conservative British counterparts. When 'Manet and the Post-Impressionists' opened in November 1910 in London, nearly everyone – the critics, the public and the British art establishment – was riled. Still they crowded in to see the exhibition, intent on experiencing the 'madness', 'pornography' and 'evil' of this louche new art movement.

On the ferry over to France, Roger and Desmond ate biscuits and sipped champagne. When they reached Paris, they not only consumed sensational French foods and wines, but also savoured the rich and remarkable visual feast of everyday life in the city that was celebrated so vividly in the art of the Post-Impressionists.

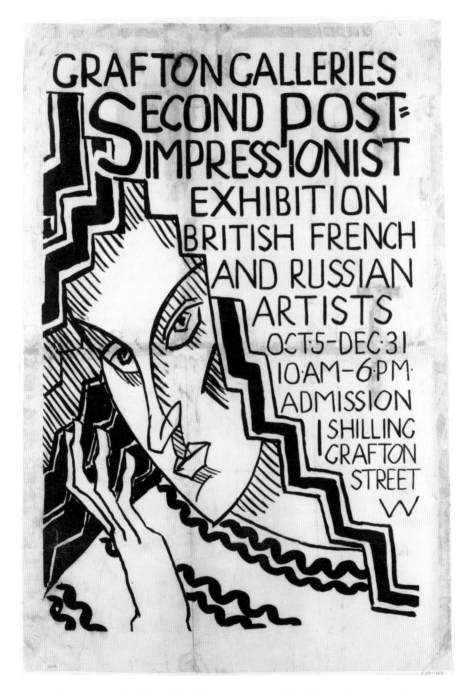

Duncan Grant and Frederick Etchells, poster for Roger Fry's 'Second Post-Impressionist Exhibition', 1912. The public's reaction to this exhibition was hostile, just as it had been towards Roger's first Post-Impressionist exhibition at the Grafton Galleries two years earlier.

Vanessa Bell, *Roger Fry*, 1912. Roger coined the term 'Post-Impressionism' in 1910, identifying a new movement by artists such as Paul Cézanne, Paul Gauguin and Vincent Van Gogh.

Post-Impressionist Barbeque Beef

'It was some time during that winter [1911] that a fancy dress dance was held at Crosby Hall which a group of us attended dressed more or less like figures from Gauguin. Roger, Clive and myself, Virginia, Adrian, Duncan and James Strachey I think were the party. We got stuffs I had lately found at Burnetts' made for natives in Africa with which we draped ourselves, we wore brilliant flowers and beads, we browned our legs and arms and had very little on beneath the draperies and when we arrived in a body at Crosby Hall the dancers stopped and applauded us. However our success was not universal for Mrs Whitehead was horrified at our indecency and I think Roger's reputation as a respectable critic, already shaky from his enthusiasm for the Post-Impressionists, must have suffered another shock.'

Vanessa Bell, 'Memories of Roger Fry', 1934

The selection of French paintings by Édouard Manet, Paul Gauguin, Vincent Van Gogh, Paul Cézanne and other artists assembled in Paris by Roger Fry and Desmond MacCarthy, and exhibited at the Grafton Galleries in 1910 and 1912, left many people visibly disturbed. They could not understand what the new paintings were about, nor did they even try. Leonard Woolf, who was secretary of the second exhibition, recalled that 'every now and then some well groomed, red faced gentleman, oozing the undercut of the best beef and the most succulent of chops, carrying his top hat and grey suede gloves, would come up to my table and abuse the pictures and me with the greatest rudeness.'

But to a few young artists Post-Impressionism was a revelation. As Vanessa Bell noted, 'here was a sudden pointing to a possible path, a sudden liberation and encouragement to feel for oneself, which were absolutely overwhelming.' The first exhibition had the effect of freeing young British artists from the restrictive conventions of Victorian painting. They were familiar with the works of the Old Masters and the Impressionists; now they were in a position to draw inspiration from both artistic schools, thereby creating form, 'not to imitate life', explained Roger, but 'to arouse the conviction of a new and definite reality'. 'All art depends upon cutting off the practical responses to sensations of ordinary life,' Roger argued, 'thereby setting free a pure and as it were disembodied functioning of the spirit'.

When he organized the 'Second Post-Impressionist Exhibition' in 1912, works by Duncan Grant, Vanessa and Roger himself hung defiantly alongside paintings by Cézanne, André Derain, Henri Matisse and Pablo Picasso. Although the public's reaction was once again hostile, one thing was certain: Post-Impressionism was not going to go away.

This is my own recipe for Post-Impressionist beef. The colourful peppercorn seasoning was created with those revolutionary artists in mind.

Garlic butter
75 G UNSALTED BUTTER, ROOM TEMPERATURE
2 GARLIC CLOVES • ¼ TSP WORCESTERSHIRE SAUCE
1 TBS CHOPPED PARSLEY

Steaks
4 X 1 IN.-THICK STEAKS • SALT • FRESHLY GROUND BLACK PEPPER
4 RED PEPPERCORNS, CRUSHED • 4 GREEN PEPPERCORNS, CRUSHED

To prepare the garlic butter, combine the butter, garlic, Worcestershire sauce and parsley together. Mix well. Transfer to a piece of cling film and roll into an oval oblong shape. Place in the refrigerator to chill.

Season the steaks with a little salt and freshly ground black pepper and cook on a hot grill for 8 minutes, 4 minutes each side.

Place a slice of garlic butter on top of each steak and garnish with the crushed red and green peppercorns. Serves 4.

Post-Impressionist Centenary Orange Cake

'The public in 1910 was thrown into paroxysms of rage and laughter. They went from Cézanne to Gauguin and from Gauguin to Van Gogh, they went from Picasso to Signac, and from Derain to Friesz, and they were infuriated. The pictures were a joke, and a joke at their expense.'

Virginia Woolf, *Roger Fry: A Biography*, 1940

Roger Fry argued that 'form' is the single most significant feature in a work of art, 'the direct outcome of an apprehension of some [detached] emotion'. Conventional Impressionists such as Claude Monet and Pierre-Auguste Renoir were too 'self-centred' in their comprehensive studies of light and colour, which meant that their works had the effect of appealing 'only to the eye'. Like the Impressionists, Post-Impressionists applied vivid colour to their canvases – but unlike their predecessors, the Post-Impressionists were 'not concerned with recording impressions of colour, light, or anything else exactly'. The aim was to arouse a new 'peculiar quality of "reality"' – aesthetic emotion – which 'the objects themselves evoked'.

This recipe from the scrapbook of Helen Anrep, Roger's partner, appeals to the eyes and arouses the tastebuds. If you want to celebrate a century of Post-Impressionism, make these cakes, fill, stack and ice them, and then cover them all over with lots of colourful sweets.

3 CUPS SUGAR • ¾ CUP BUTTER • 1 CUP SWEET [WHOLE] MILK • 4 CUPS FLOUR
1 TSP BAKING SODA • 2 TSP CREAM OF TARTAR • 5 EGGS, SEPARATED
GRATED RIND OF 1 ORANGE • JUICE OF 1 ORANGE

Break the yolks of eggs in a large bowl, add the sugar, butter and orange juice and beat until light and creamy; then add the milk, the whites of the eggs beaten to a stiff froth, and the flour into which has been sifted one teaspoon of soda and two of cream of tartar. [Mix in the orange rind.] Bake [for 60–75 minutes at 175°C in two 8 in. (20.5 cm) or] in four deep jelly-cake tins. Icing to go between

Letter from Roger Fry to Duncan Grant on Omega Workshops letterhead.
The Omega Workshops was a collaborative venture begun by Roger in 1913
in which artists were encouraged to decorate furniture and other household
objects in Post-Impressionist style.

the layers and on top: White of one egg, one cup of granulated sugar, juice
of one orange. Put the sugar on the stove with just enough water to moisten it.
(If you put too much the icing will be thin and run.) Let this boil till it is clear
and will spin a thread. Have the white of egg beaten light; then let someone
drip the sugar while you beat, and continue beating until it is thick and white;
stir in the orange juice; if it thins too much, add pulverized sugar till it is thick
enough. This makes a very [light] and delicious cake. [Serves 8–10.]

Omega's Alpha Feast

'With Post-Impressionism in pictures we are all familiar. Like it or dislike
it as much as we may, the interesting fact has to be announced that it is to
be confined to pictures no longer.'

Pall Mall Gazette, 11 April 1913

On the crest of the excitement created by the 'Second Post-Impressionist
Exhibition', Roger Fry started the Omega Workshops. His idea was to couple
Post-Impressionism in fine art with home decoration and thereby to create a
scheme for artists to be able to work collaboratively, part-time, and so earn themselves a regular income. Omega designs were bold, focusing on colour and form,

and once applied to simple, affordable pieces such as chairs, curtains and table-ware, they succeeded in transforming the banal into imaginative works of art. Inscribed into the bottom of each original piece was the Greek omega symbol: Ω.

On 12 June 1913, a dinner was held at 46 Gordon Square to celebrate the opening of the Omega Workshops (the official opening to the public and the press was on 8 July). A delicious six-course menu – beginning with Potage Alpha and finishing with Glaces à l'Omega – celebrated the brilliant colours and flavours of Post-Impressionism. Unfortunately there is no record of who was the cook on this occasion, so most of the recipes have been selected from cookbooks of the period.

Potage Alpha Saumon

Prepare the stock of the head, bones, fins and skin of the salmon and a few veg-etables boiled ½ hour; strain it. When cold, be very careful to remove all the fat and oil; thicken the soup with a little potato flour; add some chopped parsley, also some scallops of cooked salmon and of brown bread. NB The bones of 1 or 2 raw whiting give excellent flavour to the soup. [Serves 4.]

Crème de Volaille aux Petits Pois

Take 8 ozs. of raw fowl, weighed after it has been pounded and passed through a wire sieve, add 2 ozs. of cold white sauce, and pound it again, add fresh-ground white pepper and salt to taste, and half a pint of very thick cream, and mix lightly; fill a border mould previously buttered and garnished with truffle cut fancifully, place over it a piece of buttered paper cut a little larger than the mould, and steam in a shallow stewpan very gently for half an hour or until set; fill the centre with nicely cooked green peas, and pour *espagnole* sauce around the base. [Serves 4.]

To make the espagnole sauce

Cut up into rough dice one carrot, one small turnip, two onions, two or three ozs. of raw ham, put into a stewpan with two ozs. good *poularde* fat or dripping, one sprig of thyme, one bay leaf, two parsley roots, one sprig of marjoram, fry all together until a nice brown colour, then add three pints of good stock made from bones and carcasses of poultry, bring to the boil, and thicken with one dessertspoonful of potato *fécule*, mixed with a little cold water, add fresh-ground white pepper and salt to taste; if not a rich brown, add a few drops of Parisian essence [i. e., gravy browning], allow it to boil, and skim it well until it clarifies itself, strain and use. It should be the consistency of thin glaze sauce.

Cotelettes d'Agneau

Cut and trim some cutlets off a well-hung neck of mutton, brush them over with melted butter on both sides, and grill very quickly in front of a bright fire three minutes on each side, then have some green figs cut in two and cook until soft in a little *consommé* or chicken broth, drain off, and place half a fig on each cutlet. Place the cutlets around a *croûton* of bread made as below, and pour Cumberland sauce over them.

Omega Workshops invitation card, probably designed by Duncan Grant with lettering by Roger Fry, 1913.

Carve a *croûton* of bread, and fry in boiling lard a nice golden colour. Stick it to the dish with flour and white of egg mixed together. The dish should be hot when the *croûton* is fixed. Fill the top of the *croûton* with green figs, and garnish with fancy skewers, with figs and truffles, and serve very hot.

David Garnett's Cumberland Sauce

4 TBS RED CURRANT JELLY • 1 GLASS PORT [230 ML]
2 SHALLOTS • 1 ORANGE • ½ LEMON • TSP [FRENCH] MUSTARD
PINCH POWDERED GINGER

Skin orange & lemon as finely as possible & slice skins into fine strips. Drop into boiling water for 2 minutes & drain. Chop shallots finely.

Melt redcurrant jelly, add port, shallots & orange & lemon peel. Squeeze juice from orange & lemon & add mustard & powdered ginger. Let it simmer & serve either hot or cold. I prefer cold. [Serves 6.]

MENU

Dîner du 12 Juin 1913
—

Potage Alpha
Saumon
Crème de Volaille aux
Petits Pois
Côtelettes d'Agneau
Haricots Verts

Galantine
Salade Russe
Glaces à l'Oméga
Dessert
—

Vanessa Bell or Duncan Grant, menu card for the opening of the Omega Workshops, 1913.

Frances Partridge's Haricots Verts

Dress [lightly cooked, chilled] haricot beans with chervil, tarragon, chives, parsley, 5 tbs olive oil & tarragon vinegar, teaspoon French mustard, chopped raw onion, ½ tin anchovy fillets in oil and seasoning.

Galantine

Procure a nice large fowl, after plucking and drawing it split it down the back and remove all the bone, then lay it out flat on a board. Cut the flesh and make it an equal thickness all over. Put a thick layer of forcemeat as below, then a truffle here and there, then another layer of forcemeat, and then place some strips of fat bacon which have been blanched, that is, put in cold water and brought to the boil, then strain and dry it, then more forcemeat and a few blanched and skinned pistachio kernels and more forcemeat, then roll it up tight and tie it in a napkin. Boil it two hours, then undo the string and tie it again very tight and allow to get quite cold. Remove the napkin and mask it over with *chaudfroid* sauce, allow it to set, then coat it well with liquid aspic jelly. Place it on a rice stand, then pipe it with *mayonnaise* butter and decorate with cucumber fans. The cucumber fans are made by vandyking the skin, then cut in thin slices, fold in two, then fold again. [Serves 6–8.]

To make the forcemeat

Take one pound of lean veal, four ozs. of fat, two ozs. of breadcrumbs, pass the fat and lean veal through a mincing machine, add the breadcrumbs, and season well with fresh-ground white pepper and salt. Bind with the whites of two eggs; use as directed above.

To make the chaudfroid *sauce*

Fry together two ozs. of butter and two ozs. of flour without acquiring any colour, add half a pint of light stock or chicken broth and half a pint of cream, stir until it thickens, add salt to taste, boil ten minutes, dissolve three leaves of gelatine in the sauce, strain and use while cooling. It should be of a sufficient consistency for masking.

To make the aspic jelly

Take eight pounds of shin of beef, cut the meat off the bone, reserving about two pounds of the lean part. Put the remainder in a large stewpan with the bone chopped up, add one calf's foot and six quarts of water, bring to the boil, and skim well. Allow it to simmer slowly six to eight hours, when it should be reduced to about three-quarters, then strain it off through a colander, and leave it to the following day; it should then be a firm jelly. Remove all the fat off the top, and rub the jelly with a napkin, put the jelly into a clean stewpan, add half a bottle of hock and one and a half ozs. of gelatine. A little discretion is required here, as the amount of gelatin depends on the firmness of the jelly stock. Add the two pounds of lean meat passed through a mincing machine, also add one carrot, one turnip, onion, all cut up rather fine, add a small bouquet of herbs, one bay leaf, one sprig of thyme, one sprig of marjoram, two sprays of parsley, add the whites of two eggs. Stir over the fire with a wire whisk, withdraw the whisk and bring it to the boil, then put the stewpan where it will merely simmer for half an hour, then strain it through a soup cloth, add salt to taste.

To make the rice stand:

Put a pound of Carolina rice into a stewpan, cover it with water, and bring to the boil, add more water as it is reduced until the rice is done and pretty dry, then pound it in a mortar until it is a perfectly smooth paste, put it on a slab, and flatten it out to the size required; an oz. of lard may be boiled with it, and helps to facilitate the working of it; leave it until the following day, carve it by hand with a small knife, or cut the desired size with a fluted cutter.

To make the mayonnaise butter:

Blanch a bunch of parsley, a sprig of tarragon, a spray of chervil, until slippery to the touch; add a little salt and soda to the water. When done, strain off and press all the water out, and pound it in a mortar with two hard-boiled yolks of eggs, four ozs. of butter, a tablespoonful of capers. Add pepper and salt to taste, and a teaspoon of lemon juice; pound all together, and pass through a hair sieve.

Salade Russe

Take equal quantities of [lightly] cooked carrots, parsnips, beetroot, potatoes, cut in neat pieces, a few stoned French olives, some fillets of anchovy cut in two. Mix all together with four tablespoonfuls of salad oil, two tablespoonfuls of vinegar, one saltspoonful of dry mustard, a little fresh ground white pepper and salt; pile in the centre of the dish, and garnish with small three-cornered pieces of fried bread spread with caviare. Any kind of poultry may be cut up into small pieces and added.

Glaces à l'Omega

A. Basket of cream ice: Make a vanilla ice. When frozen, work it well with the ice spade, press the ice into a basket-shaped mould, adding some dried fruits, such as nectarines, pears, *glacé* cherries, angelica. An ice mould is best for this that takes to pieces when the ice has been placed on the dish. Pour a nice fruit sauce around and serve.

B. Vanilla Ice: For one quart of ice-cream put one pint of milk and cream mixed to boil, then pour it gradually on six yolks of eggs, stirring all the time. Put it into the saucepan on the stove, keep stirring until it begins to thicken. Strain it into a basin and allow it to cool, then add four ozs. of castor sugar, and two teaspoonfuls of essence of vanilla. Add one pint of thick cream, mix well all together and freeze as directed. [Pour into a Tupperware container and leave in the fridge to chill for two hours. Cover and transfer to the freezer. When the mixture is half frozen, remove from the freezer and beat for one minute. Return to the freezer.] This quantity is sufficient for twelve persons.

Vanessa Bell, *Summer Camp*, 1913. This work was painted during a group holiday to Suffolk in August 1913. Duncan Grant, who was also there, painted *Tents*, a similar work, which marked both the beginning of Vanessa and Duncan's shared artistic subject matter and the start of their intimate relationship.

Brandon Camp Poulet Provençal

'I am sitting over the fire keeping watch on a wonderful stew R. has made with a chicken, bacon, potatoes, a touch of apple, mint, etc.! We also had an omelot [*sic*] made by him for lunch.'

Vanessa Bell to Clive Bell, 12 August 1913

Roger Fry played a major role in Vanessa Bell's evolution as an artist and as an independent thinker. He opened her eyes to the colourful styles and ideologies of the modern French painters, whose expressive forms conveyed an honest, informal depiction of everyday life. This was a far cry from the drab orthodoxy of the techniques she had learned in her training under Sir Arthur Stockdale Cope and at the Royal Academy Schools. With Roger's encouragement, Vanessa matured and diversified her techniques, and ultimately distinguished herself as a modern colourist. She later recalled: 'That autumn of 1910 is to me a time when every-thing seemed springing to new life – a time when all was a sizzle of excitement, new relationships, new ideas, different and intense emotions all seemed crowding into one's life. Perhaps I did not realize then how much Roger was at the centre of it all.' In 1911, Vanessa and Roger became secret lovers and she grew to be a more confident and free-thinking artist and individual.

At Brandon Camp in Suffolk in 1913, on a camping holiday attended by Vanessa, Roger, Duncan Grant, John Maynard Keynes, Adrian Stephen and others, Roger impressed Vanessa with his culinary expertise. This fricassée, from *The Dudley Book of Cookery and Household Recipes*, dates from the time.

> Cut into neat joints a small Surrey fowl. Fry in a little butter, without allowing it to colour at all. Sprinkle on the pieces about two ounces of flour; let it cook a lit-tle, then wet with a light good chicken stock. Let it boil, stirring until it thickens, then add a faggot of herbs, one small onion, a few button mushrooms and some white wine – chablis is best. Let it simmer gently. When cooked [about 1 hour], dish up the chicken and mushrooms and strain the sauce, which has been sea-soned, over the pieces, adding about a gill of cream. Serve very hot. [Serves 4–6.]

Tunisian Citrus Fruits with Pork Chops and Crushed Sage

'Your basket of oranges and lemons came this morning. They were so lovely that against all modern theories I suppose I stuck some into my yellow Italian pot and at once began to paint them. I mean one isn't sup-posed nowadays to paint what one thinks beautiful. But the colour was so exciting that I couldn't [resist] it. I took what was left round to the Omega for Roger this afternoon and no doubt he'll soon be doing likewise. It was very clever of you I think to send them on stalks.'

Vanessa Bell to Duncan Grant, 25 March 1914

In 1913, after the waning of her affair with Roger Fry, Vanessa Bell fell in love with Duncan Grant. Here at last was a man who could nearly always make her happy and with whom she could lead an inspired life as an artist, day in and day out. He was young, charming and talented and their vision, energies and ambitions matched perfectly – apart from the fact that he was homosexual. The sexual aspect of their affair lasted only a short while and ended with the birth of a baby girl, Angelica, on Christmas Day 1918. Even so, for forty-seven years Vanessa and Duncan lived and

Vanessa Bell, *Oranges and Lemons*, 1914. Vanessa painted this still life
after receiving a box of Tunisian fruit sent to her by Duncan Grant.

worked side by side as artists, interior decorators and best friends. Despite Duncan's liaisons with other men, Vanessa was tolerant and understanding. A 'stoical warmth' was part of her very essence, as her daughter later recalled: 'She sat and sewed or painted or listened; she was always sitting, sometimes at the head of the table, sometimes by the fire, sometimes under the apple tree. Even if she said little, there emanated from her an enormous power, a pungency like the smell of crushed sage.'

When Vanessa received a box of oranges and lemons at 46 Gordon Square, sent by Duncan from Tunisia in the spring of 1914, she was so overjoyed that she painted them. Later, in her house at Charleston, Duncan's room often smelled of the fruit he left to ripen on his window sill. He delighted in the texture, flavour, form, colour and aroma of most things and was always quick to share his enthusiasm.

Thoughts of Tunisian citrus fruits and crushed English sage inspired me to create this colourful fragrant pork dish.

4 PORK CHOPS • ZEST OF 1 LEMON, GRATED • ½ TSP SALT
¼ TSP PEPPER • 2 TSP SAGE, FINELY CHOPPED • 2 TSP OLIVE OIL
1 TSP BROWN SUGAR • 3 ORANGES, CUT INTO ¾-INCH WEDGES

Wash the chops under cold running water and pat dry. Combine the lemon zest, salt, pepper, sage and 1 teaspoon olive oil in a mixing bowl with a fork. Cover the chops with the paste and place under the grill for 10–12 minutes, depending on the thickness of the meat. When a small pool forms in the centre of each chop, turn over and grill for approximately another 8–10 minutes.

Meanwhile, drizzle the orange wedges with the remaining oil and half the sugar and place under the grill for 2–3 minutes. Turn over wedges, sprinkle with the rest of the sugar, and return to grill for another minute or so to heat through. Serve with the chops. [Serves 4.]

Tender Cutlets with Aphrodisiac Sauce

Mr and Mrs Clive Bell's early months of marriage were extremely happy. They entertained frequently and sexuality seemed to radiate from Vanessa's every pore. Her bawdy sense of humour reflected her honest, happy, sensual self and soon a son, Julian, arrived. Vanessa continued to paint but most of her spare time was now dedicated to caring for the child. Clive, however, was not happy with the new situation and in late 1908 confided to his sister-in-law Virginia Stephen: 'I see nothing of Nessa … I do not even sleep with her; the baby takes up all her time.'

Virginia was feeling a similar sense of jealousy and it was not long before she and Clive began to see quite a lot of one another. Although Clive and Virginia's affair was not consummated on a physical level, they became sufficiently intimate for Vanessa to feel considerably aggrieved. But she behaved stoically, and the affair eventually blew itself out. 'You know', Virginia once observed, 'only very rich soft natures like Nessa's absorb their experiences.'

But Clive Bell's flirtation with his sister-in-law had not been his first extra-marital affair. Indeed, soon after he and Vanessa married, he resumed relations with a Mrs Raven-Hill, with whom he had had a previous relationship. In 1914, when the Bell–Stephen marriage was essentially over (by this point Vanessa had had an affair with Roger Fry and was in love with Duncan Grant), Clive began a long-term love affair with Mary Hutchinson, Lytton Strachey's cousin. In 1925 Virginia wrote to the painter Jacques Raverat describing Mary's exquisite feasts: 'Clive came in late, having been dining with Mary at her new house in Regent's Park. She has a ship's steward to serve at table, & whether for this reason or another, provides the most spicy liquors, foods, cocktails, & so on – for example,

Virginia Stephen and Clive Bell, on the beach at Studland Bay, Dorset, 1910. In 1908–9, Virginia and Clive began an intimate, albeit unconsummated, love affair.

an enormous earthenware dish, last time I was there, garnished with every vegetable, in January – peas, greens, mushrooms, potatoes; & in the middle the tenderest cutlets, all brewed in a sweet stinging aphrodisiac sauce – I tell you, I could hardly waddle home, or compose my sentiments. So Clive gets a little warm & very red about the gills towards midnight.'

But Mary could assemble more than just a few admirable dishes. She was a liberal-minded woman who shared Bloomsbury's contempt for conventional morality. Despite her marriage to the barrister and King's Counsel St John Hutchinson, a well-known patron of the arts, she felt no compunction about entering into simultaneous affairs with Clive, the writer Aldous Huxley and his wife, Maria. Moreover, in 1934, she fell in love with Virginia, telling her: 'I must love – can you bear such hunger – for I believe it is really this that I feel and I pine for you sometimes.' But Virginia, though seduced by Mary's tender cutlets and aphrodisiac sauce, would not be seduced by Mary herself.

Meat Bobbity

'Walked to Buttawa expecting to camp there for breakfast. Pleasantly surprised to find that by a misunderstanding my carts had gone to Palatupana. This meant another 8 miles in the heat of the day and I have never known anything like the heat of the jungle now. It is absolutely parched up and after an hour in it, it seems to dry up every drop of moisture in one's body. I always thought I could go from 6 to 10 without feeling it at all, but by 7.30 now one feels so weak that if there were game, which there is not – the deer have all gone to the thick jungle – one could scarcely lift one's rifle to shoot at it. Luckily my pony was behind me and I rode on fast, to Palatupana, and *en route* into the backside of an elephant who was strolling down the track near Velapalawewa. Before I knew what had happened the pony's head was facing the way we had come by. The elephant strolled on apparently oblivious and we followed him for a considerable distance. I at last sent on a bitch who was with me and she drove him out of the path like a big sheep.'

Leonard Woolf, *Diaries in Ceylon*, 2 April 1911

In 1903, after obtaining their Bachelor of Arts degrees from the University of Cambridge, Leonard Woolf and Saxon Sydney-Turner stayed on to prepare for the Civil Service Examination. They passed and were offered positions: Saxon joined the Treasury (where he worked for the rest of his life) and Leonard

14. மீட் பாபிட்டி

1 பவு. கொத்தின மீட்.

2 பெரிய மேசைக்கரண்டி நெய் அல்லது பொரிக்கும் கொழுப்பு.

2 பெரிய வெங்காயம்.

½ தேங்காய்.

1 எலுமிச்சம்பழ ரசம்.

½ கோப்பை வாதுமை முதலிய பருப்புகள்

2 முட்டை.

1 பெரிய மேசைக்கரண்டி கறிப் பவுடர்.

வெங்காயத்தை நன்றுய்ச் சிவக்கும்வரை கொழுப்பில் பொறித்துக்கொண்டு அதில் கறிப் பவுடரும் மீட்டும் சேர்த்து 15 நிமிஷம் நிதானமான தீயில் வேக வை. தேங்காயை உடைத்து இளநீரை ஒரு கோப்பையில் சேர்த்துக்கொண்டு கொஞ்சம் உப்பு சேர்த்துக்கொள். பிறகு ஆழமாயுள்ள புடிங் டிஷில், ஃப்ரை யிங் பானிலும் கோப்பையிலும் உள்ளவைகளைப் போட்டுக்கொண்டு அதில் எலுமிச்சம்பழ ரசமும், அடித்த முட்டைகளும், துருவிய தேங்காயும் மீட்டும் சேர்த்துக் கலக்கிக்கொண்டு வாதுமை முதலிய பருப்புகளை மேலே தூவி 15 நிமிஷம் பேக் பண்ணி, சூடாகவே பரிமாறு.

Recipe for Meat Bobbity in Tamil. In Ceylon, Leonard Woolf was served 'rice and curry' at every meal.

accepted an Eastern Cadetship in the Colonial Service. In 1904 he set sail for Ceylon, where he remained for the next seven years.

'Colombo was a real Eastern city,' Leonard recalled in his autobiography, 'swarming with human beings and flies, the streets full of flitting rickshas and creaking bullock carts, hot and heavy with the complicated smells of men and beasts and dung and oil and food and fruit and spice.' The quality of cooking and the array of flavours to which Leonard was introduced in Ceylon varied enormously, but what never changed was the certainty that 'rice and curry' would be served at every meal. There were fish curries, vegetable curries, meat curries and the 'eternal aged stringy curried chicken'. Sometimes, thick rice pancakes, known as hoppers, appeared at table, but after one particularly nasty episode with a greasy typhoid-infested hopper, which nearly killed him, Leonard avoided eating them.

In Jaffna, flies and the smell of rotting flesh made food consumption virtually impossible. 'Every particle of food had to be kept closely covered until the last moment before you popped it into your mouth.' But in Galle and in the jungles of Hambantota, in the southern part of Ceylon, Leonard found eating easier and a lot more pleasant: the food was fresher, the menu more varied and the overall quality of his meals much improved. He frequently contributed something to the pot after going out hunting with his gun.

This Ceylonese curry recipe was published in the 1930s in a bilingual cookbook with instructions in both English and Tamil (the latter so that the family cook could make the recipes). The dish consists of curried beef and eggs and is not too spicy – just right for the European palate.

1 LARGE TBS CURRY POWDER • 1 LIME (JUICE ONLY) • 1 LB MINCED BEEF •
½ COCONUT • 2 EGGS • 2 LARGE ONIONS
2 LARGE TBS GHEE OR FRYING FAT • ½ CUP NUTS

Fry the onions in the fat until well browned, add curry powder and meat and allow to simmer for fifteen minutes. Break the coconut and pour the milk into a cup and add a little salt to taste. Then into a deep pudding dish put the contents of the frying pan and cup, and also lime juice, beaten eggs, grated coconut meat and stir. Sprinkle nuts on top and bake [190°C] for fifteen minutes [or until cooked through]. Serve hot. [Serves 4.]

Supper at 46 Gordon Square

'There had certainly been a profound revolution in Gordon Square. I had dined in 46 Gordon Square with Thoby and his two sisters, the Misses Stephens, in 1904 only a few days before I left England for Ceylon. Now seven years later in the same rooms meeting again for the first time Vanessa, Virginia, Clive, Duncan, and Walter Lamb I found that almost the only things which had not changed were the furniture and the extraordinary beauty of the two Miss Stephens'.

Leonard Woolf, *Beginning Again*, 1964

When Leonard Woolf returned from Ceylon in May 1911, London was in the grip of an artistic tsunami. Post-Impressionism, Sergei Diaghilev's Ballets Russes and Richard Wagner's *Ring* cycle were together ushering in the dawn of a new artistic and social age. Leonard's London friends were embracing it wholeheartedly.

For the nature of friendship within Leonard's circle had changed as well. Since 1904, and especially since Lytton Strachey's 'semen' comment in 1907, polite conventions had been replaced by 'manners based on honest feelings'; first names had replaced last names; friends held no secrets from each other and conversation was frank and free. Moreover, so similar were Bloomsbury members' thoughts on love and friendship, and so intimate had they all become, that marriage, cohabitation and living within close proximity to one another seemed obvious and natural.

For Leonard, after seven years living 'a world apart' from his friends, the change was something of a shock. But it was his meeting with Virginia Stephen again, one evening over supper at 46 Gordon Square that would significantly alter the course of his life more than the new frankness of Bloomsbury. '[I]t would be worth the risk of everything to marry you', Leonard professed to Virginia in early 1912. And so it was.

Vanessa Bell, *Virginia Woolf,* 1912.

Brunswick Square Tray Food

'Brunswick would come round to Gordon when tired of the tray system of meals and in those easy days the larder always held enough for two or three unexpected guests, and servants seemed to welcome them with delight. So it was natural to say "stay to dinner" and to sit and talk as of old till all hours, either in the familiar room at No. 46 or in the Square garden.'

Vanessa Bell, 'Notes on Bloomsbury', 1951

Dec. 1911

29,
Fitzroy Square,
W.

38 Brunswick Square
W. C.

Meals are:

Breakfast.   9 A.M.
Lunch   1.
Tea .   4·30· P.M.
Dinner   8· P.M.

Trays will be placed in the hall punctually
at these hours.   Inmates are requested
to carry up their own trays; & to
put the dirty plates on them &
carry them down again as soon as
the meal is finished.

Inmates are requested to put their initials
upon the Kitchen Instruction Tablet hung
in the hall against all meals required
that day before 9·30· A.M.

Virginia Stephen's handwritten instructions to Leonard Woolf
about 'meals on trays' at 38 Brunswick Square, 2 December 1911.

Virginia Stephen was twenty-nine when she moved to 38 Brunswick Square in Bloomsbury with her brother Adrian, John Maynard Keynes and Duncan Grant (who shared Maynard's rooms). In 1911 it was scandalous for an unmarried woman to share a house with two single men to whom she was not related, but Virginia had a steely will and would not be dissuaded. 'To be intimate with Virginia Stephen in those days was not to be on easy terms,' Duncan recollected later. 'Indeed the greater the intimacy, the greater the danger – the danger of sudden outbursts of scathing criticism…. This shyness or fierceness was a necessary self-defence in her war with the world. The world must, she surmised, accept her on her own terms or not at all.'

On 4 December Leonard took the top floor of No. 38 and signed up to Virginia's communal living regime. With a shared passion for literature, they ate most of their meals together (on trays) in her room and discussed books and writing. Virginia even showed Leonard pages from *Melymbrosia*, the novel she was working on. He fell deeply in love and proposed marriage to her three times before she consented. Eventually, on 10 August 1912, they married at St Pancras Registry Office in London, in the middle of a violent thunderstorm. Clive and Vanessa Bell hosted the wedding reception afterwards at 46 Gordon Square.

This Frances Partridge pudding is very good and is ideal for serving at teatime, at a picnic, or alongside any dish that is eaten off a tray.

> **Peel & cook apples (cookers) with least possible water & brown sugar or golden syrup. When pulped fill the bottom of a baking dish & leave in fridge.**
> **When cold make a thick layer of white sugar over it & brown under grill. When brown & bubbling return to fridge till quite cold.**

Melymbrosia

'Meanwhile Helen herself was under examination, though not from either of her victims. Mr Pepper considered her; and his meditations, carried on while he cut his toast into bars and neatly buttered them, took him through a considerable stretch of autobiography. One of his penetrating glances assured him that he was right last night in judging that Helen was beautiful. Blandly he passed her the jam. She was talking nonsense, but not worse nonsense than people usually do talk at breakfast, the cerebral circulation, as he knew to his cost, being apt to give trouble at that hour.'

Virginia Woolf, *The Voyage Out*, 1915

Why did Virginia Woolf choose the title *Melymbrosia* for her early versions of her first published novel, and what is the meaning of this strange word? The literary scholar Louise DeSalvo suggests that 'it might have been intended as an ironic combination of the Greek words for *honey* and *ambrosia*: Woolf refers to the ambrosial fields of Greece in a diary she kept on a journey there.' Whatever her reason, *The Voyage Out* was the published title of the novel, and the manuscript of *Melymbrosia* is now merely an appetiser for that work, though curiously heavenly in parts. Here is my own culinary take on the meaning of *Melymbrosia*. It is naturally sweet and creamy and makes a delicious and invigorating breakfast meal.

90 G WHOLE ALMONDS • 300 G PITTED MEDJOOL DATES
150 ML GREEK HONEY • 75 ML WATER • JUICE OF 1 LEMON
1 VANILLA POD, SEEDED • 500 G GREEK YOGURT • 2 TBS POMEGRANATE ARILS

Toast the almonds in the oven and, when cool, chop roughly. Combine dates, honey, water, lemon and vanilla seeds in a saucepan and cook over medium flame for 10–12 minutes. Macerate with a fork and set aside to cool. To serve, place the yogurt in a dish, pour over the date sauce and garnish with the almonds and pomegranate arils. Serves 4–5.

Ye Olde Cock Steak Pie

'And then? Go on looking. Nothing much happens. But the dim light is exquisitely refreshing to the eyes. Let us watch little Miss Frend trotting along the Strand with her father. They meet a man with very bright eyes. "Mr Blake", says Mr Frend. It is Mrs Dyer who pours out tea for them in Clifford's Inn. Mr Charles Lamb has just left the room. Mrs Dyer says she married George because his washerwoman cheated him so. What do you think George paid for his shirts, she asks? Gently, beautifully, like the clouds of a balmy evening, obscurity once more traverses the sky, an obscurity which is not empty but thick with the star dust of innumerable lives.'

Virginia Woolf, *The Common Reader*, 1925

After their marriage, the Woolfs lived in a flat at Clifford's Inn, just off Fleet Street in London. Leonard and Saxon Sydney-Turner frequently met on Saturday evenings at Fleet Street's Ye Olde Cock Tavern for a traditional pub pie and a friendly game of chess. It is said that the writers Samuel Pepys, Charles Dickens and Alfred, Lord Tennyson had also frequented this pub, and that the playwright Oliver Goldsmith's ghost still haunts the place. Apparently, Goldsmith's disembodied head was seen lurking around at the back of the pub in 1984.

Leonard and Virginia enjoyed many a meal there. Situated just around the corner from their flat, it was convenient and, as Virginia could not yet cook, practical too. But marriage and the hubbub of Fleet Street soon took their toll on Virginia's nerves, leading to a severe nervous breakdown. On the advice of a physician, she and Leonard moved out of central London to quieter Richmond in October 1914. This move, and the outbreak of the First World War in August, effectively brought 'Old Bloomsbury' to a close.

This pie recipe from *The Official Handbook of the National Training School of Cookery* dates from 1915.

1 ½ LB BUTTOCK STEAK • ½ LB BULLOCK'S KIDNEY • ¾ LB FLOUR
½ LB CLARIFIED DRIPPING • SEASONING (FLOUR, SALT AND PEPPER)

1. Take one pound and a half of buttock steak, put it on a board, and cut it in thin slices.
2. Cut away all the skin.
3. Take half a pound of bullock's kidney, put it on a plate, and cut it in slices.
4. Put one tablespoonful of flour, one teaspoonful of salt, and a teaspoonful of pepper on to a plate, and mix them well together.
5. Dip each slice of meat and kidney into the seasoning, and roll them up into little rolls.
6. Arrange these rolls of meat and kidney in a quart [23 cm (9-in.)] pie dish, and fill up the dish two-thirds with water.
7. Put three-quarters of a pound of flour into a basin.
8. Add half a saltspoonful of salt to the flour, and mix them well together.
9. Take half a pound of clarified dripping, cut it in small pieces, and rub it well into the flour with your hands.
10. Then add by degrees enough cold water to make it into a stiff paste.
11. Take a rolling-pin and flour it. Also sprinkle flour on the board, and flour your hands to prevent the paste from sticking.
12. Take the paste out of the basin and put it on a board.
13. Roll out the paste once to the shape of the pie-dish, only rather larger, and to the thickness of about one-third of an inch.
14. Wet the edge of the dish with water.
15. Take a knife, dip it in flour, and cut a strip of the paste the width of the edge of the pie-dish, and place it round the edge of the dish.
16. Wet the edge of the paste with water.
17. Take the remaining paste and place it over the pie-dish, pressing it down with your thumb all round the edge.
18. Take a knife, dip it in flour and trim off all the rough edges of the paste round the edge of the dish.
19. Take a knife, and with the back of the blade make little notches in the edge of the paste, pressing the paste firmly with your thumb to keep it in its proper place.
20. Make a hole with the knife in the centre of the pie to let out the steam while the pie is baking.
21. Put the pie into the oven to bake gently for two hours [at 170°C]. Watch it occasionally, and turn it to prevent its burning. It should become a pale brown. It is then ready for serving. [Serves 6.]

CHAPTER THREE

Bloomsbury in Wartime

(1914–19)

Vanessa Bell, *Leonard Sidney Woolf*, 1940. In 1917 Leonard visited the Co-operative Society in Lancashire where he 'drank quantities of tea and ate splendid plates of fried fish'.

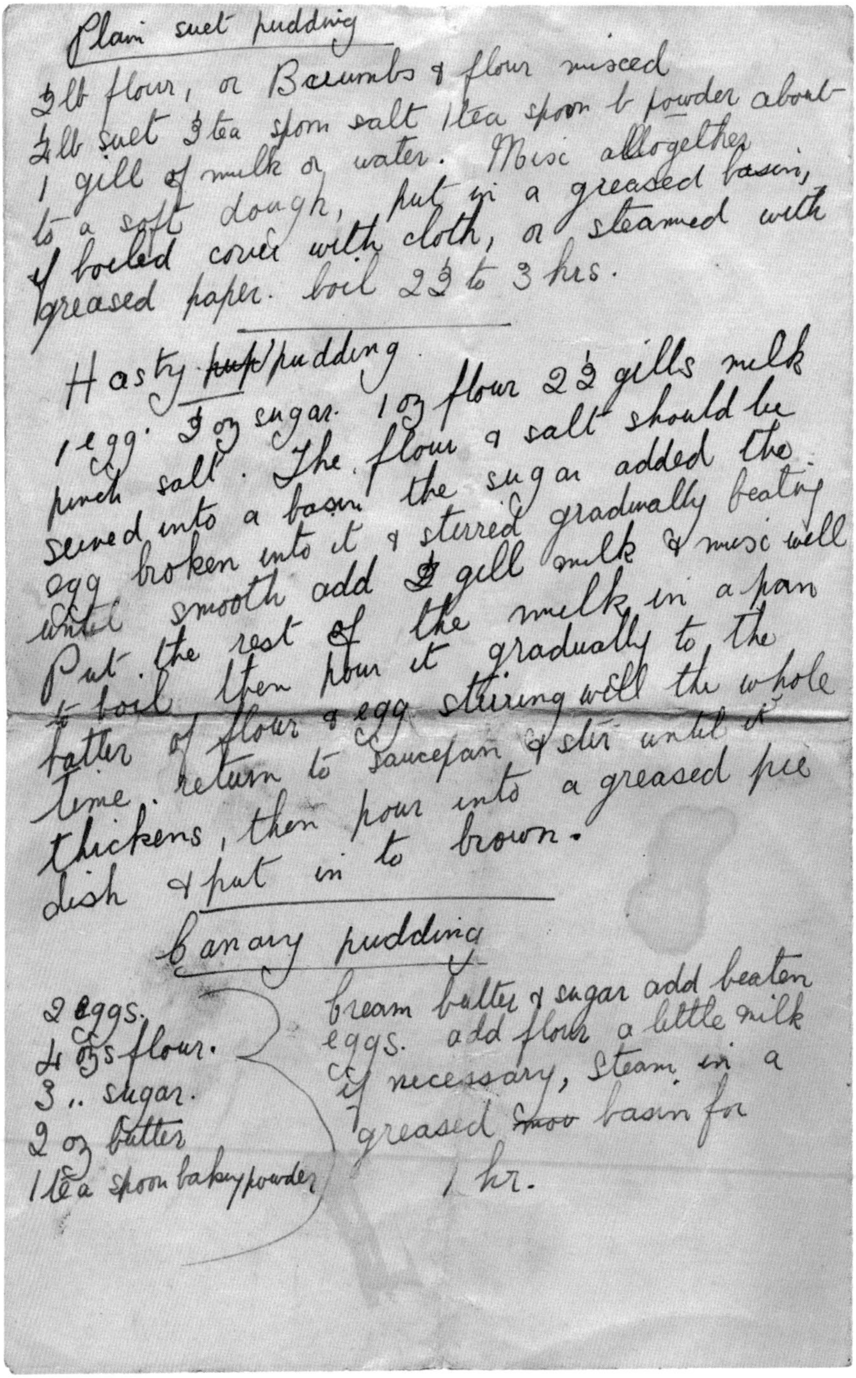

Plain suet pudding

½ lb flour, or Bcrumbs & flour mixed
½ lb suet 3 tea spoon salt 1 tea spoon b powder about
1 gill of milk or water. Mix altogether
to a soft dough, put in a greased basin,
& boiled cover with cloth, or steamed with
greased paper. boil 2½ to 3 hrs.

Hasty pudding

1 egg. 3 oz sugar. 1 oz flour 2½ gills milk
pinch salt. The flour & salt should be
sieved into a basin the sugar added the
egg broken into it & stirred gradually beating
until smooth add ½ gill milk & mix well
Put the rest of the milk in a pan
& boil then pour it gradually to the
batter of flour & egg stirring well the whole
time. return to saucepan & stir until it
thickens, then pour into a greased pie
dish & put in to brown.

Canary pudding

2 eggs.   cream butter & sugar add beaten
4 ozs flour.   eggs. add flour a little milk
3 .. sugar.   if necessary, Steam in a
2 oz butter   greased basin for
1 tea spoon baking powder   1 hr.

Three recipes, including Plain Suet Pudding, from Helen Anrep's
scrapbook. Virginia Woolf accidentally cooked her wedding ring into
such a suet pudding while on a cookery course in 1914.

Plain Suet Pudding

'She liked good talk, good food (and plenty of salt with it) and good coffee.'

William Plomer, 'Reminiscences of Virginia Woolf', 1941

The early years of Virginia and Leonard Woolf's marriage were stressful and extremely fraught. During their first night together on 10 August 1912 Virginia became notably 'unhinged', and Leonard resigned himself to a rocky 'white' marriage. After completing her first novel, *The Voyage Out*, in July 1913, Virginia became increasingly unstable, suffering from acute feelings of paranoia, insomnia and an inability to eat. Leonard was worried and took her to see a number of Harley Street doctors, but none of them was particularly helpful; one even recommended the removal of her teeth. Her mental state slipped into rapid decline, and in September she suffered a complete breakdown that culminated in her taking an overdose of the barbiturate Veronal at their flat in Clifford's Inn. Fortunately, Leonard arrived home in time to save her and, with continuous round-the-clock care, she was better by 1914, when the Woolfs moved to Richmond. But in 1915 Virginia suffered another breakdown. She refused to eat, and Leonard had to force her into taking tidbits from the end of his fork or spoon. He made her rest, and stipulated exactly when she could see friends, when she could work, and when she could write. He encouraged her to take up manual hobbies (such as cooking and typesetting) to keep her mind away from her writing. He watched her every move, monitored her mood swings and took detailed notes of her eating habits. Eventually, nine months and four psychiatric nurses later, and with a strict regime of food, sleep and rest, she rallied, and once again, the Woolfs resumed their 'normal' life together.

In 1914, when Virginia was relatively well, she took cooking lessons. She enrolled at a cookery school in Victoria and immediately, as she admitted in a letter to Janet Case, 'distinguished myself by cooking my wedding ring into a suet pudding'. This traditional recipe for Plain Suet Pudding is from Helen Anrep's scrapbook. Use the freshest suet available and, if possible, remove all rings beforehand.

2 LB FLOUR, OR BREADCRUMBS AND FLOUR MIXED

2 LB SUET • 1 TSP SALT • 1 TSP B[AKING] POWDER

ABOUT 1 GILL OF MILK OR WATER.

Mix together to a soft dough, put in a greased basin, if boiled [cover] with cloth, or steamed with greased paper. Boil 2½ to 3 hours.

Leonard's Fish and Chips

'Every morning, therefore, at about 9.30 after breakfast each of us, as if moved by a law of unquestioned nature, went off and "worked" until lunch at 1. It is surprising how much one can produce in a year, whether of buns or books or pots or pictures, if one works hard and professionally for three and a half hours every day for 330 days. That was why, despite her disabilities, Virginia was able to produce so much.'

Leonard Woolf, *Downhill All the Way*, 1967

Much attention has been given to Leonard Woolf, the devoted companion. He deserves commendation for his role as Virginia's husband – it could not have been easy coping with her mental illness and suicide attempts. For twenty-nine years he did everything to keep her safe, happy and sane: he loved her, cared for her and nurtured her literary genius. But Leonard was so much more than just Virginia Woolf's husband: he was a notable publisher, an excellent writer and a formidable political theorist.

He co-founded the Hogarth Press in Richmond with Virginia and was responsible for keeping the books, making all the management decisions and running the business on a day-to-day basis. Under his careful hand and watchful eye, the Hogarth Press grew into a successful and well-respected publisher. He also wrote and published over twenty-three works of his own: novels, short stories, autobiographies and essays. Politically, he was anti-imperialist and anti-fascist and, as a staunch socialist, his interests encompassed broad domestic, social and international issues, which he covered as literary editor of the *Nation and Athenaeum* and joint editor of the *Political Quarterly*.

Leonard's leftist leanings led him to the conference table over and over again, where he discussed his ideas with like-minded Labour politicians and union leaders. In July 1913 he attended his first Fabian Society lunch and ate his 'first of many plates of mutton at Grosvenor Road'. In 1916 he outlined a new system for international peace and collective security, *International Government*, which led directly to the formation of the League of Nations at the Paris Peace Conference in 1919. During the General Strike of 1926, he collected signatures and lobbied on behalf of the workers: 'Of all public events in home politics during my lifetime, the General Strike was the most painful, the most horrifying.'

On a trip to Lancashire in 1917, he met with the Co-operative Society, where he 'drank quantities of tea and ate splendid plates of fried fish'. This excellent recipe for fish and chips comes from a small booklet, *Handy Hints by Famous Broadcasters and Writers*, published in 1954.

Suggested ingredients

4 × 180 G HADDOCK OR COD FILLETS • 1 TBS PLAIN FLOUR
2 EGGS, BEATEN • 125 G BREADCRUMBS • 400 G POTATOES
1.5 L GROUNDNUT OIL • SALT AND PEPPER

First place a spoonful of plain flour in a large paper bag with salt and pepper. Drop in the dried fillets, and shake. Lift out, and shake off excess flour. Dip in beaten eggs, then breadcrumbs. Repeat if you like. Have a large pan half filled with fat. When really hot but not burning, drop in slices of potato, a third of an inch thick. If they rise with a jump you can put in the fish. Brown both sides and remove as soon as you dare. In time you will learn just when the fish is ready. Drain on absorbent paper.

Here is the secret of crisp chips. Cook them before the fish. Cut longish potatoes into slender fingers and dry well. When the fat is just showing a haze, drop in a few at a time so as not to cool the fat too much. When cooked through but not browned, remove and drain. Now fry fish and keep hot in the oven. Get the fat very hot again and drop in the cooked chips. In seconds they will be golden brown and crisp. Drain on the paper. For thin game chips and straw potatoes, fry only once. [Serves 4.]

Nellie's 'Good Soup'

'I particularly remember one noisy night when the bridge was bombed. I was sleeping on Virginia's rest couch in her room on the top floor and Leonard called out to me to bring my blankets down to the kitchen in the basement and make up a bed under the table. When I had staggered down with the bedding I found Virginia tucked into a camp-bed on one side of the range, Lottie and Nellie in an equally small bed on the other side, and

Dora Carrington, *The Servant Girl*, 1917. This was one of several woodcuts that appeared in Leonard and Virginia's Woolf's *Two Stories,* published by the Hogarth Press in 1917.

Leonard, looking most unhappy, was lying on a mattress on top of the kitchen table. We tried to settle down, but the noise from the anti-aircraft guns was so intense that sleep was out of the question. We were all rather alarmed, especially Lottie and Nellie, but Virginia managed to make them laugh by joking about Leonard who was precariously balanced on top of the table.'

Barbara Bagenal, Recollections of Virginia Woolf, 1972

The first book published by the Hogarth Press was *Two Stories*, written by Leonard and Virginia Woolf and hand-printed in 1917. They bought an old-fashioned press with the idea of providing Virginia with a relaxing manual pastime; but their hobby rapidly developed into a full-time business as manuscripts from their talented friends kept flooding in. Leonard hired Alix Sargant-Florence* (who later married James Strachey) to help Virginia set the type, but she lasted only a few hours. Their next employee, Dora Carrington's friend Barbara Hiles (later Bagenal), remembered Virginia offering 'a season ticket to Richmond, a share of the profits on the publications, and lunch and tea', and then adding, 'For lunch there will be meat, two veg and pudding!' Barbara stayed longer, and was present (and pleased) at the delivery in 1921 of the Minerva, a new press that was more efficient and much less labour intensive. Nine years later, the Hogarth Press purchased an even better machine, and the Minerva was given to Vita Sackville-West and Harold Nicolson as a housewarming gift when they moved to Sissinghurst Castle in 1930. It is still there.

In 1917, German air raids on London left the Woolfs running for cover. Leonard and Virginia took refuge in their basement workshop-cum-kitchen, where Barbara, Lottie Hope, the parlourmaid, and Nellie Boxall, the cook, were already bedding down with the press. 'We don't dine so much as picnic,' Virginia wrote to Vita a few years later, 'as the press has got into the larder and into the dining-room'.

In 1956 Nellie appeared in a BBC radio interview and spoke of Virginia's fondness for 'good soups'. Certainly, a bowl of Nellie's homemade soup would have been comforting fare at this particular picnic. This vegetable soup recipe comes from Herman Senn's *War Time Cooking Guide*, published in 1915.

I LEEK • I ONION • ¼ SMALL CABBAGE

2 OZ DRIPPING OR BUTTER • 1½ LB POTATOES • I PT MILK

I HEAPED-UP TBS CRUSHED TAPIOCA OR SAGO

SALT AND PEPPER

---

* Alix Sargant-Florence, Barbara Hiles and Dora Carrington (all Slade art students) cut their hair short and were thereafter collectively referred to as 'the Cropheads' by Virginia Woolf and 'the Bloomsbury Bunnies' by Molly MacCarthy.

Wash and trim the leek and the cabbage, peel the onion, cut all into small slices. Wash and peel and slice the potatoes. Put all the vegetables in a large saucepan with the dripping or butter, and stir over the fire for some minutes. Moisten with three or four pints of water, and leave to simmer for about an hour; season to taste with pepper and salt, and rub through a colander or wire sieve. Boil up, and add the milk to the soup. Let all come to the boil, skim, then stir in the tapioca or sago, and simmer for another ten minutes. Stir occasionally. A teaspoonful of celery seed, or a few outside leaves of fresh celery washed and cut into shreds, can also be added, if liked. [Serves 4.]

War Rations

'My steak was admirable – tender and juicy as … whose shall we say? – Mr Trott's? … bottom, my health quite recovered apparently, Virginia enchanting…. I don't think any more butter or sugar will be wanted, as they seem to be holding out.'

Lytton Strachey to Dora Carrington, 1 April 1918

Much of the food eaten in Britain during the First World War was imported from the United States and Canada. Until 1916 merchant ships transporting goods across the Atlantic had arrived safe and unscathed, but in 1917 Germany's devastating U-boat campaign sank so many ships that British food and coal supplies dipped to worryingly low levels.

Leonard and Virginia Woolf felt the pinch. They lived at Hogarth House in Richmond during the week and spent weekends and holidays in Sussex at Asheham House, a Regency farmhouse they had discovered while walking on the Downs in 1912 and subsequently rented for seven years. Finding sufficient coal and food to run one house, let alone two, was difficult, and in February 1917 Virginia wrote to her sister Vanessa Bell to see if she knew of any 'cheap dishes'. Their situation was becoming dire, she said: 'Last week we ran out of coal, and managed to get one ton, which is now almost finished, and it seems impossible to get any more. During the worst of the frost we had to live on coal bricks, bought from an old woman in the street; then our milk gave out, and then the telephone.'

Towards the end of the war, the food and coal shortages worsened and by July 1917 the Woolfs were bartering icing sugar with Vanessa for potatoes and greens. Even after the government introduced compulsory rationing (in January 1918) Virginia still found it 'impossible to get any milk'. Entertaining was awkward and friends were asked to bring their ration books with them when they came to stay: 'I think if you want meat, sugar or butter you must bring your cards,' Virginia wrote to Lytton Strachey in March 1918.

In 1918, despite wartime shortages and rationing, Virginia still managed to send provisions to Vanessa (who was pregnant with Angelica), to Duncan (who had wasted away after long hours of compulsory farm work in place of military service) and to her two young nephews (who were rapidly growing). On 15 November Vanessa, deeply grateful for Virginia's food parcel, told her: 'You wicked, wicked, extravagant and monstrous ape. You deserve a good beating and shutting up in your cage for a week, and if I were there you'd get it. How dared you send off such a parcel – cakes, soups, shortbreads, anchovies, sardines, sausages, I don't know what all. I'm simply overcome. While there you sit yourself shaking milk in a bottle to keep yourself alive. It's I who ought to be bombarding you with food from the country, instead of calmly eating up a pig and eggs and honey and all. Well, I suppose I must thank you instead of merely cursing, but you *are* wicked, Billy.'

These meat patties from Herman Senn's *War Time Cooking Guide* are an example of economical wartime food and, recalling Lytton's letter to Dora Carrington, tender and juicy too.

4 OZ BEEF [RUMP] OR MUTTON • 6 OZ FLOUR • 2 OZ DRIPPING
½ TSP BAKING POWDER • SALT AND PEPPER • [MILK/EGG]

Cut meat into small dice, season with salt and pepper, and moisten with a little water. Put the flour, baking powder, and a pinch of salt into a basin. Rub in the dripping, add enough water to mix to a stiff paste, roll out, cut into rounds, put 6 or more aside for covers. Roll out the trimmings, and stamp out 6 or more linings for the patty-pans [in all, 12 x 3½ in. (9 cm) rounds], which must be ready greased. Put a dessertspoonful of meat in each, wet edge of paste, put on the covers, press edges together, and make a hole on the top to let out steam. Decorate with little leaves, etc., made from the scraps of paste left over. Brush over with milk or beaten egg, and bake in a fairly hot oven for about ½ an hour. [Serves 2.]

Asheham Scrambled Eggs

'One week-end, when Virginia and Leonard were staying at Asheham, I walked over from Charleston to stay the night with them. When I arrived, Virginia said that she did not know what we could have for supper because the woman who came in to cook for them was ill. I suggested that I made some scrambled eggs. Virginia was amazed and said, "Can you really cook scrambled eggs?"'

Barbara Bagenal, in *Recollections of Virginia Woolf*, 1972

Vanessa Bell, *Still Life with Milk Jug and Eggs, Asheham*, 1917. At Asheham, Virginia Woolf was amazed to discover that her friend Barbara Hiles (later Bagenal) knew how to cook scrambled eggs.

It was a function of Virginia Woolf's social class ('the lower division of the upper middle class', according to her nephew Quentin Bell) that she was ignorant in the ways of cooking and cleaning. In the house where she grew up, at 22 Hyde Park Gate, her father employed seven servants to take care of the eleven members of his family. Not until 1934 did the Woolfs finally do away with live-in help altogether.

In addition to being free from having to perform domestic chores, Virginia also had the luxury of breakfasting in her own bedroom each morning. At eight o'clock, Leonard made a pot of fresh coffee and Louie, their daily in Sussex, cooked their eggs and bacon 'just right' – using two separate frying pans. When everything was ready, Leonard and Louie carried the breakfast things out to Virginia's bedroom.

Dora Carrington, sketch of a dining table in a letter to Julia Strachey, 1929. At a weekend party at Asheham, Carrington, Lytton Strachey, Vanessa and Clive Bell, Mary Hutchinson and Duncan Grant enjoyed drinking 'good' rum punch in the evenings.

Asheham Rum Punch

'I have just come back from spending three days on the Lewes downs with the Clive Bells, Duncan [Grant], Mrs Hutchinson and Lytton Strachey. God knows why they asked me!! It was much happier than I expected. The house was right in the middle of huge wild downs, four miles from Lewes, and surrounded by a high hill on both sides with trees. We lived in the kitchen for meals, as there weren't any servants, so I helped Vanessa cook. Lytton is rather curious. I got cold, and feel rather ill today. They had rum punch in the evenings which was good. Yesterday we went for a fine walk over tremendous high downs. I walked with Lytton. I like Duncan, even if you don't! What traitors all these people are! They ridicule Ottoline!'

Dora Carrington to Mark Gertler, December 1915

It was at Asheham, at a weekend party organized by Vanessa Bell, that the young artist Dora Carrington (always known to Bloomsbury as 'Carrington' because she disliked her first name) was first introduced to Lytton Strachey. She had just left the Slade School of Art, where she had showed enormous promise. Her artist friends there had included Paul Nash, Christopher Nevinson, Dorothy Brett, Alix Sargant-Florence, Barbara Hiles and Mark Gertler, who became her long-standing boyfriend. With a special gift for figure composition and painting, she had earned the respect and admiration of her peers.

Her first impressions of Bloomsbury and of Lytton, in particular, were not favourable. Annoyed when he kissed her while they were out walking on the South Downs, she was determined to get her own back. The following morning, armed with a pair of scissors, she sneaked into his bedroom and prepared to cut off his beard – but just as she was about to snap the long blades shut, Lytton opened his eyes and Carrington's loathing turned, miraculously, to love.

This is Mrs Beeton's heartwarming punch recipe from 1915.

1 QT VERY OLD ALE • 1 PT BOILING WATER • ¼ PT RUM
½ PT WHISKY • ¼ PT GIN • 1 LEMON, THINLY SLICED
SUGAR, TO TASTE • A PINCH OF GROUND CINNAMON
A PINCH OF GROUND CLOVES • A PINCH OF GRATED NUTMEG

Put all these ingredients into a large stewpan and bring nearly to boiling point. Strain into a punch bowl, add a few fresh thin slices of lemon, and serve.

Carrington's Virgin Salad

'I spent a wretched time here [at Garsington] since I wrote this letter to you. I was dismal enough about Mark [Gertler] and then suddenly without any warning Philip after dinner asked me to walk round the pond with him and started without any preface, to say, how disappointed he had

Garsington Manor, present day. Garsington was the home of Lady Ottoline and the Liberal MP Philip Morrell from 1913 to 1928.

been to hear I was a virgin! How wrong I was in my attitude to Mark and then proceeded to give me a lecture for quarter of an hour! Winding up by a gloomy story of his brother who committed suicide. Ottoline then seized me on my return to the house and talked for one hour and a half in the asparagrass [*sic*] bed, on the subject, far into the dark night. Only she was human and did see something of what I meant.'

Dora Carrington to Lytton Strachey, 30 July 1916

At Alderney Manor in Dorset, Dorelia John and her riotous, earring-wearing artist husband, Augustus, immersed themselves in a life of free love and communal living. Surrounded by 60 acres of heathland and a bevy of blue and yellow gypsy caravans, they began a bizarre salad-tossing ritual, which Virginia Nicholson writes about in *Among the Bohemians*: 'The family and their guests feasted on sorrel soup, huge casseroles flavoured with garlic, cooked in olive oil, washed down with rough red wine. The "disagreeably flavoured bulb" [garlic] was lavished on salads, which were prepared and served with fantastic rituals, the leaves being finally tossed with her bare hands by the senior virgin present.'

One can only assume that it was regularly Carrington's hands that were covered with salad oil.

Dora Carrington (centre) at Garsington Manor with (from left to right) Alix Strachey, Ottoline Morrell, Dorothy Brett and Juliette Huxley. Carrington eventually lost her virginity aged twenty-three to Lytton Strachey in Wales.

Fruition in Wales

'Oh! I am feeling so desolate! Lunch is over, tea is over, dinner is over, and here I am lying in my solitary state on the sofa among the white cushions – silent, nieceless,* sad!'

Lytton Strachey to Dora Carrington, 1 September 1916

Lytton Strachey and Dora Carrington joined Barbara Hiles and her soldier friend Nicholas Bagenal on a two-week trip to Wales in August 1916. '[E]verything was perfectly civilized,' Lytton wrote to David Garnett, 'parquet floors, spring beds, air cushions, delicious meals [cooked by Barbara], and an old hag to wash up…. As for Carrington – we seemed to see a great deal of each other.'

In Wales, Lytton and Carrington's attraction for each other came to fruition. Although a physical expression of their love was unsustainable, it was tenable in every other respect. There are 'A great deal of many kinds of love', proclaimed Lytton. Indeed, despite great differences in age, sexual preference and level of education, Lytton and Carrington's unique and profound love flourished until their deaths in 1932.

After the war Nick Bagenal became a horticulturist who, according to Quentin Bell, knew everything there was to know about fruit trees.

Sugar

Carrington: [I am going] to make some puddings & good dishes to cook for you when I come back, as I am sure in time we will get tired of eggs on plates.
Mark Gertler: [Y]ou certainly ought to learn something about cooking. I should always prefer my girl friends to be better cooks than artists. Don't let this annoy you.
Carrington: You don't care a bit whether I paint a good picture or not! But I *will* learn to cook, so that you will have no fault to find in me.

Dora Carrington–Mark Gertler correspondence, January 1915

Food was one aspect of the relationship between Dora Carrington and her boyfriend Mark Gertler where they had little disagreement: both liked good food and both had hearty, healthy appetites. Mark's appetite for sex, or *sugar*, as the two of

---

Early on in their relationship Lytton and Carrington often referred to one another using familial terms of endearment: uncle–niece, grandfather–grandchild or 'votre grand-bébé'.

them called it, was very different from Carrington's, however. They argued about it endlessly: he was all for it; she was not. For seven years Mark tried to make love to Carrington and when she did finally consent to sleep with him in the autumn of 1916 (after her visit to Wales with Lytton Strachey), she could see that 'sugar' had benefits, but still felt no overwhelming desire for any herself. For the time being, 'sugar' was best rationed.

She wrote to Mark in December 1916: 'I read Marlowe again last night and knew what one thing meant more than I did last week! It certainly is a necessity if one wants to understand the best poets. No she's not going on to say that is *why* she takes sugar in her coffee now. But taking sugar incidentally does not make one appreciate those poets more fully. But I only like sugar some times, not every week and every day in my coffee. I think you would like it so much and take it so often in your coffee that you wouldn't taste anything in time, and miss the taste of the coffee. But darling I shall look after that alright and only allow you three lumps a month. You've had more than three for this month. So no more till next year, you sugar-eater you!'

Of course, another reason why Carrington did not want to sleep with Mark was that she had fallen in love with Lytton. Mark was devastated and bitter when he learned the news and told her he could not understand how she was able to love a man who could not love her as 'completely' as he did. Hadn't Lytton once been in love with *him*? Mark wrote to Carrington: 'After the first course I waited and waited and nothing else came. Now, I simply must have sweets. After waiting for about fifteen minutes I gave my mouth a final wipe, got up and walked off in despair. What if I never get sweets! I sat and brooded all the afternoon about it and couldn't work.'

Teatime in Tidmarsh

'Tea was served in the dining room – a wonderful spread with farm butter, honey in the comb, home-made cakes and currant loaf, served in a pink lustre tea service.'

Gerald Brenan, *Personal Record*, 1974

After months of searching, Dora Carrington finally found a house where she and Lytton Strachey could live: the Mill House in the village of Tidmarsh, Berkshire. It was a small, romantic farmhouse set in an acre of land with an apple orchard, fruit trees, a vegetable garden and a little stream. To Carrington's well-trained eye, it was idyllic. In October 1917 she took out a lease (paid for by John Maynard Keynes,

Mark Gertler, *Portrait of a Girl Wearing a Blue Jersey* [Dora Carrington], 1912. Mark and Carrington began sleeping together in 1916 and referred to their lovemaking sessions as 'sugar'.

Saxon Sydney-Turner, James Strachey and Harry Norton*) and immediately began making pots of delicious jams and jellies for their new life together. In November she was ready to move in. She wrote to Lytton: 'Everything is packed with apples, artichokes and potatoes, instead of straw and paper! This method will probably insure [*sic*] all the china being smashed. But anyway the food supply is guaranteed for some months!'

Carrington's goal was to make everything perfect for Lytton. She decorated the house lovingly: the walls, the doors, and the bookcases – even the tiles around the fireplace were painted with the utmost care and attention. She hired Mrs Legg to help her with the housework, but she did most of the cooking herself. She made sure that Lytton was continually stimulated by a bevy of young, beautiful and intelligent men, and that he took regular exercise, drank plenty of milk

* *Harry – H. T. J. Norton, the mathematician – was Lytton's friend and financial sponsor. Lytton dedicated* Eminent Victorians *to him and paid him back with the proceeds from the sales of his book.*

and ate his rice pudding. She looked after him, cared for him and fed him like a god – because to her that is what he was. Breakfasts were lavish, lunches sublime, dinners 'indescribably grand'. Teatimes were heavenly: cakes, pies, breads, jams, butter and runny honey appeared extravagantly before Lytton each afternoon.

Their devotion was mutual. In 1918 Virginia Woolf wrote to her sister, Vanessa Bell, 'after tea Lytton and Carrington left the room ostensibly to copulate; but suspicion was aroused by a measured sound proceeding from the room, and on listening at the keyhole it was discovered that they were reading aloud Macaulay's Essays!'

Unfortunately Carrington's collection of recipes has been lost. These two recipes are from Helen Anrep's scrapbook. They are very good, but nobody ever put together an afternoon tea quite like Carrington.

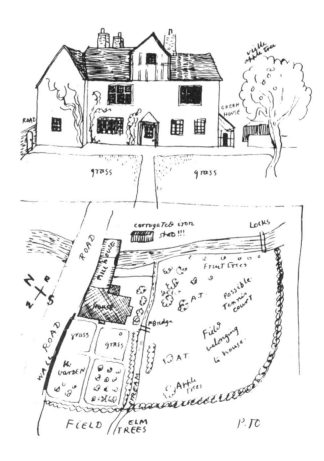

Dora Carrington, sketch of the Mill House, October 1917. When they moved to Tidmarsh in 1917, Carrington treated Lytton Strachey like a god.

Jam Roly Poly

2 LB SUET CRUST [6 OZ SHREDDED SUET, 1 LB FLOUR,
PINCH OF SALT, COLD WATER] • JAM

[Sift the flour and salt together. Mix in the suet. Add sufficient water to make a stiff paste.] Roll crust in a long strip about twice as long as wide, spread jam on to within 1 inch of edge, roll up, seal the edges well. Put in a scalded floured cloth [and] tie up ends [and] put in saucepan of boiling water, and boil 2 hours. [Serves 6.]

Johnny Cake

Two thirds of a teaspoonful of soda, three tablespoons of sugar, one teaspoonful of cream of tartar, one egg, one teacup of sweet milk, six tablespoonfuls of Indian meal, three tablespoonfuls of flour and a little salt. [Preheat oven to 175°C. Combine the Indian meal, sugar and milk. Whisk in the egg. Sift together the baking soda, cream of tartar, flour and salt. Mix well. Combine with the egg mixture. Transfer to a small, greased and floured baking tin and cook for 30–40 minutes. Slice, spread with butter and serve. Serves 6.]

Pickled Pears

'But beside the rooms created for Lytton and visitors there was a string of others which were her [Carrington's] special province. The kitchen, of course, and the still-room where she made country wines. Her cowslip wine was nectar, her sloe gin unequalled. Then the jams, bottled fruit and vegetables, chutneys, pickles, preserves. Her pickled pears were a revelation. The making of these was part of Carrington's secret life. I was in her confidence in all such occupations, for I shared her tastes, and it was I who had introduced her to Cobbett's *Cottage Economy*. Sometimes things went wrong. Her first attempt at bottling broad beans led to a series of explosions and to the most nauseating smell.'

David Garnett, *Great Friends*, 1979

Like Carrington's pickled pears, this recipe, adapted from *Mrs Beeton's Book of Household Management*, published in 1915, is a (pleasant) revelation.

8 LB FIRM, SOUND PEARS • 6 LB PRESERVING SUGAR
FINELY GRATED RIND AND JUICE OF 3 LEMONS
2 IN. WHOLE [ROOT] OF GINGER

Select a stew jar with a close-fitting lid, cover the bottom to the depth of one inch with cold water, put in the fruit and sugar in layers, and add the ginger, lemon rind and lemon juice. Cover closely, place the jar in a saucepan of boiling water, and cook slowly until the pears are quite tender [about an hour], but not broken. Put them carefully into jars, strain the syrup over them, and cover with papers brushed over on both sides with white of egg. The pears will keep good for three or four months if stored in a cool, dry place. [Serves 8.]

Bloomsbury Jam

Dora Carrington and Virginia Woolf were the great Bloomsbury jam makers. Jars and punnets of fresh fruit cluttered their larders and littered their kitchen cupboards and shelves. This traditional recipe from *May Byron's Jam Book* (1923), is excellent, especially when made with fresh, locally sourced fruit. Preparation time is roughly an hour.

To every four pounds of raspberries add one pint of red-currant juice. Let boil for half an hour, stirring well, and mashing the fruit with a wooden spoon. Press through a fine sieve, so that no seeds can pass; weigh, and for each pound of fruit allow twelve ounces of sugar. Boil up the fruit again, then add the sugar, and boil till the jam will set, which should be in twenty minutes.

Cowslip Wine and Sloe Gin

According to David Garnett, Dora Carrington's cowslip wine was 'nectar'; her sloe gin 'unequalled'. This delicate medium-sweet cowslip wine is made from the aromatic flower of the plant and is deliciously refreshing when served chilled on a warm summer's evening. Wild cowslips have declined dramatically in Britain in recent years and, although one can still find them growing on roadside verges and in nature reserves in April and May, they should therefore not be picked, and the recipe below is for historical interest only.

Sloe gin is a warming alcoholic drink, ideally served 'neat' in the depths of the winter. These recipes are from two classic cookery books of the period, *The Dudley Book of Cookery and Household Recipes* (1913) and Isabella Beeton's *All About Cookery* (1915), respectively.

Mark Gertler, *Still Life with Apples and a Mixing Bowl*, 1913. In 1915 Mark encouraged his then girlfriend, Dora Carrington, to learn how to cook, which she duly did.

Dora Carrington, 1920s. Carrington bottled fruits and vegetables and made delicious homemade wines and liqueurs.

Cowslip Wine

Pull the yellow flowers off the cowslips. To every gallon of water weigh 3 lb of lump sugar. Boil the quantity for half an hour, taking off the scum as it rises. When cool enough, put to it a crust of toasted bread dipped in thick yeast. Let the liquor ferment in the tub for thirty-six hours, then into the tub put for every gallon the juice of 2 lemons and the rind of 1 lemon, and both the juice and the rind of 1 Seville orange. Take 1 gallon of the cowslip flower tips and pour on them the liquor. This must be carefully stirred every day for a week, then to every 5 gallons of the liquor put in 1 bottle of brandy. Let the cask be closely stopped and stand only six weeks before you bottle it off. Be careful to use the best corks. PS Boil the rind of the lemon and orange with the sugar; it makes the wine a better colour.

Sloe Gin

Half fill clean, dry wine bottles with the fruit [sloes] previously pricked with a darning needle. Add to each, 1 oz of crushed barley-sugar, a little noyeau, or 2 or 3 drops of essence of almonds. Fill the bottles with good unsweetened gin, cork them securely, and allow them to remain in a moderately warm place for 3 months. At the end of this time strain the liqueur through fine muslin or filtering paper until quite clear, then bottle it, cork securely, and store away in a cool, dry place until required for use.

Tipsy Chicken

'I've just picked some peas. The beans frighten me. As for the raspberries, I feel as if I should never worm my way under the nets. La Legg [the cook] confesses herself baffled by the hens – after pretending last night that she could catch them without the slightest difficulty. I am in favour of making them tipsy – it seems to me, short of shooting them, the only plan. She, of course, thought I was mad to suggest it'.

Lytton Strachey to Dora Carrington, 6 July 1918

Once, while Dora Carrington was away, Lytton Strachey was obliged to pick his own vegetables for his supper. Unused to such tasks, he just about coped, managing to pick a few peas. The cook, on the other hand, failed to catch a hen!

This chicken recipe is from Frances Partridge's scrapbook and is attributed to Helen Anrep. If you wish, marinate the chicken pieces first in a little gin before cooking; this tenderizes the meat and infuses the flesh with delicious 'tipsy' botanicals. Serve with peas and, for the brave, beans.

Suggested ingredients

1 LARGE CHICKEN • 2 TBS BUTTER • 1 ONION, ROUGHLY CHOPPED
1 CLOVE GARLIC, FINELY CHOPPED • STOCK • 1 CUP BASMATI RICE
½ TSP SAFFRON THREADS • 1 TBS OLIVE OIL
1 SMALL TIN PIMENTOS

Cut up chicken & brown in butter. Put them in a warm casserole; add browned onions & garlic. Just cover chicken with stock & water which has rinsed frying pan. Cook slowly for about 1½ hours; but after 1 hour add a cup of rice, saffron if any, a spoonful of olive oil & a small tin of sliced pimentoes.

above: **Page from Frances Partridge's recipe book containing cooking instructions for Hunter Chicken.** *left:* 'We caught 4 rabbits in the garden last week and Partridge shot a pheasant', sketch in a letter from Dora Carrington to Poppet John (daughter of Augustus John), *c.* 1928, depicting Ralph Partridge shooting a pheasant from a window at Ham Spray House.

Hunter Chicken

'Of course your grandfather [Clive Bell] loved shooting; a brace of pheasants, or snipes were a favourite delicacy – he was a very good shot; and rabbits of course at that time were free of all myxomatosis.'

John Higgens in conversation with Virginia Nicholson, *c.* 2000.

Lytton Strachey may have been a hopeless hunter – even of beans and hens – but Dora Carrington was a good shot. In fact, Bloomsbury counted several good hunters among its members: Clive Bell and his son Julian were very good, while Thoby Stephen, Desmond MacCarthy, Ralph Partridge and Leonard Woolf were all competent. At the other end of the spectrum was David Garnett: 'Bunny always had guns lying around,' recalled Henrietta Garnett. '[H]e knew how to load a gun but he couldn't somehow connect the bird in the air with the bird in the bush.'

Fortunately one doesn't have to be a good shot to appreciate Frances Partridge's recipe for Hunter Chicken. It is *very* good.

Fry the pieces of a jointed chicken (coated in flour) in butter. Remove & fry one or 2 large onion[s] gently. Add 1 15 oz tin tomatoes & a glass of white wine. Blend well, pour over chicken, season, add bay leaf & 1 teasp. caster sugar & cook gently for 1 to 1½ hours. Add thick cream before dishing up. Try adding 12 green olives & some chicken stock, 2 cloves crushed garlic. [Serves 4–6.]

Savoury Loin of Pork

'[G]ather here – all who have passion and who desire to create new conditions of life – new visions of art and literature and new magic worlds of poetry and music. If I could but feel that days at Garsington had strengthened your efforts to live the noble life: to live freely, recklessly, with clear Reason released from convention – no longer absorbed in small personal events but valuing personal affairs as part of a great whole – above all to live with passionate desire for Truth and Love and Understanding and Imagination.'

Ottoline Morrell on Garsington Manor, *c.* 1914

Such was Lady Ottoline Morrell's dream when she graciously opened the doors of her Elizabethan manor house to friends and guests from its purchase in 1914 until she and her politician husband, Philip, sold up and moved back to Bloomsbury

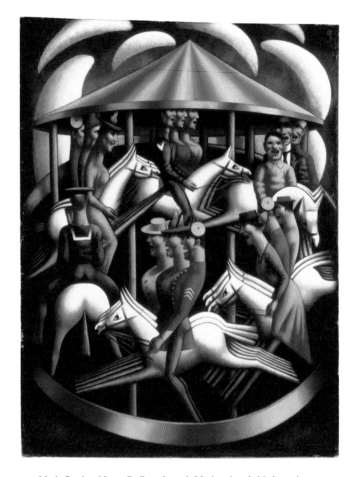

Mark Gertler, *Merry-Go-Round*, 1916. Mark painted this haunting depiction of a futile, mechanized world at war while working as a conscientious objector at Garsington during the First World War.

in 1928. During the First World War, she and Philip were pacifists and, as such, invited conscientious objectors to work as agricultural labourers on their farm. Clive Bell, Lytton Strachey, Bertrand Russell, Aldous Huxley and Mark Gertler were among the semi-permanent workers and residents at Garsington in 1916.

'The war has done some funny things among our friends,' wrote Virginia Woolf. '[Clive] sits in a farmhouse and occasionally turns over a vegetable marrow.' In fact, labour at Garsington was somewhat more intellectual than manual. Clive wrote an anti-war pamphlet, *Peace at Once*, which was confiscated and destroyed by the police. Mark painted *Merry-Go-Round*, a haunting depiction of the horrors of war. Lytton researched and continued to work on *Eminent Victorians*.

Bertrand, Ottoline's on-off lover, co-founded the Union of Democratic Control, a powerful anti-war organization. Aldous collected copy for his first novel, *Crome Yellow*, published after the war, which cruelly satirized Ottoline.

But Ottoline and Philip were not enormously rich and by 1918 had serious cash-flow problems. Despite her hospitality, Ottoline was criticized for being 'stingy with the food', and wild stories on this theme began to circulate. Quentin Bell, in *Elders and Betters*, recalled 'the story of a peacock which died a natural death and then appeared [as a] roast at table'. On another occasion, Lytton complained that there was far too little food on the breakfast table. He lost his temper, and was thereafter given 'breakfast in bed, with two eggs to it'. To Leonard Woolf

Clive Bell and two farm workers at Garsington Manor, 1917. In 1915 Clive wrote an anti-war pamphlet that was confiscated by the police and banned and burned under orders issued by the Lord Mayor of London.

he confessed: 'The rest continued to starve.' In truth, the food at Garsington was probably perfectly adequate, as Ottoline's biographer Robert Gathorne-Hardy remembers: 'The simple excellence of the food – a modest example of fine English country-house cooking – seemed altogether appropriate.' Home-baked milk bread was a Garsington teatime speciality. Pork would certainly have been on the menu in 1916, since Ottoline and Philip kept pigs. This loin of pork recipe from the Helen Anrep collection may be served with the Garsington Pickled Cabbage that follows.

> Have a small loin of pork very deeply scored and press some sage and onion stuffing between the scorings. Brush with olive oil and put in a hot oven [240°C] for the first fifteen minutes to make the crackling brittle. [Reduce the temperature to 190°C and cook for a further twenty minutes per 550 g.]

Garsington Pickled Cabbage

> 'Only is the sunlight ever normal at Garsington? No, I think even the sky is done up in pale yellow silk, and certainly the cabbages are scented.'
>
> Virginia Woolf to Barbara Bagenal, 24 June 1923

Red Cabbage Pickle is the title of a newspaper cutting from Helen Anrep's scrapbook. According to the article, this pickle is 'very appetizing' and will 'keep a few weeks'.

> Choose firm [red cabbage] heads, cut them into quarters, and after removing the stalk cut the cabbage across into very thin slices; spread it upon large platters, scatter salt with a liberal hand over it. The next day, drain through a colander. Then put the cabbage into a jar, and pour vinegar heated to the boiling point over it, some whole black pepper or curry powder or ginger may be put into the vinegar and be heated with it.

Chicken Pancakes

> 'Philip [Morrell] is fairly contented, though I think terrified of bankruptcy, and makes ineffectual attempts to economize by dividing one and a quarter chicken between 9 grown ups and 3 children!'
>
> Vanessa Bell to Roger Fry, 27 December 1915

Dora Carrington, *Picking Vegetables*, 1912.

This Frances Partridge recipe is a delicious and economical way to make a chicken go that little bit further.

> Cut [the leftover] meat in small cubes, toss in butter, season & sprinkle with red pepper. Add a little cream, chopped mushrooms, onions, pimentos, tomatoes or any available cooked vegetables. [Cook on a gentle heat until onions are soft and transparent. If the meat has previously been cooked, add to the pan later and heat through.] Make some very thin pancakes with no sugar [see Blinies, p. 248], place some of the mixture in each, roll & brown for a few minutes in a fireproof dish in the oven. Keep back a little sauce & pour it over the pancakes.

Duncan Grant's long-haired lurcher, Henry, painted by Grant under a window in Vanessa Bell's bedroom (now the library) at Charleston, *c*. 1916–17.

Little Henry's Honey Cake

'He [Bunny] races swiftly, vigorously, before the mind's eye pursuing a puppy [Henry] with half a cake in its mouth; they were both going at a tremendous rate. I wonder who won? We shall never know. That was at Wissett Lodge in Suffolk. Thither we had gone to grow fruit.'

Quentin Bell, Elders and Betters, 1995

Late in the winter of 1914, Duncan Grant met the shy, handsome blue-eyed son of Edward and Constance Garnett, David (or Bunny, as he was known), and it was not long afterwards that they became lovers. Bunny, who initially worked for the Friends War Victims Relief Mission in northern France, returned to England in 1916 and made plans to work, with Duncan, as a fruit farmer in the hope of avoiding conscription. As pacifists, they were eligible to be exempted from military service if they were able to prove to a tribunal that their work was of national importance. With this in mind, they went to Wissett Lodge in Suffolk to plough, prune and be together. There they laboured with innovative style. They nursed poorly chicks back to health by placing them in the warm kitchen cooker. They painted the tail feathers of leghorn chickens a distinguishing blue colour as a theft deterrent when their numbers dwindled suspiciously. If that didn't raise eyebrows, the sight of Bunny (and Barbara Hiles) strapped to the plough when tilling the soil certainly did.

Bunny found a recipe book and a book on beekeeping, and immediately began cooking meals and supplementing meagre wartime sugar rations with quantities of golden honey, some of which went to Duncan's long-haired lurcher, Henry. Soon afterwards, Vanessa Bell (who was also in love with Duncan) arrived with her sons Julian and Quentin, aged eight and six, their nanny, Flossie, and Vanessa's cook, Blanche. Survival mode switched to creative mode. Brushes and paint were unpacked and soon walls, furniture and curtains – just about all paintable surfaces – were transformed into vibrant works of art.

In May 1916, however, the local military tribunal rejected Duncan and Bunny's pleas for military exemption. Although they won their case on appeal, their labour as self-employed fruit farmers was deemed unsuitable war work. So, after harvesting the autumn fruit at Wissett Lodge, Duncan and Bunny moved to East Sussex to work on a farm belonging to someone else – a Mr Hecks. Vanessa took out a lease on Charleston, a neighbouring farmhouse, and the rest, as they say, is history.

This honey cake recipe is adapted from *Mrs Beeton's Book of Household Management* (1915). It is so good you'll want to keep it away from thieving dogs.

1 LB SELF-RAISING FLOUR • 5 OZ SOFT BROWN SUGAR
6 OZ CLEAR HONEY + 3 TBS FOR GLAZE • 8 OZ BUTTER • 3 EGGS
1 TSP GROUND CINNAMON • ½ TSP GROUND CLOVES
¼ CUP BRANDY

Boil the honey and sugar together, stir in the butter, cinnamon and cloves. Remove from the fire, add the brandy, and leave mixture to cool for 10–15 minutes. Beat the eggs and stir into the mixture. Sift the flour and add to the contents of the stew pan, and stir well. Pour into a 20 cm buttered/floured cake tin, and bake in a preheated 150°C oven for approximately 1 hour. Turn onto a wire rack to cool. Heat 3 tablespoons honey and spoon over the cake to glaze. [Serves 8.]

Charleston Coffee Pot

> 'It has a charming garden, with a pond, and fruit trees, and vegetables, all now rather run wild, but you could make it lovely.'
>
> Virginia Woolf to Vanessa Bell on Charleston farmhouse, 14 May 1916

Vanessa Bell's first impressions of Charleston and its grounds were not entirely favourable: the place was too big, too remote and far too cold and inhospitable. She soon changed her mind, however, and in October 1916 she and her two children, Julian and Quentin, Duncan Grant and Bunny Garnett moved into the farmhouse at the foot of Firle Beacon.

During the day, Duncan and Bunny worked on Mr Hecks's neighbouring farm, as directed by the military tribunal. Endless days hauling turnips out of the ground, hoeing beans and harvesting hay were physically exhausting. Moreover, in 1917, as a result of the German U-boat blockade of food shipments, their bodies ached not only from overexertion but also from lack of calories. Their health began to deteriorate.

At Charleston, life was basic with few comforts. Water was pumped manually to fill the cistern, or collected from the nearby spring in buckets when the pump froze; it was then heated on the range for washing, cooking and bathing. The outdoor earth closet needed regular emptying, and so did the chamber pots. The coal-fired kitchen range and the fireplaces were the only sources of heat; daylight, candles and oil lamps the only sources of light.

Despite these hardships, however, Vanessa and her entourage were better off than most. They cultivated their own potatoes and other vegetables. Apples proliferated in the orchard, and pears, peaches and plums grew in the walled garden at the back of the house. Bunny kept bees for honey and there were ducks in the pond, chickens in a run and, in the fields, rabbits that they could shoot and eat.

The one luxury that the Charlestonians enjoyed was freshly ground coffee (available from Fortnum & Mason and the Army & Navy Stores). During the lean war years, hot coffee provided much solace and comfort. No wonder Duncan made a painting of the coffee pot in the Charleston dining room in 1918.

This is a recipe by Igor Anrep, the son of Boris and Helen Anrep. He also knew the delicious benefits that come from grinding one's own coffee beans: 'The English generally make coffee much too weak or they use powdered coffee which is also fairly nasty.'

Duncan Grant, *The Coffee Pot*, *c.* 1918. Coffee was a comforting
beverage at Charleston during the war.

1 OZ COFFEE • NORMANDY COFFEE POT OR STRAINER

Grind the coffee finely but not to a powder, according to the method of straining.
Coarsely ground coffee is wasteful. Always warm the pot thoroughly with boiling
water. Throw this away and put the coffee in the strainer. Pour on a little, almost
boiling, water and leave for about one minute to allow the grounds to swell. Then
pour on boiling water more generously and leave to strain through into the pot.
Two or three fillings are sufficient before the liquid becomes water and weak.
Coffee beans are often under-cooked. They should be plain chocolate brown.

Bunny's Honey

'[I]f he [Bunny] had been edible he would have had a strong flavour. If he were to be compared to an animal then I should liken him to a bear, a creature with an endearing weakness for berries and honey but also a carnivore.'

Quentin Bell, *Elders and Betters*, 1995

'One evening he [Mr Tebrick] went to a cottager who had a row of skeps, and bought one of them, just as it was after the man had smothered the bees. This he carried to the foxes that they might taste the honey, for he had seen them dig out wild bees' nests often enough. The skep full was indeed a wonderful feast for them, they bit greedily into the heavy scented comb, their jaws were drowned in the sticky flood of sweetness, and they gorged themselves on it without restraint. When they had crunched up the last morsel they tore the skep in pieces, and for hours afterwards they were happily employed in licking themselves clean.'

David Garnett, *Lady into Fox*, 1922

David 'Bunny' Garnett was not part of the Bloomsbury Group at its inception around 1904. Nor did he go to Cambridge or attend any of Thoby Stephen's 'Thursday evenings' at 46 Gordon Square. His enduring appeal to Bloomsbury, however, and his unrelenting love for its members, are legendary.

Dora Carrington's honey label for David Garnett, 1917.

The hearth designed by Roger Fry in Clive Bell's study at Charleston.

At Charleston, on 25 December 1918, Vanessa gave birth to Angelica. Angelica was Duncan Grant's biological daughter, but it was Bunny who claimed her for his own. He wrote to Lytton Strachey about the baby: 'Its beauty is the remarkable thing about it … I think of marrying it; when she is twenty I shall be forty-six – will it be scandalous?'

It was. Bunny Garnett and Angelica Bell married in May 1942, and thus his second liaison with Bloomsbury began. Twenty years later, in 1962, his daughter, Henrietta Garnett, married Lytton Burgo Partridge, Bunny's nephew through his first marriage to Rachel ('Ray') Marshall. Within nine months, Sophie Vanessa was born and Bunny became grandfather to Bloomsbury's fourth generation.

Just as a bear (or a fox) is drawn to a nest of honey bees, so Bunny was drawn to Bloomsbury – and to beekeeping. In 1917 Dora Carrington designed the woodcut for his honey label that appears opposite.

Marrow and Ginger Jam

'Art is significant deformity.'

Roger Fry to a reporter soon after the opening
of the Omega Workshops on 8 July 1913

The bizarre-looking hearth in Clive Bell's study at Charleston was supposed to jettison heat effectively into the surrounding room. It was designed during the Bells' first winter there in 1916–17 by Roger Fry, constructed by Bunny Garnett, and appreciated by all – for in that bitter winter, the hearth was the only source of heat in the house (apart from the coal-fired kitchen range). At teatime, everyone would huddle around it; a pot of tea would be produced and, Quentin recalled, 'a confection called marrow jam' would appear, 'the vegetable marrow being made more palatable – that at least was the intention – by being flavoured with ginger.' This recipe from Grace Higgens is not at all unpleasant, although Quentin 'never conquered the dislike of vegetable marrows'.

4 LB MARROW, DICED (WEIGHED AFTER REMOVING SEEDS AND SKIN)
3½ LB SUGAR • JUICE OF 2 LEMONS • 3–4 OZ ROOT GINGER

Steam the marrow until tender, this takes 15–20 minutes. Put marrow into basin in layers with sugar and lemon juice, leave to stand for 12 hours. Put marrow and sugar into preserving pan, bruise the ginger well and tie in a muslin bag, add the ginger to the marrow. Stir over a low heat until sugar has dissolved. Boil jam rapidly until setting stage, this takes 20–30 minutes. Remove the bag of ginger, test for setting, pot and cover.

A Forsterian Salad
(with Quentin Bell's Chapon Seasoning)

'A pageant requires not only splendour, but a touch of the grotesque, which should lurk like onion in a salad.'

E. M. Forster, *Abinger Harvest*, 1936

E. M. Forster ('Morgan' to his friends) is one of the better-known members of Bloomsbury, but he was always on the outside of the group, grazing at the periphery. His thoughts on love, honesty, social conventions, civil liberties and religion were all very much in tune with Bloomsbury, but there were differences too. Morgan preferred Italy to France, Beethoven to Mozart, and was, in himself, diffident, non-confrontational and retiring. 'Lytton nicknamed him the Taupe, partly because of his faint physical resemblance to a mole, but principally because he seemed intellectually and emotionally to travel unseen underground and every now and again pop up unexpectedly with some subtle observation or delicate quip which somehow or other he had found in the depths of the earth or of his own soul,' recalled Leonard Woolf in his autobiography *Sowing*.

Dora Carrington, *E. M. Forster*, 1920. In the cold winter of 1939–40, Morgan (who was trying to keep warm) burnt his trousers by standing too close to Leonard and Virginia Woolf's 'cosy stove'.

Of all his Bloomsbury friends, Morgan was closest to Lytton Strachey and Leonard and Virginia Woolf. He was a regular guest at their country houses and once, on a visit to Monk's House (the Woolfs' Sussex home from 1919 onwards), he burnt his trousers on their 'cosy stove', while trying to keep himself warm. Fire seemed to be the order of the day, however, for when Morgan went out for dinner that evening to Charleston (still wearing his burnt trousers), the beam between the kitchen and the hall also caught fire. Fortunately the fire brigade was quick to arrive and serious damage was averted.

Quentin Bell used to season his salads by rubbing a piece of bread with a clove of garlic and placing it at the bottom of the salad bowl. Either the bottom of the bowl was reached and someone would eat the *chapon*, recalled Virginia Nicholson, or one would unceremoniously burrow down into the verdant depths and fetch it out. Here is her recollection of how her parents liked to prepare and season their salads.

'They always insisted that the dressing (which was made at the bottom of the salad bowl) was made as follows: Salt, pepper, mustard, vinegar. Mix well to dissolve the salt. Then add oil (proportions 1 x vinegar : 3 x oil) and whisk well to emulsify. Then add the optional "chapon" of garlic bread, and put the wooden salad servers into the bowl at an angle. Then place the salad leaves on top of the servers, and only toss when ready to serve. My parents and grandparents preferred very simple salads – just lettuce leaves, or chicory, or frisée, without onion'.

Asheham – 'Such a Dinner'

'Saxon is now as I write wandering disconsolately in the garden with a Badmington [*sic*] racket and B[attle]D[ore] and S[huttle] Cock. But the ladies have taken to the pen and there is no one for him to play with. I think there can be few people with such natures as he possesses, or it would be different.'

Dora Carrington to Lytton Strachey, 4 February 1917

Duncan Grant, *Asheham, Still Life*, 1912.

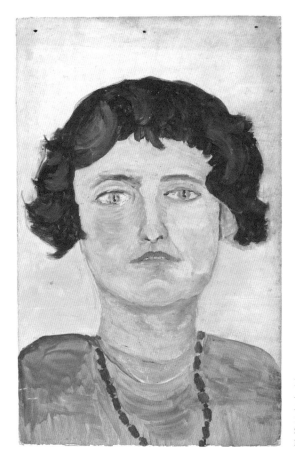

Rachel ('Ray') Strachey, *Barbara Bagenal (née Hiles)*, late 1920s or early 1930s. In 1917 Saxon Sydney-Turner fell in love with Barbara Hiles.

In January 1917 Saxon Sydney-Turner borrowed Asheham House from Leonard and Virginia Woolf. He invited Dora Carrington and Lytton Strachey (who declined because of the recent cold snap) as well as Barbara Hiles, an artist with whom he had recently fallen in love. The weather was sunny, but chilly, and they kept themselves warm by going for long walks and tobogganing down the South Downs on tea trays and on John Maynard Keynes's despatch case. In the evenings, Saxon read aloud, and on one occasion they collaborated on a series of amusing poems that they sent to Barbara's friend Nicholas Bagenal, who was serving with the Irish Guards in France.* One afternoon, Duncan Grant, Bunny Garnett, Adrian Stephen and his wife, Karin, walked over from Charleston and 'ate the most tremendous tea. Like starving stags, and brought a dog', noted Carrington. A few days later, Duncan and Bunny returned with Vanessa Bell and Maynard. They ate, said Carrington, 'Such a dinner. Soups, Beef sausages and Leeks, Plum Pudding, Lemon Jellies, and Punches afterwards!!!'

* *Nicholas Bagenal transferred to the Irish Guards from the Suffolk Regiment in 1916 and was seriously wounded in April 1918.*

Almost exactly a year later, on 1 February 1918, Barbara married Nicholas. Saxon never loved anyone else and never married. He and Barbara did, however, remain good friends for the rest of their lives.

Lytton Soup

'Lytton had written a book called *Eminent Victorians* "which blackened the reputation of decent and distinguished people". This sounded fun; we looked forward to his appearance with pleasure and here he was drinking soup at our table. How, I wondered, would he deal with it? It was thick white soup. How would it get past his beard? He seemed unaware of the difficulty and then, sure enough, he had a thick snowy growth on his upper lip. Did he realize how absurd he looked? Perhaps he did for with one deft wipe with his napkin he removed it, whereupon Vanessa said to him: "Lytton, how do you like being famous?" He considered this briefly and then, with what sounded like an expiring croak he replied: "Vaguely pleasant".'

Quentin Bell's memory (as a seven-year-old) of
Lytton Strachey visiting Charleston, *Elders and Betters*, 1995

Lytton Strachey visited Charleston in the winter of 1917. One evening he was reading aloud from the manuscript that would soon be published as *Eminent Victorians* when Duncan Grant fell asleep. This, Duncan later explained, was due to his exhaustion from having worked on Mr Hecks's farm all day.

and cold soup too!

Last night I dreamt of Queen Victoria!

Dora Carrington, sketch of Lytton Strachey in a soup bowl, 1920.

PRAY worthy Poet do not laugh at this somewhat curious scarf

Dora Carrington, sketch of Lytton Strachey, 7 November 1918.

When *Eminent Victorians* appeared in print in May 1918, however, it became an overnight sensation and a bestseller. According to the preface: *Je n'impose rien; je ne propose rien: j'expose.* ('I impose nothing, I propose nothing: I expose.') By exposing the truth, which often sullied the reputations of four eminent figures of nineteenth-century Britain – Cardinal Manning, Florence Nightingale, Thomas Arnold and General Gordon – Lytton proved that 'Discretion is not the better part of biography.' Indeed, he made biography a lot more interesting.

As Nightingale revolutionized nursing with steely determination by transforming its standard of cleanliness, so Lytton revolutionized biography by introducing a higher standard of honesty. To quote him on Nightingale: 'The ill-cooked hunks of meat, vilely served at irregular intervals, which had hitherto been the only diet for the sick men, were replaced by punctual meals, well-prepared and appetizing, while strengthening extra foods – soups and wines and jellies ("preposterous luxuries," snarled Dr Hall) – were distributed to those who needed them.'

Cressida Bell, Quentin's daughter, remembers having delicious potato and leek soup flavoured with rosemary at Charleston. This soup recipe, adapted from *King Edward's Cookery Book* (1920), is also nice served cold, especially with thin slices of Grace's melba toast (see p. 327).

2 TBS FLOUR • 6 [LARGE] POTATOES • 3 TBS VEGETABLE OIL
2 LEEKS, THINLY SLICED • ¾ OZ FLOUR • 2 PT STOCK • SEASONING •
1 PT [WHOLE] MILK • 1 SPRIG ROSEMARY

Bake the potatoes (in their skins), rub the inside through a sieve, put into a saucepan with the stock, add the milk. [Heat gently but do not boil. Meanwhile, in a frying pan, heat the oil and sauté the leeks and rosemary until soft. Add them to the pot.] Cook for ten minutes, thicken with flour [then remove the rosemary and put through a moulis], season and serve. Enough for 6 persons.

Armistice Chocolate Creams

'I'm glad you are fat; for then you are warm & mellow & generous & creative. I find that unless I weigh 9½ stones I hear voices & see visions & can neither write nor sleep. This is a necessity, I suppose, to part with youth & beauty, but I think there are compensations—'

Virginia Woolf to Jacques Raverat, 10 December 1922

Virginia Woolf's weight oscillated when she was unwell. In 1913, when her 'flu'-like symptoms began, she refused to eat and her weight dipped dramatically; on 9 September 1913 she tried to take her own life. By the end of September 1914, she was back to a healthy weight and well enough to take cookery classes. In 1915, however, she was again painfully thin and had become so violent and incoherent that Leonard committed her to a nursing home where she could receive professional round-the-clock care. By 1916, she was strong and sane again, back at Asheham in Sussex and consuming plenty of food. In fact, she grew so large that Lytton Strachey wrote to Ottoline Morrell 'she rolls along over the downs like some amphibious monster'. Cruel, perhaps, but at least she had regained her mental equilibrium. Her weight dipped again slightly, then it stabilized and she managed to maintain a healthy nine-and-a-half stone, more or less, until her final breakdown, in 1941.

Virginia could not stand greedy behaviour. She herself was a slow eater and often had to force herself to eat when she was not hungry. Her weakness, if indeed it was one, was chocolate. On Armistice Day 1918, she and Leonard celebrated the end of the war by eating chocolate creams at home by the fire at Hogarth House in Richmond. This classic recipe is from *McDougall's Cookery Book*, published in 1930.

2 OZ MCDOUGALL'S SELF-RAISING FLOUR • 3 OZ CASTOR SUGAR
1 OZ CHOCOLATE POWDER OR COCOA • 2 EGGS

For the cream filling:
3 OZ BUTTER • ½ TSP VANILLA ESSENCE • 4 OZ ICING SUGAR
A LITTLE LEMON JUICE

Sift the flour and chocolate powder thoroughly together, put the eggs into a basin, add the sugar, and whisk until thick and creamy. Stir the flour and chocolate powder in as lightly as possible without beating. Spread the mixture over a 9 x 13 in. [23 x 33 cm] baking tin greased and dusted with flour. Bake in a hot oven (400°F) for seven minutes. Turn out, top downwards on to a clean towel liberally sprinkled with castor sugar. Leave to cool. [Beat all the cream filling ingredients together.] Then spread the filling on and roll up and trim the ends with a sharp knife. (If preferred, whipped cream, sweetened and flavoured can be used instead of this filling.) [Serves 2.]

Roger Fry, *Clive Bell*, *c.* 1924. Clive's *Pot-Boilers*, 'an odd lot' of essays, was published in 1918.

Pot-Boilers

'Obliged by hunger and request of friends'.

Clive Bell's explanation for publishing his collection *Pot-Boilers*, 1918

In 1918 Clive Bell published a collection of seventeen of his essays under the title *Pot-Boilers*. By his own admission, they were 'an odd lot, and I think there are but two – the last two – that I am not a little ashamed of reprinting'. Indeed, not all of his arguments were perfectly sound, nor were the essays written in the clearest of styles, but they did boil the author's pot, having kept his belly from grumbling too loudly throughout the lean war years.

Poulet en Casserole

'"Have you ever tasted such chicken and salad?" he said presently, starting on a wing. "I hope you're romantic about food, Miss Villiers; I find myself praising and magnifying for ever the Walhalla-like dishes these lackeys keep bearing in."

"Oh, well, I don't know; I think I shall go in for keeping up the English reputation for being austere about food," said Perdita, laughing.

"That austerity probably only comes from long training in having, from politeness, to rise above the tastelessness of English meals," said Mr Fitzgerald reflectively.

Perdita laughed. She thought Mr Fitzgerald delightful.'

Molly MacCarthy, A Pier and a Band, 1918

In Molly MacCarthy's first novel, published in 1918, Mr Fitzgerald has an insatiable appetite for French cuisine, including *poulet en casserole*. He is sensitive and charming, 'a very good fellow, but too lazy'. He is also incorrigible: 'Perdita sometimes felt as if he were a full jug without a handle – full of precious liquid, but with no means of pouring it out.' In all this Mr Fitzgerald bears more than a passing resemblance to Molly's husband, the literary critic Desmond MacCarthy.

This is a delicious chicken casserole recipe from the Frances Partridge collection.

Suggested ingredients

1 CHICKEN • 2 TBS BUTTER • 3–4 SPRIGS FRESH TARRAGON
1 GLASS WHITE WINE • 1 PT STOCK • SALT AND PEPPER

Cut up chicken & fry the pieces in butter. Fill a casserole with them sprinkling freely with tarragon. Season. Add a good glass of wine, or 2, & some stock & cook gently about 1½ hours. [Serves 4–6.]

Mill House Christmas Chicken

'We had quite a mouvementé Christmas – two very gay visits from [fellow Apostle and his wife, a poet] Gerald and Fredegond [Shove] – and then, on Xmas Eve, Harry arrived, carrying in a neat satchel a turkey and four bottles of claret. He has lingered on, I am glad to say, and is at the present moment sitting on the other side of the fire'.

Lytton Strachey to Clive Bell, 31 December 1917

Harry Norton (Lytton Strachey's Cambridge friend and literary sponsor), John Maynard Keynes, Oliver Strachey and Saxon Sydney-Turner all paid Lytton's rent at the Mill House in Tidmarsh, on the understanding that they could come and stay whenever they wanted. So, on Christmas Eve 1917, Harry arrived at their front door bearing a turkey. This first Christmas at the Mill House was celebrated in style, with good friends, good cheer and all the festive trimmings.

However, when Harry arrived on their doorstep a year later, soon after the end of the First World War, he brought with him neither drop nor crumb – just one small gift for Lytton: the Omega Workshops' *Original Woodcuts by Various Artists*. His friend was fully appreciative of the present, but he was also hungry and somewhat disappointed there was so little food about. 'We eat large chickens,' Lytton grumbled to Ottoline Morrell, 'which pretend to be turkeys not very effectively, and drink grocer's wine.' Post-war austerity and rationing made Christmas 1918 an occasion for culinary improvisation, with rumblings – although none had been heard from the guns across the Channel for some weeks – still coming from Lytton's tummy.

These instructions on how to roast or bake meat are from Herman Senn's *War Time Cooking Guide*. The method is the same, regardless of whether one is cooking a turkey or a chicken.

Wipe and trim the meat, tie up if necessary, put in a baking tin (on a trivet if possible) with a little dripping and flour on top, and put in a very hot oven

above left: **Vanessa Bell,** *Nude*; and *above right:* **Roger Fry,** *The Cup*, both from the Omega Workshops' *Original Woodcuts by Various Artists*, 1918.

[220°C] for the first ten minutes, so as to harden the outside and keep in the juices. The meat requires to be frequently basted. When the meat is browned, move it to a cooler part of the oven [190°C] until it is quite done. The time allowed for baking is usually ¼ hour for each pound of meat and ¼ hour over.

When done, take up the meat and make the gravy. To do this, pour off nearly all the dripping in the tin, and keep in a jar for future use. Pour into the tin about a gill or more of hot water, season with salt and pepper, stir over the fire until it boils, and pour the gravy round the meat. [Serves 4–6.]

Unusual Oysters

'He appeared, I seem to think, in a large ulster coat, every pocket of which was stuffed with a book, a paint box or something intriguing; special tips which he had bought from a little man in a back street; he had canvasses under his arms; his hair flew; his eyes glowed. He had more knowledge and experience than the rest of us put together.... And at once we were all launched into a terrific argument about literature.... We had down Milton; we re-read Wordsworth. We had to think the whole thing over again. The old skeleton arguments of primitive Bloomsbury about art and beauty put on flesh and blood. There was always some new idea afoot; always some new picture standing on a chair to be looked at, some new poet fished out from obscurity and stood in the light of day.'

Virginia Woolf's sketch of Roger Fry for the Memoir Club, 1922

Once, just after the end of the war, Roger Fry ran into Osbert Sitwell in London. Seeing how desperately pale and emaciated his friend looked (Osbert had just been released from military hospital), Roger invited him to his studio for lunch. This meal with Roger was recounted twenty years later in Osbert's autobiographical volume *Laughter in the Next Room*: '"What *unusual* oysters these are, Roger! Where did you get them?" "I'm glad you like them," he replied, with the spirit and intonation of the quarter [Fitzrovia]. "They come from a charming, dirty little shop around the corner!" After that, I somehow curbed my hunger, and hid the oysters under their shells. As he cleared away the plates, he took a tin out of some steaming water, and said, "And now we will have some *Tripes à la Mode de Caen*." Setting my jaw, I ate on.'

The Omega Wine Cup

'He cooked; he washed up; he made pots; designed rugs and tables; showed visitors round the Omega; found work for Conscientious Objectors; fought on their behalf with politicians; did what he could to pay his artists their thirty shillings a week; and in one way or another he tried his best to make the Omega, though chairs were lacking, a centre in which some kind of civilized society might find a lodging.'

Virginia Woolf, *Roger Fry: A Biography*, 1940

Roger Fry masterminded the opening of the Omega Workshops in mid-1913 and, for a year, Omega was a remarkable success. Post-Impressionist décor made an impact on British society and tastes began to shift away from the staid and banal Victorian aesthetic towards Omega's bright, fun and adventurous designs. But the

Duncan Grant, *The Blue China Plate*, 1949. In 1919 the Omega Workshops closed, as the British public had been reluctant to undertake the aesthetic upheaval of its drawing rooms during wider upheaval of the First World War.

outbreak of war in 1914 impeded the success of the workshops: the men went off to fight; the artists dispersed; and the concerns of the nation were now focused on more pressing matters. By 1919 it was clear that the British had been unable to cope with both the upheaval of war and the upheaval of their drawing rooms. The Omega Workshops were too radical and too revolutionary for the austerity and conservatism of post-war Britain.

In the summer of 1919, Roger closed down the workshops and the bold and brightly coloured dresses, fabrics, tables, chairs and plates were sold at huge discounts. The closure was a sad occasion, especially for Roger. In her biography of Roger written in 1940, Virginia Woolf recalled Omega's demise: 'But some of the things he made still remain – a painted table; a witty chair; a dinner service; a bowl or two of that turquoise blue that the man from the British Museum so much admired. And if by chance one of those broad deep plates is broken, or an accident befalls a blue dish, all the shops in London may be searched in vain for its fellow.'

Economical Fish Dish

'The danger confronting us [after the First World War], therefore, is the rapid depression of the standard of life of the European populations to a point which will mean actual starvation for some (a point already reached in Russia and approximately reached in Austria). Men will not always die quietly. For starvation, which brings to some lethargy and a helpless despair, drives other temperaments to the nervous instability of hysteria and to a mad despair. And these in their distress may overturn the remnants of organization, and submerge civilization itself in their attempts to satisfy desperately the overwhelming needs of the individual. This is the danger against which all our resources and courage and idealism must now co-operate.'

John Maynard Keynes, *The Economic Consequences of the Peace*, 1919

In 1918–19, John Maynard Keynes was certain that the prospect of starvation would undo post-war Germany. The punitive damages against Germany agreed at the Versailles peace treaty in 1919, where Maynard was present as an official of the British Treasury, were too severe, he strongly argued. In disgust at the treaty, Maynard resigned from his post and returned to Charleston, where he wrote *The Economic Consequences of the Peace*. The book was an immediate international bestseller and, as it turned out, Maynard was absolutely right: the punitive damages *were* unfair and Germany's later retaliation, although brutal and irrational, was not

Duncan Grant, *John Maynard Keynes*, 1908. Maynard argued that under the terms agreed at the Treaty of Versailles, Germany would have no chance of economic recovery and its people would, as a consequence, starve.

altogether surprising – least of all to Maynard. Hunger, Maynard knew, can so often bring out the beast in humans.

This recipe for creamed cod is from a Second World War-era newspaper article (author and date unknown) found in the Grace Higgens archive. On the back are printed detailed instructions for how to put on a gas mask correctly.

[360 G] COD FILLET • 300 ML MILK • 2 CLOVES • ONION • PARSLEY
15 G CORNFLOUR • LEMON JUICE • 1 EGG

Put a slice of cod in a small saucepan, cover with milk and add two cloves, a small piece of onion and a piece of parsley. Cook slowly, then take out the fish, remove skin and bone and put on a hot dish. Strain the milk, thicken with cornflour, add a teaspoon of lemon juice and a beaten egg, and stir over a low heat until it thickens. Do not let it boil. Pour over the fish and garnish with parsley. [Serves 2.]

CHAPTER FOUR

An Appetite for Bloomsbury

(1920s)

Duncan Grant, *Portrait of John Maynard Keynes*, 1917. When Maynard set all the clocks at Charleston back by one hour in the summer of 1920, the result was 'extremely Tchekhovesque'.

Hasty Pudding

'The clock cannot be set back.'

John Maynard Keynes, *The Economic Consequences of the Peace*, 1919

Despite this famous assertion, John Maynard Keynes performed a bizarre experiment with time at Charleston in the summer of 1920: he set all the clocks in the house back by one hour. According to his biographer Robert Skidelsky: 'The servants rebelled, and refused to wind up the kitchen clock: as a result they had no time at all. Clive went on living and eating on normal time. "How mad they all are", Lytton wrote to Carrington. "The result is extremely Tchekhovesque. But luckily the atmosphere is entirely comic. Everyone laughs and screams and passes on."'

This recipe for Hasty Pudding from Helen Anrep's scrapbook is timeless.

1 EGG • 2 OZ SUGAR • 1 OZ FLOUR • 2½ GILLS MILK • PINCH SALT

The flour and salt should be sieved into a basin the sugar added the egg broken into it and stirred gradually beating until smooth add 2 gill milk and mix well. Put the rest of the milk in a pan to boil then pour it gradually [in]to the batter of flour and egg stirring well the whole time. Return to saucepan and stir until it thickens, then pour into a greased pie dish and put it in to brown. [Place under the grill for 10–15 minutes. Serves 4.]

Picasso Dines with Bohemia

'As it happened, continental civilization came to us before we had a chance of going to it; for early in the summer of 1919 Diaghileff's troupe arrived in London, with *La Boutique fantastique* and *Le Tricorne*, with Picasso, Derain, Stravinsky and Ansermet…. Suddenly the arts became the preoccupation of Society (with the capital S) which twelve months earlier had been preoccupied with military and political intrigues. French became the language of the Savoy where Diaghileff, Massine, Stravinsky, Picasso and Picasso's very beautiful and rather aristocratic wife were staying for the season. Abruptly and unexpectedly the wheels of civilization began to turn.'

Clive Bell, *Old Friends*, 1956

As a result of the First World War, 'civilization' – as defined by Bloomsbury – took a knock; indeed, the Bloomsbury members believed another major war would ruin civilization for ever. According to Clive Bell, writing in 1928, 'Civilization requires the existence of a leisured class, and a leisured class requires the existence of slaves – of people … who give some part of their surplus time and energy to the support of others.' Virginia Woolf was not so convinced: 'in the end it turns out that civilization is a lunch party at No. 50 Gordon Square', she said privately.

The 'civilized' classes were present at a dinner party hosted by John Maynard Keynes and Clive Bell at 46 Gordon Square in 1919. At this party, the Picassos were introduced to London's bohemian set and brushed shoulders with others they already knew: André Derain, Swiss conductor Ernest Ansermet and Russian ballerina Lydia Lopokova, in addition to forty of London's less fashionable writers, painters and students. Clive described the event: 'Maynard, Duncan Grant, our two maids and I waited on them. Picasso did not dress. We rigged up a

Pablo Picasso and his wife, Olga, in his London workshop where he made the curtain for *Le Tricorne*, 1919. The Picassos were introduced to London's bohemian set at a dinner party given by Clive Bell and John Maynard Keynes in 1919.

couple of long tables: at the end of one we put Ansermet, at the end of the other Lytton Strachey, so that their beards might wag in unison.'

This menu is from *Lovely Food* (1931), a cookery book by Ruth Lowinsky. In her introduction to the menu she writes of 'a dream party of some of the most celebrated people of the day, whom one can never hope to meet, or, if met, be remembered by: Einstein, Mr Charles Chaplin, Freud, Virginia Woolf, Stella Benson, Mussolini, P. G. Wodehouse, Mistinguett, Lydia Lopokova and Jean Cocteau'. Such a menu seems perfect for the dinner party Maynard and Clive put together for the Picassos. The quantities for each recipe may be increased or decreased according to the number of guests present.

Tomates à l'Espagnol

Cut in strips some cheese, tongue, apples, celery, truffles. Mix with mayonnaise, [cut the tomatoes in half, mix the tomato insides into the mixture] and fill the tomatoes.

Consommé à l'Indienne

One quart of good [chicken] stock. Slice into it two onions, one large cooking apple, and add one tablespoonful of desiccated cocoanut, one dessertspoonful curry powder (more if liked hot) and bones of roast chicken or game. Simmer

Duncan Grant, *Ballet Decoration*, unknown date. Lydia Lopokova dazzled her audiences with her large personality but she was only five feet tall.

one hour, strain, clarify, reboil; serve [with] pieces of game or chicken and a little plain boiled rice. [Serves 2.]

Saumon en Surprise

2 LB SALMON • ¼ LB BUTTER • 4 YOLKS OF EGG • ½ PT CREAM
[FEW DROPS ANCHOVY ESSENCE]

Cook the salmon in water with oil, [drain] and pass through a sieve [or macerate in a blender]. Mix well with ingredients. Put in a soufflé case and stand on ice before serving [or simply chill]. Decorate with [additional] whipped cream flavoured with anchovy essence. Enough for six people.

Poulet aux Choux

3 SPRING CHICKENS • I PT CONSOMMÉ • I LARGE WHITE CABBAGE
PEPPER AND SALT • ½ LB HAM OR BACON • 2 OZ BUTTER

Fry in a stewpan a large white cabbage, half a pound of ham or bacon cut in squares, and three chickens for ten minutes. Add a pint of consommé, a little pepper and salt, and let the whole stew for an hour or, if *old* chickens, an hour and a half. Take out the cabbage and chickens, cut up the cabbage and add two ounces of butter, pepper and salt to taste, reduce the stock, put the chickens in the stock to get thoroughly hot, place the cabbage in the centre of the [serving] dish, cut the chickens in half and place round the cabbage and pour the stock round the dish. Enough for five or six people.

Glacé aux Fruits

5 EGGS • 1¼ PT MILK • 1 LB CASTOR SUGAR • 1 PT CREAM
[GLACÉ CHERRIES, ANGELICA, RAISINS] • [BRANDY] • [RUM]

Make a custard with eggs, sugar and milk, and let it cool. Cut up some glacé cherries, angelica, raisins and glacé fruit and sprinkle with brandy. Whip cream very thick, add some custard and sufficient good rum to flavour. Put the mixture alternately with fruit into an ice mould and freeze for four hours. [Serves 8.]

A Bloomsbury Stew

'I again fell very much in love with her. She seemed to me perfect in every way. One of her new charms is the most knowing and judicious use of English words. I am going to the ballet tomorrow, and am asking her to sup with me afterwards at the Savoy.'

John Maynard Keynes to Vanessa Bell, 22 December 1921

In 1918, night after night crowds flooded into the London Coliseum to see Sergei Diaghilev's doll-like protégée, prima ballerina Lydia Lopokova. They were beguiled by her natural charm, impish wit and refreshingly modern style. Osbert Sitwell recalled her 'grace, pathos, entrancing cleverness' and 'true comic genius'. Clive Bell flirted with her shamelessly at a dinner party that he and John Maynard Keynes hosted for the Ballets Russes, and later, in a review in the *New Republic*, likened the 'new ballet' to 'a symphony', praising Lydia's performance as follows: 'We are in world of purest art and about as far from "stageland" as one well could be.'

In 1921, Diaghilev staged a colourful rendition of *The Sleeping Beauty* with Lydia in the title role. Maynard attended each performance, and fell further and further in love. On 11 December he and Lydia lunched together. On the 16th they dined together at the Savoy. And on the 28th Maynard left his lover, Sebastian Sprott, and went to have tea with Lydia at the Waldorf. By January, the ballerina and the economist were deeply in love, and in April Lydia moved into the heart of Bloomsbury, at 50 Gordon Square.

Lydia had a large appetite for food – the physical exertion of her art demanded it. This is a recipe she later contributed to *The Ballet Cook Book*.

3 LB MUTTON, CUT IN 1½-IN. CUBES • 1 TSP SALT
½ TSP PEPPER • 12 SMALL WHITE ONIONS • ½ TSP THYME
6 LARGE POTATOES, DICED • 1 CUP DICED TURNIPS • ¼ CUP COLD WATER
1 CUP FROZEN PEAS • 1 CUP DICED CARROTS • ¼ CUP FLOUR • 1 BAY LEAF

Place meat in a Dutch oven; cover with boiling water and simmer covered over low heat for 1½ hours or until tender. Add carrots, turnips, potatoes, onions, herbs and seasonings; simmer covered for 25 minutes. Add peas, and cook for five minutes. Combine cold water and flour and stir into stew. Bring to a boil over low heat stirring constantly. Continue cooking until thickened and clear for 3–5 minutes. Serves six.

New Year's Oyster Feast

One food Lytton Strachey could not stomach was oysters. So it was disappointing for him when John Maynard Keynes arrived on his doorstep in Tidmarsh in January 1922 with a box of fifty oysters. Although Lytton abstained from the oyster feast, the others – Dora Carrington, Ralph Partridge and, of course, Maynard – certainly did not.

This classic oyster recipe has been adapted from *Success: 1500 New Economy Cookery and Household Recipes*, published in 1933.

50 OYSTERS • BROWN BREAD AND BUTTER • LEMONS • PEPPER • VINEGAR

Open the oyster, take away the top shell entirely, remove the beard, plunge in water, release the oyster from the under shell by inserting knife. Spread the oyster on the shell neatly and serve on the shell with thin brown bread and butter. Allow each person to season his own oysters.

Maynard's Parties at No. 46

'[A]fter the end of the first war there was a frenzied kind of excitement and relief from everything. The parties were mostly fancy-dress parties, and there were charades, and people wrote plays for them. They went on absolutely all night, and were very enjoyable. I can remember a marvellous party, called the Sailors' Party, in which we all had to go wearing naval costume.

Dora Carrington, *Lytton Strachey Reading*, 1916.

I went as a lower-deck type, and Lytton went as a full Admiral of the Fleet. As you can imagine, with his beard and his cocked hat and his sword he was impressive. Well then, there used to be parties given by the Keynes's at which we did theatricals, and Keynes used to appear as the Prince Consort and his wife, Lopokova, as Queen Victoria. On one occasion I wrote a satirical account of what went on in the Hogarth Press basement, the series of people who had been there and only lasted six months and been thrown out – of which I, needless to say, proved to be one…. And then there was another party that I gave with two other friends at which we had about two hundred people…. There was nothing much to eat except heaps of straw-berries and cream and cheap white wine. We didn't mind much in those days what we ate and drank as long as there was plenty of everything.'

George Rylands, quoted in *Recollections of Virginia Woolf*, 1970

John Maynard Keynes was as generous as he was brilliant. All his theories of economics, his studies on probability, and his ideas on government interven-tion, taxation and expenditure were formulated, according to Clive Bell, for the

Vanessa Bell, *The Keynes-Keynes*, *c.* 1927. John Maynard Keynes's parties were 'the grandest' and 'most elaborately conceived' in Bloomsbury.

benefit 'of Civilization'. In 1940 Maynard founded CEMA, the Council for the Encouragement of Music and the Arts (later the Arts Council of Great Britain). But his generosity extended beyond the public realm to incorporate the unique needs of his friends. He contributed towards the cost of Dora Carrington and Lytton Strachey's lease on the Mill House in Tidmarsh, and he paid a third of all running costs at Charleston. He paid for the education of David 'Bunny' Garnett's two sons and helped Duncan Grant support his elderly mother in her old age. He also entertained Bloomsbury with his brilliant mind and clever conversation and threw, Bunny recalled, '"the grandest" parties in Bloomsbury, as well as the most elaborately conceived', with dinner, champagne, costumes, conversation and theatrical entertainment.

Virginia Woolf described Maynard's *Twelfth Night* party in 1923 in her diary, as follows: 'Let the scene open on the doorstep of number 50 Gordon Square.

We went up last night, carrying our bags and a Cingalese sword. There was Mary H in lemon coloured trousers with green ribbons, and so we sat down to dinner; off cold chicken. In came Roger and Adrian and Karin; and very slowly we coloured our faces and made ready for number 46.... Suppose one's normal pulse to be 70: in five minutes it was 120: and the blood, not sticky whitish fluid of daytime but brilliant and prickly like champagne.... Shakespeare I thought would have liked us all tonight'.

Sunday Lunch at Cambridge

'Keynes's intellect was the sharpest and clearest that I have ever known. When I argued with him, I felt that I took my life in my hands, and I seldom emerged without feeling something of a fool. I was sometimes inclined to feel that so much cleverness must be incompatible with depth, but I do not think this feeling was justified.'

Bertrand Russell, *Autobiography*, 1967–69

The University of Cambridge pulsated in John Maynard Keynes's veins from the beginning of his life through to the very end. He was born into the university community (his father was a professor of economics) and spent his formative years, after attending Eton, mixing with the Cambridge intelligentsia, including his fellow Apostles. When his friends regrouped in Bloomsbury after 1904, Maynard certainly became part of the group, but he never let go of his Cambridge roots and always remained involved in the university – as a researcher, writer, college fellow, Apostle and bursar. When he died in 1946, he bequeathed his manuscripts and letters to the library of King's College, Cambridge, and also gave King's his collection of Impressionist paintings and drawings (now on long-term loan to the Fitzwilliam Museum in Cambridge).

On Sundays, Maynard typically ate lunch in Cambridge at 8 Harvey Road with his parents or at the Cambridge Arts Theatre restaurant with his wife, Lydia. But on 11 November 1923 (Armistice Day), he ate in his rooms at King's College with his fellow King's graduate, Apostle and great friend, Roger Fry. He wrote to Lydia: 'In a few minutes I have a large luncheon party in honour of Roger who is here. We eat

Oysters	Hock
Salmon Mayonnaise	Grand Marnier
Chicken Chaudfroid	Coffee
Damson Pie, cream.'	

Teetotalism at Tilton

'But when Maynard, having invited to dinner two of his big-wigs (Austen Chamberlain and McKenna I seem to remember*), discovered at the last moment that all his champagne had been drunk by Duncan Grant and his boon companions – Duncan's mid-day champagne-parties in Brunswick Square were a feature of that memorable summer [1914] – he took it well enough.'

Clive Bell, *Old Friends*, 1956

'Would you believe it? Not a drop of alcohol appeared. The Charlestonians declare that Il gran Pozzo** is now immensely rich probably £10,000 a year; I can believe it and water, water everywhere! Such is the result of wealth.'

Lytton Strachey to Dora Carrington, 29 September 1925

Nobody could amuse, charm or infect John Maynard Keynes with a sense of fun better than Duncan Grant. When Duncan drank all of Maynard's champagne, he was forgiven. When Maynard was advised to give up alcohol for his bad knee, only Duncan could convince him to crack open a bottle of the old stuff. 'I had an enormous Sunday lunch with Maynard & Lydia to-day, rather good, *with* wine after some difficulty,' Duncan wrote to Vanessa Bell in 1926. Neither the delightfully comic Lydia nor Lytton with his camp wit could quite get their way with Maynard to the extent that Duncan could.

Tilton – the place where Lytton complained of teetotalism – was Maynard and Lydia's country house in Sussex, only a five-minute walk from Charleston. It was a working farm and, according to Maynard's biographer Robert Skidelsky, Maynard and Lydia occasionally took their pigs to market in Lewes themselves – in the back of their Morris Cowley!

Tilton Grouse

'It was the common opinion of Bloomsbury that the Keyneses were remarkably economic in their hospitality.'

Nigel Nicolson, quoted in Hugh Lee, *A Cézanne in the Hedge*, 1992

* *Austen Chamberlain was Chancellor of the Exchequer in 1903 and a contender for the premiership in 1911. Reginald McKenna was Home Secretary from 1911 and Chancellor in Herbert Asquith's coalition government of 1915–16.*
** *Lytton's nickname for Maynard Keynes; Italian for 'The Great Well'.*

For all John Maynard Keynes's generosity and extravagance, he also had a con-
tradictory streak of miserliness. Once, just after the First World War, Maynard
arrived at Charleston with a crate of tinned meat, purchased at discount from an
army surplus store in London. It did not matter to him that the meat was barely
edible, for at a penny a tin this was a deal too good to miss. However, as Clive Bell
sardonically noted, 'the bargain-hunter himself could barely keep it down'.

Another penny-pinching incident occurred in 1927. '[L]ast night, at Tilton',
Virginia Woolf recounted to Lytton Strachey, 'we picked the bones of Maynard's
grouse of which there were three to eleven people. This stinginess is a constant
source of delight to Nessa – her eyes gleamed as the bones went round.'

Vanessa Bell, *Snow at Tilton*, 1941. In 1925 John Maynard Keynes took out a long-term lease
on Tilton, a farmhouse not far from Charleston. In 1942 he accepted a peerage and adopted
the title 'Lord Keynes of Tilton'.

This useful tip for tenderizing a fowl (such as particularly tough old grouse that must be picked to the bone) is from Helen Anrep's scrapbook.

The French have a way of making a tough fowl tender in roasting which is worth following. It should be seasoned and tied up securely in two thicknesses of soft white or pale brown paper and put into the oven half an hour earlier than the time one would choose to assure its being done. It will steam slowly in this way, and if delicately dredged with flour when the paper is taken off at the end of the half hour in a hot oven, it will come out brown and easily carved.

Lytton's 'Victoria'

'Lytton's "Victoria" has been a great success in every periodical and paper in England and Scotland. Even the "Times" and "Daily Mail" bow before him! Many say it can't be so good as EV [*Eminent Victorians*] to receive this adulation. But it is I think, much better. His fortune will soon be immense, if a revolution does not come and cut short his life. For he is definitely joining the Upper Classes I regret to say. He's charming to me. I think he is walking on air for the moment and can't be disagreeable!! Last Tuesday he hired a private motor and took Ralph and me to Hampton Court. It was fun whirling through London, pretending to be one of the idle rich…. We had lunch in an inn over-lapping the river, and then motored back to London, dropping the private secretary at the Woolves' Lair on the way back'.

Dora Carrington to Alix Strachey, 15 April 1921

In 1921 Lytton Strachey came out with *Queen Victoria*, his second biographical triumph. He wrote about the fat baby who was christened Victoria (much to the disgust of her father) and grew to be a wilful and headstrong child. He portrayed Victoria as the truthful adolescent, the devoted wife, the mother, the widow, the grandmother, the friend and, of course, the accomplished monarch. Her eccentricities, her temper, her stubbornness and her emotionality were exposed as never before. For the first time the reader saw her for who she really was: a complex, courageous and stubborn woman who held her own as a queen reigning in a male-dominated world.

While mourning the loss of her beloved Albert in 1861, Queen Victoria retreated to Osborne House on the Isle of Wight. Each day at around five o'clock, she took 'tea' – a recent craze begun and popularized by her lady of the bedchamber, Anna Russell, duchess of Bedford. The Queen liked cake with her tea: a sponge cake with a whipped cream and jam centre was named the

Vanessa Bell, *Lytton Strachey, c.* 1912. Lytton's <u>*Queen Victoria*</u> was published in 1921. It was an unprecedented candid biography in which he divulged details of the Queen's hitherto private life.

'Victoria Sandwich' after her. Victoria herself was small in stature (standing a mere five feet tall), and was rumoured to be nearly as wide. So she presumably much enjoyed eating her favourite cake. For a really good Victoria sponge recipe see Grace Cakes, pp. 171–73.

Tidmarsh Triptych

'I seem to see Lytton, elegant in his dark suit, with his squeaky voice that faded out at the end of the sentence and his strongly stressed pronunciation of certain words, seated remote and fantastic at the head of the table. Then I see Ralph with his look of a Varsity rowing man and his stylized way of speaking, which contrasted with his general air of gaiety and high spirits.

And lastly Carrington with her coaxing voice and smile and gaily teasing manner and the extraordinary deference and attention she paid to her god.'

Gerald Brenan, *Personal Record*, 1974

No sooner had Lytton Strachey and Dora Carrington established life *à deux* in 1917, than a new person entered their life at the Mill House in Tidmarsh: Major Rex Partridge. He was handsome and masculine and had just returned from the First World War. He was studying at Oxford, not far from Tidmarsh, and was introduced to Carrington by her brother Noel, a fellow rower at Oxford.

Initially, Major Partridge's militaristic stance grated on Lytton and Carrington's pacifist ideals, but in time his outlook began to change. He developed a conscientious objection to war; his literary and artistic tastes matured; and he changed his name to Ralph. (Lytton thought 'Rex' had imperialistic overtones.) And he fell head over heels in love with Carrington.

Carrington did not exactly reciprocate Ralph's passion, but she did harbour strong feelings of affection for him. She also knew that without Ralph, Lytton, who was now in love with their golden boy, would soon get bored of her solo company. As Lytton remarked, 'everything at sixes and at sevens – ladies in love with buggers, and buggers in love with womanizers…. Where will it all end?' Furthermore, Ralph was responsible for producing most of the food for their ménage: pots of delicious runny honey, gooseberries, cherries, apples, eggs, broad beans, new potatoes and masses of other seasonal vegetables. Without Ralph at the Mill House, their food supplies would dwindle.

Butter

'Carrington introduced me to Lytton who, mumbling something I did not catch, held out a limp hand, and then led me through a glass door into an apple orchard where I saw Ralph, dressed in nothing but a pair of dirty white shorts, carrying a bucket. He came forward to meet me with his big blue eyes rolling with fun and gaiety and carried me off to see the ducks and grey-streaked Chinese geese that he had recently bought. He had discovered the pleasure of growing vegetables and keeping domestic poultry – anything that provided food appealed to him – and got a sensuous enjoyment from watching the processes of their generation and from handling their smooth, finely grained eggs.'

Gerald Brenan, *Personal Record*, 1974

Dora Carrington, *Eggs on a Table, Tidmarsh Mill, c.* 1924. In 1918 Major Rex (later Ralph) Partridge was introduced to Carrington and Lytton Strachey's ménage at the Mill House in Tidmarsh.

Ralph Partridge and Dora Carrington married in May 1921 and honeymooned in Venice, where Lytton Strachey joined them. A few months later, Ralph's friend Gerald Brenan began a torrid affair with Carrington that threatened to destabilize the complicated love triangle already established between Lytton, Carrington and Ralph. Initially, Ralph was furious and felt betrayed by their disloyalty; but he had not been entirely faithful, either. He later agreed that it was probably best to preserve the domestic arrangement they already shared with Lytton at the Mill House and accept that an honest, open marriage was the way forward. Carrington and

Gerald continued to see one another, but as Gerald had now moved to Spain as his primary base, Carrington's domestic life continued much as before.

Gerald, however, was lonely, hungry and miserable. Carrington sent him puddings, pots of apple jelly and delicious marmalade pies, but this food only tantalized him. He told her in return: 'I discover that there are two things necessary for my happiness: 1. the company of women, 2. butter. or else 1. butter, 2. women. I can't decide on the order.' Gerald wanted Carrington, but also butter, which was equally unavailable.

This is my own recipe for homemade butter. Make sure the cream is at room temperature before you begin churning. It makes all the difference.

1 PT DOUBLE CREAM, ROOM TEMPERATURE • SALT

The easiest way to make butter is to over-whip double cream in a food mixer (the old-fashioned way was to use a butter churn, but even a glass jam jar will do). Once it is firm, wash it under cold water and place it into a bowl or colander. Knead it with a wooden spoon until all the buttermilk has been released. Drain. (The buttermilk can be retained and used for baking.) Rinse under cold water and repeat the process until the butter is uniform and there is no buttermilk residue. To help preserve the butter, knead in a little salt. Transfer to a ramekin or small serving dish. If you have a butter stamp, press firmly over the top of a level surface. This butter will keep in the refrigerator for up to two weeks.

Cockerel for Virginia

'I will kill our one and only cock, the pride of the village, cockerel then, as you will have such an obscene mind, and a bottle of sloe gin will be opened for your pleasure over a vast wood fire at night.'

Dora Carrington to Virginia Woolf, 31 October 1918

In many of her letters, Dora Carrington used tempting descriptions of food and drink to entice her friends and lovers to her. To Mark Gertler, in 1915, she promised to learn to cook 'so that you will have no fault to find in me'. To Lytton Strachey she guaranteed 'vast quantities of food and drink, and raiment for the night season'. She baited Gerald Brenan with 'strawberry ices, & cream, & cheese straws & home made marmalade'. She wrote of homemade pies, roast partridges, succulent joints of lamb, freshly baked sweet suet puddings, sipping-chocolate, marrow tart, layered ices and savoury omelettes. Her line drawings also infuse her correspondence with a delectable tongue-in-cheek flavour and render her seductions irresistible.

much later. 5 och
I have reached Tidmarsh o now.
tea is over The Mill House, o we sit
on the lawn Tidmarsh, where for near
a month every afternoon you have
Pangbourne.
sat with me .. lunch was
awful the weather had turned
everything bad. my most lovely
steak o kidney Pie had to be
given to the Hens

and it was such a delicious
Pie full of eggs, rare spices, kidneys
& steak. Then Lytton thought
the cocheral which we had
the minuet the pie vanished
from the table was bad, so
that had to whisked away

Dora Carrington, sketch of hens feeding on a pie that went bad in hot weather, 1922.

This tantalizing chicken dish is from the Frances Partridge archive.

Cold roast chicken. Cut in quarters. Cover with lemon juice, plenty of thick honey, parsley and pats of butter. Heat through in moderate oven of about 20 minutes.

Ham Spray Triangles

'Ralph Partridge took over the vegetable garden, the greenhouse, the orchard and the bees. In all these pursuits they shared, and they became the chief bond between them. When Ralph went to live in London with Frances Marshall, Carrington felt betrayed by a partner in the vegetable garden bed as much as in the matrimonial. He did what he could to help in the garden during weekends for he loved Ham Spray. Between them they produced much of the food which they ate.'

David Garnett, *Great Friends*, 1979

The *ménage à trois* at the Mill House in Tidmarsh – consisting of Lytton Strachey in love with Ralph Partridge, Ralph in love with Dora Carrington, and Carrington in love with Lytton – moved to Ham Spray House in Wiltshire in 1924. There the three became even more interdependent. Triangular relationships have stresses, strains and growing pains just like any other relationship, and theirs was further complicated by the fact that other people were brought in to satisfy certain inherent sexual incompatibilities: Lytton, for example, was homosexual; Carrington was bisexual and Ralph was heterosexual. In 1926 Ralph began living in London during the week with Frances Marshall (whom he eventually married, after the deaths of Lytton and Carrington), returning to Ham Spray at weekends. What began as a simple love triangle eventually became a complicated web of infidelity, passion and sex. Still, the three managed to incorporate changing interests and new lovers remarkably well.

Ham Spray Triangles are adapted from a recipe found in Frances Partridge's recipe book. They make a delicious light meal or hors d'oeuvre.

Suggested ingredients
120 G HONEY-CURED HAM, THINLY SLICED • 6 TBS FISH ROE
1 TBS BUTTER • 1 CUP SHALLOTS, CHOPPED • PAPRIKA
6 SLICES WHITE BREAD, CRUSTS REMOVED • A SPLASH OF WHITE WINE
1 CUP BÉCHAMEL SAUCE

Fold thin slices of honey-cured ham round soft roes & slice in half. Heat them in the oven in a fireproof dish in a creamy béchamel sauce [see p. 193], to which has been added finely sliced shallots (cooked in butter & white wine) & seasoned with paprika, salt and pepper. Brown slightly under grill. Serve rolls on toasted white bread, sliced twice, diagonally. [Serves 6.]

Ham Spray Breakfast Rolls

'Breakfast was lavish. Ham and eggs, kedgeree or kippers, coffee, a large bowl of fresh cream just skimmed from the pans of milk, hot rolls, butter, marmalade, damson cheese and honey in the comb. During the morning I would go for a walk with Lytton on the downs, while Ralph strayed about – in spring looking for plovers' eggs or in the autumn gathering mushrooms. Or else we were driven to some hidden Wiltshire village, or to one of Carrington's favourite spots. Then towards evening the games of bowls and after dinner sitting watching the parent barn owls ferrying mice from the stack-yard on an average of one every three minutes, to the owlets in the great beech.'

David Garnett, *Great Friends*, 1979

Ralph Partridge, Dora Carrington, Lytton Strachey and Saxon Sydney-Turner having breakfast on the lawn at Ham Spray House, Wiltshire, 1927. Photograph by Frances Partridge.

Dora Carrington discovered Ham Spray House at the end of a long farm track, past tumbledown barns and a scattering of outbuildings, while visiting Wiltshire in October 1923. The two-storey house, with its high-corniced ceilings, tiled fire-places and large, south-facing sash windows, was built around 1830. The rooms were bright and well proportioned with charming period alcoves, curved doors, a first-floor library and space for an artist's studio above the granary. For sale with two acres of land and situated only seventy miles from London and three miles from Hungerford, it was the perfect country house. In January 1924, Lytton Strachey and Ralph Partridge purchased Ham Spray House, in Ralph's name, for £2,300.

Carrington saw to the renovations. Electricity and central heating were installed; the front hall was painted yellow. Carrington also painted the 'arches in the passage to the kitchen Giotto blue', the tiles in the kitchen and the larder yellow and blue, and 'the letters of the alphabet from Z to A' on Lytton's library bookshelves. She monogrammed the fireplace tiles, painted a trompe-l'oeil book-case into a hidden alcove and selected paintings to hang on the walls. By July 1924 the house was sufficiently comfortable for Lytton to move in, whereupon 'a con-tinual stream of guests' was invited to stay, noted David 'Bunny' Garnett, 'all lazily enjoying Lytton's conversation … and *la douceur de vie* provided by Carrington.'

Outside, a verandah opened out onto a spacious lawn, a ha-ha, acres of long, green grass and, in the distance, rolling downland hills. It was here, sitting at carefully laid tables on the lawn on warm summer mornings, that the residents of Ham Spray House and their guests ate breakfast.

This précis from William Cobbett's early nineteenth-century cookbook *Cottage Economy* – Carrington's cookery bible – has been adapted from 'loaf' to 'rolls', but beware, unless one has a continual stream of guests to feed, the quanti-ties are quite substantial.

Suggested ingredients

1 BUSHEL (APPX. 19 KG) WHOLEMEAL BREAD FLOUR • 1 PT YEAST
1 PT WARM WATER • APPX. 22 PT WARM WATER OR MILK • ½ LB SALT

Suppose the quantity to be a bushel of flour. Put this flour into a *trough* that people have for the purpose. Make a pretty deep hole in the middle of this heap of flour. Take (for a bushel) a pint of good fresh yeast, mix it and stir it well up in a pint of *soft* water milk-warm. Pour this into the hole in the heap of flour. Then take a spoon and work it round the outside of this body of moisture so as to make a *thin batter*. Continue to stir for a minute or two. Then take a handful of flour and scatter it thinly over the head of this batter, so as to *hide* it. Then cover the whole over with a cloth to keep it warm. When the batter has raised enough to make *cracks* in the flour, begin to work the flour into the batter. Grad-ually pour in the soft water milk-warm, or milk. Scatter the salt (*half a pound* per bushel of flour) over the heap. When you have got the whole *sufficiently moist, knead well.* To do this the *fists* must go heartily into it. It must be rolled over, pressed out, folded up and pressed out again, until it be completely mixed and formed into a *stiff* and *tough dough.* I have never quite liked baker's bread since I saw a great heavy fellow in a bake house in France, kneading bread with his *naked feet!* His feet looked very *white* to be sure: Whether they were of that colour *before he got into the trough* I could not tell....

When the dough is made, form it into lumps and scatter dry flour thinly over it. Cover it again, keep warm and allow it to ferment for 15 or 20 minutes.

[Thereupon Cobbett expounds on the art of heating a brick oven correctly using faggot sticks, brushwood and woody furze or ling, the common heather.]

When both the dough and the fire are ready, divide the dough into four pieces and knead again, sprinkling flour over your board, to prevent the dough adhering to it. Roll each piece out into a thin cylinder; divide each into eight, roll into separate parcels. Once the rolls are formed, place in the oven as quickly as possible and bake for about *twenty minutes.* And what is the *result?* Why, good, wholesome food, sufficient for a considerable family for a week, prepared in three or four hours. [Serves 100–150.]

Kedgeree

'Ralph has become a hen-maniac and secretly I have a complex against them. Because I don't like the taste of eggs.... Annie [the cook] has taken a turn for the good, and now makes us delicious bread, suet puddings and other inventions. Morally she has taken a turn for the bad; lies, and loafs about with young boys. But I've decided now to interest myself in her morals no more, only in her cooking.'

Dora Carrington to Gerald Brenan, 18 December 1921

On April Fool's Day in 1928, all eggs on the breakfast table at Ham Spray House were curiously hollow and the eggs in the nearby nests painted. A more practical 'fool', and one that egg-lovers and non-eggs lovers alike can enjoy, is to disguise the flavour of the egg with other, stronger flavours. This Grace Higgens recipe

Dora Carrington, sketch of food and glass, 1917.

Dora Carrington, *Annie Stiles*, 1921. Annie came to help with the cooking and housekeeping at the Mill House in Tidmarsh in 1921, when she was sixteen years old.

will do just the trick. One may even wish to add chopped onions, curry powder, cardamom, parsley and/or the juice of half a lemon to conceal the egg flavour completely.

I TEACUPFUL RICE • SALMON, COD OR HADDOCK • PEPPER • SALT
CAYENNE PEPPER • I OZ BUTTER • I EGG

Cook rice, then strain. Put in saucepan, add fish, seasoning, Butter & stir in 1 egg, keep hot until served. Serve on toast. Chopp [*sic*] hard boiled egg & sprinkle over. [Serves 2.]

Epoch-Making Dinners at Ham Spray

'The dinner [celebrating Helen Anrep's visit] was indescribably grand. Epoch-making: grapefruit, then a chicken covered with fennel and tomato sauce, a risotto with almonds, onions, and pimentos, followed by sack cream, supported by Café Royal red wine, *perfectly* warmed…. I shall repeat this grand dinner for our next weekend. We all became very boozed…. [The following evening] we again had a *superb* dinner ending with crème brûlé[e] and two bottles of champagne and more sherry afterwards!'

Dora Carrington to Lytton Strachey, 26 September 1925

Christine Kühlenthal, *Dora Carrington Cooking*, *c.* 1915. Carrington started to learn how to cook in 1915, for Mark Gertler, and by 1925 was preparing 'epoch-making' dinners for Lytton Strachey.

While Dora Carrington was wining and dining Helen Anrep, Dorelia John, Henry Lamb and neighbours Mr and Mrs Darcy Japp at Ham Spray House in late September 1925, Lytton Strachey was visiting his Bloomsbury friends at Charleston. There he enjoyed delicious candlelit dinners with Vanessa and Clive Bell and Duncan Grant, and scintillating conversation that carried on until late in the evening. Leonard and Virginia Woolf popped over from Monk's House to see him (despite Virginia's recent breakdown – her nerves had frayed considerably since she started writing *To the Lighthouse* in August). After a few days Lytton ventured over to Tilton to see John Maynard Keynes, and his wife, Lydia, whose recent marriage was causing considerable consternation within the Bloomsbury fold. Maynard and Lydia seemed to be very happy, Lytton noted, but on the whole his visit was 'lugubrious' and 'sober' – without a drop of alcohol.

True to her word, when Lytton returned home a few days later, Carrington had prepared for him another epoch-making and equally impressive (alcoholic) dinner. Lytton, Carrington and Ralph had a well-stocked wine cellar. They bought barrels of wine in France and bottled it themselves at home. Most evenings at Ham Spray House were therefore usually quite merry.

Dodo's Quince Marmalade

'[Augustus] John is encamped with two wives and ten naked children....
I saw him in the street today – an extraordinary spectacle for these parts.'

John Maynard Keynes in Cambridge, 23 July 1909

Dorelia ('Dodo') McNeill was the beautiful lover of the wild, eccentric and talented portrait painter Augustus John. She lived with Augustus and his wife, Ida Nettleship (Ida died giving birth to her fifth child in 1907), in a ménage in which they embraced not only each other but also a life of complete bohemianism. Like gypsies they moved from campsite to campsite, living out of brightly coloured caravans, tents and wagons, and maintaining an unconventional, carefree existence of drinking, brawling and sex (Augustus is rumoured to have fathered over a hundred illegitimate children).

Bloomsbury members often met with a broader circle of artists, intellectuals and writers to party, picnic and exchange new ideas. Raucous behaviour sometimes ensued, occasionally resulting in fisticuffs (see Gin Sling, p. 259), broken bottles, stolen drawings and overwrought emotions. Later on, recipes were exchanged, and Dodo's quince marmalade, for example, found its way to Helen Anrep's dining table. This recipe was enclosed in a letter sent by Dodo to Helen in the 1960s.

Dorelia ('Dodo') McNeill (also known as Dorelia John), 1909. Dodo, Ida and Augustus John lived in a ménage in which they embraced a life of gypsy-style bohemianism.

Peel [quinces] as thin as possible, cut in quarters, core & cut up in small pieces not too thin. Boil till soft in water which does not quite cover cuttings, about 10 minutes. Weigh fruits and water & allow ¾ lbs. sugar to every 1 lb. of fruits and water. Boil again till the marmalade turns a nice pink colour. From ¾ to 1 hr it took me. Is really delicious.

'Males'

'There was a dish of spring onions on the table. Julia said suddenly: "What are those little long things some people have got?" Carrington: "Those mean they are males, dear. Ask Tommy if he'll lend you his." Julia: "Oh no, not unless I'm offered."'

Frances Partridge, *Memories*, 1981

above left: **Henrietta Bingham and Stephen Tomlin, 1920s;** *above right:* **Lytton Strachey and Ralph Partridge, 1920s; both possibly photographed by Dora Carrington.**

Bloomsbury relationships were rarely straightforward. But the complicated web of affairs centred around Ham Spray House in the mid-1920s was astonishing even by the standards of Bloomsbury. The growing liaison between Ralph Partridge and Frances Marshall caused considerable friction between Ralph and Dora Carrington, whom he had married in 1921. But romance was soon rampant in Carrington's corner as well. In 1924 she fell in love with Henrietta Bingham, the beautiful daughter of the American ambassador, and they became lovers. Before long, however, Henrietta ran off with the bisexual sculptor Stephen ('Tommy') Tomlin, to whom Lytton Strachey was also attracted. Carrington was devastated, yet soon got over it when she developed a crush on Lytton's niece Julia Strachey, who was also Frances's best friend from school. When that ended, Tommy re-entered Carrington's life and they became lovers, but their relationship ended a year later, in 1927, when Tommy and Julia married. Around this time, Lytton, too, found a romance, of a sort, with the literary figure Roger Senhouse. Their affair – Lytton's last – involved secret beatings and mock crucifixions and lasted, intermittently, for four or five years.

Spring onions, or 'males', are to be eaten whole. They add a sprightly edge to summer salads and stir-fries, and are also highly nutritious and versatile. One should accept one if offered, but be cautious about having too many.

Breakfast with Clive

'Every morning, a gong summoned us to the breakfast room, at one end of which, seated upon leather sofas and armchairs, was the family, while at the other end, seated in a row, were the servants – about six women all spotless in black and white. Grandfather read the "collect" for the day and a selected passage from the Bible, then with one accord we fell upon our knees and examined the upholstery of our chairs. I was always fascinated by the neat precision with which the servants executed this manoeuvre. They looked like a flotilla of moorhens diving head down into a pond. When the Lord's Prayer had been said they rose and, in the same disciplined fashion, filed out of the room to return with porridge, scrambled eggs, coffee and tea.'

Quentin Bell, Elders and Betters, 1995

If Ham Spray House differed from Charleston, the residents of Cleeve House in Wiltshire inhabited a different world altogether. What a shock it was when Vanessa, Julian, Quentin and Angelica arrived there to play happy families with Grandmother and Grandfather Bell.* Formality, religion, family unity and propriety were distinctly foreign to the three Bell children and regarded by them as amusingly farcical. Vanessa was not amused, however, and found the pompous antics of her in-laws loathsome. Shooting and hunting conversation bored her, so Clive's family seemed to have nothing interesting to talk about.

Even at Charleston, Clive maintained his sense of Bell propriety, according to Angelica Garnett (née Bell). 'A bad sleeper but of regular, predicable habits,' Angelica wrote in *Deceived with Kindness*, 'Clive took time, after Grace had brought his jug of hot water and had drawn his curtains, to wash and dress. Unlike Vanessa's, his toilet was a semi-public affair, and he could be heard shuffling on his carpeted floor from bathroom to bedroom … blowing his nose, gargling, brushing his teeth and talking to himself…. Finally, pink as a peach, perfumed and manicured but in old darned clothes of once superlative quality, he would enter the room and tap the barometer, the real function of which was to recall his well-ordered Victorian childhood. After greeting Vanessa he would help himself to coffee and settle down with deliberation to eat an orange, dry toast and marmalade.'

* Clive Bell's parents were William Heward Bell (1849–1927) and Hannah Taylor Bell, née Cory (1850–1942).

Clive's favourite breakfast dish, according to Virginia Woolf, was eggs and sausages. At Charleston Grace Higgens prepared such a cooked breakfast and kept it warm for Clive inside the Aga.

Clive Bell's Significant Form

'Clive, who has nothing Christlike about him, has had to give up eating tea, because, when Lady Lewis gave a party the other night and Rosenthal played Chopin, a waistcoat button burst and flew across the room with such impetuosity that the slow movement was entirely spoilt. The humiliation, which would have killed you or me – the room was crowded with the elite of London – only brushed him slightly – he won't eat bread and butter anymore; but his spirits are superb, and he says that life grows steadily more and more enchanting, the fatter one gets.'

Virginia Woolf to Barbara Bagenal, 24 June 1923

In 1914 Clive Bell propounded in his book, *Art*, that 'significant form' is the universal quality present in all outstanding visual art. 'What quality is common to Sta. Sophia and the windows at Chartres, Mexican sculpture, a Persian bowl, Chinese carpets, Giotto's frescoes at Padua, and the masterpieces of Poussin, Piero della Francesca and Cézanne?' asked Clive. 'Only one answer seems possible – significant form. In each, lines and colours combined in a particular way, certain forms and relations of forms, stir our aesthetic emotions.'

Was it aesthetic emotion roused by Clive's own significant form that prompted Virginia Woolf to gossip so vividly about his bursting button at a piano recital of Chopin?

This chocolate jelly recipe from the Grace Higgens archive probably had something to do with Clive's expanding waistline. He loved chocolate and according to his granddaughter, Virginia Nicholson, he would often break off from his walk across the South Downs Way to buy a bar of chocolate from the Firle village shop. Afterwards, he would resume his trek.

1 PT MILK • 2 OZ VANILLA CHOCOLATE • ⅓ OZ GELATIN
1 DSP CASTER SUGAR • 3 DSP CREAM

[G]rate chocolate, melt gelatine in milk, & choc & sugar. Boil gently for 8 minutes. leave until nearly cold. then whip with whisk for four minutes. pour into mould & leave to set. decorate with whipped cream. [Serves 4.]

The Bloomsbury Pot

'When the door was opened, a warm stream of Clive's hospitality and love of the good things of life poured out, as ravishing as the smell of roasting coffee on a cold morning. Heaviness, dullness, coldness, the besetting sins of English people and of the English climate, were impossible in Clive's house and Clive's company. Such jolly hearty good-fellowship is traditionally associated with fox-hunters and shooting parties and it was, in fact, from that milieu that Clive inherited his temperament. His tastes had led him into the chillier world of philosophers, mathematicians, critics and artists where the spiritual virtues of the hunt breakfast were unknown. Clive therefore provided an essential element in the formation of Bloomsbury.'

David Garnett, *The Flowers of the Forest*, 1955

Following the Cambridge tradition of G. E. Moore, Clive valued 'good' states of mind above all else, and argued that 'there is no state of mind more excellent or more intense than the state of aesthetic contemplation'. In practice, he aesthetically contemplated just about every aspect of his life: art, wine, women, conversation, friendship and food. Some have labelled him a womanizer and a hedonist, but it was his insatiable appetite for good things – including the intelligentsia of Cambridge and the Stephen sisters of Bloomsbury – that made him what he was. Although he had been a Latin and Greek scholar at Cambridge, he never claimed to be as intellectual as some of his university friends. But he outshone them in his social skills, 'the secret of which was that he liked his guests to shine, and that food, wine and conversation were all equally good', recalled Frances Partridge. Thus Clive added a delicious appetizing flavour to the Bloomsbury pot.

Grace Cakes

'By the grace of God came Grace.'

David Garnett, quoted in *Bloomsbury at Home*, 1999

For many years Vanessa Bell had difficulty finding good domestic help. Many cooks came and went. The Zany was unreliable; Mrs Pitcher hated the governess; Trissie was socially ambitious; Emily was a bad-tempered, brick-wielding sugar thief; and Mad Mary was always just a little too fun, and sadly ended her days in a lunatic asylum.

Grace Germany arrived at Gordon Square in August 1920 at the age of sixteen. She was forgetful and naïve, and one could almost have added her to the list of incompetent 'exes' but for her willingness to lend a hand to anything. In a letter to Clive written a year after Grace's arrival, Vanessa remarked: 'Our French cook … is very practical and I think looks upon Grace as a hopeless amateur – as indeed she is, trapesing about in exquisite transparent clothes, with a handker-chief tied round her head, very lovely and quite incompetent. However she picks up a few words of French occasionally and makes herself understood with the help of a dictionary.' (As witness, see the early French text by Grace, above.) As Angelica's nursemaid, Grace was immature, scatty and inept, but she soon devel-oped into a reliable parlourmaid, cook and housekeeper. In 1971 she retired as the long-serving, much relied-upon 'treasure' of Charleston.

Grace became an excellent cook, taking inspiration from her visits to France and from the finest cookbooks of her day: *Kitchen Essays with Recipes and their Occasions* by Lady Jekyll (1922), *A Second Helping* and *The Finer Cooking* by X. M. Boulestin (1925 and 1937), the *Good Housekeeping Cookery Book* (1925) and Chester's *French Cooking for English Homes* (1927). Today this culinary archive survives on a kitchen shelf at Charleston.

'When I was a child at Charleston', recalled Virginia Nicholson, 'we always had "Grace Cakes" for tea. Grace explained the recipe to my mother [Anne Olivier Bell] – it was 2 eggs + the weight of 2 eggs in flour, butter, sugar – in other words, a classic sponge; it was sandwiched with jam.'

Grace's Algerian Omelette

'Lydia, like everyone who knew Grace at all well, became much attached to her'.

Quentin Bell, foreword to *Grace at Charleston*, 1994

above: **Vanessa Bell,** *The Kitchen*, **1943. Grace Germany was a shy sixteen-year-old when she began working for Vanessa in 1920. She retired fifty years later, the much relied-upon 'treasure' of Charleston.** *opposite:* **Simple instructions (in French) for setting the table in Grace's handwriting, 1920s. In Cassis, Grace learned a little French and made herself understood with the aid of a dictionary.**

Duncan Grant, *Still Life with Jug, Knife and Onion*, 1920.

Once Lydia Lopokova realized that she was not welcome in Vanessa Bell's studio for spontaneous conversation and cups of tea (Vanessa did not wish to be distracted from her work and she considered chatting with Lydia a waste of time), she ventured downstairs to the kitchen in Gordon Square and found more receptive ears in the young Quentin Bell and Grace Germany. Among the clutter of pots and pans and (dare I say it) the occasional cockroach, Lydia would spend hours in the kitchen regaling the two of them with 'stories of Old Russia, of samovars and droshkis and boyars', Quentin recalled. 'She gave us both tickets for the London Coliseum, where the variety programme included ballet, and I cherish the memories of splendid afternoons there, when our talkative Russian friend from the kitchen was transformed into a silent but miraculously expressive beauty.' Even as Quentin grew older, he and Lydia 'never lost that early friendship' that had begun in the basement kitchen at 50 Gordon Square.

'I have a passion for an omelette that Grace prepares; today I had it twice,' Lydia wrote to John Maynard Keynes in June 1922. This is a Grace Higgens recipe for an omelette with a slightly exotic flavour.

I ONION • BUTTER • I LARGE SPOONFUL RICE • I CUP STOCK
SALT AND PEPPER • 4 EGGS • TOMATO SAUCE

Mince up an onion very finely. Fry in butter but do not let it get brown. Put some more butter into the pan and when the onions are cooked add a large spoonful of rice. Turn and stir it so that it is all well browned to a warm biscuit colour. Then pour in a good cup of good stock and after mixing all well together with pepper and salt to taste, cover the pan and let the contents simmer very gently for about fifteen minutes.

Make an omelette of four eggs and when it is cooked spread the cooked rice and onions over the whole surface of the omelette, and when well warmed through fold in two and serve on a hot oval dish surrounded with tomato sauce. [Serves 2.]

Mrs Harland's Fruit Fool

'What shall we do without a cook? Karsavina* can make scrambled eggs. But can I?'

Lydia Lopokova to her mother-in-law, Florence Keynes, 5 January 1931

Having travelled and lived in hotels for much of her life, Lydia Lopokova had little opportunity to cultivate many domestic skills. Fortunately, her husband John Maynard Keynes's long-standing cook and housekeeper, Mrs Harland, was extremely able and competent.

* *Tamara Karsavina was Lydia Lopokova's fellow ballerina, friend and rival.*

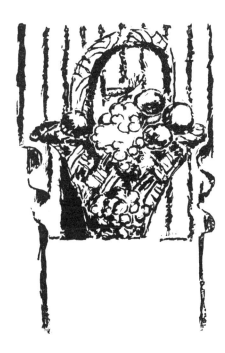

Vanessa Bell, linocut of
a basket of fruit, 1950.

In the summer of 1922, Maynard loaned Mrs Harland to Charleston where she cooked so many outstanding dishes that Clive Bell was 'obliged … to work in the garden each day to keep down his weight. Duncan took to doing exercises in the nude every day before dinner,' according to Duncan Grant's biographer Frances Spalding. On a separate occasion at 46 Gordon Square, Lydia invited Frederick Ashton, her choreographer, and Harold Turner, her dance partner, to lunch, where they feasted on quantities of Mrs Harland's delicious liver and soufflé. Despite the lightness and airiness of her soufflé, that afternoon's ballet rehearsal was rendered impracticable: 'the food was so prominent in our insides,' Lydia wrote to Maynard, 'that hysterical laughter accompanied every step. I couldn't be lifted.'

Mrs Harland's fruit fool found its way into Frances Partridge's recipe book. It is one of her lighter dishes. Still, it would be unwise to pirouette or to attempt any serious lifting afterwards.

> Cook fruit [1 lb summer berries] till soft with least possible quantity of water. Put through mixer & add 2 beaten-up whites of egg, & sugar last. [Serve chilled. Serves 4–6.]

Afternoon Tea in the Garden at Charleston

'Charleston is as usual. One hears Clive shouting in the garden before one arrives. Nessa emerges from a great variegated quilt of asters & artichokes; not very cordial; a little absent minded. Clive bursts out of his shirt; sits square in his chair & bubbles. Then Duncan drifts in, also vague, absent minded, & incredibly wrapped round with yellow waist-coats, spotted ties, & old blue stained painting jackets. His trousers have to be hitched up constantly. He rumples his hair. However, I can't help thinking that we grow in cordiality, instead of drifting out of sight. And why not stand on one's own legs, & defy them, even in the matter of hats & chaircovers? Surely at the age of forty…. As for Duncan he requires, I think, peace for painting. He would like it all settled one way or the other. We saw a perfectly black rabbit, & a perfectly black cat, sitting on the road, with its tail laid out like a strap. "What they call an example of melanism" said Clive – which amused me very much, & also made me like him.'

Virginia Woolf's diary, 26 August 1922

The Woolfs and the Bells often met up for tea on Sundays. Occasionally, if the weather was fine, Leonard and Virginia would cycle the nine miles from Monk's House to Charleston. In 1924 Grace Higgens met them on their bicycles: 'they looked absolute freaks, Mr Woolf with a corduroy coat which had a split up the back.... Mrs Woolf in a costume she had had for years.' At Charleston, if the weather was fine, they would gather outside in the walled garden, and sit in Rhorkee chairs amidst the profusion of poppies, zinnias, rambling pink albertines, white hydrangeas, hollyhocks and delphiniums. Figs, apples, pears and damsons clung espaliered against the red-brick and flint garden walls, and waterfalls of white clematis and fragrant jasmine blossoms cascaded down the sides of the eighteenth-century farmhouse. Alliums, artichokes and other bright, tall stemmed flowers stood among the green vegetable foliage. Italianate statues, colourful mosaics, gravel paths and neatly planted rows of box hedging contained, barely, the extravagant mass of delinquent colour.

Clive Bell recalled Virginia's teatime visits in *Old Friends* as follows: 'She might be divinely witty or outrageously fanciful; she might retail village gossip or tell stories of her London friends; always she was indescribably entertaining; always she enjoyed herself and we enjoyed her. "Virginia's coming to tea": we knew it would be exciting, we knew that we were going to laugh and be surprised and made to feel that the temperature of life was several degrees higher than we had supposed.'

Adults gossiped, laughed and bantered freely with one another, while the children played about near the pond. A refreshing cup of tea, a second slice of cake, a gentle walk around the garden: a perfect afternoon tea in the garden at Charleston.

Vanessa Bell, *Tea Things*, 1919. This painting hung on a wall in Clive Bell's flat from 1919 and moved back to Charleston with him in 1939. The tray, the cups, and the saucers were all 'tea things' at Charleston.

Here are three of Grace's delicious teatime favourites.

Seed Cake

1 LB FLOUR • 8 OZ MARGARINE • ¼ TSP BICARBONATE OF SODA
2 OZ CANDIED PEEL • 7 OZ SUGAR • 2 EGGS • 5–6 FLUID OZ MILK
1 OZ CARAWAY SEEDS

Grease a cake tin and line it with greased paper. Sieve the flour with the bicarbonate of soda into a basin. Rub the fat into the flour. Cut the peel into small pieces. Add the sugar, caraway seeds [2 teaspoons is sufficient] and candied peel to the flour mixture. Mix all the dry ingredients well together. Beat the eggs well, mix with the milk. Add the eggs and milk to the dry ingredients. Mix well together and beat thoroughly, adding more milk if required. Place the mixture in the prepared cake tin and bake in a moderately hot oven [180°C] for about about 1½ hours. [Serves 6–8.]

Hurry Cake

4 OZ BUTTER • 2 OZ [OR 4 OZ] SUGAR • 4 OZ GROUND ALMONDS
2 OZ SELF-RAISING FLOUR • [2–3 DROPS] ALMOND ESSENCE • [2 EGGS]

Cream butter and sugar [and eggs] together and gradually add the almonds, flour and essence. [Place in a small round buttered cake tin and] bake in a moderate hot oven [180°C] for 15–20 minutes [or until a knife comes out clean. Serves 6].

Walnut and Coffee Slices

2 OZ WALNUTS • 4 OZ MARGARINE • 3 OZ SUGAR
2 LEVEL TSP MAPLE SYRUP (OR GOLDEN SYRUP WITH 2 OZ BROWN SUGAR)
7 OZ FLOUR • 1 TSP [INSTANT] COFFEE

Chop the walnuts. Cream margarine, sugar and syrup together. Work in the flour, coffee [dissolved in 10 ml hot water] and walnuts and knead together. Add 2–3 drops of milk if necessary. Roll out thinly and bake in oven for 30 minutes at 180°C. [Serves 6.]

Tea Party Fooling

'Was she the bewitched princess, or the wicked little girl at the tea party – or both, or neither? I can't tell.'

Christopher Isherwood, *Virginia Woolf*, 1941

Virginia Woolf's niece, Angelica Bell, remembered that her aunt 'could cook, and bottle fruit – well do I remember the pride she took in her cupboard of jade-green gooseberries and sad-purple raspberries on the stairs at Monk's House.'

Her aunt also devised a language, 'Pixerina-Witcherina', which she used to communicate secretly with her niece. The game was typical of Virginia's intellect: she would warp and twist reality to amuse herself and her young friends. Adults weren't always so lucky. She sometimes teased them mercilessly, telling T. S. Eliot, for example: 'It's such a pity, Tom, that you started being a poet instead of remaining in a bank. By now you might have been the Manager of the Bank of England.' But with children, Virginia's playfulness was sensitive and empathetic.

Whether she was the 'bewitched princess' or the 'wicked little girl' mentioned by Christopher Isherwood, or both at the same time, Virginia could always be relied upon to liven up a tea party with her fooling.

Virginia Woolf with Angelica Bell, 1932. Virginia and Angelica shared a secret language, 'Pixerina-Witcherina', which they used to the exclusion of all others.

From **Leonard Woolf, Monk's House, Rodmell, Lewes, Sussex.**

Many thanks for the delicious cake which we
both enjoy every day at tea. Could you be so good
some time as to write out the recipe, as I cant get
any cakes made excpet yours that I like to eat?
We go to London tomorrow.   V. Woolf.

Virginia Woolf's thank-you card to Grace Higgens, 1936.

Monk's House Tea

'Tea was set out on a long refectory table, with purple lustre ware, home-made bread and cakes, and honey from their hives. There were crumpets, too: these Mrs Woolf had specially bought to toast there and then herself, because it was her fancy, she said, to do so, as few, she continued, understood the pleasure of having crumpets for tea. The talk was richly embroidered by her humour and wit.'

G. E. Easdale, 'Tea with Virginia Woolf', 1931

When Virginia and Leonard Woolf bought Monk's House in Rodmell, Sussex, in 1919, the house had no electricity, lavatory, bath or running water. Its 'ground floor' was actually several feet below the level of the garden; if there was rain, a river flowed through the kitchen.

Initially a neighbour cooked and prepared meals for the Woolfs and brought trays of food around at designated intervals. A new cooker was installed in 1926 and in 1931 they fitted electricity and purchased a Frigidaire. There were other improvements as well, such as flush lavatories and central heating, but the house was never very comfortable. The ceilings were low and the green painted walls made the house feel 'like a sea-shell through which the water flows,' wrote Angelica Garnett, 'leaving behind it a taste of salt'.

But for Leonard and Virginia, Monk's House was home, and they liked the leisurely pace of Rodmell after the bustle of London. Still, their daily routine was more or less the same as it had been in the city: they wrote in the mornings, and went for a walk or worked in the garden most afternoons. If they had guests for tea, friends and family were subjected to a competitive game of lawn bowls, which Leonard usually won.

The author Enid Bagnold, though never close to the Woolfs, recalled having tea at Monk's House after a disastrous* day at the races: 'Virginia leant, listening magically, her face on her hand, laughing. Leonard, his hand trembling** on the way to his mouth with a scone, egged me on, picking over the disaster, finding new bits, looking for more.' Virginia's friend (later lover) Vita Sackville-West described another Monk's House scene in a letter to her husband, Harold Nicolson: 'Virginia has gone to talk to the servants, and I sit alone in her friendly room with its incredible muddle of objects, so crowded that I am terrified of knocking something over. I've already broken a chair. Leonard has departed for the market, laden with baskets of apples and carrots. They *are* nice. Leonard has now got a cat, which means that the rooms are further crowded by tin dishes on the floor.' Virginia herself touchingly re-created their workaday teatime in her novel *The Waves*: 'Yet Byron never made tea as you do, who fill the pot so that when you put the lid on the tea spills over. There is a brown pool on the table – it is running among your books and

* Her hat had blown off her head and become caught in the horses' legs at the start of a race at Goodwood Racecourse.
** Leonard had a mild congenital tremor.

Duncan Grant, Quentin Bell and Angelica Bell enjoying a game of bowls on the lawn at Monk's House, unknown date. From the Monk's House photograph album.

papers. Now you mop it up, clumsily, with your pocket-handkerchief. You then stuff your handkerchief back into your pocket – that is not Byron; that is you; that is so essentially you that if I think of you in twenty years' time, when we are both famous, gouty and intolerable, it will be by that scene: and if you are dead, I shall weep.'

This traditional recipe from G. F. Scotson-Clark's *Kitchenette Cookery* (1926) is the best method for brewing tea that I have ever come across.

Tea

Always use an earthenware teapot. Heat it before putting in the tea. Use India or Ceylon tea, but even if you like China tea, avoid green tea, which has a bad effect on the nerves.

Use a teaspoonful for each person, or a little less if you do not like it too strong. Put the tea in a tea-ball, as this keeps the tea leaves together and makes the washing-up of the teapot much simpler. Pour *freshly boiled water*, that is *absolutely boiling*, on the tea; let it stand three minutes; stir it and pour it out immediately. Use milk and sugar or lemon and sugar.

If you do not take milk and sugar or lemon, it is better to have the tea weaker. Another advantage of using the tea-ball is that it can be removed from the pot after five or six minutes. In this way the tea does not steep and become bitter.

Every year on 26 November Leonard's mother sent him a birthday cake. This cake would adorn the Woolfs' tea table where usually, Angelica Garnett noted, 'there were biscuits instead of cake'. This Grace Higgens cake is delicious with a dollop of homemade jam on top.

Banana Fruit Loaf Cake

4 OZ MARGARINE • 4 OZ CASTER SUGAR • 1 HEAPED TBS GOLDEN SYRUP
1 LB RIPE BANANAS, MASHED • 2 EGGS • ½ TSP SALT
PINCH MIXED SPICE • 2 OZ CHOPPED PEEL
2 OZ GLACÉ CHERRIES, QUARTERED • 2 OZ CHOPPED WALNUTS
8 OZ SELF-RAISING FLOUR

Cream margarine and sugar. Stir in syrup, bananas and eggs. Mix in cherries, peel and nuts. Fold in sifted flour, salt and spice. Stir well. Put in a greased 2 lb. tin (loaf tin) and bake No. 4 gas [180°C] about 1¼ hours. Very nice spread with butter. [Serves 8.]

Hogarth Eccles Cakes

When Leonard Woolf remembered the beginning of the Hogarth Press in 1917 in his autobiography, he recalled the yearning he and Virginia felt when they found themselves gazing at a shop in Farringdon Street, wondering what printing

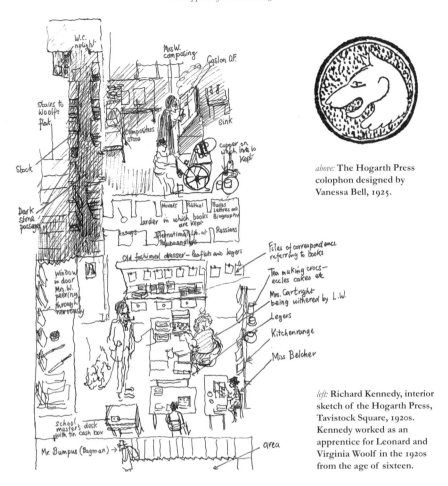

above: **The Hogarth Press colophon designed by Vanessa Bell, 1925.**

left: **Richard Kennedy, interior sketch of the Hogarth Press, Tavistock Square, 1920s. Kennedy worked as an apprentice for Leonard and Virginia Woolf in the 1920s from the age of sixteen.**

equipment to buy: 'Nearly all the implements of printing are materially attractive and we stared through the window at them rather like two hungry children gazing at buns and cakes in a baker shop window.'

The delivery and positioning of their new equipment at Hogarth House in Richmond were as disruptive as any new arrival, and everyone in the household had to adapt. Leonard recalled the upheaval in his autobiography: 'When the printing machine was delivered, we had it put in the corner of the dining-room, but, when McDermott [a local printer in Richmond] saw it there, he shook his head and said it was much too dangerous – the machine was so heavy that if we worked it there, it would probably go through the floor on to the cook's head in the kitchen. So we had to have it all dismantled again and erected in a small larder at the back of the house in the basement. The invasion of the larder was not popular with Nellie and Lottie, the cook and the house-parlour-maid, but at least it was safer for them to have it there than over their heads in the dining-room.'

The Hogarth Press, like any well-loved child, soon had the run of the entire house. Virginia and Leonard were devoted to their beloved press and came to live, eat and drink alongside the printed word. They 'printed in the larder, bound books in the dining-room, interviewed printers, binders, and authors in a sitting-room', recalled Leonard. It united them as a couple and introduced them to many new and interesting people, including a series of assistants. One of the latter, Richard Kennedy, drew the charming sketch plan of the Hogarth Press reproduced on the preceding page, in which Eccles cakes are indicated as suitable sustenance for type-setting and printing. Eccles cakes are also suitable for the entire family. This recipe from *The Golden Book of Confectioners' Recipes* (*c.* 1920) dates from around the time that the Hogarth Press was established.

For the puff dough
½ LB FLOUR • ½ LB PASTRY BUTTER [REAL BUTTER]
½ GILL [10 ML] OF [COLD] WATER

Put flour in mixing bowl, rub butter in but not very fine, and then add the water and make into dough, after this roll the dough out, fold each end over one another, and roll again, do this three times, and then place the dough for about two hours in a cool place.

To make the Eccles cakes (suggested ingredients)
5 OZ CURRANTS • 1 TBS CASTER SUGAR • 1 EGG YOLK
1 TBS MILK • ¼ TSP ICING SUGAR

Weigh off 1½ oz. pieces of puff paste dough, roll these out round, and then put 1 oz. of currants on each round (the currants must be mixed with fine sugar beforehand), fold the ends of the dough over to the centre and twist them. Then place on your board and roll them out. After this egg-wash them [with beaten egg yolk, milk, ¼ teaspoon icing sugar] and bake in a sharp oven, when they come out of the oven, sprinkle with caster sugar. [Makes 24.]

Veal Schnitzel with Mushrooms

'All human relations have shifted – those between masters and servants, husbands and wives, parents and children.'

Virginia Woolf, *Mr Bennett and Mrs Brown*, 1924

Nellie Boxall went to work for Virginia Woolf as live-in cook and housekeeper at Hogarth House in 1916. Their mutually dependent relationship was fraught with equally mutual resentment, and there are many instances in Virginia's diaries and

Vanessa Bell, *Interior with Housemaid*, 1939. After the First World War the demarcation between social classes became increasingly less distinct.

letters when the two of them were at loggerheads. 'I am sick of the timid spite-ful servant mind,' she wrote to Vanessa. And in her diary she commented: 'She doesn't care for me, or for anything.' This difficult relationship between mistress and servant was more than personal; it was indicative of the social changes taking place at large all over England. The demarcation between the social classes was shifting and, in some cases, fading, as both employer and employee found them-selves jostling for more freedom and less dependence.

Nellie worked for the Woolfs for eighteen years. She served Virginia through the latter's intermittent bouts of madness and witnessed her development into a literary genius. She knew how to wind Virginia up, and equally how to placate her. When asked later what was Mrs Woolf's favourite dish, Nellie recalled that 'she liked veal schnitzels and mushrooms with the trimmings and was very fond of good soups'. This classic Viennese recipe from the Frances Partridge collection is simple and easy to prepare – an appeasing sort of dish.

Wiener Schnitzels

Cut very thin, one per person. Put butter in a frying-pan & while it is heating (not before) flour the escalopes both sides. Cook them 2 mins one side, turn & cook 2 mins, turn again & cook three.

… with mushrooms

Chop, & fry mushrooms [in plenty of butter] before cooking the escalopes; add a tablespoonful of thick cream & some parsley to the sauce.

A Welcome Night In

'I was thinking (among other things) that this is a lazy life. Breakfast in bed. Read in bed. Bath. Order dinner. Out to Lodge. After rearranging my room (turning table to get the sun: church on right; window left: a new very lovely view) tune up, with cigarette: write till 12: stop: visit L.: look at papers; return; type till 1. Listen in: Lunch. Sore jaw: can't bite. Read papers. Walk to Southease. Back 3. Gather and arrange apples. Tea. Write a letter. Bowls. Type again. Read Michelet or write here. Cook dinner. Music. Embroidery. 9.30 read (or sleep) till 11.30. Bed.'

Virginia Woolf's diary, September 1940

By late 1923, after nine years living in Richmond, Virginia Woolf was sufficiently stable mentally for Leonard to acquiesce to her pleas to return to central London. They moved to 52 Tavistock Square in Bloomsbury in January 1924. Leonard feared that the excitement of the city would bring on Virginia's 'influenza', so he devised a strict daily routine that would not be too taxing:

8.15–9 a.m. – Breakfast
10 a.m. – 1 p.m. – Fiction Writing
1 p.m. – Lunch/Walk/Non-Fiction Writing
4.30 p.m. – Tea
8.00 p.m. – Dinner/Reading/Listening to Music
11.30 p.m. – Bed

He also kept a watchful eye on her. 'He completely arranged his life and hers so that she would have the minimum of mental strain. I think she needed someone as firmly anchored mentally as he was and I am sure that he was the only person who could have kept her going,' wrote Alix Strachey in *Recollections of Virginia Woolf.*

From 1923 onwards the Woolfs' personal and professional lives flourished. The Hogarth Press published many celebrated writers: Sigmund Freud, T. S. Eliot, E. M. Forster, John Maynard Keynes, Vita Sackville-West, Edith Sitwell, Roger Fry, Clive Bell, George Rylands and, of course, many books by the Woolfs: *Mrs Dalloway*; *To the Lighthouse*; *The Waves*; *Orlando*; *The Years*; *Fear and Politics*; *Quack, Quack!*; *Barbarians at the Gate*; *Imperialism and Civilization*; *Hunting the Highbrow*; and *War for Peace.*

Virginia and Leonard worked hard, but they also enjoyed an active social life. They lunched at Kettner's and Simpson's (Lytton Strachey's favourite restaurant) and The Ivy (Clive Bell's favourite restaurant), Boulestin and L'Etoile. They went to exhibitions, concerts, lectures and ballets, and attended costume parties, tea parties, birthday parties, literary parties and dinner parties. London was in the midst of a jazz and cocktail craze, and feminists, flappers and trades unionists were leading social change. But for Virginia, all this excitement had to be rationed. The Woolfs were usually seen leaving parties early and going home for a night in.

Evenings at home were a welcome break. In her letters, Virginia often described the meals she was 'dishing up' (but had not necessarily prepared herself): 'an omelette with good coffee', 'grilled herring', 'roast mutton', 'ham and eggs and an odious pudding called Canary with a mop of bright red jam on its head', '2 chops, broiled in gravy'. After dinner, she and Leonard would retire to their sitting-room to sit and talk, smoke (Virginia rolled her own shag cigarettes) and listen to classical music on their gramophone.

The first of these two simple recipes is from Lucy Yates's classic cookery book, *Cooking for 2*, published in 1930. The second is from Helen Anrep's scrapbook.

Ham and Eggs

This ever popular dish is very often spoilt by want of care. The ham should be fried in a little fat and then closely covered so that it may steam through. This can be done by putting it between two hot plates while the eggs are being fried in the pan. Place an egg on each slice of ham and pour a little hot fat over, and the fat is improved by having a dash of vinegar and made mustard heated with it.

When frying eggs, have a sufficient depth of fat partially to cover the egg, which can be done by tilting the frying pan. Break each egg separately into a cup, and while holding the pan tilted to get a 'cup' of fat, slide the egg into this. Eggs should *poach* in fat just as they would poach in water. To do this there must be a sufficient depth to set the egg in a ball directly it goes into the fat.

Canary Pudding

2 EGGS • 4 OZ FLOUR • 3 OZ SUGAR • 2 OZ BUTTER
1 TSP BAKING POWDER • [MILK] • [JAM OR CUSTARD]

Cream butter and sugar. Add beaten eggs. Add flour [and baking powder] and a little milk, if necessary. Steam in a [well-greased] basin for 1 hour. [Turn out onto a serving plate. Serve with a nice dollop of jam or custard. Serves 4–6.]

A Bloomsbury Tea Party

'Straight lines go too quickly to appreciate the pleasures of the journey. They rush straight to their target and then die in the very moment of their triumph without having thought, loved, suffered or enjoyed themselves. Broken lines do not know what they want. With their caprices they cut time up, abuse routes, slash the joyous flowers and split the peaceful fruits with their corners. It is another story with curved lines. The song of the curved line is called happiness.'

René Crevel, *The As Stable Pamphlets*, 1926

Among the lectures attended by the Woolfs, and Bloomsbury in general, were those organized around teatime by Molly MacCarthy in 1925. She invited a broad range of speakers including Francis Birrell, who spoke on 'Women in French Literature', and the young French novelist and surrealist René Crevel, who chose 'L'esprit contre la Raison'. Needless to say, some lectures were better received than others. At the gathering to hear Crevel, 'The whole thing – the brazen pretentious boy and the anxious pretentious audience, was extremely funny,' reported Logan Pearsall Smith (author of *Stories from the Old Testament*, which was published by the Hogarth Press in 1920) to the literary critic Cyril Connolly.

Each lecture was followed by the tea, which was served promptly at five o'clock.

Finger sandwiches, scones with clotted cream and a selection of homemade cakes and pastries were among the foods typically offered at English tea parties in 1925. Here are three teatime classics. These chocolate biscuits are from *Fry's Chocolate Recipes*.

Chocolate Tea Biscuits

2 BREAKFAST CUPS FLOUR • 4 TBS FRY'S BREAKFAST COCOA
4 TSP BAKING POWDER • 3 TBS MARGARINE • ½ TSP SALT
⅔ CUP MILK, TO MAKE A FIRM BUT NOT STIFF DOUGH
2 TBS SUGAR

Molly MacCarthy, photographed by Ottoline Morrell, 1923. In 1925 Molly organized a series of tea-party lectures. Some were better received than others.

Mix and sift dry ingredients, flour, sugar, cocoa, baking powder and salt. Cut in margarine or work it in with tips of fingers. Add gradually the liquid, mixing to a soft dough. Toss on floured board, roll lightly to one-half inch in thickness, cut in small biscuits. Place on greased and floured pan, chill. Bake in hot oven [220°C] 12–15 minutes. [Makes 24.]

Lady fingers can be quite tricky to make. If possible, use a pastry bag to pipe the batter onto a piece of parchment paper – this way you will have a neater result.

Helen Anrep's Lady Fingers
½ LB BUTTER • 1 LB FLOUR • ½ LB SUGAR
JUICE AND GRATED RIND OF 1 LARGE LEMON • 3 EGGS, SEPARATED

[Preheat the oven to 180°C]. To make Lady Fingers for afternoon tea, rub half pound butter into a pound of prepared flour; to this add half pound sugar, the juice and grated rind of one large lemon, and, lastly, three eggs, the whites and yolks beaten separately, and the whites stirred in after all the other ingredients are well mixed together. This dough should be stiff enough to make rolls about the size of a lady's finger; it will spread when in the oven so that it will be of the right size and shape. If you wish them to be varied and inviting, dip them in chocolate icing after they are baked, and harden for a moment in the oven. [Makes about four dozen 3 in. (7.5 cm) lady fingers.]

The following traditional English recipe is from *Five Hundred Sandwiches*, published in 1929.

Cucumber Sandwiches
Peel a cucumber and slice into cold salted water. Drain after an hour. Pour over vinegar to cover and let stand five minutes. Drain and serve between thin slices of buttered bread. Salad dressing may be used if desired. Variation: Sprinkle finely chopped fresh mint on the cucumber.

Dining Out

'In the evening we had dinner with old Augustus [John] at the Eiffel Tour [*sic*]. Rather fun. Very late, at 9.30. Such a delicious meal. Snails. Wild duck and orange salad, and real iced raspberries and cream and two bottle[s] of Burgundy.'

Dora Carrington to Julia Strachey, 29 October 1929

The Bloomsbury Group enjoyed dining out and in the 1920s and 30s patronized London's most fashionable eating establishments: Simpson's, the Café Royal,

Kettner's, Boulestin, The Ivy and the Eiffel Tower. The British typically did not dine out much before the 1950s – it was neither affordable nor fashionable. Therefore Bloomsbury – even when it came to dining out – was ahead of its time.

Poor Gerald Brenan (Dora Carrington's friend) could not afford fancy restaurants, so satisfied his hunger at less reputable eateries on Charlotte Street. Later he recalled two of these that stood exactly opposite each other. The one on the west side was called Bertorelli's: 'Here one sat at a bare marble-topped table and was served with a substantial plate of appetizing food, followed by an orange. There were no frills and the napkin provided was a paper one.' The other one, on the east side, which was called Vaiani's, ran according to a different principle: 'Mr Vaiani, a small bird-like Italian, believed that the style in which meals were served was of more importance than the materials of which they were made and thus saw to it that every table should be spread with a spotless white tablecloth, set off with a glass vase of paper flowers, and every cover have an elaborately folded linen napkin and a roll of fresh bread placed beside it.' Mr Vaiani also liked to offer his customers rare and exotic foods, such as pheasant, grouse and capercaillie. But since his prices had to compete with Bertorelli's, he was obliged to cut his costs on something, and so the game was half rotten while the sauce on the spaghetti would consist of nothing but a mulch of tinned tomatoes. Gerald, however, saw flashes of genius in the cooking: 'It was this aspiring strain in Mr Vaiani that made him such a touching figure. All the creative instincts of the great chef were there, struggling to assert themselves against their economic limitations and now and then bursting out in some surprising invention, as for example in the dish to which he proudly gave the name of Pêche Vaiani. This consisted of tinned peaches with chocolate poured over them.'

L'Etoile Fish Cakes

'I was woken up properly by Blanche putting my breakfast-tray down on the table beside me, and pulling the curtains. It was eight o'clock. I was happy – as usual – to find food before me, all ready to be eaten; I certainly wanted nothing else in the world just then; but, having put on my eye-glasses, I saw two letters crouching under a plate…. I thought that before reading it I'll have my breakfast. And then, as I ate my boiled egg and drank my rather thick tea – but the toast was on its accustomed royal scale – I suddenly remembered the dubiousness* of my position'.

Lytton Strachey, 'Monday June 26th 1916',
describing 'a day in the life' at Wissett Lodge

* The 'dubiousness' of Lytton's position was due to the intricate tangle of affairs unfolding at Wissett Lodge.

'I delighted in him [Lytton] because I could see in imagination the enormous rich hunk he was about to cut from the cake of life. What we talked about I cannot remember, but that was the residual impression. I must, of course, have asked him if he did not know "So-and-So, and So-and-So", mentioning those younger Cambridge "Apostles" who, as I said, also proved to be roads leading to "Bloomsbury" – Lytton Strachey certainly was one of them. Anyhow we got on so well together that he asked me to lunch with him the next day. One other thing interested me in him, the orientation of his life at the moment seemed to resemble what my own had been when I first went up to Cambridge.'

Desmond MacCarthy, *Bloomsbury, an Unfinished Memoir*, 1933

'Perched away in a corner of Duncan Grant's studio, he [Desmond] had a suit-case open before him. The lid of the case, which he propped up, would be useful to rest his manuscript upon, he told us. On he read, delighting us as usual, with his brilliancy, and humanity, and wisdom, until – owing to a slight wave of his hand – the suit-case unfortunately fell over. Nothing was inside it. There was no paper. He had been improvising.'

E. M. Forster, 'Tributes to Sir Desmond MacCarthy, II', 1952

Molly MacCarthy began the Bloomsbury 'Memoir Club' in 1920. This was her second and more successful attempt to get her husband, Desmond, to *write down* his recollections. Her initial idea, a 'Novel Club', was abandoned after Desmond was caught 'spilling' onto the floor his brilliant – but actually nonexistent – manuscript: an incident later immortalized by a listening E. M. Forster in a paper for the Memoir Club.

At some small restaurant in Soho, at The Ivy or at L'Etoile, or possibly at Charleston, Gordon Square, Tilton or the MacCarthys' house in Wellington Square, Bloomsbury members would convene once or twice annually (their final meeting was in 1956) to catch up, gossip and reminisce. After the bread rolls, the salad, the meat and the wine, after the coffee and after all the news and current affairs had been divulged and discussed at length, they would retire to a room – maybe the drawing room or the studio – to listen to a memoir. Sometimes there would be two memoirs.

Autobiographical stories, anecdotes, recollections and sketches of the past were read aloud. Here, the Bloomsbury wit, the Bloomsbury honesty, the Bloomsbury eloquence and the Bloomsbury sense of fun were dished out for them all to enjoy. On one especially entertaining occasion, Desmond turned to Clive Bell and said: 'After all *we* – at any rate for ourselves – are the best company in the world.'

On another occasion, John Maynard Keynes said to Clive: 'If everyone at this table, except myself, were to die tonight, I do not think I should care to go on living.'

Here is the signature dish of that classic French bistro, L'Etoile, on Charlotte Street. In addition to hosting the Memoir Club, it was also the meeting place of the Cranium Club, an informal dining club founded by David 'Bunny' Garnett in 1925. At the time of writing L'Etoile is still open for business.

500 G SALMON FILLET (SKIN OFF) • 100 G MARIS PIPER POTATOES
1 SMALL LEEK • ½ TBS TOMATO KETCHUP
1 TBS COARSE-GRAIN MUSTARD • 200 G JAPONAISE BREADCRUMBS
1 BUNCH DILL

For the béchamel sauce
100 G FLOUR • 100 ML MILK [HEATED] • 50 G UNSALTED BUTTER
PINCH NUTMEG • SALT AND PEPPER

Place salmon in oven on a hot tray, 200°C Gas Mark 6, for 5–7 minutes so it is still pink inside. Put into a bowl. Sweat finely chopped leeks in butter. Add to salmon then add 50 g mashed potato. Add 2 tablespoons béchamel sauce and flavour with salt and pepper. Add 1 tablespoon coarse grain mustard and ½ tablespoon tomato ketchup, plus any juice from cooking [the] salmon.

Mix together in the container. Press it into symmetrical shapes (approximately 4 in. wide) with a pastry cutter. Place in freezer to set until firm (up to 2 hours). Once firm, cover first in flour, next in beaten egg, finally in breadcrumbs blended with dill to obtain an attractive green colour. Deep or shallow fry for 2 minutes to retain moisture and flavour. Then cook in oven for 8 minutes to heat all the way through at 180°C Gas Mark 4.

For the béchamel, melt butter in pan. When bubbling, but before turning brown, add the flour through a wire sieve. Stir gently with a wooden spoon into a thick creamy substance. Add hot milk, stir vigorously. Season with salt, pepper and a little nutmeg. Add the salmon juice retained from cooking. The sauce should be thick. Serves 4.

Boulestin's Summer Luncheon

'Ah, what better luncheon on a summer day than an omelette, cold chicken or a well-spiced home-made galantine, a lettuce salad flavoured with fines herbes and spring onions and a cream cheese? It has the excellence of simplicity, and I like to think that the eggs come from our hens, the salad and the herbs from our garden, and, of course, we have made the vinegar ourselves – as it should be in every perfect household.'

Marcel Boulestin, *What Shall We Have To-day?*, 1931

Boulestin is a well-known eating establishment, originally located in Covent Garden, that was popular with the Bloomsbury Group and other writers, artists, politicians and well-known personalities of the day. It came into being in 1927 as a result of Virginia Woolf's dislike of crowded restaurants. Dorothy Todd, editor of *Vogue*, who was aware of Virginia's aversion, arranged an informal luncheon party with her and a few other guests at the private flat of the French writer and boutique owner Marcel Boulestin. When dish after sumptuous dish appeared before them, it was suggested to Boulestin that he open a small boutique restaurant. By the time that the pudding and coffee had arrived, finance had been secured and Boulestin's future as a celebrated restaurateur, television chef and cookery-book writer lay ahead.

Omelette à la Crème

This is an ambitious omelette, and when *réussie*, a delicious one. Beat the eggs as usual, add to the mixture a few fresh mushrooms, previously cooked in cream or in butter, fry quickly, fold it in the usual way, pour over your omelette – which must be light, soft and not too well cooked – a Béchamel sauce, well seasoned, and to which cream and a little grated cheese has been added, and brown lightly under a gas grill (if you have not got a salamander). Needless to say all these operations must be done in a few minutes. No omelette should be made slowly or kept waiting a second. You can decorate it, if you want it more elaborate, with a few slices of truffles.

Salade Parisienne

Mix in equal parts watercress, batavia [lettuce] and beetroot, season with salt, pepper, oil and vinegar, add parsley, chervil and tarragon finely chopped together.

Crème de Framboises

Whip to a stiff froth the white of one egg, add to it half a pint of fresh cream and go on whipping till the mixture is like a *mousse*. Squash through a hair sieve a handful of raspberries, mix the *purée* obtained with fine caster sugar (enough to sweeten both the cream and the fruit). Add this lightly, together with a few whole raspberries, to the whipped cream, keep on ice for half an hour and serve.

German Ragout

'We [Vanessa and I] both learnt the rules of the game of Victorian society so thoroughly that we have never forgotten them. We still play the game. It is useful. It has also its beauty, for it is founded upon restraint, sympathy, unselfishness – all civilized qualities … my tea-table training.'

Virginia Woolf, 'A Sketch of the Past', 1939

Duncan Grant, *Still Life (Table with Fruit and Vegetables)*, 1930.

Although Bloomsbury took a firm stance against many Victorian conventions, there was one that they could not quite bring themselves to renounce completely: table manners. Virginia Woolf famously pronounced that she was going 'to do without table napkins' – but she never actually did. Desmond MacCarthy, Virginia observed with approval, had 'perfect manners'. John Maynard Keynes, however, did not. Clive Bell was critical of Maynard's manners, and his son Quentin concurred: 'It was true that he [Maynard] was an acquisitive eater and would gather toast, marmalade, butter, sugar and condiments into a small area around his plate, helping himself as the occasion demanded.' David 'Bunny' Garnett added: 'Maynard would help himself from the nearest dish with his own knife and fork when dining with his friends, instead of passing his plate—'

But Maynard found an ideal eating companion in his wife, Lydia Lopokova. Both of them were very relaxed about table manners, and greedily gobbled up their food. Sometimes, if she was really hungry, Lydia did not even bother with a knife and fork, and shovelled food into her mouth with her fingers!

This recipe is from an article written by Lydia for the *Evening News* in 1927. Despite Lydia's habitual disregard for cutlery, it is advisable to have a napkin and a fork to hand, just in case. Maybe also a spoon.

Suggested ingredients

2 LB ROUND STEAK • 2 CELERY STICKS • I CARROT • PARSLEY
2 ONIONS • I CALF'S BRAIN • 2–3 CLOVES • 3 PEPPERCORNS
¼ TSP SALT • I ONION, SLICED • ½ GLASS [⅓ CUP] VINEGAR
2 OZ BUTTER • 2 TBS FLOUR • FRESHLY GRATED LEMON PEEL
I WINE GLASS [⅔ CUP] RHINE WINE • 2 EGG YOLKS

Cut up some raw beef as finely as possible, add several sticks of celery, a carrot, a few sprigs of parsley, and a large onion, all cut up without salt. Cover with water, and steam for one or two hours, [remove scum] then pour through a sieve. Let it stand till cold, and remove any surface fat.

Next, take a calf's brain, put it in a saucepan with two or three cloves, a few peppercorns, a spoonful of salt, a sliced onion, half a glass of vinegar, and enough water to cover all; bring to the boil and drain and cut into pieces.

Melt two ounces of butter with two tablespoons of flour, stir in some of the broth, some grated lemon peel, and a wineglassful of Rhine wine, pour this over the brain, and cook for a short time, add the yolks of two eggs, and serve with the rest of the broth. [Serves 4.]

Pâté Maison

'She [Virginia] seemed to hate her dinner parties to come to an end. Sometimes they would go on until two a.m. She gave her guests an impression of gaiety which could plunge at any moment into the deepest seriousness. She would tell stories of things which amused her until the tears ran down her cheeks.'

Stephen Spender, *World Within World*, 1951

At the Woolfs' house in Tavistock Square, after their nine years of 'exile' in Richmond, Leonard and Virginia lived on the top two floors, 'looking at all the glories of London'. The Hogarth Press and Virginia's study were in the base-ment, while the middle two floors of the house were rented out to a firm of solicitors. Each day, Mabel Haskins came in to cook, clean and wash up. She so irritated Leonard with her clumsiness and bad cooking that he sent her off on a Marcel Boulestin cookery course. Soon Mabel was making 'the crèmes, soufflés and fresh sauces, which the Woolfs favoured'. Nevertheless, she continued to irritate Leonard.

Stephen Spender was one of the young writers who Leonard and Virginia published and with whom they became friends. *The Backward Son*, his broadly autobiographical novel about a young boy who was persecuted and bullied at school, was published by the Hogarth Press in 1940. This is Stephen's pâté recipe, which he contributed to *Celebrity Cooking* in 1967.

8 OZ CHICKEN LIVERS • 4 OZ BUTTER • I OZ BRANDY • 2 OZ CREAM
A GOOD PINCH OF GROUND CLOVES • A PINCH OF MACE
A PINCH OF NUTMEG • A PINCH OF THYME • BLACK PEPPER
SALT • ½ PT ASPIC JELLY • PARSLEY

Sauté the chicken livers [6–7 minutes] in 1 oz of butter. Put in a liquidizer with the remaining butter, cream, brandy, cloves, mace, nutmeg, thyme and season-ing, and blend. Leave to cool. [Make the aspic jelly by melting 4 sheets gelatin in 570 ml chicken stock. Stir in 1 raw egg white and bring gently to the boil, stir-ring constantly. Once it boils, pour through a fine sieve lined with a paper towel. When cool and syrupy, but not set, it is ready to use.] Coat a mould with aspic jelly and put in the refrigerator to set. When set, put pâté into the mould and return to the refrigerator to harden. Then turn out and decorate with parsley. Serve with black olives, radishes and hot toast. Serves four.

Mrs Dalloway's Dinner

'It made no difference at this hour of the night to Mrs Walker among the plates, saucepans, cullenders, frying-pans, chicken in aspic, ice-cream freezers, pared crusts of bread, lemons, soup tureens, and pudding basins which, however hard they washed up in the scullery, seemed to be all on top of her, on the kitchen table, on chairs, while the fire blared and roared, the electric lights glared, and still supper had to be laid. All she felt was, one Prime Minister more or less made not a scrap of difference to Mrs Walker.'

Virginia Woolf, *Mrs Dalloway*, 1925

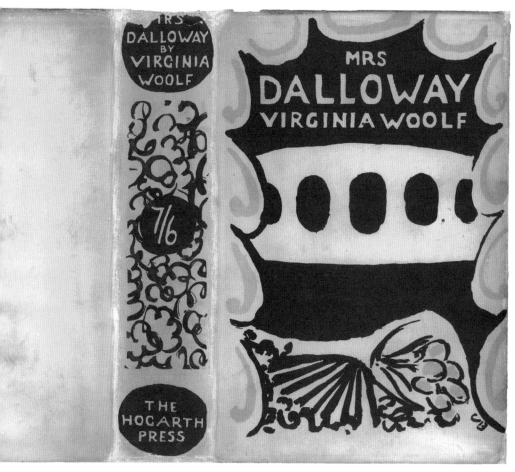

Jacket design by Vanessa Bell for *Mrs Dalloway* by Virginia Woolf, 1925.

Virginia Woolf was an ardent walker, and through her novels one sees London and tastes it as she herself did. *Mrs Dalloway* walks its readers across the post-war city in 1923. Big Ben strikes the hour, the standard flies high at Buckingham Palace, the buses on Piccadilly roll along and the park gates remain inert: a place to pause before moving on. Apart from the visual landmarks, there is a stream of thoughts and reflections, as the MP's wife Mrs Dalloway inhales the sweet, earthy smell of a flower shop, tosses a shilling into the Serpentine, remembers her father's tailored suits and feasts her eyes on 'salmon on an iceblock'.

Clarissa Dalloway is an unhappy person because she is preoccupied with social rank and worldly success. She married not for love but for position and is therefore 'nothing … not even Clarissa anymore; this being Mrs Richard Dalloway'. Her world is superficial; she knows it, and her servants know it.

When the undercooked salmon arrives at her resplendent dinner table, she sees how her life has fallen short of perfection. She has no identity of her own and her life has no purpose, despite the excellence of her food (described in the novel) and the importance and influence of her guests. The following five recipes re-create Mrs Dalloway's famous dinner party.

This recipe was co-written by Henrietta and David 'Bunny' Garnett.

Cucumber Vichyssoise
3 LEEKS • 1 MEDIUM SPANISH ONION • 2 OZ BUTTER
5 POTATOES, MEDIUM SIZED • 1 CUCUMBER
[½–1 PT CREAM, OR A COMBINATION OF MILK AND CREAM]

Slice the white parts of the leeks finely. Discard the green. Slice the onion. Peel the potatoes & chop them. Put all into a saucepan & cover with water or with veal or chicken stock. [Boil gently until the potatoes are soft.]

Peel cucumber & add to the rest. Put through moulé or liquidizer. Add ½ pint or pint of milk & cream. Season. Put in refrigerator for several hours & serve very cold. Sprinkle with chopped chives. [Serves 6.]

The following was published in 1927, two years after *Mrs Dalloway*. It is from Chester's *French Cooking for English Homes*.

Mayonnaise of Cold Salmon
Remove skin and bones from the remaining pieces of cold boiled salmon. Let them soak for an hour in a mixture of [50ml] vinegar and [1 tbs] fresh tarragon leaves. Then wipe them dry on a soft cloth. Wash and pick two long or round lettuces and cut the outer leaves into shreds reserving the hearts.

Make a thick mayonnaise sauce (*see below*) and cut three or four hard-boiled eggs into eight pieces. Put these around a long oval dish as a garniture. In the centre place the shredded lettuce upon which the pieces of salmon must be laid. Cut each lettuce heart into four and place at the ends of the dish. Pour the mayonnaise sauce over the fish and lettuce. Serve the rest of the sauce in a boat to be handed with the fish.

Serve with pared crusts of bread and slices of lemon.

For the mayonnaise:
Mix together the yolks of two eggs, the juice of a lemon [or 2 tablespoons], salt, pepper, [1 tablespoon] mustard and spices; pour some [25 ml light olive] oil, drop by drop, over the mixture, stirring meanwhile. If the sauce turns, add a little vinegar. The sauce must be of the consistency of thick cream. Vinegar may be added to taste.

Aspic moulds remained popular in British cooking until the 1950s. This chicken dish is from *King Edward's Cookery Book*, 1920.

Chicken in Aspic

1 GILL CREAM • SMALL CRESS • ½ PT ASPIC [SEE PÂTE MAISON, P. 197]
½ LB COOKED CHICKEN • 3 OZ TONGUE • PEPPER, SALT AND CAYENNE

Whip the cream until stiff. Pour a little jelly into a mould or cake-tin, arrange strips of tongue (cut in fancy shapes) and cress in a pattern, set with more liquid jelly. Whip the aspic until quite white and stiff, and mask the mould with it. Mince the chicken and tongue, mix with the cream and seasoning, fill mould with it. Cover with a layer of whipped aspic. Leave until set, then turn out, and serve with salad or chopped jelly. [Serves 6.]

This deliciously rich, soft ice cream is from *The Cookery Book of Lady Clark of Tillypronie*, which was published posthumously in 1909 and was still popular when *Mrs Dalloway* came out in 1925. Serve with Ottoline's Plum Pudding, p. 64.

Chocolate Ice Cream

Make a custard of six yolks of egg to 1 oz (i.e., 6 or 7 bits) of broken lump sugar and 1 pt. cold milk in which some [100 g dark (70%) cocoa] chocolate has already been melted. Stir on the stove for about five minutes till thick (but do not let it boil). Then pass through a tammy and pour into a basin to get cold and mellow. Do this after breakfast, and let it stand till after luncheon or even longer. First freeze alone for 10 minutes; then add whipped cream [made from 1 cup double cream]; and freeze it again for 1 hour. [Serves 4–6.]

The following recipe is also from *The Cookery Book of Lady Clark of Tillypronie*.

Homemade Gateau de Pommes

2 LB APPLES • 2 LB LUMP SUGAR • 2 LEMONS • BLANCHED ALMONDS
CREAM OR CUSTARD

Sharp, freshly gathered apples answer best: Golden Pippins, Ribston Pippins, or old English unreformed Russetins.

Peel, quarter, and core; so prepared, weigh 2 lbs. Take a large stew pan, and just cover the bottom with cold water in which pips, peel, &c. have been stewed and the water then strained; add the apples, 1½ or even 2 lb of lump sugar, and the whole rind of 2 lemons free from white; some add the pulp and juice as well.

Shake the pan gently over the fire till all comes to the boil; then stir constantly with a wooden spoon till the mixture will drop off the spoon like jam (20 or 30 minutes). Take out the lemon peel, and pour the apple into a hollow mould well rubbed with olive oil or clarified butter. If possible, make the day before it is wanted, and do not turn it out till quite cold.

Stick the 'cake' all over with spikes of blanched almonds. *Smother* in thick plain cream or rich custard (cold). It requires a great deal of sauce. [Serves 2.]

Lady Millicent Bruton's Luncheon

A second 'political' meal – Lady Millicent Bruton's luncheon – is also described in *Mrs Dalloway*, as follows: 'And so there began a soundless and exquisite passing to and fro through swing doors of aproned white-capped maids, handmaidens not of necessity, but adepts in a mystery or grand deception practised by hostesses in Mayfair from one-thirty to two, when, with a wave of the hand, the traffic ceases, and there rises instead this profound illusion in the first place about the food – how it is not paid for; and then that the table spreads itself voluntarily with glass and silver, little mats, saucers of red fruit; films of brown cream mask turbot; in casseroles severed chickens swim; coloured, undomestic, the fire burns; and with the wine and the coffee (not paid for) rise jocund visions before nursing eyes....'

Lady Bruton invites the MP Richard Dalloway and the Buckingham Palace courtier Hugh Whitbread to lunch. She is an experienced society hostess who effortlessly conjures up a magnificent meal of turbot, casserole, fresh fruit and soufflé. Like magic, she makes the slippery one-sided turbot vanish beneath a

Vanessa Bell, *Apples and Vinegar Bottle*, 1937. Sharp, freshly gathered apples are best for Homemade Gateau de Pommes.

thick gravy sauce and, again like magic, she disguises the true purpose of her hospitality: to procure a letter from her guests. Her world is just as superficial as the pretentious presentation of the dishes in her luncheon menu.

Turbot is a left-eyed flat fish with a delicious, delicate flavour. This recipe is from Marcel Boulestin's *A Second Helping*, published in 1925.

Turbot en Aspic

Cook your turbot in a well-seasoned *court-bouillon* and let it get cold. Then remove it, drain it well and cut it in pieces of equal size (taking care to remove bones and skin). Put this in a dish and dispose on and around the fish a few capers, or slices of truffles, mushrooms or gherkins.

Return the *court-bouillon* in which the turbot has been cooked and the head and bones of the fish to the fire, and boil it fast for about twenty-five minutes. Pass it through a fine sieve and a muslin; add a flavouring of either port, champagne or hock when the liquid is only tepid, and pour it over the pieces of fish. Having previously tested the consistency of the jelly (by dropping a little on a cold plate where it ought to jellify after a few seconds), add a little gelatine if necessary, but the jelly should not be too stiff; needless to say, whatever wine you use for flavouring must be of the best quality.

The following is another classic recipe from *The Cookery Book of Lady Clark of Tillypronie*.

Chicken 'en Casserole'

Suggested ingredients

I CHICKEN • I PT CHICKEN STOCK • I BAY LEAF
FRESH HERBS [PARSLEY, CHIVES, TARRAGON] • [2 LARGE] CARROTS
2 ONIONS • [¼ TEASPOON GROUND] MACE • SALT AND 6 PEPPERCORNS

Take a young chicken and braise it in the oven [160°C] for 1½ hours or until tender, in about 1 pt of good stock, a bay-leaf and bunch of herbs, carrots, onions, and a little mace, and a very little salt, also ½ doz. peppercorns.

When the chicken is tender cut it up into neat joints, remove the herbs, and skim off the fat; return it to the oven again for about ½ hour, with the vegetables and stock, [season with salt and pepper] and serve in the jar in which it was cooked. [Serves 4.]

These soufflés from Lady Clark's cookbook are very easy to make. Instead of flouring your baking tin, try coating the inside surface with melted butter and then sprinkling it with a little caster sugar. This helps the soufflé to grip the sides and rise.

Small Soufflés

½ PT MILK • 2 OZ BUTTER • ½ PT FLOUR • 4 EGGS • SUGAR • VANILLA
FRESH RASPBERRIES OR STRAWBERRIES

Put ½ pt. of milk and 2 ozs. of butter on the fire. When it boils, add ½ pt. of flour, and stir it till it comes off the sides of the pan. Let it cool; add 4 eggs and a little sugar, and beat till it is quite smooth. Flour a baking tin, and put teaspoonfuls of this mixture on the tin, leaving a little space between each (for each teaspoonful is a pudding). Glaze the tops with egg and sugar flavoured with vanilla. The oven must not be too hot [190°C for 30 minutes]. They should rise quite high in the oven. [Serves 8.]

Serve with fruit juice, or custard, or cream flavoured with coffee [or with red fruits, such as raspberries or strawberries].

The Lighthouse Dinner Menu

'It is always helpful, when reading her, to look out for the passages which describe eating. They are invariably good. They are a sharp reminder that here is a woman who is alert sensuously. She had an enlightened greediness which gentlemen themselves might envy, and which few masculine writers have expressed. There is a little too much lamp oil in George Meredith's wine, a little too much paper crackling on Charles Lamb's pork, and no savour whatever in any dish of Henry James's, but when Virginia Woolf mentions nice things they get right into our mouths, so far as the edibility of print permits.'

E. M. Forster, Rede Lecture, 1941

In 1908, when she was in her mid-twenties, Virginia Stephen visited Italy and France with Vanessa and Clive Bell. 'We drank an immense amount of coffee and sat out under the electric light talking about art. I wish we were 10 years younger, or 20 years older, and could settle to our brandy and cultivate the senses', wrote Virginia. New sights, sounds and smells awakened Virginia's sensual awareness and titillated her taste buds. English food was unadventurous, bland and overcooked, but to eat foreign foods and wines was to be enraptured by a symphony of flavours and desires.

In her novels, Virginia Woolf often employed 'the dinner party' situation to bring her characters together and to expose social inequalities; food can be used to influence and to manipulate. In *To the Lighthouse*, for example, William Bankes is seduced by 'Mildred's masterpiece': 'It was rich; it was tender. It was perfectly cooked'. 'But how do you make *Boeuf en Daube*?' Vanessa wrote to her sister about this episode, five days after *To the Lighthouse* was published. 'Does it have to be eaten on the moment after cooking 3 days?' It is clear that by this time Virginia had most definitely cultivated her senses. The three dishes in the sections that follow are all inspired by this particular novel.

Vanessa Bell, jacket design for *To the Lighthouse* by Virginia Woolf, 1927.

Augustus Soup

"'Ellen, please, another plate of soup," and then Mr Ramsay scowled like that.

And why not? Mrs Ramsay demanded. Surely they could let Augustus have his soup if he wanted it. He hated people wallowing in food, Mr Ramsay frowned at her. He hated everything dragging on for hours like this. But he had controlled himself, Mr Ramsay would have her observe, disgusting though the sight was.'

Virginia Woolf, *To the Lighthouse*, 1927

Butter and good stock are what make this soup recipe from *Good Things in England* so good.

> 1. Cut some carrots in fine match-like shreds. 2. Cook for five minutes in a little butter. 3. Keep them as whole as possible. 4. Add sugar and salt. 5. Drain and put them into clear stock: just before sending to table squeeze the juice of 3 or 4 grated carrots rubbed through a tammy, add a little boiled rice and serve.

Mildred's Masterpiece (Boeuf en Daube)

'[A]n exquisite scent of olives and oil and juice rose from the great brown dish as Marthe, with a little flourish, took the cover off. The cook had spent three days over that dish. And she must take great care, Mrs Ramsay thought, diving into the soft mass, to choose a specially tender piece for William Bankes. And she peered into the dish, with its shiny walls and its confusion of savoury brown and yellow meats, and its bay leaves and its wine, and thought, This will celebrate the occasion – a curious sense rising in her, at once freakish and tender, of celebrating a festival, as if two emotions were called up in her, one profound – for what could be more serious than the love of man for woman....'

Virginia Woolf, *To the Lighthouse*, 1927

This recipe for *Boeuf en Daube* is my own. Provençal beef stew does not have to be eaten 'on the moment after cooking 3 days', as Vanessa Bell thought. In fact, it tastes better after it has been chilled and reheated.

1.5 KG TOP RUMP OF BEEF • 1.5 KG SKIRT OF BEEF
• 60 G BACK BACON, TRIMMED OF FAT
3 TBS PLAIN WHITE FLOUR SEASONED WITH 1 TSP SALT
AND ¼ TSP FRESHLY GROUND PEPPER
¾ CUP SALT CURED NIÇOISE OLIVES, STONES REMOVED
500 ML FULL-BODIED RED WINE • 45 ML COGNAC
2 TBS EXTRA VIRGIN OLIVE OIL
2 CUPS GOOD QUALITY BEEF STOCK • 1 TBS TOMATO PASTE
1 ONION, STUCK WITH 3 CLOVES • 3 MEDIUM TOMATOES, HALVED
1 HERB BOUQUET, AS BELOW • SALT AND PEPPER

For the marinade
1 HERB BOUQUET: 3 SPRIGS PARSLEY, 2 SPRIGS THYME,
1 BAY LEAF, 1 STALK CELERY
2 OR 3 STRIPS ORANGE ZEST, WITHOUT PITH
½ TSP GROUND BLACK PEPPER

Vanessa Bell, door in the Spare Room, Charleston, 1936, depicting a bowl of seasonal fresh fruit.

2 RED ONIONS, THINLY SLICED
3 FRESHLY CRUSHED CLOVES • 3 CLOVES GARLIC, CHOPPED
4 CARROTS, ROUGHLY CUT • 10 G FRESHLY CHOPPED PARSLEY
10 G FRESHLY CHOPPED THYME
¼ TSP FRESHLY GROUND NUTMEG
⅓ CUP OLIVE OIL

Three days in advance, prepare the marinade by combining all the ingredients together in a non-metallic bowl. Cut the top rump into 3 cm cubes and the skirt into similar sized pieces. Toss all the meat, including the bacon, into the marinade mixture. Pour the wine and cognac over the top and mix again. Cover and place in the refrigerator for 24 hours, stirring occasionally.

Next day, preheat the oven to 140°C. Remove the meat from the marinade, separate, and dry the beef pieces on sheets of kitchen towel. Roll the rump in seasoned flour. Cut the bacon into bite-sized pieces. Heat the olive oil in a large cast-iron casserole dish (Le Creuset is perfect) and quickly brown the skirt, followed by the bacon and the rump. Transfer meat to a plate. Pour the beef stock into the pot, add the tomato paste and scrape off all the delicious brown bits from the bottom using a wooden spoon. Remove the orange peel from the marinade and replace the old bouquet garni with a fresh one. Pour the marinade, fresh tomatoes, onion and olives into the pot and bring it gently to the boil. Simmer for 20 minutes. Add the meat and cover with foil. Place the lid of the casserole on top to seal the dish. Place in the middle of the oven for 1½ hours.

Remove from the oven and cool. Discard the bouquet garni and the onion. Refrigerate.

On the day of serving, skim any residual fat off the top. Reheat gently and season with salt and pepper. Serve with basmati rice and peas. Serves 6–8.

Neptune's Fruit Banquet

'Rose's arrangement of the grapes and pears, of the horny pink-lined shell, of the bananas, made her think of a trophy fetched from the bottom of the sea, of Neptune's banquet.... Augustus too feasted his eyes on the same plate of fruit, plunged in, broke off a bloom there, a tassel here, and returned, after feasting, to his hive. That was his way of looking, different from hers. But looking together united them.'

Virginia Woolf, *To the Lighthouse*, 1927

The natural fruit season in Britain runs from June to November. Apples and pears are picked in late summer and autumn and stored and eaten throughout the winter months, and unforced rhubarb is harvested in the spring; but one has to wait until summer to enjoy the mouth-watering flavours of ripe strawberries, plums, currants, loganberries and blackberries. In 1927 the banquet of fruit described in *To the Lighthouse* would have been a rare visual feast, perhaps occurring only once or twice a year when the fruit season was at its peak. This is my own interpretation of it.

FRESH, SEASONAL FRUIT • 2 BUNCHES GRAPES • PEARS • APPLES

The important thing when composing this dish is to arrange your fruits in a casual but organized fashion, being careful to offset the colour of one fruit against the size and shape of another. Begin by placing a large seashell at one end of the platter. Next place a large fruit next to it, branching out with other fruits, covering the base of the plate. Fruit should be placed in small piles of threes or fours to create depth and height. Lay one or two large bunches of grapes over the top, voluptuously draping the fruit beneath. If smaller fruits are in season, add them at this stage. A certain amount of creativity is required when arranging the fruit and it is always advisable to use fruit that is fresh and in season.

A Room of One's Own: Two Menus

'It is part of the novelist's convention not to mention soup and salmon and ducklings, as if soup and salmon and ducklings were of no importance whatsoever, as if nobody ever smoked a cigar or drank a glass of wine. Here, however, I shall take the liberty to defy that convention'.

Virginia Woolf, *A Room of One's Own*, 1929

In 1928 Virginia Woolf visited the University of Cambridge. She was disappointed to see how the men's colleges had so much more money and their members enjoyed so many more privileges than the women's colleges. The difference became blatantly obvious when she was invited to Newnham College for dinner and was served an uninspiring meal of plain soup, muddy beef rump, yellow sprouts, custard, prunes and water; while at King's College, in George Rylands's private suite of rooms, she had an inspirational lunch of freshly prepared foods and fine wines.

In defense of the cuisine at Newnham, however, 'The visit of Miss Strachey's close friend, Virginia Woolf, in 1929 to read us a paper was a rather alarming occasion', recalled her hosts E. E. Duncan-Jones and U. K. Stevenson. 'As I remember it she was nearly an hour late; and dinner in Clough Hall, never a repast for gourmets, suffered considerably. Mrs Woolf also disconcerted us by bringing a husband and so upsetting our seating plan'.

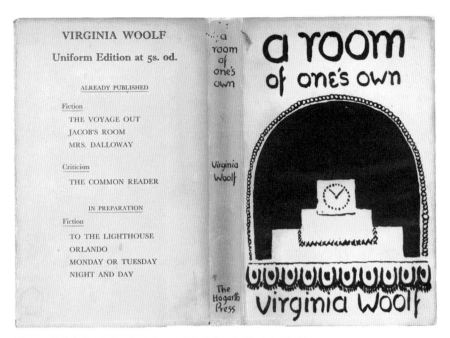

Vanessa Bell, jacket design for *A Room of One's Own* by Virginia Woolf, 1929.

A week later, Virginia returned to Cambridge with her friend Vita Sackville-West to speak to the women of Girton College. She delivered *A Room of One's Own*, a paper in which she argued that 'Intellectual freedom depends on material things' and that a 'woman must have money and a room of her own if she is to write fiction'. Furthermore, she concluded, 'One cannot think well, love well, sleep well, if one has not dined well. The lamp in the spine does not light on beef and prunes.' In the following sections are two very different menus: the first not so good and recommended only for its economy and practicality; the second very good. These two separate dining experiences at Cambridge collectively provided the impetus Virginia needed to write her feminist classic.

Menu 1: Dinner at a Women's College

'Here was the soup. It was a plain gravy soup. There was nothing to stir the fancy in that. One could have seen through the transparent liquid any pattern that there might have been on the plate itself. But there was no pattern. The plate was plain. Next came beef with its attendant greens and potatoes – a homely trinity, suggesting the rumps of cattle in a muddy market, and sprouts curled and yellowed at the edge, and bargaining and cheapening, and women with string bags on Monday morning. There was no reason to complain of human nature's daily food, seeing that the supply was sufficient and coal-miners doubtless were sitting down to less. Prunes and custard followed…. Biscuits and cheese came next, and here the water-jug was liberally passed around, for it is the nature of biscuits to be dry, and these were biscuits to the core. That was all. The meal was over.'

Virginia Woolf, *A Room of One's Own*, 1929

This classic soup recipe is from A. H. Adair's *Dinners: Long and Short* (1928).

Consommé

Having prepared your *pot-au-feu*, pour the stock through a sieve into a saucepan and let it reduce; see that it is well seasoned. You may clarify it further by adding the beaten white of an egg to the boiling stock. The sediment will all drop to the bottom of the saucepan, leaving a perfectly clear *consommé*, which should be passed through a muslin. [Serves 4.]

For the pot-au-feu

Put two or three pounds of stewing beef into a large thick saucepan with a knuckle of beef and a few marrow bones. Add three quarts of cold water, salt, and pepper and bring slowly to the boil, skimming constantly. When there is no scum left, add two or three carrots and two leeks, cleaned and cut into pieces, an onion stuck with two cloves, and a head of celery, also cut into small pieces. Bring to the boil, and then remove to a cooler part of the stove and let the soup boil very gently for six or seven hours.

Remove the grease and pass through a sieve. Should you have any chicken bones, feet or giblets, these may also be used in making the *pot-au-feu*.

This simple recipe from the Grace Higgens archive may be served hot or cold.

Beef Loaf
1 LB BEEF • ¼ LB FAT BACON • 1 ONION
1 CUP WHITE BREADCRUMBS • 1 TBS CHOPPED PICKLES
SEASONING • 1 EGG

Mince the beef & half the bacon & put in a basin, add the onion, finely chopped, the breadcrumbs, chopped parsley and pickles. Season well with pepper & salt. Mix well & moisten with beaten egg or some gravy. Form the mixture into a long loaf & put in a greased tin, cover with greased paper & bake in a hot oven for ½ hour, the[n] put rest of bacon on top & cook until bacon is brown & crisp, remove meat onto hot dish and & make gravy. [Serves 4.]

You may wish to cook your sprouts more briefly (5 minutes should suffice) than the 12–15 minutes in this recipe from G. F. Scotson-Clark's *Kitchenette Cookery* (1926).

Sprouts

Pick over the sprouts and take away any stale or discoloured leaves. Have ready a saucepan of absolutely boiling water in which is a tablespoon of salt. Put in the sprouts and turn down the gas so that the water still bubbles briskly but not sufficiently to break the sprouts. Do not on any account let the water cease to bubble. Do not cover the pan but let the sprouts boil for twelve or at the outside fifteen minutes, just long enough to thoroughly cook the largest of the sprouts.

Then strain them in a colander and allow them to drain, gently pressing them with a saucer to force out any excess of water but not to break the little sprouts. You will find your sprouts are thoroughly cooked and a beautiful bright green. On no account allow them to remain in the water after the time mentioned or they will turn an unpleasant brownish-pink colour, lose their flavour and become indigestible.

The reason for not covering the pot while they are cooking is to prevent, to a very large extent, the unpleasant odour arising from the cooking of any of the cabbage family. [Allow 6–10 sprouts per person.]

Most British adults remember prunes and custard from their school dinner days. These simple instructions for preparing prunes are from the Grace Higgens archive; the custard is from a booklet produced by a corn-flour manufacturer in the 1930s.

Prunes

Allow [½ cup prunes per person.] to soak for 24 hours with an orange cut in slices peel and all and then stewed without sugar [remove orange slices first]– with [dry red] wine if possible – till quite tender, then reduce the juice adding sugar and boil prunes up again.

Custard

¾ OZ BROWN & POLSON'S 'PATENT' CORN FLOUR • 1 PT MILK •
½ OZ BUTTER • 2 EGGS • 1½ OZ CASTOR SUGAR
½ TSP ESSENCE OF VANILLA

Mix the corn flour to a smooth cream with a little of the milk. Bring the rest of the milk to the boil. Pour the mixed corn flour into the milk, stirring vigorously. Add the butter. Beat the two yolks of eggs with the sugar and stir into the corn flour. Boil for six minutes, stirring all the time. Remove from the fire. Beat up the whites of the two eggs to a stiff snow, and stir lightly to the rest. Add the essence of vanilla, beat up well, and serve [pour over the prunes]. [Serves 6–8.]

These recipes for sour-milk cheese and biscuits are from *Complete Guide to Sound, Successful and Attractive Food Reform* (1929).

Savoury Biscuits and Sour Milk Cheese

For the biscuits:

½ LB WHOLEMEAL FLOUR • 2 OZ NUT FAT [GROUNDNUT OIL]
4 OZ MILLED CHEDDAR CHEESE • 1 TSP MARMITE

Rub fat into flour lightly, add grated cheese. Dissolve Marmite in a little warm milk and water, stir into the mixture, but keep it rather dry. Roll out thinly. Cut into small rounds. Prick well with a fork. Bake in a sharp oven for 10 minutes. [Makes 20 biscuits.]

For the cheese

Wholesome sour milk is made as follows: Put the milk into a wide-mouthed vessel or earthenware crock and keep it in fairly warm place for two days in summer and about three days in winter. Do not cook it. Protect it from dust, etc. by a piece of clean muslin kept from blowing off by having cheap beads or something of the sort sewn on to the edges.

If the milk is covered with anything less porous than muslin the lactic acid bacteria will not get at it and it will go bad through putrefaction. It is ready when it is of the consistency of junket. [2 pints sour milk yields approximately 100 g cheese.]

To make the cheese

Place a square of strong muslin, butter muslin or cheese cloth over a colander, pour the sour milk into this, tie up the corners and allow to drain (or use a muslin bag), standing the colander (or hanging the cheese) over a bowl, in a cool place. It may be left overnight, and then squeezed, thus getting rid of practically all the whey, producing a more solid result. The muslin used must be kept sweet by boiling it. If the muslin smells sour it is not fit to use.

Menu 2: Lunch at a Men's College

'[L]unch on this occasion began with soles, sunk in a deep dish, over which the college cook had spread a counterpane of the whitest cream, save that it was branded here and there with brown spots like the spots on the flanks of a doe. After came the partridges, but if this suggests a couple of bald, brown birds on a plate you are mistaken. The partridges, many and various, came with all their retinue of sauces and salads, the sharp and the sweet, each in its order; their potatoes, thin as coins but not so hard; their sprouts, foliated as rosebuds but more succulent. And no sooner had the roast and its retinue been done with than the silent serving-man, the Beadle himself perhaps in a milder manifestation, set before us, wreathed in napkins, a confection which rose all sugar from the waves. To call it pudding and so relate it to rice and tapioca would be an insult. Meanwhile the wineglasses had flushed yellow and flushed crimson; had been emptied; had been filled.'

Virginia Woolf, *A Room of One's Own*, 1929

The following recipes have been selected from *Dinners: Long and Short* (1928).

Fillets de Sole à la Crème

Cook the fillets of soles in butter with salt [about 2 minutes each side], pepper, and paprika, remove them, and keep them hot. Add a glassful of cream and boil until quite thick. Put back the fish and serve. [Allow 2 sole fillets per person.]

Perdrix en Cocotte

This is a delicious dish for which an older bird can be used. Pluck and clean the partridge, singe it, bone it and stuff it with pork sausage-meat; sew the partridge and tie it to keep it in shape, and put it in a casserole on a bed of carrots, onions, and its bones. Cook for a few minutes, add a cup of stock, salt, and pepper, and let it simmer gently for three-quarters of an hour. While this is proceeding peel and parboil a handful of small 'button' onions. Then remove the partridge, pass the gravy through a sieve and put it back into the casserole with the partridge, adding the 'button' onions. Let all this simmer again until the bird is quite tender. A few minutes before serving 'bind' the sauce with a little flour and water. It is better to serve this dish in the casserole in which it has cooked. [Serves 2.]

Salade de Haricots Verts

Dress the cold boiled French beans with a *vinaigrette* and add a little chopped onion or garlic. [Allow 120 g green beans per person.]

For the vinaigrette

This is simply made of olive oil, wine vinegar, salt and pepper. Dissolve the salt in the vinegar, add the oil (one tablespoon of vinegar to two of oil) and then sprinkle with pepper to taste.

Pommes Sautées

Cut the potatoes into rounds (you may use either raw or freshly boiled ones, but they must be of the soapy and not the floury kind) and fry them in butter, shaking the pan constantly. Season with salt and pepper.

Gateau de Riz en Moule

Put quarter of a pound of well-cleaned rice in a saucepan with half a pint of milk, quarter of a pound of sugar and the grated rind of an orange. Boil slowly until the rice is soft. Then add two beaten eggs, stirring hard. Take a well-buttered mould and cover the bottom with grated toast. Pour the rice mixture into this and cook *au bain-marie* for three quarters on an hour. Allow the mould to cool a little, and then turn the contents into a dish. [Serves 4.]

Polite Wine Drinking

It is unnecessary to have more than three wines with dinner: a light dry white wine with the fish – Moselle, Pouilly, or the slightly heavier white Hermitage, good, but not necessarily expensive; a really good château-bottled claret (Château Latour, Haut Brion, or Mouton Rothschild) … or a fine old Burgundy (or even Châteauneuf du Pape or Côte Rôtie, if really beautiful) with the *rôti*; and Champagne with the sweet, unless you prefer to serve with it a very cold bottle (the sweeter it is the colder it must be) of one of the big Sauternes: Yquem, Suduiraut, Vigneau de Rayne or Guiraud. As for the dessert wines, none is rather a good rule with a dinner served as described above and not with Champagne throughout; but if the master of the house is a lover of port he will have almost aggressively firm views and traditions. On the whole, this is a question of taste, but the provincial French people show some wisdom when they drink humble, natural Porto Blanc half an hour before dinner by way of a change from the usual Vermouth, Quinquina, or the pernicious cocktail.

A Picnic in the Old Umbrella

'Did Leonard tell you how our entire life is spent driving, cleaning, dodging in and out of a shed, measuring miles on maps, planning expeditions, going [on] expeditions, being beaten back by the rain, eating sandwiches on high roads, cursing cows, sheep, bicyclists, and when we are at rest talking of nothing but cars and petrol?'

Virginia Woolf to T. S. Eliot, 24 August 1927

Leonard and Virginia Woolf have been called many things: elitist, self-centred, intellectuals – even snobs – but never car enthusiasts. Yet that is exactly what they became after they bought their first motorcar, a second-hand Singer. 'The Umbrella' (as Ottoline Morrell dubbed her) soon took the Woolfs everywhere: to lunch at Charleston, to tea in Hampstead with Gladys Easdale (and into her gatepost), to France, to Germany and, of course, back home to Sussex. According to Virginia, 'The Singer runs so fast on French roads that we got here early. It is undoubtedly what one will do in Heaven – motoring all day, and eating vast meals, and drinking red wine and liqueurs.' (The drink-drive limit was not introduced in the United Kingdom until 1967.)

A leisurely afternoon by the side of a quiet country road, feasting on delicious views, soup, sandwiches and cake does indeed sound heavenly. This menu is from a chapter entitled 'A Motor Excursion Luncheon' in an excellent cookbook kept by Grace Higgens at Charleston.

Leonard and Virginia Woolf and their Singer car, Cassis, 1928. The Woolfs bought the second-hand Singer in July 1927. From Vanessa Bell's photograph album.

Potage à la Écossaise

Suggested ingredients

1 QT GOOD LIGHT STOCK • 2 TBS PEARL BARLEY
1 CARROT • 1 TURNIP 1 LEEK • 1 ONION • CELERY
2 CABBAGE LEAVES OR 3–4 BRUSSELS SPROUTS
LAMB OR MUTTON CUTLETS • CHOPPED PARSLEY • CREAM
SALT AND PEPPER • PEAS AND SMALL NEW POTATOES, FOR GARNISH

Put into rather more than a quart of good light stock some two tablespoons of pearl barley (previously washed in cold water), a carrot, turnip, leek, onion, celery, a little cabbage or 3 or 4 Brussels sprouts, and let them cook gently together with the required number of nice cutlets from a well-selected and trimmed neck of mutton or lamb. Season with a little chopped parsley, cream, salt and pepper to taste, and a couple of teaspoons of green peas, and some of those tiny new potatoes which the prudent housewife will have bottled like her gooseberries, or buried in a tin of dry sand for a winter luxury. The 6 ½ d. bazaar again sells charming quite small square or round white metal tins and nice horn or wooden spoons for the appropriate consumption of this dish. [Serves 4.]

Stuffed Salmon Rolls

½ LB SALMON • MAYONNAISE • 1 PICKLED GHERKIN, CHOPPED
SALT AND PEPPER • BREAD ROLLS • BUTTER • LETTUCE LEAVES

First cook a slice of salmon (about ½ lb, and Norwegian might do [for 2 sand-wiches]), and when cold pass through a wire sieve and mix with a little mayon-naise sauce or whipped cream flavoured with a drop of Worcester sauce and tarragon vinegar. Add a pickled gherkin chopped small, and salt and pepper. Cut off the tops of the rolls or scones, remove the soft inside and butter them sparingly. Fill in with the prepared salmon, place a little shredded lettuce on top, and replace the lid with a thin slice of the buttered inside. A filling of egg and sardine, of minced chicken or game with cream and chopped walnut or beetroot, celery or gherkins, could be substituted, or some pickled prawns or lobster with a little chopped aspic and salad.

Winter Cake

1 LB FLOUR • 1 LB BLACK TREACLE • 1 DSP GROUND GINGER
½ LB BROWN SUGAR • ½ LB BUTTER • ½ PT MILK
½ TSP CARBONATE OF SODA • 4 EGGS
A LITTLE FINELY CHOPPED CITRON [OR 2 HEAPED DSP MIXED PEEL]
WHITE WHOLE ALMONDS, FOR TOP

Mix the dry ingredients together, warm the milk and dissolve the butter in it, beat up the eggs, then add treacle and stir into the dry ingredients, beat well, bake for three quarters of an hour [180° C in a 11 in. (28 cm) round tin for 50 minutes]. This mixture should be of a running consistency before baking, so add more milk if necessary. Bake in a flat brick-shaped tin or if preferred round and deep, a saucepan will serve. [Serves 8.]

A Bohemian Picnic

'Boris Anrep had completed a mosaic in a chapel at the Military Academy, Sandhurst, and this was the object of our pilgrimage. Julian and I were allowed seats in a charabanc which also contained Augustus John, Mary Hutchinson, Lesley Jowett, Maynard, Duncan, Clive, Vanessa and Boris himself. There were lots of other people. We set off fairly early and went to see the decorated chapel. We then proceeded into the open country, stopping at a very beautiful place where there was open downland together with a noble forest. Here the grown-ups gathered in a circle around a bonfire, ate lunch and washed it down with champagne. Then they played kiss-in-the-ring – I remember Duncan catching and kissing Lesley Jowett. Finally they played another game: they set up a dozen or so empty bottles and bombarded them with others (also presumably empty). Vanessa excelled at this sport. Soon the ground beneath the trees was littered with a carpet of smashed glass. Julian and I, having helped ourselves to victuals, wandered away on our own, but not so far that we could not see the grown-ups at play. We were deeply shocked and distressed. We had always been told that places of outstanding natural beauty were to be respected. Only the worst kind of hooligan – or tripper – would leave broken glass behind him. This in our scale of morality was a crime; we were not in the least offended by what followed on the journey home.

'On that journey I was seated between Vanessa and Maynard. There was some trouble at the beginning of it. John had made drawings of everyone on paper plates provided for the picnic (two of these are still at Charleston); the man sitting next to Vanessa stole a drawing belonging to the man in front of him and refused to give it back. Vanessa, in her best Hyde Park Gate manner, said she wanted to look at the drawing, got it, and at once handed it back to its rightful owner. The thief exploded in fury, but they didn't come to blows so I lost interest and began to pay attention to Maynard.'

Quentin Bell, *Elders and Betters*, 1944

Picnicking at High and Over, Sussex, 1928. Clockwise from left: Francis Birrell, Clive Bell, Angelica Bell, Angus Davidson, Virginia and Leonard Woolf, Richard Kennedy, Quentin Bell, and, with their backs to the camera, Duncan Grant and Julian Bell. From Vanessa Bell's photograph album.

These recipes, from several Bloomsbury members, make ideal picnic fare.

Boris Anrep's Frankfurt Sausages

Heat a tin of Heinz tomato soup till boiling. Cut sausages into slices about an inch long & simmer in the soup for 5 to 10 mins. Stir in cream to thicken. Fried onions can be added to the soup. Cabbage is good with this dish. [Serves 1–2.]

Virginia Nicholson's Stuffed Charleston Vine Leaves

'A vine grew over a pergola outside the studio door that leads into the Folly Garden. When I was a child and we spent holidays at Charleston we occupied the outer studio (now the café) which also led out onto the Folly Garden. I can remember my mother going out to pick handfuls of bright green fleshy leaves from the vine which she blanched, stuffed with savoury rice and baked in the oven. I still make "dolmades" her way.'

Virginia Nicholson to Jans Ondaatje Rolls, 26 February 2013

BLANCHED VINE LEAVES, STEMS REMOVED • BOILED ROUND OR RISOTTO RICE
A SMALL ONION OR A COUPLE OF SHALLOTS, FINELY CHOPPED AND FRIED
HANDFUL OF SOAKED CURRANTS • OLIVE OIL • DRIED OREGANO
SALT, PEPPER, GRATED NUTMEG

Mix the rice and other ingredients, moistened with olive oil. Stuff the vine leaves by placing a spoonful of stuffing at the 'base' of the leaf where the veins join. Carefully fold in the leaf to either side, then starting at the base, roll it up and squeeze to seal. Lay the stuffed vine leaves in a shallow baking dish. Moisten with water, stock, a little tomato purée and lemon juice. Bake for about half an hour, serve warm or cold.

Igor Anrep's Marinade of Mushrooms

½ LB BUTTON MUSHROOMS • 2 SMALL ONIONS
JUICE OF 2 LEMONS • 3 TBS OLIVE OIL • 2 CLOVES GARLIC
THYME, ROSEMARY, CORIANDER SEEDS • ¼ PT WATER • SALT, PEPPER

Chop onions and garlic, put in saucepan with oil, herbs, lemon juice, water and seasoning. Simmer ten minutes. While boiling, put in the mushrooms for another two minutes. Pour into bowl and serve cold.

Helen Anrep's Lemon Jelly Cake

One cup of sugar, mixed with butter the size of an egg, one cup of milk, one egg, well beaten, and [12 oz] flour enough to make rather stiff, sifted with a heaping teaspoonful of baking powder, and bake in three jelly-cake tins [at 190°C until a knife comes out clean. Transfer to a wire rack to cool]. For the jelly, take the juice and grated rind of one lemon, one small cup of sugar, three teaspoonfuls of cornstarch [cornflour], mixed smoothly with a little water.

Let all boil together until thick, and spread on the cakes. This quantity makes two layers. [Serves 6.]

Angelica Garnett's Cherry Tart

Seive [*sic*] nine ounces of flour into a bowl. Add a pinch of salt or 2 oz of sugar if desired. Mix thoroughly with 3–4 oz lard, then make a hole in the middle and stir in the yoke [*sic*] of one egg & a little cold water; just enough to make it stick together, but be careful to leave it as crumbly as possible. Form into a ball and leave for one hour. Have your oven ready, roll out the pastry and fill a round tin with it. Cook slowly and when half done fill with [drained, sweetened and pitted] Morello cherries covered with 2 oz sugar. Finish baking. When cold you can, if liked, add the white of egg on top beaten to a froth with a little sugar.

CHERRY TART

8ᵗʰ July 1942

Seive nine ounces of flour into a bowl. Add a pinch of salt or 2 oz of sugar if desired. Mix thoroughly with 3–4 oz lard, then make a hole in the middle and stir in the yoke of one egg & a little cold water; just enough to make it stick together, but be careful to leave it as crumbly as possible. Form into a ball and leave for one hour. Have your oven ready, roll out the pastry and fill a round tin with it. Cook slowly and when half done fill with Morella cherries covered with 2 oz sugar. Finish baking. When cold you can, if liked, add the white of egg on top beaten to a froth with a little sugar.

Angelica Garnett's recipe for Cherry Tart from the Garnetts' cookery book.

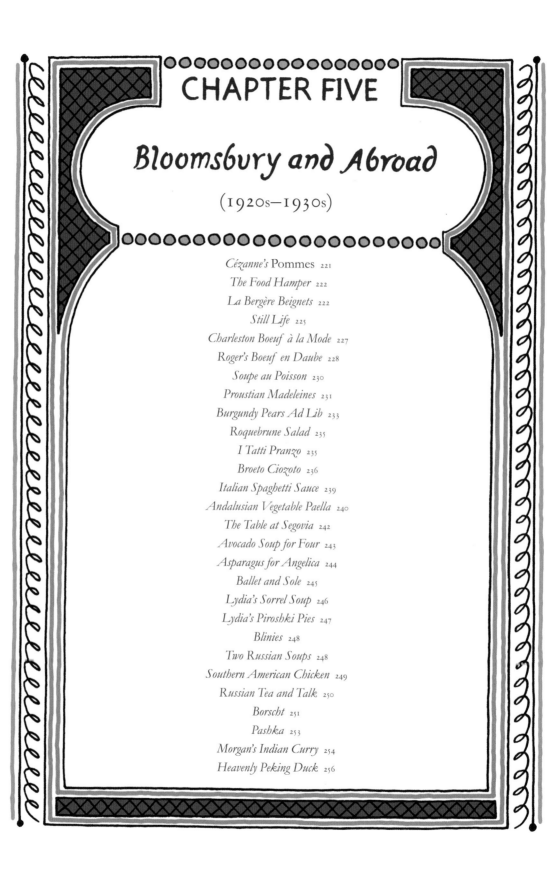

CHAPTER FIVE

Bloomsbury and Abroad

(1920s–1930s)

Paul Cézanne, *Still Life with Apples*, 1877–78. John Maynard Keynes attended the auction of the late Edgar Degas's estate in Paris in 1918 and returned to Charleston with a Cézanne in his suitcase.

Cézanne's Pommes

'I've got a Cézanne in my suitcase. It was too heavy for me to carry, so I've left it in the ditch, behind the gate.'

John Maynard Keynes, quoted in David Garnett, *The Flowers of the Forest*, 1955

France was always the chief source of foreign inspiration for Bloomsbury – whether in art or food. The auction of the art collection of Edgar Degas, who died in 1917, coincided with an Allied conference held in Paris in March 1918. Both events were attended by John Maynard Keynes as chief adviser to the Chancellor of the Exchequer. The British Treasury had been persuaded by Maynard – who had been convinced by his art-loving friends Duncan Grant, Clive Bell and Roger Fry – that the auction was a not-to-be-missed opportunity to purchase a few important paintings for the nation. So, with the director of the National Gallery at his side, Maynard bid for, and won, thirteen pictures for the Gallery and six for himself, including one small Cézanne, *Pommes* (also known as *Still Life with Apples*).

Maynard received a lift back to England a few days later in Austen Chamberlain's motor car, and was dropped off at the bottom of the Charleston drive. With the prospect of having to lug his heavy suitcase all the way up to the house, he decided instead to hide it – and the Cézanne inside – in the hedge by the gate, no doubt speculating that at least one of his friends would be curious enough to go and fetch the suitcase. If that was his plan, it worked a treat. David 'Bunny' Garnett and Duncan Grant dashed out and returned triumphant, having carried the suitcase between them, while Maynard was given a hot meal and a celebratory glass of wine. If Bunny and Duncan were a little surprised to discover that Cézanne's *Pommes* was only 19 x 27 cm (7½ x 10½ in.) in size, they never said so.

The Food Hamper

'The children are as happy as crickets and we all feed out of doors on the terrace – in two parties…. There is hardly any food which is a trouble but any quantity of the most delicious red wine – sold for 1 franc 50 a bottle, about sixpence which makes up for the lack of marmalade for which I hanker from time to time.'

Duncan Grant to David Garnett, 20 October 1921

Paul Cézanne, Henri Matisse, Paul Bonnard, André Derain and Pierre-Auguste Renoir had all painted in the Provence region of France. The Bloomsbury artists also felt the appeal of Provence. The promise of warm colours coupled with bright sunlight enticed them south to the land of *Les Impressionistes*.

From October 1920 to January 1921, Vanessa Bell and Duncan Grant rented La Maison Blanche, a villa in the foothills of St-Tropez overlooking the Mediterranean. By day they filled their canvases enthusiastically with light and colour, and by night they delighted their palates with the flavours of the Côte d'Azur, washed down with liberal quantities of red wine. Family breakfasts and lunches were prepared by their French cook and enjoyed out on the terrace, while dinners were eaten there too, or at a restaurant in town with Roger Fry, who was staying nearby. But there were foods they hankered after, so Vanessa wrote to John Maynard Keynes asking him to send them various items from England. According to Frances Spalding, Duncan's biographer, 'The food hamper arrived, causing the greatest excitement, a large tin of golden syrup producing whoops of joy.' There were also tins of powdered egg, Quaker Oats, potted meat, jam and tins of tea in the Army & Navy hamper Maynard sent.

La Bergère Beignets

'She [Elise Anghilanti] was an excellent cook, her specialty the traditional *boeuf en daube*. As great a treat was my favourite, *beignets*; she used to dip a gauffering [*sic*] iron first into batter and then into steaming olive oil, then the liberated fritter would slip its moorings and float off to sizzle on its own. At lunchtime, Elise would bring a whole pile of them onto the terrace, where we devoured them as quickly as possible, since they had to be piping hot.'

Angelica Garnett, *Deceived with Kindness*, 1984

Later in the 1920s, the heat, the light and the easy living of the French Mediterranean coast lured Vanessa Bell and Duncan Grant south to Cassis sur Mer, year after year. In 1928 they leased La Bergère, a rickety stone cottage in the middle of a vineyard, not far from the centre of town. Here they painted without interruption, basking in the sunshine, drinking local wines and eating traditional

Vanessa Bell, *La Bergère, Cassis*, 1930. Duncan Grant and Vanessa rented La Bergère from 1928 to 1938. It was there that 'she would establish "Charleston in France",' according to Leonard Woolf's biographer Victoria Glendinning.

Elise Anghilanti and Grace Germany in Cassis 1928. Elise Anghilanti cooked for Vanessa Bell and her family at La Bergère from 1928. She was responsible for teaching Grace Higgens many French recipes. From Vanessa Bell's photograph album.

Provençal meals prepared by their cook, Elise Anghilanti. 'I admire that woman's [Vanessa's] gifts more and more,' Duncan wrote to David 'Bunny' Garnett in 1929. 'They are unrivalled. Anyhow there is precious little for any of us others left to do – but paint, eat, drink, sleep and bathe – and with the heat I tend to become idler and idler.' Other Bloomsbury members came and went in Cassis: Clive Bell, Lytton Strachey, Dora Carrington, and Virginia and Leonard Woolf; Julian, Quentin and Angelica Bell came as often as their school schedules permitted. (Angelica was frequently removed from school to accompany Vanessa and Duncan to France.) Bloomsbury by the Med was in high season when the smell of *boeuf en daube* wafted out onto the terrace and mingled with the aroma of Elise's freshly baked *beignets*. And, of course, the smells of turpentine and oil paint were never very far away.

    This recipe from Lady Gage (Vanessa leased Charleston from a Lord Gage of Firle in 1916) was published in *Food from Firle* (1978). Despite a few differences from Angelica's memory of Elise's recipe, these English *beignets* are excellent.

Suggested ingredients
½ PT WATER • 3 OZ BUTTER • 5 OZ FLOUR • 3 EGGS
FAT OR [GROUNDNUT] OIL FOR BOILING • WHIPPING CREAM • VANILLA
CASTER SUGAR • APRICOT JAM (OPTIONAL)

Put ½ pt of water into a stew pan with 3 oz butter. Let them boil together till the butter has melted, then stir into it 5 oz sifted flour. When it is quite smooth, beat in 3 eggs. Let the mixture get quite cold, then have some boiling fat and drop the mixture into it with a teaspoon and fry until a light brown. Whipped cream with a little vanilla and caster sugar to be served with them, or a hot apricot sauce. [Serves 6.]

Still Life

'Oh why do I admire you – my dear it would take ages to tell you all I do admire you for but you see I think you go straight for the things that are worthwhile – you have done such an extraordinarily difficult thing without any fuss, but thro' all the conventions kept friends with a pernick-ety creature like Clive, got quit of me and yet kept me your devoted friend, got all the things you need for your own development and yet managed to be a splendid mother…. You give one a sense of security of something

Vanessa Bell, *Still Life*, 1933. The rustic textures and earthy warm colours of southern France were tantalizingly depicted on Vanessa's canvases.

solid and real in a shifting world…. You have genius in your life as well as in your art and both are rare things.'

Roger Fry to Vanessa Bell, 16 September 1917

Vanessa Bell composed both her life and her art in much the same way – with constructive application and due consideration of form, light and colour. All aspects of her professional and personal life coexisted harmoniously. In *Still Life*, Vanessa's

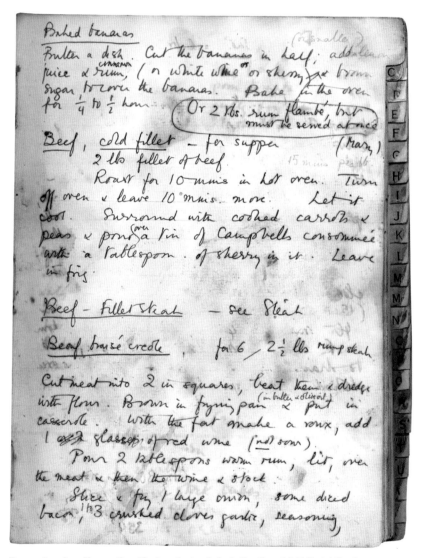

Four recipes from Frances Partridge's recipe book, including Beouf [*sic*] Braisé Creole.

use of colour is bold and confident and evokes the ripe existence that she and Duncan enjoyed in the autumn of 1931 while staying at La Bergère in Cassis. It depicts a tantalizing display of fresh local produce, carefully arranged on a swathe of white table linen, with a folded napkin and an assortment of hand-crafted Provençal crockery. The pears look so sweet and succulent that one would like to pluck a pear from the picture and take a bite.

Charleston Boeuf à la Mode

'And the food which is partly very good but monotonous is better than English restaurant food, but not nearly as good as French. I thought of you in Paris where we spent three days and had thick steaks. I really think you ought to go to at least to Dieppe simply to eat its so easy we got there in no time from Charleston, one could hardly believe it, and then you'd get just as good food as in Paris and its a very nice old town and you could bathe on the beach.'

Vanessa Bell to Grace Higgens, from Perugia, Italy, 1952

During the 1920s and 30s Vanessa and Duncan divided their time between Charleston, Bloomsbury and France. They also visited Italy in 1952 and feasted on its splendid landscapes, colourful frescoes, mosaics and ancient historical and architectural gems. Italian cooking was also appreciated by them – although Vanessa did not rate it as highly as French cooking.

These two French beef recipes are from the Frances Partridge archive.

Beouf [sic] Braisé Creole

For 6. 2½ lbs rump steak. Cut meat into 2 in. squares, beat them & dredge with flour. Brown in frying pan (in butter & olive oil) & put in casserole. With the fat make a roux, add 1 glass of red wine (not sour). Pour 2 tablespoons warm rum, lit, over the meat & then the wine & stock. Slice & fry 1 large onion, some diced bacon, 1 to 3 crushed cloves garlic, seasoning, 1 small tin black olives, 1 ditto pimentos, herbs & bay leaf, 1 tablespoon tomato purée. Cover & cook very gently for 3 hours. (or more?) Liquid should just cover meat.

Boeuf Bourguignon

For 4, 1½ lbs rump. Cut meat in squares (2 in.), brown in butter with 2 sliced onions. Add 1 tablesp. flour & mix together for 1 or 2 mins over medium heat. Add 2 crushed cloves garlic, 1 (or 2) glass[es] of red wine, & stock or water to cover the meat. Cover & cook gently for 2½ hours, adding during the process ½ cup diced bacon, bouquet, seasoning – & after about 2 hrs 2 doz baby mushrooms & ½ cup sliced raw mushrooms.

Roger's Boeuf en Daube

'As for the cooking, he announced triumphantly, "I've made a *boeuf en daube* which is a dream and will last us about five days so all I need do is to boil peas or something", and he could read or write while he watched the pot.'

Virginia Woolf, *Roger Fry: A Biography*, 1940

In 1940, six years after Roger Fry's death, Virginia Woolf wrote a comprehensive biography of him. Not surprisingly, it discussed his ideologies, his achievements, his love of France and his insatiable 'museum appetite'. But the book also conveyed a sense of his selfless, inquisitive and enthusiastic nature. Virginia revealed Roger's independence, impatience, gullibility, loneliness and integrity. As a husband and as a lover, he cut a tragic figure: his wife was committed to a mental asylum and his lovers routinely left him; one even jumped off a cliff. But in his later years, he found comfort and companionship with Helen Anrep, who had left her unfaithful husband, Boris. As for the details of her subject's everyday existence, Virginia made, for example, over forty different references to food alone. Eating habits, as she knew so well, are significant and reveal important aspects of an individual's life and personality.

Roger enjoyed Sunday sirloins and tea-cakes as a child; at Clifton College 'he tried unsuccessfully to make omelettes in a machine of his own invention', to which his roommate objected; and at Cambridge he ate out frequently with friends. He also attended annual Apostolic dinners in London and, while holidaying in Turkey with the Bells, he nursed an ill Vanessa, 'ventured into the kitchen, and returned triumphant with a new dish or two'. When she got better, the two of them became lovers.

In the centre of Roger's small Bloomsbury studio was 'an arrangement of flowers or of fruit, of eggs or of onions'. In one corner was a lone bed, and in another corner a gas ring to cook 'odd meals for himself with the smell of paint hanging over the frying-pan'.

In his last years Roger became less solitary. Helen was intelligent and completely devoted to him. In 1933 he was appointed to the Slade Professorship at Cambridge. He wrote, painted and lectured. At home, he made time to cook: the wild ducks he roasted for Leonard Woolf, the French translator Charles Mauron and Oliver Strachey (Lytton's elder brother) were, he admitted, 'a trifle tough', but at his little house Mas d'Angirany in St Remy, his *boeuf en daube* was, he enthused, 'a dream'.

Roger Fry, *Roquebrune and Monte Carlo from Palm Beach*, 1915–16.
Roger's love for France and all things French was infectious, and it was
he who first introduced Boeuf en Daube to his Bloomsbury friends.

Soupe au Poisson

'It was now, in these last years of peace, that France became for him [Roger] what for the rest of his life she remained – his second country; and there he made friends, deep, affectionate and charming....'

Clive Bell, *Old Friends*, 1956

The recipe for Soupe au Poisson from Helen Anrep's scrapbook.

Roger Fry sometimes carried his Francophilia to extremes. In London, he abandoned dirty saucepans under chairs and allowed them to get mixed up with tubes of paint, but in France he was known to carry around with him a huge clay Provençal cooking pot known as a *diable*. On one occasion, noted Virginia Woolf, he arrived on the doorstep of a hotel in Royat 'clasping in his arms' his *diable*. In the last ten years of his life, when he and Helen Anrep were lovers, both enjoyed cooking. Presumably they took turns using the *diable*, which would have been perfect for this recipe for fish soup, given here in translation from the French original opposite.

> **Fry an onion until it just starts to brown. When it is yellow add one or two tomatoes; afterwards add the (cleaned and scaled) 'poisson de roche' – little rock fish [250g]. Brown them a little and then add water – one large glass per person, plus one for the pot. Add four or five cloves of crushed garlic, parsley, bay leaves, salt and enough pepper to taste. Leave to boil for one hour (lid on), then strain everything through a cheesecloth. Once strained, return to heat and add the pasta or rice, saffron (two packets) and boil for a quarter of an hour, then add [grated Gruyère] cheese. Alternatively, one may add some slices of fresh white fish at the same time as the pasta. Serves two people.**

Proustian Madeleines

'She [Mother] sent out for one of those short, plump little cakes called "petites madeleines", which look as though they had been moulded in the fluted scallop of a pilgrim's shell…. I raised to my lips a spoonful of the tea in which I had soaked a morsel of the cake. No sooner had the warm liquid, and the crumbs with it, touched my palate than a shudder ran through my whole body, and I stopped, intent upon the extraordinary changes that were taking place. An exquisite pleasure had invaded my senses, but individual, detached…. And suddenly the memory returns. The taste was that of the little crumb of madeleine which on Sunday mornings at Combray … when I went to say good day to her in her bedroom, my aunt Léonie used to give me, dipping it first in her own cup of real or of lime-flower tea … and the whole of Combray and of its surroundings, taking their proper shapes and growing solid, sprang into being, town and gardens alike, from my cup of tea.'

Marcel Proust, *Remembrance of Things Past*, 1913

'Everyone is reading Proust,' Virginia Woolf wrote to E. M. Forster in January 1922. Indeed, Proust's interior meanderings and the way in which he recalled the

Roger Fry, *The Round Table*, 1920. Painted while Roger was staying at Maison Barrière, Vence, the picture shows Marcel Gimond, Julie Gimond (née Sorel, centre) and Sonia Lewitska.

smallest and most seemingly insignificant biographical details were a novelty and an inspiration to all Bloomsbury intellectuals. In May, Virginia told Roger Fry: 'Proust so titillates my own desire for expression that I can hardly set out the sentence. Oh if I could write like that! I cry. And at the moment such is the astonishing vibration and saturation and intensification that he procures – there's something sexual in it – that I feel I *can* write like that, and seize my pen and then I *can't* write like that. Scarcely anyone so stimulates the nerves of language in me: it becomes an obsession.'

Virginia's reading of Proust may well have enhanced her next two novels, *Mrs Dalloway* and *To the Lighthouse*. In these she shares Proust's stream-of-consciousness technique and adopts his introspective musings on life, the human condition and the passage of time. Clive Bell was also influenced by Proust. In an essay, he explores the French author's 'tedious' and 'clumsy' style of writing but concludes that Proust's interminable meanderings are actually an effective and necessary means by which to conjure up an accurate reflection of one's past: 'From the unsurveyed mines of sub-conscious memory he dragged up experience vital yet stingless and made the past live sterilized in the present.'

Burgundy Pears Ad Lib

'We had breakfast in my room, and entered on a heated argument about men & women. V. is curiously feminist. She dislikes the possessiveness and love of domination in men. In fact she dislikes the quality of masculinity. Says that women stimulate her imagination, by their grace & their art of life.'

Vita Sackville-West, 'A Week in France with Virginia Woolf', 1928

In 1925 Virginia and Vita Sackville-West began a passionate love affair that lasted on and off for three years. 'Dear Vita has the body and brain of a Greek God', Virginia wrote to Clive Bell. Inspired by Vita's beautiful legs, brains and aristocratic background, Virginia wrote the book *Orlando* (1928) an 'elaborate love-letter, rendering Vita androgynous and immortal: it transformed her story into a myth',

Virginia Woolf and Vita Sackville-West, 1933. In September 1928 Virginia and Vita went to Burgundy together and feasted on 'pears ad lib' and other French delicacies. From the Monk's House photograph album.

Vanessa Bell, *Still Life with Pears and Everlasting Flowers, c. 1945.*

according to Vita's son Nigel Nicolson. There she writes: 'For it would seem – her case proved it – that we write, not with the fingers, but with the whole person. The nerve which controls the pen winds itself about every fibre of our being, threads the heart, pierces the liver.'

In September 1928, two weeks before *Orlando* was published, Virginia and Vita went to Burgundy. These two talented women, glowing in the solidarity of friendship following the end of their affair, feasted together in France. There they ate the 'vastest most delicious meal I have ever eaten', Virginia wrote to Leonard. It 'began with paté of duck, went on to trout, gnocchi, stuffed chicken and spinach made with cream and then sour cream and a delicious cake and then pears ad lib'.

These Burgundy pears are my own 'ad lib' creation, inspired by Virginia and Vita's deep friendship and their holiday in France together in 1928.

2 RIPE PEARS • 30 ML ORANGE JUICE • 350 ML BURGUNDY WINE
180 ML CRANBERRY JUICE • 3 X 1.5-CM SLICES FRESH ORANGE, WITH SKIN
1 CINNAMON STICK • 2 CLOVES • 2 TBS WHITE SUGAR
A PINCH OF GROUND NUTMEG

Peel the pears but do not remove the attractive stem at the top. Cut a slice off the bottom so that the pears can stand upright. Dip them in orange juice and set aside. In a deep pot, combine the wine, cranberry juice, orange slices, sugar and cinnamon stick, cloves, sugar and nutmeg and bring to the boil. Gently immerse the pears into the pot and boil for 15 minutes. Remove, and set aside.

Simmer the wine sauce for another 15 minutes. To serve, stand the pears upright on a serving dish and drizzle with wine sauce. Delicious with vanilla ice cream. [Serves 2.]

Roquebrune Salad

'I had last seen the house when I was seventeen, and it held for me potent memories of Dorothy Bussy, Lytton Strachey's sister, hunched in an armchair reading, her straight grey hair falling over her spectacles, occasionally regarding me with a look of intelligent sympathy. Her husband, Simon, was like a little owl, fierce and stubborn. It was he who did the housekeeping, scolding the cook without mercy for such culinary *faux pas* as putting too much salt in the salad – I seem to remember that it was a fault she committed rather too often'.

Angelica Garnett, *Deceived with Kindness*, 1984

In 1933 Molly MacCarthy went on holiday without her husband, Desmond. His irresponsible charm had once again taken its toll on her nerves and she was depressed, frustrated and, on top of everything else, her hearing was getting worse. So with a little money and a single train ticket in her pocket, she headed south to Roquebrune on the Côte d'Azur, to stay with Dorothy and Simon Bussy.

Their house, La Souco, was situated just below the terracotta-tiled town. Cypress, olive, lemon and orange trees dappled delicate colour and light on the fragrant garden and from her green-shuttered bedroom window Molly could look out to the Mediterranean, the drifting day boats, the blue mountains and, at night, the brilliant lights of Monaco. For Molly, the view was as therapeutic as it was breathtaking, and soon she began to feel better.

Despite their troubles, Molly and Desmond's marriage endured. Their grandson, Hugh Cecil, claimed it was their 'instinctive power of sympathetic understanding' that kept them together. This is true – but the fresh sea air of the Riviera and generous servings of (liberally salted) green salad must have had restorative powers too.

I Tatti Pranzo

'I was hardly halfway across the terrace [at the Villa I Tatti], when I heard behind me a scrunch on the gravel and the voice of Mr Loeser saying "Mr

Keynes"! "One minute please Mr Keynes"! My heart stood still. My head spun. I must turn round. I must make a decision. The whole desperate situation was instantly clear to me.'

Duncan Grant, 'I Tatti: A Question of Labels', for the Memoir Club, *c.* 1950

While Molly MacCarthy was recuperating with the Bussys at La Souco in 1933, her husband, Desmond, was living the high life with the art connoisseur Bernard Berenson and his wife, Mary, at their famous villa, I Tatti, just outside Florence. I Tatti was not a Bloomsbury outpost, but it was on the 'Bloomsbury map'. It was here, for example, in the summer of 1920, that Duncan Grant, Vanessa Bell and John Maynard Keynes dined, the day after a party at which Berenson's neighbour, Charles Loeser, had mistaken Duncan for Maynard, and shown Maynard the pictures in the villa while asking Duncan about the European financial situation. When the truth surfaced, Loeser was not impressed, and relations between him and Bloomsbury were rather strained when they all met up for dinner. When Lytton Strachey visited I Tatti the following summer, however, there were no incidents and his visit was quite pleasant.

Desmond stayed with the Berensons for two weeks in 1933. According to Desmond's biographers, Hugh and Mirabel Cecil, he took daily walks around the villa's extensive gardens and enjoyed coffee with 'BB' in his study each morning. The collection of Renaissance paintings, books and *objets d'art* at I Tatti was a feast on which Desmond would 'gaze in an ecstasy of depression, feeling how little I know and how old I was and that I need however never be *bored* again'. Mealtimes, the Cecils detailed, were just as impressive.

Broeto Ciozoto

'[Duncan's] *Doorway* is brilliant. It is like champagne: effervescent and sparkling: whereas Mark Gertler's work may be described as having *great strength and grip*, like the advertisements of some brands of kitchen tea.'

Gwen Raverat, 1 November 1929

The art of Duncan Grant has a flavour that is hard to specify. It is like a colourful fantasy food, a dish composed of the finest fresh ingredients, selectively chosen from and inspired by the most fertile regions of France, Italy and beyond, fragrantly seasoned with herbs of Provence and as lyrical and as imaginative as a mellow Florentine sauce.

Duncan was nineteen when he travelled to Italy and was enchanted by the frescoes of Piero della Francesca. At twenty-one he journeyed to France and drew inspiration from Pablo Picasso and, on a second visit four years later in 1911, from Henri Matisse. He also travelled to Sicily, Tunisia, Greece and Turkey and absorbed the art of Byzantium, echoes of which would appear on his canvases and in his murals, over and over again. The effect of light on colour intrigued him, and his interest resonated with the vibrant hues of southern Europe.

This Italian recipe for fish soup is from Ristorante Giorgione, a Venetian restaurant visited by Duncan in 1926. Broeto Ciozoto means 'broth from Ciota'.

Duncan Grant, *The Doorway*, 1929. Duncan drew inspiration from his trips to Europe and North Africa, and from artists such as Henri Matisse, whose influence is apparent in the composition of this painting.

Duncan Grant, *Bathing*, mural for the dining room at the Borough Polytechnic, Elephant and Castle, London, 1911. Grant's art frequently reflects the romantic flavours of the people and places he encountered on his travels.

Ciota is a small village near Chioggia in the Veneto region of Italy. This dish is a speciality of the region, belonging, according to the restaurant, 'to the family of "fish soups" that are prepared all along the lagoon coast, but it is particularly in Chioggia that it is a speciality'.

You need several different types of fish. First, into a terracotta pot put two red scorpion fish heads, six angelfish heads, scorpion fish and the heads of a handful of grey prawns, and 300 g of goby fish heads. All of these heads must be well cleaned and washed. You can also add other types of fish, but those mentioned are the classic ones for this dish. Cover the fish heads with plenty of water, one whole sliced lemon and two whole tomatoes. Slowly bring to the boil and simmer for one hour, remembering that a quarter of an hour before the fish heads have finished cooking, you must also add the whole bodies of the fish (these are added after the heads because they require less cooking time). Separately, boil a plump grey mullet. When it is done, place to one side to cool. 1) Remove all the bones from the broth and crush [bones] in a pestle and mortar. When it becomes a paste, pass through a sieve. 2) Cut the mullet into small pieces and remove all the bones. Add the mullet pieces to the purée. 3) Pass the broth through a sieve. Crush all the solid fish bits and add to the broth. 4) Put it all back onto the heat, until you start to see the water begin to tremble; then pour this warm soup over charcoal-toasted slices of bread. Scatter over a handful of cheese and serve.

If you prefer a more meaty broth, leave the whole fish in the broth. Make sure, however, that there is just enough broth to moisten the bread and keep the fish mixture moist.

NB: You won't find another broth (it would be more correct to call it a 'soup') as good as this one. Therefore, you must hold onto this precious forgotten recipe from Ciota, because I guarantee that the dish is really good.

Italian Spaghetti Sauce

'For the youth was hungry, and his lady filled his plate with spaghetti, and when those delicious slippery worms were flying down his throat his face relaxed and became for a moment unconscious and calm. And Philip had seen that face before in Italy a hundred times – seen it and loved it, for it was not merely beautiful, but had the charm which is the rightful heritage of all who are born on that soil.'

E. M. Forster, *Where Angels Fear to Tread*, 1905

E. M. Forster's essential tenet was 'only connect'. In his novels and essays, he contrasted classes, cultures and civilizations, exposing many of the hypocritical, narrow-minded and alienating divisions within the English class system.

Morgan's writings frequently describe meals and dishes that have been poorly prepared and are therefore tasteless and unappetizing. There are the 'bullety bottled peas' in the Julienne soup in *A Passage to India*, served with 'pseudo-cottage bread' and a 'fish full of branching bones, pretending to be plaice'. In his essay 'Porridge or Prunes, Sir?', the porridge appears 'in pallid, grey lumps', the prunes 'in grey juice', the toast 'like steel' and the marmalade as 'a scented jelly'. English food, when superimposed on a foreign culture, reflects the malaise afflicting English society. When pretentious English values are inflicted upon others, the results are aesthetically and emotionally stultifying. For Morgan the Italians were by comparison with the English unreserved and passionate, which was reflected in their gastronomy. Gino, in *Where Angels Fear to Tread*, devours his spaghetti with uninhibited gusto, because it is succulent, flavourful and satisfying.

This is an authentic Italian recipe from Maria Luisa Taglienti's *The Italian Cookbook.*

½ CUP OLIVE OIL • 2 CUPS WATER • I CLOVE GARLIC
⅛ TSP MARJORAM (OPTIONAL) • 2 TINS TOMATO PASTE (6 OZ)
2 LEAVES FRESH SWEET BASIL, OR ⅛ TSP DRIED BASIL
SALT AND PEPPER TO TASTE

Sauté the garlic in oil until golden. Discard the garlic. Mix tomato paste with water and add to oil in saucepan, together with basil and marjoram. Cook uncovered over low flame for 35 to 45 minutes, or until sauce is thick. Season to taste. Enough for one pound of macaroni or rice [or spaghetti]. [Serves 4.]

Andalusian Vegetable Paella

'Nowhere have I seen wheat grow thicker or taller than on its *bancales* or terraces, nowhere were the figs and apricots and persimmons and melons and trellis-grown grapes better to the taste. A little higher up the slope, above the chestnut level, there grow cherry trees whose dark red succulent fruit no one bothered to pick, while from the next village came walnuts and pears and apples. This meant that in summer, if one liked fruit and vegetables, one lived well.'

Gerald Brenan, *Personal Record*, 1974

In 1919 Ralph Partridge's army friend, Gerald Brenan, packed up his belongings and two thousand books and went to live and educate himself in the remote Spanish mountain village of Yegen, in Andalusia. Money was scarce, friends were few and far between and the food, once cooked, diabolical.

Getting to Gerald's hilltop abode was arduous and time-consuming. Still, friends came to visit. The ménage from Tidmarsh – Lytton Strachey, Dora Carrington and Ralph – made the effort in the spring of 1920, but the trip was a disaster from the outset. The ferry crossing from Liverpool to Lisbon, followed by an arduous back-breaking journey in a rickety old train, an uncomfortable bus ride and a meandering trek on the back of a mule across swollen streams and along thirty-five miles of rugged mountain trails was just too much, especially for Lytton. Carrington and Ralph arrived tired and irritable, and poor Lytton was quite ill. 'It was "death"' Lytton later warned Virginia Woolf.

But Gerald continued to receive visitors: the photographer John Hope-Johnstone, Augustus John and his son Robin, Bertrand Russell, short-story writer Victor Pritchett, Roger Fry, David 'Bunny' Garnett and, in April 1923, Leonard and Virginia Woolf. John Hope-Johnstone disparaged the food situation but Robin John argued, according to Gerald, 'that anyone who could not see that Spanish bread and olive oil and lentil pottage and stews of salt cod and potato omeletes were better than roast beef and *sole meunière* and *steak au poivre* was a degenerate who did not understand the true values of life'.

Dora Carrington, *Soldiers at a Stream*, 1919. Carrington painted this work while on a walking holiday in Spain with her brother Noel and Rex Partridge. One year later, she returned to the region with Rex (now Ralph) and Lytton Strachey.

Virginia, perhaps surprisingly, found no fault with Spanish cuisine and praised the Andalusian way of life: 'I don't want to come back to meat meals, servants, and telephones,' she wrote to Molly MacCarthy from Spain.

Getting to Yegen is still complicated, although one can now get there in a day from London. In creating this vegetable paella, I have attempted to incorporate the delicious flavours and spices of Gerald's Andalusia.

¼ CUP OLIVE OIL • 1 ONION, SLICED • 3 CLOVES GARLIC • 1 GREEN PEPPER
1 RED PEPPER • 1 YELLOW PEPPER • 1 JAR ARTICHOKE HEARTS
1 CUP FRESH PEAS • 2 PLUM TOMATOES, CUT INTO WEDGES
1½ TSP PAPRIKA • ¼ TSP CAYENNE • SALT AND PEPPER
4–5 CUPS VEGETABLE OR CHICKEN BROTH
1 TSP SAFFRON THREADS • 2 CUPS ARBORIO RICE
CHOPPED FRESH PARSLEY

Chop the vegetables. Heat the oil in a paella pan and cook the onions and garlic gently until soft. Add the peppers, artichokes and peas and cook for four or five minutes. Add the tomatoes, paprika and cayenne and season. In a separate pot heat the broth and when boiling add the saffron. Pour into the paella pan. Add the rice 'dry' and simmer until cooked, 18 to 20 minutes. Do not overcook. Allow to rest for five minutes and, just before serving, stir in the parsley.

The Table at Segovia

'I was really rather surprised to see Saxon Turner approach the table at Segovia where I was seated with one Trend, a Cambridge musician; he approached the table in perfect style with just a little guttural noise, a sort of burble which expressed everything the moment demanded and sat down'.

Roger Fry, quoted in a letter from Virginia Woolf
to Barbara Bagenal, 24 June 1923

Saxon Sydney-Turner's intellectual prowess was quite astonishing, even for Bloomsbury. He was a brilliant Greek scholar and had a comprehensive knowledge of the ancient classics and equally of modern literature. He won prizes for solving crosswords and making acrostic puzzles in Latin verse. He played the piano and could cite, unaided, from every concert and Wagnerian opera that he had ever attended.

But Saxon found communication difficult. 'He seemed to glide, rather than walk, and noiselessly, so that one moment you were alone in a room and next moment you found him sitting in a chair near you though you had not heard the door open or him come in,' recalled Leonard Woolf. His conversation 'was extremely spasmodic, elusive and allusive'. Gerald Brenan thought he had never met such a bore. Barbara Bagenal, however, noted that Virginia Woolf could 'make him almost voluble'. He 'ate very little and at the most erratic hours', said Leonard. Given Saxon's usual awkwardness, one can understand why Roger was so astonished to see him approach his table 'in perfect style' at Segovia.

Avocado Soup for Four

'Avocado pears' were not readily available in England until the early 1960s. Before then, one had to travel to southern Spain or to other Mediterranean climes to enjoy this soft, versatile, nutrient-rich fruit. Today, one can pick them up in most supermarkets and greengrocers, in any season. If necessary, one can speed up the ripening process by placing an avocado in a brown paper bag with a banana or an apple and, in a day or two, it will be soft and ready to eat.

Vanessa Bell, *Saxon Sydney-Turner at the Piano, c.* 1908. Saxon spoke very little and had an encyclopedic knowledge of Wagnerian opera.

Frances Partridge was first introduced to avocados *in loco* in the 1920s and was still very much around to see them arrive on the shelves of her local super-market in London in the 1960s, by which time she was the proud owner of a modern electric mixer. During her lifetime, which spanned 103 years (she died in 2004), she saw an unprecedented number of changes – social and technological, not to mention culinary. This is her recipe.

> **2 ripe avocado[s]. 4 oz single, 4 oz double cream. Chicken stock to required consistency, [glass dry sherry], parsley, salt, pepper. Put avocados & cream in mixer & add stock. When required heat, add sherry, seasoning & parsley.**

Asparagus for Angelica

'When I was very small, I was invited to tea by Roger [Fry] at Dalmeny Avenue, in London. Several other little girls were there as well as his bearded, deep-voiced sister, Margery, who kept house for him. Expecting the spread of jellies, cakes and biscuits that were usually put before chil-dren, we each sat down to a plate bare of all but a baked potato. Discovering that these were made of cardboard, everyone but myself burst into tears. Somehow aware that this was what the grown-ups called a joke, I opened mine and found it filled with hundreds and thousands, multi-coloured sweets the size of a pin's head, impossible to eat without scattering them all over the floor – indeed impossible to eat at all. Dismayed that their attempt to amuse us had fallen so flat, poor Margery bustled away to get the real tea, hidden behind a curtain, and the rest of the evening, no doubt spent more normally, was forgotten by me.'

Angelica Garnett, *Deceived with Kindness*, 1984

To Angelica Bell, Roger Fry was like 'a grandfather with paternal and avuncu-lar overtones'. He was patient and kind and spent many hours with her, making, mending and sticking interesting things together. His voracious appetite for knowl-edge, coupled with his astonishing patience, rendered their time together both amusing and educational. Furthermore, only Roger could persuade Angelica to try eating those 'limp rods' that appeared before her one mealtime at Charleston. 'It was to Roger that I owe my first taste of asparagus; he brought bundles of it down to Charleston, having obtained it cheaply from some unusual source,' she recalled. 'I had made up my mind to dislike it simply because everybody was so concerned I should do otherwise, but when it appeared on the table, limp rods of jade and ivory, I allowed him to persuade me to try it – and then, naturally, could not have enough.'

Frances Partridge, 1930s. Frances saw many changes in her long life (103 years), including the arrival of supermarket chains and the invention of the electric mixer.

Quentin Bell was also very fond of asparagus and grew it in his garden. 'He loved it steamed, simply with melted butter,' recalled Virginia Nicholson.

Ballet and Sole

'Living in Spain, I grew to love Spanish food, the dinners with their many courses, the omeletes [*sic*] with pimentos, the chicken with rice, and snails, and mussels.'

Lydia Lopokova, 'Snails in Spain', 1927

When Sergei Diaghilev and his Russian troupe took refuge from the First World War in Spain in 1916, the ballet revolution was about to advance one step further.

above left: Lydia Lopokova in costume for Sergei Diaghilev's *Petrushka*, 1919. Soon afterwards, Lydia disappeared from public view until 1921, when she performed as Aurora in *The Sleeping Princess. above right:* Duncan Grant, *Lydia Lopokova,* 1923. When Lydia took refuge in Spain with Diaghilev's Ballets Russes, she became influenced by Spanish dancing styles and was appreciative of the local cuisine.

The impact on the Ballets Russes of flamenco dancing from Andalusia was enormous – not only on its choreography but also on its costumes, stage design and music. 'I, too, watched the dancers and learned how to use my hands and arms – how to put them akimbo as if in defiance of a Moor ready to touch me!' noted Lydia Lopokova. But castanets and heel-clicking were not the only things to inspire the ballet revolutionaries – they were also fully appreciative of the flavours of Spanish cuisine. In an article for the London *Evening News* in 1927, Lydia provided this recipe for King Alfonso Sole.

> Fry a sole in butter with a little lemon juice. Then cut a banana in two, sauté in the juice of the fish, with a little slice or two of tomato. Lay the banana and the tomato on the fish, and pour melted butter over all before serving. [Serves 2.]

Lydia's Sorrel Soup

According to the memoirs of David 'Bunny' Garnett, in the mid-1920s John Maynard Keynes – Lydia Lopokova's husband – asked him if he would be willing to ghost-write for Lydia an article on her taste in cookery, to be published in the *Evening News*. It turned out that she did not need very much help. 'It was delightful. We talked it over,' Bunny recalled. 'I think I gave Lydia confidence – but I hardly wrote anything myself – the whole point seemed to me not Lydia's ideas about cookery but her enchanting use of the English language. I haven't seen the article for forty years or so, but I remember that she began her recipe for sorrel soup with the words: "You can find a bland grass growing in the fields…"'.

The next five sections are all based on recipes in Lydia's series of newspaper articles. The first is her recipe for sorrel soup, which is delicious when eaten with *piroshki* pies, the subject of her second recipe.

Suggested ingredients
200 G SORREL • 2 TBS BUTTER • ½ TSP SALT • ½ PT WATER
½ PT STOCK • 1 TBS FLOUR • 2 EGGS • 1 CUP SOUR CREAM

There is an amiable grass called sorrel with an acid taste to it that springs everywhere in Russian fields. I have found it wild in Sussex also, when I was gathering mushrooms under the downs, and I was so delighted I plucked it and brought it home. What for? To make soup.

Pick a basket of wild sorrel, look it over carefully, wash it, chop it up finely and put it with its juice into a pan. Add a spoonful of butter, a spoonful of salt, a glass or two of water, and boil it until it is so soft that you can rub and wash it through a sieve with cold water. Then add some stock, add a tablespoonful of flour to thicken, and a spoonful of butter. Stir it well, mix it into the soup, and then boil it up again.

Just before serving, shell as many lightly-boiled eggs as there are persons and slip them into the soup. Then you may add half a glass of sour cream, or, if you have no sour cream, add the thickest fresh cream that you can get. We also serve with this soup buckwheat rusks. [Serves 2–3.]

Lydia's Piroshki Pies

Russian *piroshki* pies are ideal with soup, at breakfast or as a delicious snack at any time of day.

It is time I told you about the little pies, or pastries – we call them *piroshki* – which we Russians eat with soup. We have much imagination in making dough – that is, with yeast, or puff paste or pancakes. The stuffing for these little pies must be juicy, and the dough must be absolutely cold when you put the stuffing in.

Here is a recipe for making a dough with ½ lb of flour, an egg, a spoonful of butter, a little salt, and 2 oz of yeast.

Melt the yeast in a quarter of a glass of milk with a spoonful of flour in it … and put it by the fire for a quarter of an hour before using. Beat up the egg, adding it with salt to the yeast. Then mix into the flour and make a dough. You may have to add a little more milk to get the right consistence. Work the butter in last of all with your fingers. Then roll several times, cut into small pieces, the right size for your pies, fill them with a spoonful of stuffing and set them aside for the pastry to rise for a quarter of an hour before you put them into the oven. Take them out of the oven at the last moment; they must be hot. The stuffing is very varied. Minced meat, fish, chopped eggs and rice, sour cream and spinach, and so on, are all used. One of these pasties is served on a side-dish with every plate of soup. [Makes 12 little pies.]

Blinies

'Your English food is so dignified,' joked Lydia Lopokova in the *Evening News* in 1927. For contrast she put forward this recipe for Russian pancakes, known as *blinies*, 'the friendly little dishes of my greedy country'.

Pancakes are amongst the Russian's favourite dishes; and here is a good substitute for the true Russian Pancake (*blinie*).

Make a batter, as for English pancakes [recipe below], and take a very small frying pan with boiling lard in it. Pour in the smallest quantity of batter which will cover the pan, so that you shall have the thinnest little pancake possible.

Build up a pile of these pancakes, spreading, between each two, a layer of jam and what in England is Devonshire cream, and serve.

This is an English cook's version of *blinies*, and is not at all bad.

Angelica Garnett's English Pancake Recipe or 'Extra Good Pancakes'
2 WHITES OF EGG • 3 YOLKS OF EGG • 6 OZ FLOUR
3 OZ BUTTER • ½ PT MILK

Separate whites from yolks [and] beat [whites] stiffly. Warm milk add butter & yolks then flour. Stir in whites. Fry as small pancakes.

Two Russian Soups

In an article on her favourite Russian soups, Lydia remarked disarmingly, 'I do not think the English people like soup: they think it is thin, "cold," and economical. In England there is thick soup with potatoes, and there is thin soup, with carrots which one has to dodge.' These two recipes of hers are for *oolia*, an exquisite Russian fish soup, and *shee*, a hearty pickled cabbage soup.

Oolia

Here is a recipe for a Russian soup called Oolia (I do not know how you spell it). First you catch some small fish, [such] as perch or rudd, or you may buy small fish from the fishmonger.

Wash and clean 3 lbs. of the fish, put them into a saucepan with many glasses of cold water; add a few sticks of celery, an onion, a few herbs, a spoon-ful of salt. Then boil over a slow fire until the fish are boiled to rags – that is, from two to three hours. Next sieve through and boil once more. You may serve your soup with chopped parsley sprinkled over it.

Or, better still, you may make it transparent and free from all the sordid-ness of ordinary fish. Take 2 oz. of pressed caviare, grind it in a mortar till noth-ing is left of the little pips of the caviare. Mix a little cold water with the caviare, and by degrees dilute this with your soup. Lastly, add the whole mixture to the soup, stirring it well with a wooden spoon. Boil for ten minutes; take the pan off the fire and then bring to the boil once more. Then serve – and behold! not soup, but the majestic offer of a plate of amber! [Serves 3–4.]

Shee

So I will tell you about Shee. There are two kinds: fresh Shee and sour Shee, made with fresh or with pickled cabbage. It is almost the national food.

To prepare pickled cabbage soup, first add milk to some stock, making a white broth. Put in a few pieces of meat. Take two pounds of pickled cabbage, squeeze it, rinse it thoroughly in hot water, squeeze it again, turning it over well.

Chop four or five onions, fry them in butter, and add the cabbage, frying it too. Add a spoon of flour, some pepper and pieces of bay leaf.

When the cabbage has been well fried add your mixture to the broth and boil the whole until the cabbage becomes tender. Half an hour before serving put in five potatoes. Add half a glass of sour cream when serving.

This soup is always served with buckwheat in a side-dish by each plate – either plain boiled buckwheat or boiled buckwheat fried and pressed into little round cakes.

Without Shee Russians could not face life! [Serves 16.]

Southern American Chicken

Not all of Lydia Lopokova's recipes were from Europe. One of her articles for the *Evening News* enthused about the United States, where she had lived for a considerable time. In America, she wrote, '[Water] tastes like the first frost of autumn, makes the blood tingle in one's veins; one's forehead aches for a moment with ecstasy as one gulps it down.' She was also very complimentary about some local dishes, 'particularly the cookery in the Southern States'. Here are two of her chicken recipes from the Deep South.

Smothered Chicken

Split a young chicken down the back and dust with salt and pepper. Put a tablespoonful of lard in a frying pan and put the chicken into the boiling lard. After it has been frying gently for a quarter of an hour add half a glass of water, set on the side of the stove and keep it simmering for an hour. Serve with fried parsley. [Serves 4–5.]

Creole Chicken

Creole chicken is cooked the same way, except that two sliced onions, a table-spoonful of flour and three or four sliced tomatoes are added in succession to the slowly frying chicken, and it is allowed to simmer with herbs, bay leaf, parsley, a clove of garlic, and green peppers, if you have them. [Serves 4–5.]

Russian Tea and Talk

'The Russians love to talk … but when I ask an English lady to lunch she begins to put on her gloves – what a horrid, rude, unsocial, by-the-clock custom that is! How I hate to see it! – almost as soon as we leave the table…. In Russia they stay on to tea and dinner…. The servants would be shocked – it would be against their principles. But the Russians have no principles – it is only a question if the conversation is good and flowing and disinclined to come to a terminus.

'Being so conversational, we naturally drink more tea, very weak tea, but always fresh, poured down the larynx with two drops of lemon, just enough to readjust that organ to a fresh starting point of words. Conversation gives life fullness and variety, and is one of the best creations of the human mind….

'I am so used by now to English customs (and climate) that I almost (not quite) take milk with my tea.'

Lydia Lopokova, 'We Russians – You English', unpublished draft article, 1921–34

Despite the fact that Lydia Lopokova was one of the most talented, famous, popular and loveable figures of her day, Bloomsbury never quite came to accept her. Clive Bell claimed that she 'destroyed all conversation at Gordon Square' and Vanessa Bell, as mentioned earlier, found her intrusive – especially when she arrived, uninvited, in her studio for tea and talk. John Maynard Keynes, however, fell ever more in love with her. She was no intellectual, but her unique use of the English language, her effusive charm, and her physicality, rendered her Maynard's perfect complement. With Lydia by his side, his busy life acquired a sense of balance: she looked after him and gave him much-needed respite from the gruelling demands of his government position. Their marriage was very happy and, despite the criticisms from the rest of Bloomsbury, the Keyneses remained completely devoted to one another.

Lydia liked her tea very hot, and lots of it. Nevertheless, she noted, 'It will be no good for you to have a samovar and Russian tea, unless you sit up all night talking and talking as Russians do!'

Russian tea has a unique smoky flavour; this is because the tea has become infused with smoke from the campfires along the caravan trading route between Russia and China. On a trip to Leningrad (now St Petersburg) in 1987 I discovered how to make tea the Russian way:

> To make Russian tea, one requires a samovar. This traditional urn heats water to boiling point and is brought to the table after lunch, where it will remain until the early hours of the morning. At the top of the samovar is a small pot of tea-concentrate, or 'zavarka'. A tiny amount of zavarka is poured into a small glass teacup and then diluted (roughly to the ratio ten to one) with hot water from the samovar. It is then flavoured with lemon and sugar.

Borscht

Helen Anrep was not an artist, a writer or an intellectual, but from 1924 she was welcomed into the Bloomsbury fold as the friend and companion of Roger Fry. Married to the Russian artist Boris Anrep, she found herself unhappily sharing their home with his live-in mistress, and left her wayward husband soon after meeting Roger at a party. In the period leading up to his death in 1934, and for many years after, Helen was a good friend and confidante to many Bloomsbury members.

She was also an excellent cook. This recipe for borscht is from Helen's scrapbook. Whatever its original source – which may have been her Russian-born husband Boris or his Ukrainian girlfriend, the poet Anna Akhmatova – it is authentic, easy to make and delicious.

1 [LB] BEETROOT • 2 LARGE ONIONS • 4 SMALL ONIONS
2 DESSERTSPOONS OIL • 1 TSP SALT • 12 PEPPERCORNS • 1 SMALL BAY LEAF
1 GARLIC CLOVE • ½ MEDIUM CABBAGE

Peel and cut in to half inch cubes the large beet. Peel and cut in slices 2 large and 4 small onions [and] put both together into large white [?] saucepan with

two dessertspoons of oil, salt level teaspoon, 12 peppercorns, one bay leaf, one clove of garlic cut in slices, shake well; put on the closed stove till hot through, and add hot water enough to cover; stew gently till onion is tender; add boiling water ⅔ full; when all comes to the boil put in ½ (or ¼ if large) cabbage and allow to boil gently for an hour or more.

The craze for Sergei Diaghilev's Ballets Russes after the First World War accounts for the fact that borscht made its way into many English recipe books at this time. This second recipe comes from the Frances Partridge collection. It is more refined than either Helen Anrep's 'Borstch' or Lydia Lopokova's Russian soups, as it is blended to a smooth, silky consistency.

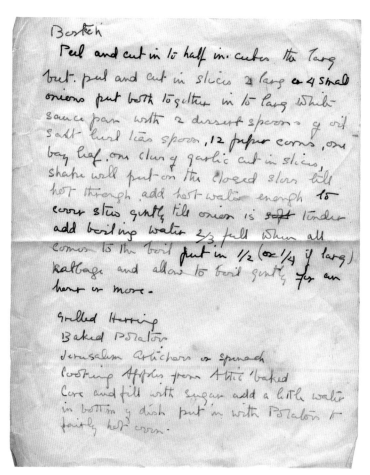

Recipe for 'Borstch' [*sic*] from Helen Anrep's scrapbook.

I LB BEETROOT • I LB POTATOES • I SMALL ONION • I OZ BUTTER
[I LITRE] WATER & STOCK CUBES • SALT & PEPPER • 4–6 TBS CREAM

Skin beetroot & peel potatoes; dice both & chop onion. Add all to the melted butter in a saucepan, cook for 5 mins very gently with lid on, shaking occasionally. Stir in stock and bring to boil. Simmer for one hr. Put through liquidizer, return to saucepan & season. Serve with a spoonful of cream in each plate. This reheats well. For 4–6. [NB – 'less' noted between 'beetroot' and 'potatoes'.]

Pashka

'It is said that when Lytton Strachey happened to arrive at Naples on Easter Sunday he caused a commotion. The "better" class of people was shocked and turned away in disgust, but the *lazzaroni* [beggars] greeted him joyously with a murmur of: "Yea indeed he is risen".'

Quentin Bell, *Elders and Betters*, 1995

Lytton Strachey undoubtedly had a 'divine' aura about him. His unusual physical features often attracted unsolicited attention, and his effeminate mannerisms, the eternal length of his legs, his bard-like beard, his omniscient eyes and the way he pressed his fingers together when thinking, as if in prayer, turned many a head.

To celebrate his first Christmas with Dora Carrington and Ralph Partridge at Ham Spray House in 1924, Lytton wrote a play, which the residents and guests acted out. Boris Anrep brought along a Russian Easter cake, but this traditional pudding, made with cottage cheese, candied fruits and nuts, was too rich to eat, especially after all the festive feasting. In Russia, the initials 'XB' – meaning 'Christ is Risen' – are traditionally written in blanched almond slivers over the top of the cake. But at this Christmas party in 1924, Christ Himself would have had difficulty in eating any of this sweet confection, let alone in rising afterwards.

Here is my own recipe for *paska*, or pashka. It is incredibly rich, so small servings suffice.

I CUP THICK DOUBLE CREAM • 3 EGG YOLKS, BEATEN
I ½ CUPS SUGAR • 2 LB CREAMED COTTAGE CHEESE
8 OZ CREAM CHEESE, AT ROOM TEMPERATURE
2 OZ WHOLE ALMONDS, TOASTED • 3 OZ CANDIED FRUITS, CHOPPED
I TBS FRESH LEMON ZEST, GRATED
½ TSP VANILLA EXTRACT • ½ CUP RAISINS
BLANCHED ALMONDS CUT INTO SLIVERS, FOR DECORATION • CHEESECLOTH

Gently heat the cream in a pan on the stove (do not boil) and whisk in the egg yolks and the sugar. Remove from the heat and integrate well with the cottage cheese and cream cheese; a food processor makes this easy. Add the almonds, candied fruits, lemon zest and vanilla extract.

Line a sufficiently large flower pot (6 in. [15.5 cm] would be fine) with a rinsed and wrung cheesecloth. Scoop the mixture into the pot and place a weighted saucer on the top (a can of beans will suffice) and leave in the refrigerator for 2–3 days, with a bowl beneath to catch the liquid pressed out.

Remove the *pashka* from the flower pot and turn out onto a serving plate, carefully removing the cheesecloth. Decorate with almond slivers. 'XB' is the traditional Easter message. Serve chilled. Serves 6–8.

Morgan's Indian Curry

'It is odd that I should have seen so much of the side of [Indian] life that is hidden from most English people.'

E. M. Forster, *The Hill of Devi*, 1953

Parading elephants, pools of pink lotuses, mangoes, spiced milk, cymbals, ritual singing, evaporating ink (from the heat), mounds of delicious sweet rice – this was E. M. Forster's India – not the India of Anglo bottled peas and cutlets he depicted in *A Passage to India*. In *The Hill of Devi* he recounts his adventures as personal secretary to the Maharajah of Dewas and details aspects of the royal court to which only he and the Prince's entourage were privy. Morgan respected the state's religious traditions and customs and participated in its many fasts, feasts and celebrations. With an enthusiasm that was both rare and perceptive, and by virtue of his own impartiality and judiciousness, he was able to make personal connections with people from other cultures in a way that few of his characters, or his contemporaries, were capable of.

On 29 December 1913, Morgan was guest at a marriage banquet given at court in Dewas. He arrived on a large painted elephant and, bedecked in fine Indian silks and muslins, he feasted upon the following, as he reported in a letter to his mother, later published in *The Hill of Devi*.

1. A mound of delicious rice – a great standby.
2. Brown tennis balls of sugar – not bad.
3. Golden curlicues – sweet to sickliness.
4. Little spicy rissoles.
5. Second mound of rice, mixed with spices and lentils.
6. Third mound of rice, full of sugar and sultanas – very nice.
7. Curry in metal saucer – to be mixed with rice no. 1.

we went to the Banquet-Room. This
again I must try to describe to you.
Mr. Forbes, Mrs. Raja, Mr. D. R's brother, Darling

Marathas.

Open Space.

Brahmins.

Marathas.

We all sat on the floor, cross-legged, round
the edge of a great hall, the servants running
about in the middle. Each was on a legaless
chair and had in front a tray like a bed tray
on which was a metal tray, on
which the foods were arranged. The Brahmins
ate no meat, and were waited on by special
attendants, naked to the waist. The rest
of us had meat as well as the other dishes. Round

each man's little domain, an ornamental pattern
was stencilled in chalk on the floor. My tray
was arranged some what as follows, but
"Jane, Jane, however shall we recollect
the dishes" as Miss Bates remarked.

1. A mound of delicious rice – a great standby.
2. Brown tennis balls of sugar – not bad
3. Golden and curlicues – sweet to sickliness.
4. Little spicy rissoles.
5. Second mound of rice, mixed with spices [and lentils]
6. Third mound of rice, full of sugar and
   sultanas – very nice.
7. Curry in metal saucer – to be mixed with
   rice no. 1.
8. Sauce, as if made from apples that felt
   poorly. Also to be mixed with rice, but only
   once by me.
9. Another sauce, choosy hooey and brown

top: E. M. Forster in Indian dress, 1921. In 1912–13 and 1921, Morgan worked as private secretary to a young maharajah of the Indian state of Dewas Senior. He was privy to a side of life in India that most foreigners never saw. *above:* Morgan's diagram, in a letter written to his mother on his birthday, of the marriage banquet he attended in Dewas in 1913.

8. Sauce, as if made from apples that felt poorly. Also to be mixed with rice, but only once by me.

9. Another sauce, chooey-booey and brown.

10, 11, 12. Three dreadful little dishes that tasted of nothing till they were well in your mouth, when your whole tongue suddenly burst into flame. I got to hate this side of the tray.

13. Long thin cake, like a brandy snap but salt.

14. It may have been vermicelli.

15. As for canaries.

16. Fourth mound of rice to which I never came.

17. Water.

18. Native bread – thin oat-cake type.

Heavenly Peking Duck

'My cook tried a Chinese lunch yesterday, but he's not nearly as good as other people's at Chinese food. This – and the wine – is very good indeed. Some dishes, like bird's-nest soup, sugar water and gelatine, [are] exaggerated. Others, like sharks' fins, as good as reputed. Preserved eggs, one version very good, another a combined sour-sweet too much for me. But the ordinary basic food is heavenly. Everything comes on at once, and the order is roughly cold dishes, soup, some hot dishes, sweet, more hot dishes, fish, rice. Then one eats fruit in the drawing-room. But it varies. One helps oneself from a central bowl with spoon or chopsticks – at these I'm fairly good, but can't yet take large quantities.'

Julian Bell to Vanessa Bell, from China, 31 October 1935

After reading history at Cambridge, and completing two postgraduate dissertations (one on Alexander Pope's poetry and the other on political and aesthetic ethics), Julian Bell took a teaching post at Wuhan University in China. While extolling the virtues of perfect punctuation and William Shakespeare to Chinese students, he learned to read and write Mandarin to a considerable extent, and to appreciate many of the finer aspects of Chinese culture.

He sailed down the Yangtze, watched the tense China–Japan political situation unfold and enjoyed a love affair with Ling Shuhua, a well-known (married) Chinese short-story writer. She acquainted him with the delectable flavours of sweet dried cabbage soup and heavenly Peking duck. In January 1936, Julian wrote to his mother: 'The nicest dish in the world is Peking duck. You have first of all a sort of sour, flat paste pancake affair; taste of new, home-made bread. You pick one up with chopsticks and spread it on the palm of your hand. Then you put on it an outside slice of very fat, crackling, roast duck (or goose?). You add some sort of raw shallot-endive vegetable dipped in a heavy soy-piquant sauce. You fold round the pancake and eat as a sort of big messy sandwich. Also good is sweet walnut soup, spiced mutton galantine. And fifty dishes past investigating. The beauty of the duck is that *all* the tastes *and textures* persist in the mouth.'

Duncan Grant, *Julian Bell Reading, c.* 1930. After spending sixteen months teaching English in China (from October 1935 to January 1937), Julian returned to England and signed up to drive ambulances for the International Brigade in Spain.

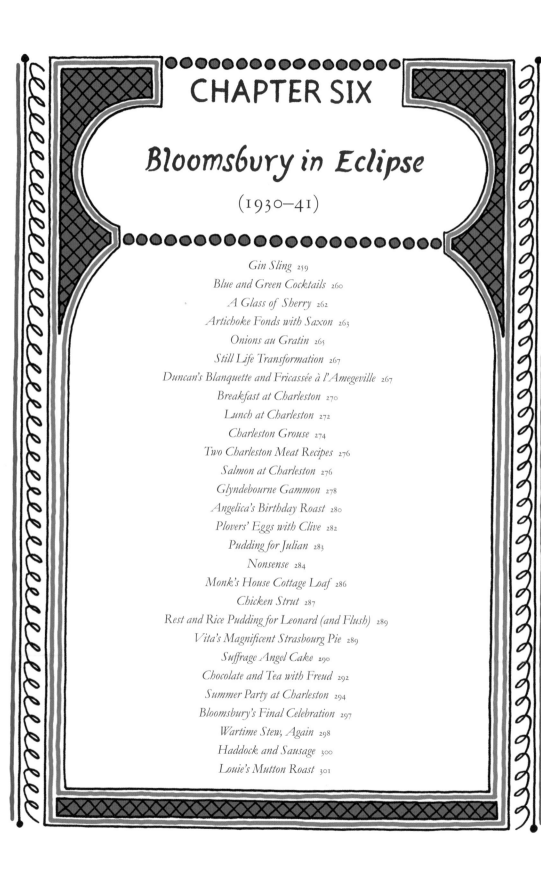

CHAPTER SIX

Bloomsbury in Eclipse

(1930–41)

Augustus John, 1909. Augustus was a free spirit, which sometimes led to raucous behaviour and the occasional punch-up.

Gin Sling

'Henry [Lamb] was entertained by Dodo to a gala night at the Eiffel Tower, where Clive turned up, and Augustus in his cups leaned across the table and struck Clive in the face twice, which Clive took extremely well in the rest of the company's opinion.'

Ralph Partridge to Frances Marshall, 13 December 1931

At the beginning of the 1930s, the London restaurant known as the Eiffel Tower, whose proprietor, Rudolf Stulik, had been chef to the Habsburg emperor Franz Joseph I, 'was a favourite resort of poets, painters, actors, sculptors, authors, musicians and magicians; not to speak of members of the fashionable and political world,' said Augustus John. Indeed, the place's fervid décor – its brilliant yellow walls hung with defiant Vorticist paintings contrasting with its white tablecloths and continental aromas – was as bright and as lively as its vivacious clientele, the more bohemian of whom would occasionally let loose a roar of laughter and/or an ill-directed fist.

The Café Royal was another favourite watering hole of Augustus in the 1920s and 30s, and it was also frequented by members of the Bloomsbury Group. If one requires a good strong drink, perhaps to recover from an unforeseen blow, try this gin sling from the *Café Royal Cocktail Book*.

1 TSP SUGAR DISSOLVED IN WATER
1 GLASS DRY GIN • 1 LUMP ICE
Serve in a long tumbler and fill with water.

Blue and Green Cocktails

In December 1932, there was a grand London reception in St James's, organized by Vanessa Bell and Virginia Woolf, to celebrate the new exhibition at the Lefevre Gallery. The London glitterati, literati and artisti were there, merrily imbibing the fresh new flavours of Duncan Grant and Vanessa's latest decorative creation: the autumn-themed Music Room. On the walls of the gallery hung six hand-painted panels, each festooned with colourful flowers and integrated mirrors. Ornate leaves were painted throughout the room; the bespoke rug, Art Deco chairs, modern lamps and grand piano displayed the same bold style in a riot of turquoise, yellows, blues and greens. And if this did not dazzle the crowd, the glittering cocktails certainly did. '[Y]oung men in white jackets served blue and green cocktails with what looked like gold-leaf floating on the surface', Frances Spalding noted in Duncan's biography.

Edible gold leaf has been used for centuries for culinary purposes. It has no flavour of its own and floats in liquid. These recipes come from two legendary London barmen of the period, Harry Craddock of the Savoy, and Giovanni Quaglino of the St James's Palace Hotel.

Green Dragon by Quaglino
⅓ GIN • ⅓ CRÈME DE MENTHE GREEN • ⅙ KÜMMEL • ⅙ LEMON JUICE
DASH OF ABSINTHE • SQUEEZE LEMON PEEL
Shake well and strain into cocktail glass.

Blue Devil Cocktail from the Savoy
½ DRY GIN • ¼ LEMON JUICE OR LIME JUICE • ¼ MARASCHINO
1 DASH BLUE VEGETABLE EXTRACT
Shake well and strain into cocktail glass.

Duncan Grant, *Design for the Music Room*, 1932. In 1932 Duncan
and Vanessa Bell redecorated the Lefevre Gallery Music Room in
an Art Deco-style fiesta of turquoise, yellows, blues and greens.

Charleston Cocktail from the Savoy*
⅙ DRY GIN • ⅙ GLASS KIRSCH • ⅙ GLASS MARASCHINO
⅙ GLASS CURAÇAO • ⅙ FRENCH VERMOUTH • ⅙ ITALIAN VERMOUTH
Shake well and strain into cocktail glass. Squeeze lemon peel on top.

London Cocktail from the Savoy
2 DASHES ORANGE BITTERS • 2 DASHES SYRUP
2 DASHES ABSINTHE • ⅓ DRY GIN
Shake well and strain into cocktail glass.

*Harry Craddock compiled his recipes from the existing repertoire of the Savoy's American Bar, but the Charleston Cocktail recipe is probably his own, as the 1925–26 dance craze for which it is named coincided with his becoming head barman at the Savoy in 1926.

Lytton Strachey and Dora Carrington, 1920s.

A Glass of Sherry

'Carrington, however, was the dominating personality [at the Slade], and when she cut her thick gold hair into a heavy golden bell, this, her fine blue eyes, her stutter, turned-in toes and other rather quaint but attractive attributes combined to make her a conspicuous and popular figure. But I had noticed her long before this was achieved, when, as a bored sufferer in the Antique Class, my wandering attention had been suddenly fixed by the sight of this amusing person with such very blue eyes and such incredibly thick pig-tails of red-gold hair. I got an introduction to her and eventually won her regard by lending her my braces for a fancy dress dance. We were on the top of a 'bus and she wanted them then and there.'

Paul Nash, *Outline. An Autobiography and Other Writings*, 1949

Dora Carrington was one of the most tragic figures in the story of Bloomsbury. Her artist friends were horrified when caring for Lytton Strachey became her primary concern in life. But in loving Lytton, Carrington also discovered a way forward. In him she found companionship (non-sexual, which was a relief), intellectual and emotional stimulation, and a sense of purpose. Her creative expression found its way into letters, onto the walls at the Mill House and Ham Spray House, and into every morsel of food that she lovingly prepared for Lytton and their friends.

When Lytton died of stomach cancer in 1932, Carrington could find no reason to go on. On the morning of 11 March, she shot herself in the chest and died a few hours later. She was only thiry-eight. 'We found her propped on rugs on her bedroom floor; the doctor had not dared to move her, but she had touched him greatly by asking him to fortify himself with a glass of sherry', wrote Frances Partridge.

Artichoke Fonds with Saxon

'Saxon arrived for ten days' holiday, looking very white and old. We were both delighted to see him, changed into his silk summer suit, lying out on the garden bed under the weeping ash with a detective story. We had grouse in his honour and a bottle (the last) of Châteauneuf 1923; globe artichokes, grapes, figs and plums, all homegrown.'

Frances Partridge's diary, 31 August 1940

Saxon Sydney-Turner (*right*) and Ralph Partridge (*left*), photographed by Frances Partridge at Ham Spray House, 1932. When Saxon visited Frances and Ralph at Ham Spray House in 1940, aged sixty, they celebrated his stay with fresh foods from their garden and a bottle of Châteauneuf 1923.

Duncan Grant, *Still Life, c.* 1955.

This recipe for Artichoke Fonds, or hearts, is from the Frances Partridge archive. The *Pâté Truffe* recipe is my own.

Lightly cook a tin of artichoke fonds (2 to each person) in butter, sprinkle with chopped parsley & fill each with a good teaspoonful of Amieux paté truffée [*sic*] before serving.

To make Pâté Truffe:
2 SHALLOTS, CHOPPED • 80 G BUTTER • 3 TRUFFLES
¾ TBS TRUFFLE JUICE • 100 ML DOUBLE CREAM • SALT AND PEPPER

Sauté the shallots in butter and when clear (4–5 mins), add the cream. Gently simmer and grate the truffles over the saucepan. Add the truffle juice, season with salt and pepper and simmer for ten minutes. Serves 4.

Onions au Gratin

'For all the "war depression" which sat so heavily upon him, Desmond
was a much sought-after guest for dinner and luncheon; at house-parties
and Saturdays to Mondays. He was a life-enhancer; he made a party "go":
hostesses could cease to fret that their guests might not get on. Desmond
was the magic ingredient, whose ease and charm ensured that they did.
His limitless curiosity about human nature led him to take an interest in
his least prepossessing neighbour at dinner; there was no bore so leaden
that he could not divine something of interest in him – their very tedium
could in itself be fascinating.'

Hugh and Mirabel Cecil, *Clever Hearts*, 1990

To itemize all the people with whom Desmond MacCarthy lunched, dined
and weekended is to give the A-list of the 1920s and 30s, beginning with King
George V. Desmond was the boy with the golden tongue, and a favourite with the
Asquiths, the Morrells and the Colefaxes. Diana Cooper, Neville Chamberlain,

Vanessa Bell, *Still Life in the Kitchen*, 1933.

Roger Fry, *Still Life of Fish*, 1928. Roger was an artist but excelled more as an art critic, lecturer, promoter and spokesman for modern art.

Harold Nicolson, Stanley Baldwin, Logan Pearsall Smith and Maurice Baring all vied for his company, as did John Maynard Keynes, Virginia Woolf and the rest of his Bloomsbury friends. He 'has become fascinated by *smart society* which inspires him to talk and gives him good food and drink', wrote Roger Fry in 1918. Indeed, thirty-two years later, while staying with his friend Somerset Maugham in the South of France, Desmond wrote to his wife, Molly: 'I am silent with pleasure at almost *every* dish that is put before me.' Desmond enjoyed *la douceur de vivre*, and others around him enjoyed him equally.

'I never knew my grandfather (I wish I had!),' Sophie MacCarthy relates, 'and I only recall this being a favourite dish of his because that's what my mother would say whenever she made it.' This is Desmond's granddaughter's recipe.

10 MEDIUM (BROWN-SKINNED) ONIONS • 2 PTS SEMI-SKIMMED MILK
1 BAY LEAF • GRATED NUTMEG • 2 TBS PLAIN FLOUR • 1 ½ OZ BUTTER
GRATED GRUYERE OR CHEDDAR CHEESE (OR A COMBINATION OF BOTH)
SALT & PEPPER

Carefully peel the onions and place in a wide-based pan and cover generously with milk adding a bay leaf, grated nutmeg and ½ tsp of salt. Simmer for 1 hour or until a pointed knife goes easily through. Lift the onions out with a slotted spoon and place in a gratin dish. Using the milk that the onions have cooked in, make a béchamel sauce by melting the butter and adding the flour to make a roux. Gradually add the milk to the roux until you have smooth sauce (not too thick) adding extra milk if necessary. Add the grated cheese; Gruyere if you like it lighter and more delicate, Cheddar if you prefer a stronger flavour or a combination of both works well too. A twist or two of ground black pepper then pour the sauce over the onions, sprinkle with more cheese and place in a hot oven for 15 mins until brown.

This dish is a very good accompaniment to roast beef or lamb. Serves 4–6.

Still Life Transformation

'When at last the apple, the kitchen table, and the bread-knife have come together, it is felt to be a victory for the human spirit over matter. The milk-jug and the ginger-jar are transformed. These common objects are invested with the majesty of mountains and the melody of music.'

Virginia Woolf, *Roger Fry: A Biography*, 1940

Of the three Bloomsbury artists – Roger Fry, Vanessa Bell and Duncan Grant – Roger was probably the least celebrated. There is no question that he had talent: his rhythm of line and his forms, textures and colours were aligned, proportionate and emotive, but his paintings were not quite so harmonic, nor his pots so rhapsodic, as those made by Vanessa and Duncan. Because Vanessa and Duncan worked side by side, they were able to focus primarily on their art. Roger to some extent got left behind as an artist; perhaps because he was so involved in his other work as a lecturer, art critic and public figure in the arts.

Duncan's Blanquette and Fricassée à l'Amegeville

In 1941 Duncan Grant received the highest accolade for design awarded in the United Kingdom – the Royal Designer for Industry Award, for his contribution to printed textiles. The prestigious award, first granted in 1936, recognizes the value of a designer's aesthetic work and its benefit to society.

On the back of an invitation to the Annual Reception of the Faculty of the Royal Designers for Industry, Duncan wrote down a recipe for Blanquette.

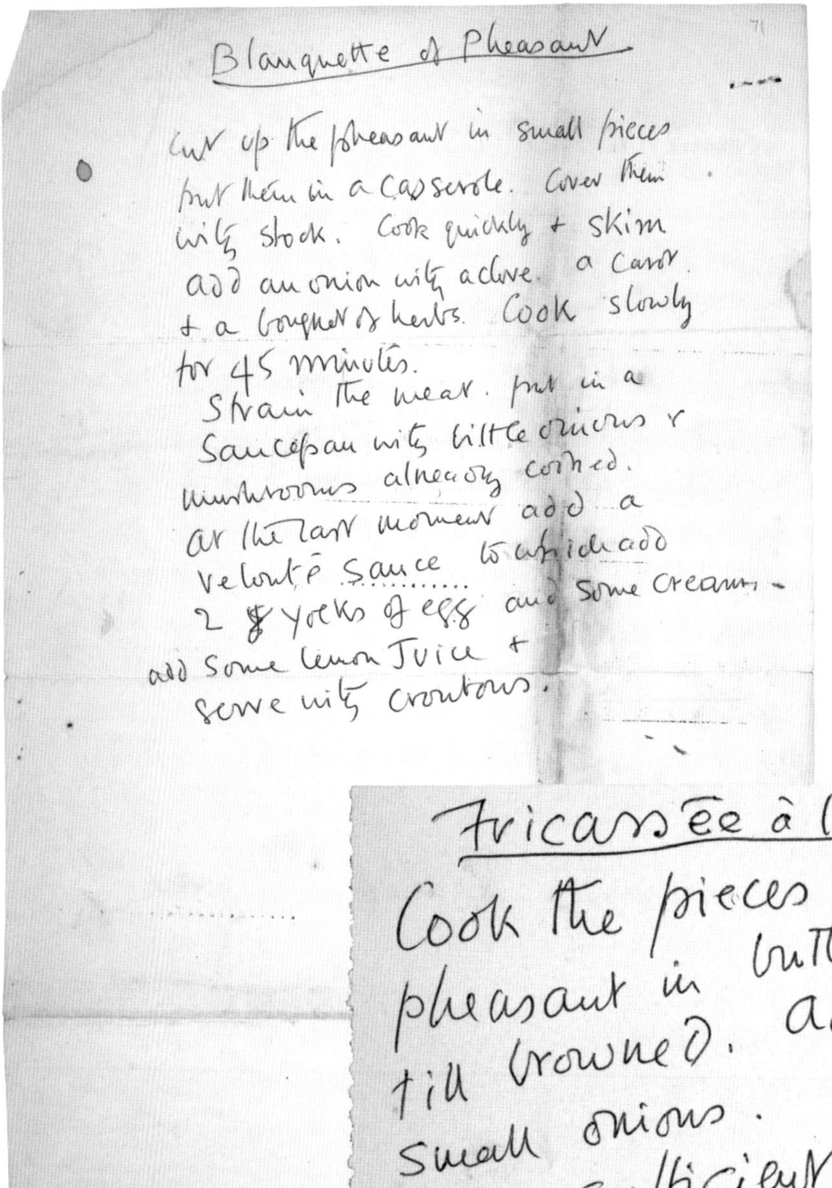

Blanquette of Pheasant

Cut up the pheasant in small pieces
put them in a casserole. Cover them
with stock. Cook quickly + skim
add an onion with a clove. a carrot.
+ a bouquet of herbs. Cook slowly
for 45 minutes.
Strain the meat. put in a
saucepan with little onions &
mushrooms already cooked.
At the last moment add a
velouté sauce to which add
2 yolks of egg and some cream.
add some lemon juice +
serve with croutons.

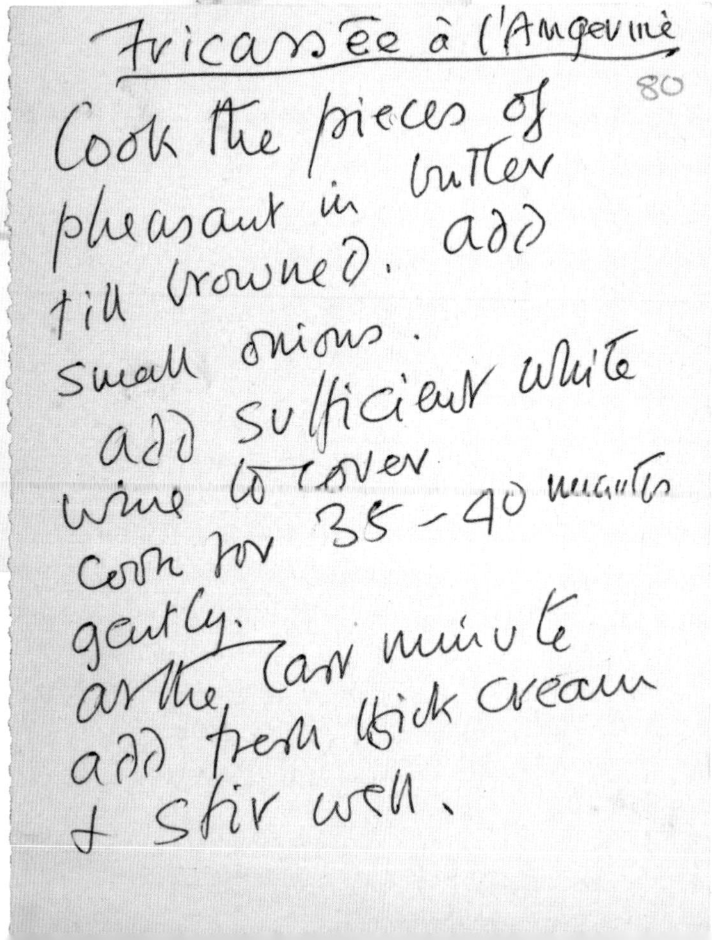

Fricassée à l'Amgeviné

80

Cook the pieces of
pheasant in butter
till browned. add
small onions.
add sufficient white
wine to cover
cook for 35 – 40 minutes
gently.
at the last minute
add fresh thick cream
+ stir well.

Duncan Grant's recipes for
Blanquette of Pheasant and
and Fricassée à l'Amegeville.

Vanessa Bell, *Pheasants*, 1931.

Another handwritten recipe of his, Fricassée à l'Amegeville, was found alongside it in the Grace Higgens archive at the British Library. Both dishes are delicious and easy to make.

Blanquette

Cut up the pheasant in small pieces. Put them in a casserole. Cover them with stock. Cook quickly & skim. Add an onion with a clove, a carrot & a bouquet of herbs. Cook slowly for 45 minutes. Strain the meat. Put in a saucepan with little onions & mushrooms already cooked. At the last moment add a velouté sauce [to make this sauce combine 2 tablespoons of clarified butter with 2 tablespoons of flour in a pot over medium heat and gradually whisk in 6 cups stock], to which add 2 yolks of egg and some cream. Add some lemon juice & serve with croutons.

Fricassée à l'Amegeville

Cook the pieces of pheasant in butter till browned. Add small onions. Add sufficient white wine to cover and cook for 35–40 minutes gently. At the last minute add fresh thick cream and stir well. [Serves 4.]

[NB: The easiest way to prepare this is to cut the breasts straight from the pheasant. Then there is no messy plucking and one can begin the cooking process immediately.]

Breakfast at Charleston

'Vanessa presided in the dining-room, the magnetic centre of all our thoughts and activities. At breakfast she was always down first, and sat for some time alone, enjoying her solitude. She had dressed and washed quietly, almost secretively, and would be in her habitual place on the far side of the round table, looking with dreamy reflectiveness at the still-life in the centre, or out of the window at the pond and the weather…. Now, as she ate a piece of buttered toast with coarse salt and held a steaming cup in long, straight be-ringed fingers, she considered her letters, absorbed the temper of the day, and braced herself to meet its demands….

'Duncan sometimes overslept, in which case someone would ask me to play a particularly irritating little *Écossaise* by Beethoven on the piano directly underneath his room. Eventually he would enter the dining-room, growling his dislike of the "beastly tune", ruffling his hair through his fingers and blowing his nose on a large red bandanna. Insouciant and natural, every day he peeled an orange, ate porridge and drank coffee with fresh appreciation, almost as though he had never done it before, conscious perhaps that each new day was a miracle that might not be repeated. For him, objects seemed alive, never simply things, just as repeated actions never bored him but became a source of reiterated pleasure. After wishing everyone good morning and hitching up his trousers, which were tied round his waist with an old red tie, he would squat to help himself to porridge, kept hot on a low trivet in front of the fire, and tell us about his dreams – often very amusing – or about the book which, tradition has it, he absorbed by putting under his pillow.'

Angelica Garnett, *Deceived with Kindness*, 1984

For breakfast at Charleston, Anne Olivier Bell, Quentin's wife, remembered 'scrambled eggs, or boiled eggs or poached eggs or eggs and bacon or sausage', and always

Vanessa Bell, *The Dining-Room Window, Charleston, c.* 1940. Vanessa was the first down to breakfast each morning. She would pour herself a cup of strong black coffee and in her mind's eye compose the day.

'bread and honey and toast and jam'. This is Angelica Garnett's recipe for brown bread. It is delicious served warm, in thick slices, first thing in the morning.

To make 4 loaves

3½ LBS COARSE BROWN FLOUR • 3 GOOD HANDFULS OF COARSE OATMEAL
1 TSP[OR 1 TBS] SALT • 1 TBS [FRESH, OR 2 TBS QUICK DRY] YEAST
2 TBS LARD OR ANY FAT • 1½ DSP BLACK TREACLE OR SYRUP
[APPX. 2 PTS WARM WATER OR MILK] • [1 TBS SUGAR]

Melt the fat and treacle in a basin and add a very little milk. Cover yeast with sugar and when liquid add to the fat. Have the flour and oatmeal in a bowl with salt, then add the other ingredients and mix together with a wooden spoon to a soft dough adding milk or water until it can be worked with the hands. Knead well on a floury board then set to rise by fire for 15 minutes [or until doubled in size]. Work well again on board [then rest, covered] for at least ½ hour then shape into [greased] loaf tins and set to rise again for 5 minutes or a bit longer. Bake in very hot oven for ¾ hour [10 minutes at 220°C and reduce to 180°C for remaining time].

Lunch at Charleston

'The round table came to Charleston in 1934. Vanessa's first decorations on it wore out and her new ones are now wearing in their turn, particularly at the end – if a round table can be said to have an end – where she habitually sat to serve the food.'

Quentin Bell, *Charleston: A Bloomsbury House and Garden*, 1987

The bell rang at one o'clock and Clive Bell and John Maynard Keynes put down their pens, Duncan Grant and Vanessa Bell set down their brushes, and the children, likewise, stopped what they were doing and ran into the house for lunch. (From the age of nine or ten the children were allowed to join the adults for meals in the dining room.)

Anne Olivier Bell recalled that 'lunch on the whole was usually ham or some salads and bread and cheese and possibly some beer'. But a letter from Angelica Garnett reveals a more varied lunchtime diet: on Sundays, heavenly aromas of roast Southdown mutton, sirloin or ham wafted through the house and mingled with the sweet smell of hot apple pie, treacle tart, roly-poly pudding, spotted dog

Duncan Grant, *Still Life with Pears*, 1929. Apples and pears grew abundantly in the garden at Charleston and were a continual source of inspiration for the Bloomsbury artists and cooks.

Duncan Grant, *The Hammock*, *c.* 1921–23.

or queen of pudding. On Mondays, they ate the leftovers from the Sunday roast (always carved by Vanessa) together with a mixed salad (usually dressed by Duncan), baked potatoes and pickled walnuts. On Tuesdays, there was fish – haddock or cod – and on Wednesdays, lamb or mutton. Grace made a shepherd's pie on Thursdays. On Fridays, she made sausages and, on Saturdays, her half-day off, it was eggs and bacon. Harveys beer, or water, was available to drink, and a freshly brewed pot of strong coffee was always enjoyed at the table at the end of each midday meal.

Here are two lunchtime recipes – Corned Mutton from Helen Anrep, and, from Grace Higgens, Queen of Pudding, which satisfied even Duncan Grant's sweet tooth. Today, one can buy mutton from speciality butchers. It has quite a strong flavour and the flesh can be a little tough, so allow extra time to prepare and cook this meat. To roast mutton, allow 40 minutes per pound (off the bone) in a 150°C oven. This corned mutton recipe is, however, for the adventurous cook. It is surprisingly good, but preparation is a little time-consuming.

Corned Mutton

I LEG OF MUTTON • 2 TBS SALT • I TSP BLACK PEPPER
I TSP GROUND CLOVES • I TSP CINNAMON • I TSP ALLSPICE
I TBS BROWN SUGAR • I GILL VINEGAR

Take a leg of mutton and corn it with the following mixture: Two heaping table-spoonfuls of fine salt, one teaspoonful of black pepper, one of ground cloves, cinnamon and allspice each, and a heaping tablespoon of brown sugar. Mix thoroughly and put the mutton in a deep pan, and rub it into it well. Sprinkle what remains over the top of the leg, and turn a gill of vinegar over it. Rub it daily for a week, taking up the brine that has drained off into the pan and pouring it over the mutton. When ready to boil wash off the salt and spices with cold water and place the leg into boiling water, letting it boil up, and remove the scum which rises; then put it back upon the stove and let it simmer slowly for three hours – if it weighs ten pounds; longer if heavier. Take it from the pot and place upon a platter with heavy weights over it and let it stand overnight before it is served. Then cut into very thin slices, thin as a wafer[.]

Queen of Pudding

2 OZ SPONGE CAKE • ½ PT BOILING MILK • 1 EGG

2 OZ CASTER SUGAR • ¾ OZ BUTTER • JAM

Soak sponge cakes well in almost boiling milk, then beat yolk of eggs [*sic*] well into mixture. [Grease ovenproof dish with butter and add cake mixture.] Put into oven until set [approximately 8–10 minutes at 180°C]. When set, cover top with jam, whip white of egg up stiffly with 1 dessertspoonful of caster sugar and spoon onto the top. Put back into oven until set [15–20 minutes]. Serve hot. [Serves 4–6.]

Charleston Grouse

'Dinner was at eight, and started invariably with soup, made with the rest of the joint. It was ample and rich, strong enough to be a whole meal in itself, and was tasted with care and appreciation by Duncan and Clive. Vanessa would change her dress and wear earrings – the men however merely washed their hands and perhaps changed their ties…. But there would also be a choice of game, shot by Clive in the neighbourhood…. And we were proud of the fact that we ate our own artichokes.'

Angelica Garnett to Anna Fewster, 5 October 2009

Once, when Leonard and Virginia Woolf and T. S. Eliot came to dine at Charleston, three enormous platters of roast grouse appeared on the sideboard. In contrast with John Maynard and Lydia Keynes's stinginess in serving grouse at Tilton (see pp. 152–54), Vanessa had inadvertently ordered 'two a mouth' instead of 'a bird between two', as Clive had suggested. This story has been improved with each retelling, and I have read accounts of eleven, sixteen and sometimes even twenty-two grouse appearing on the legendary occasion.

This recipe from *Warne's Everyday Cookery* is sufficient for three persons. Be sure to measure quantities accordingly.

1 GROUSE • 1 TSP LEMON JUICE • 1½ OZ BUTTER

1 SLICE OF FAT BACON • 2 OZ BACON FAT OR DRIPPING • SALT • PEPPER

FLOUR • WATERCRESS • FRIED BREADCRUMBS

Pluck and draw the bird, wipe it inside and out with a damp cloth. Mix a piece of butter the size of a walnut with salt, pepper and lemon juice, and put it inside the bird with the liver. Then truss as for a roast fowl, using, however, a finer trussing needle and fine string. Tie a piece of fat bacon over the breast and roast the bird in front of a clear fire or in a good oven. Baste it often with dripping, bacon fat or butter. A few minutes before serving, remove the slice of bacon and dredge the breast with flour, baste it with a little oiled butter and brown. The time for roasting depends upon the size and age of the bird. A young bird takes from 25 to 30 minutes and an older one ¾ hour.

To dish: Put the grouse on a hot dish, remove the trussing strings and skewers. Make gravy in the dripping tin as for roast beef, pour a very little round, garnish with watercress. Hand the rest of the gravy in a tureen. Chip potatoes, browned breadcrumbs and a green salad should accompany grouse.

T. S. Eliot and Virginia Woolf, 1924. Virginia set the type for Tom's *The Waste Land*, which was published by the Hogarth Press in 1923; during this time Tom, Virginia and Leonard became very close friends.

Two Charleston Meat Recipes

For many years the only utility in the kitchen at Charleston was a cold-water tap. Electricity did not arrive until 1933, and a refrigerator with an icebox did not arrive until after 1939 (Clive Bell's contribution – he liked ice with his gin). Before this, blocks of ice were used to keep the food chilled, and the coal-fired range in the kitchen was used for cooking and heating the bathing and cleaning water. Groceries were delivered on the back of a horse-drawn van from Flint's grocery store in Lewes and the local butcher delivered pre-ordered cuts of meat once a week.

Grace Higgens had many ways of preparing meat at Charleston. These are two of her recipes.

Pies Kidneys

Cut them in slices [after removing the core] and brown with onions and chopped parsley, then add stock or water and if possible any sort of wine or sherry [to cover] and allow to simmer very slowly till quite tender for ½ or ¾ of an hour. Serve with risotto or plain rice [if not used as pie filling].

Fried Steaks [Hamburger Patties]

1 LB MINCED BEEF • 1 TBS GRATED OR CHOPPED ONION
2 OZ FINELY CHOPPED SUET • 1 PINCH OF GROUND ALLSPICE
PEPPER AND SALT

Mix all ingredients together & form into cakes 3 inches in diameter & about an inch in thickness. Dip them very lightly in flour, using only enough to give a thin film on the meat.

Fry quickly on both sides in a little boiling fat, then cover over and fry slowly for ten mins can be served with mashed potatoes or fried onions.

Make the gravy by adding 1 tablespoonful of flour to the fat in pan pour in a cupful of stock or gravy stir until boiling then strain around meat.

Salmon at Charleston

Working as she was for artists and art critics, Grace Higgens felt the need to make dishes that would titillate the eyes as well as the taste buds. Her instructions for serving cold salmon are indicative of the care and attention she gave to cooking and the pride she took in presenting dishes beautifully. Her grilled salmon recipe appears here too; it can also be cooked in advance and served cold.

Vanessa Bell, *The Cook*, 1948. Grace Higgens (née Germany) was not only cook at Charleston; from 1934 she was also resident housekeeper. She and her husband, Walter, lived in 'High Holborn', the attic room above the kitchen. In 1935 their only child, John, was born.

Dishing Cold Salmon

Cover bottom of dish with salad, arange [*sic*] cold salmon on top, cut hard boiled egg into slices and arange [*sic*] on top of salmon, cut a cucumber into thin slices and put round edge of dish, cover over egg & salmon with mayonnaise, leaving cucumber uncovered like a frill round edge. A glass dish looks nicest. Stoned olives are nice placed on mayonnaise.

Grilled Salmon

Light grill about 10 mins before wanting to get hot. Grill salmon cutlets about ten minutes on each side. [Cooking time depends on the thickness of the steaks.]

Serve with cucumber cut into slices and covered with vinager [*sic*], potatoes, lettuce Salad, & mayonnaise.

Glyndebourne Gammon

Glyndebourne, that great English opera festival, not far from Charleston, began in 1934 with a performance of Mozart's *The Marriage of Figaro*. The occasion is a formal black-tie affair, and one traditionally brings food and a bottle for refreshment during the intervals. Watching and listening to virtuoso performances, dressing up and delighting in the beautiful landscaped gardens of the Christie estate, with a picnic, are just a few of the reasons why Glyndebourne is probably – still – the finest, most atmospheric operatic event of the English summer season.

In 1935 Virginia and Leonard Woolf (she in a blue silk dress, he in a black broadcloth dinner jacket) attended Mozart's *The Magic Flute* at Glyndebourne. At the end of Act 1, after Tamino, the tenor, has been ushered off to the Temple of Ordeal to prove himself worthy of Pamina, the soprano, the Woolfs stepped out of the new 330-seater auditorium and strolled down to the lake for a plate of ham.

Mozart was a favourite with Bloomsbury. The following year, Vanessa Bell, Angelica Garnett, Duncan Grant, Marjorie Strachey and the art historian Kenneth Clark went to see Mozart's *Don Giovanni* at Glyndebourne. This time, during the

The Green Room lawn at Glyndebourne, 1936.

Roger Fry, *Omega Virginal*, 1917–18. Classical music was important to the Bloomsbury members.

long interval, writes Vanessa's biographer Frances Spalding, 'Vanessa herself, as they sat over their picnic supper, gave an impromptu rendering of "What shall we do with the broken tumbler", unaware of the startled head that looked out from the door which led to the singers' quarters. The family collapsed with laughter and Vanessa, taking this as a compliment to her performance, sang on until a whole troupe of singers emerged "and I had to pull myself together and behave as a polite lady making way for them past our broken tumblers and sandwiches. Altogether it was a successful evening and the music was divine."'

It was not until after the war that picnicking at Glyndebourne became popular (most members of the audience in 1934 dined in the Christie Dining Hall). So, when Virginia and Leonard walked down to the lake during the interval, they would have enjoyed their plate of cold ham in an idyllic, tranquil location in relative privacy.

This recipe for boiled gammon (a similar cut to ham, only it has not been cured) from the Grace Higgens archive makes perfect picnic food as it can be cooked in advance, chilled, sliced and served later as required.

12 LB HAM • 1 ONION • 2 CARROTS • PEPPERCORNS • CLOVES • SUGAR
HONEY • ORANGE JUICE • ORANGE SLICES TO GARNISH

Place the joint in a large pan and cover with cold water and soak overnight.
Wash the joint and place on a shallow trivet in a pan and cover with cold water
and bring slowly to the boil. Add 1 onion peeled and cut in half, 2 carrots and a
few peppercorns. Simmer gently for 3½ hours.

To serve hot, cool for a few minutes then remove the skin. Place in a roasting tin and score the fat diagonally across and stud with cloves. Blend the sugar,
honey and orange juice and pour over the joint. Bake in a moderate oven 180°C for
thirty minutes. Baste during the cooking. Serve hot. Garnish with orange slices.

Angelica's Birthday Roast

'Here we are spending a very domestic Christmas. Really I think I shall
advertise it. "Mr and Mrs Clive Bell and family at home at Charleston,
Christmas 1923 – no one else admitted."… I haven't been here at this time
since five years ago when Angelica was born. It was very romantic then
– the first Christmas of peace and a most lovely moonlit, frosty night. I
remember waking up in the early morning after she had been born and
hearing the farm-men come up to work singing carols and realizing it was
Christmas Day, and it seemed rather extraordinary to have a baby then—'

Vanessa Bell to Margery Snowden, 1923

Angelica Bell was the love child of Vanessa Bell and Duncan Grant, the living
personification of Bloomsbury's most valued principles: love above convention;
independence, integrity, honesty and intelligence. She was the beautiful, talented,
darling baby of Bloomsbury and her arrival on 25 December 1918 was (secretly)
heralded as a victory for independent spirit.

Each year her birthday was celebrated* alongside that other significant
birthday, when turkey, plum pudding and Christmas trimmings adorned the
dining-room table. 'They didn't wish to celebrate Christmas in any way,' recalled
Anne Olivier Bell, 'they thought it was a religious festival which they didn't agree
with.' Still, if the Bells were staying at Cleeve House, Clive's family house in
Wiltshire, there would be an aspect of religiosity to their Christmas celebrations;
but at Charleston, as Vanessa, Clive and the children were non-believers, the sense
of occasion began when Clive arrived with chocolates, wine and other 'goodies'
from Fortnum & Mason. Small presents added an element of enchantment to the

* Clive Bell gave Angelica her birthday present on his own birthday, 16 September.

festivities, and the over-excited children helped to create an atmosphere of joyous celebration.

Most fourteenth birthday parties are celebrated with sleepovers and party games – but not Angelica's. In 1932 her birthday was spent in fancy dress, with Virginia and Leonard Woolf dressed as Queen Victoria and the Prince Consort. It was a fitting theme for a Christmas birthday, since Victoria and Albert have been credited with popularizing many aspects of what is now the traditional Christmas celebration, including the festive feast, parlour games and indoor Christmas trees. For those who could afford it, roast turkey with seasonal trimmings also became fashionable, along with Christmas crackers filled with sweets and holly, garlands and mistletoe decorations for the home. Thus it was that at Charleston in 1932, the Bloomsbury members, renowned for their flair and for never doing things by halves, celebrated Angelica's fourteenth birthday party in authentic royal style.

This time-honoured method for roasting turkey is from Olive Humphries's *Cook with Ease*, published in 1935.

Vanessa Bell, *Angelica Bell*, c. 1930. Angelica was born at Charleston on Christmas Day, 1918.

Draw and truss the turkey. Wipe the inside with a damp cloth. Stuff one end of the bird with veal stuffing, and the other end with either sausage or chestnut stuffing. Sew or skewer the flap of skin at the neck over the stuffing, and secure it to the back of the turkey. Sprinkle the bird with flour, salt and pepper, and spread freely with bacon fat, lard or dripping. Rashers of bacon or sausage may be placed over the breast, or the bird may be covered with a well-greased paper, removing either of these ¼ hour before dishing.

Grease the oven grid bars and place the turkey on them, allowing the fat to drip into the bottom of the oven. Allow ¼ hour to the lb. and ¼ hour over.

Serve with sausage, bread sauce and bacon rolls.

Plovers' Eggs with Clive

'If Clive had ever suffered embarrassment from our fictitious relationship, he seemed determined to disregard it now that I was growing up. For him, well-off, living half his life *en garçon* in London, it was a delight to give me my first oyster or plovers' egg, and introduce me to his cosmopolitan and society friends, with whom we would lunch at the oval mahogany table, sitting long into the afternoon under the influence of still champagne, the remains of purple passion fruit crushed on our plates, our words left floating in the air. Clive enjoyed showing me off.'

Angelica Garnett, *Deceived with Kindness*, 1984

'Truth' and 'honesty', Bloomsbury's fundamental precepts, were apparently ignored when it came to Angelica Bell's true parentage. Shortly after Julian Bell's death in 1937, Vanessa told Angelica the truth: Duncan Grant, not Clive Bell, was her biological father. That she had been deceived for eighteen years and led to believe that she was a 'Bell' was hard for her to accept, and for years she was confused and felt emotionally isolated, especially as 'no one seemed capable of talking openly and naturally on the subject'. In her autobiography, *Deceived with Kindness*, written forty-nine years later, Angelica revealed how hard it was for her to come to terms with her parents' 'lie'. 'I'm afraid,' recalled Virginia Nicholson, 'it haunted her all her life, one way or another.'

Today it is illegal to collect plovers' eggs due to the dwindling population numbers of some species, such as peewits, but pheasant eggs make an ideal substitute. They are rich and delicious and take only three minutes to boil. This recipe has been adapted from Eggs en Cocotte Pascal in the Frances Partridge collection.

4 PLOVERS' EGGS • 4 TBS CREAM
1 LEVEL TSP FRENCH MUSTARD • 4 DSP CHOPPED CHIVES

Place the plovers' eggs into a pot of cold water and bring to the boil. Remove after seven minutes and rinse under cold water. Just before serving, remove the shells and slice the eggs in half.

To make the sauce, combine the cream and mustard together and heat until hot. Remove from heat, stir in the chives (and any other fresh herbs) and pour over the eggs. Serve immediately.

Pudding for Julian

And one, my best, with such a calm of mind,
And, I have thought, with clear experience
Of what is felt of waste, confusion, pain,
Faced with a strong good sense, stubborn and plain;
Patient and sensitive, cynic and kind.
The sensuous mind within preoccupied
By lucid vision of form and colour and space,
The careful hand and eye, and where resides
An intellectual landscape's living face,
Oh certitude of mind and sense, and where
Native I love, and feel accustomed air.

Julian Bell, from the poem 'Autobiography', *c.* 1934

Vanessa Bell's gift for organization and her ability to create a stimulating environment positioned her, quite naturally, at the centre of Bloomsbury. She nurtured the group through three decades of social, political, economic and artistic reform and was instrumental in maintaining its cohesiveness.

At home she threw herself into motherhood and ran her household with calm efficiency, care and love. At times her honesty and her protective efforts towards those she cared for could be stifling, and her displays of affection were sometimes awkward and excessive. 'I longed for her to want me to be strong and independent,' wrote her daughter Angelica, 'whereas apparently all she desired was to suffocate me with caresses.'

Vanessa's special fondness for her eldest son, Julian, was all too apparent. Quentin Bell remembered an occasion, soon after Julian's return from China in 1937, when, 'while his plans were still in a state of flux, there was a meal at Charleston eaten by Vanessa, we three children and, I think, Duncan. Vanessa served a pudding;

Julian Bell and Vanessa
Bell, 1909. Vanessa's special
fondness for her eldest son,
Julian, and the way in which
she displayed her 'maternal
passion' was at times 'a little
absurd', noted Quentin Bell.

she gave half to Julian, the rest of us divided what remained. Vanessa herself realized that there was something more than a little absurd about this method of displaying affection and said something like: "You see, I have to."… Luckily he liked the pudding and ate it all up with an unembarrassed grin. He, more than any of us, was able to accept the maternal passion without confusion or irritation.'

Nonsense

'He was a wilful child, swift and erratic in his movements; he looked at one from large eyes and planned devilment…. One saw him often naked, romping in the old orchard with his younger brother; their mother following them about with a camera in her hand. Julian was shrill, sometimes noisy, always rather catlike and quick. My first row with him was when I found him standing, unconscious of evildoing, on some vegetable-marrow plants that he had trampled to pieces. My anger flared up and Julian faced me with astonished wide-open wild eyes. Taken in the midst of unconscious wrong-doing, and overwhelmed with abuse, he was white with anger and as fierce as a little spitting tiger-kitten, and yielded only because my passion equalled his and I was bigger.'

David Garnett, 'Julian', 1937

Uneasy about the rising tide of Fascism in Spain, and restless to do something about it, Julian resigned early* from his teaching post at Wuhan University in China and returned to England to sign up. His poem 'Nonsense' (published in 1936 in *Work from the Winter and Other Poems*), provides a hint of his feelings during this troubled time:

> Sing a song of sixpence,
> A pocketful of rye,
> The lover's in the garden
> And battle's in the sky.
> The banker's in the city
> Getting off his gold;
> Oh isn't it a pity
> The rye can't be sold.
>
> The queen is drinking sherry
> And dancing to a band;
> A crowd may well feel merry
> That it does not understand.
>
> The banker turns his gold about
> But that won't sell the rye,
> Starve and grow cold without,
> And ask the reason why
> The guns are in the garden,
> And battle's in the sky.

Julian volunteered to drive ambulances for the anti-Fascists, thus vaguely appeasing the pacifists and members of his family who did not want him to go and fight in the Spanish Civil War. Julian, 'fundamentally political in thought and action', as he himself admitted, left for the front in June 1937. Six weeks later, at the Battle of Brunete, a piece of shrapnel struck his chest and lodged in his lung. 'Well, I always wanted a mistress and a chance to go to the war', he said to his doctor (a friend from Cambridge days), 'and now I've had both.' He died a few hours later.

Julian was a free spirit, a poet, an Apostle and his premature death in 1937, like that of his Uncle Thoby in 1906, left a hole at the heart of Bloomsbury. This time, however, there was no marriage or collective ideology that could bridge the loss of such a rare, young and much-loved individual.

* *Julian Bell was caught having an affair with the wife of the dean of Wuhan University; hence his resignation after only sixteen months.*

Virginia Woolf, *c.* 1917, photographed by Ottoline Morrell. Virginia enjoyed making bread and taught her cooks how to do it properly.

Monk's House Cottage Loaf

'[T]here was one thing in the kitchen that Mrs Woolf was very good at doing: she could make beautiful bread. The first question she asked me when I went to Monk's House was if I knew how to make it. I told her that I had made some for my family, but I was no expert at it. "I will come into the kitchen, Louie," she said, "and show you how to do it. We have always made our own bread." I was surprised how complicated the process was and how accurately Mrs Woolf carried it out. She showed me how to make the dough with the right quantities of yeast and flour, and then how to knead it. She returned three or four times during the morning to knead it again. Finally, she made the dough into the shape of a cottage loaf and baked it at just the right temperature. I would say that Mrs Woolf was not a practical person – for instance, she could not sew or knit or drive a car – but this was a job needing practical skill which she was able to do well every time. It took me many weeks to be as good as Mrs Woolf at making bread, but I went to great lengths practising and in the end, I think, I beat her at it.'

Louie Mayer, quoted in *Recollections of Virginia Woolf*, 1972

According to Louie Mayer, who was the Woolf's cook and housekeeper from 1934, Virginia was a capable cook but 'did not want to give time to cooking and preferred to be in her room working'. She did, however, like to bake bread, and in doing so, 'She used every dish in the place and left all the washing up,' said Nellie Boxall, the Woolfs' previous cook. Despite the mess, or perhaps because of it, Virginia's home-made cottage loaf was superb – delicious, light and golden brown – every time.

Chicken Strut

'I am free for tea on Wednesday or Thursday or for dinner on Wednesday. And if any of those times suited you I should be very glad to show you what little I know about the Grizzly Bear, or the Chicken Strut.'

T. S. Eliot to Virginia Woolf, 2 June 1927

'I shall walk across the meadows to Lewes and buy a chicken.'

Virginia Woolf to Gerald Brenan, 10 August 1923

Virginia Woolf at Monk's House, 1931. Virginia spent a few hours each afternoon out of doors, usually in her garden, or walking. Occasionally, her daily walk took her into Lewes to buy a chicken, a distance of approximately four miles.

Virginia Woolf was a great walker. When in London, most afternoons she walked around Bloomsbury, through the parks, along Oxford Street and in and out of the market stalls around Covent Garden. In Sussex she would stride out purposefully with her walking stick, heading north or south along the banks of the River Ouse, over the Downs, sometimes even across the meadows to Lewes, to fetch a chicken for dinner. This was revision time and, unabashed, she would speak aloud, sounding out words, trying out phrases and re-enacting entire conversations, capturing and perfecting the rhythm, mood and cadence of her fictional characters.

In 1927 T. S. Eliot offered to show Virginia how to perform some of the more radical (and then deemed degenerate) American dance steps, including the Grizzly Bear, the Memphis Shake and the Chicken Strut. One can only but wonder if Virginia was ever tempted to Strut the four and a half miles into Lewes to buy her chicken.

This chicken recipe is from Frances Partridge, who was herself an enthusiastic dancer.

Suggested ingredients
1 LARGE CHICKEN • SALT AND PEPPER • 1 ½ PT MILK
1 ONION, CHOPPED • 250 G MUSHROOMS, HALVED OR QUARTERED
1 DSP FLOUR • 100 ML CREAM

Skin & cut up chicken; flour, pepper & salt it. Bring 1½ pints milk to the boil, put in chicken & simmer for ½ an hour. Then add onions & mushrooms, & cook for another hour. 10 mins before serving, thicken with flour & some cream.

Leonard Woolf and his dog Pinka in the garden at Monk's House, 1931. In 1937 Virginia Woolf followed doctor's orders and made pots of creamy rice pudding for Leonard, who was suffering from a strange unidentified illness. From the Monk's House photograph album.

Rest and Rice Pudding for Leonard (and Flush)

'And then she looked up and saw Flush. Something unusual in his look must have struck her. She paused. She laid down her pen. Once he had roused her with a kiss, and she had thought that he was Pan. He had eaten chicken and rice pudding soaked in cream. He had given up the sunshine for her sake. She called him to her and said she forgave him.'

Virginia Woolf, Flush: A Biography, 1933

At the beginning of 1937 Leonard Woolf developed a strange illness, which left him in bed with a temperature and the doctors and Virginia completely confounded. The doctors could do nothing but recommend plenty of R & R (rest and rice pudding). After three weeks of following their advice, Leonard's situation gradually began to improve.

Virginia diligently made quantities of rice pudding for Leonard. This traditional recipe is from *The Recipe Book of Atora* (1925). It is creamy and sweet and, in small quantities, comforting – even for dogs.

2 OZ CAROLINA RICE • 1 PT MILK • 2 OZ SUGAR • PINCH OF SALT
1 TBS SHREDDED ATORA [SHREDDED BEEF SUET] • NUTMEG

Put all ingredients into a pie-dish, pour milk over and stir well. Grate some nutmeg over the top, and bake in slow oven [140°C] for 2 hours. [Serves 4.]

Vita's Magnificent Strasbourg Pie

'Oh an English Christmas! We are not Christians; we are not social; we have no part in the fabric of the world, but, all the same, Christmas flattens us out like a steam roller; turkey, pudding, tips, waits, holly, good wishes, presents, sweets; so here we sit, on Boxing day, at Rodmell, over a wood fire, & I can only rouse myself by thinking of you.'

Virginia Woolf to Jacques Raverat, 26 December 1924

For Christmas in 1937, Vita Sackville-West sent Leonard and Virginia a delicious Strasbourg pie (a raised pie containing foie gras), which they enjoyed eating with T. S. Eliot. 'Heaven above us, what immortal geese must have gone to make it!' exclaimed Virginia. 'Complete silence reigned. The poet ate; the novelist ate; even Leonard, who had a chill inside, ate.'

The following year Vita sent the Woolfs another magnificent pie, and this time it really was a godsend: a thick snowstorm had brought East Sussex to a halt: there was no electricity, pipes froze and, on Christmas day at Monk's House, the cooker refused to start. Vita's Strasbourg pie was a blessing.

Since it proved impossible to locate a recipe dating from the 1930s, I offer instead this superb Strasbourg pie from *Lobscouse and Spotted Dog* (1997), the gastronomic companion to Patrick O'Brian's Aubrey–Maturin series of novels. This pie is a match for Vita's and quite magnificent.

1 WHOLE FRESH FOIE GRAS, ABOUT 1 ¼ LB

1 LB PUFF PASTE • 1 LB BACON

1 EGG BEATEN WITH 1 TSP WATER

Preheat oven to 450°[F]. Trim the foie gras, removing any dark spots. On a lightly floured board, roll out three-quarters of the Puff Paste until it is about ¼ inch thick. Trace the shape of a hinged metal pâté mold on a piece of paper. Cut it out to make a pattern for the top crust. Line the pâté mold with the sheet of Puff Paste, crimping and trimming as necessary. Leave a ¾-inch overhang. Line the pastry with bacon, draping it so that it covers the bottom and hangs over the sides. Put the foie gras into the mold, cutting and packing as needed to make it fit. Fold the bacon over the foie gras, and lay additional bacon strips on the top, so that it is completely covered.

Roll out the remaining Puff Paste until it is large enough to cover the pâté mold. Cut it to size using the paper pattern. Cut a small hole in the center of the top crust. Place the top crust over the mold. Bring up the overhanging edges of the bottom crust, brush them with the egg wash, and cement them over the rim of the top crust, pressing gently to seal.

Cut decorative shapes from the pastry scraps and arrange them on the crust, covering the seam, and secure them in place with the egg wash. Brush a thin layer of the remaining egg wash over the entire top of the crust.

Place the mold on a rimmed cookie sheet and bake at 450° for 10 minutes. Reduce heat to 350°[F] and bake for another 20 minutes. Cool thoroughly on a rack and unmold carefully onto a serving dish. Serves 20.

Suffrage Angel Cake

'Dame Ethel [Smyth] was a highly eccentric character. On one occasion the Woolfs invited her to dine at their house at Rodmell near Lewes, Sussex. Dame Ethel bicycled the twenty miles from the village where she lived to Rodmell, dressed in rough tweeds. About two miles from her destination she decided that perhaps she was not suitably dressed

Monk's House under snow, 1938. From the Monk's House photograph album.

for a dinner party. She thought that possibly corsets were required to smarten up her figure. Accordingly, she went into a village shop and asked for some corsets. There were none. Distressed, she looked round the shop and her eye lighted on a bird cage, which she purchased. About twenty minutes later, Virginia went into her garden to discover Dame Ethel in a state of undress in the shrubbery struggling with the bird cage, which she was wrenching into the shape of corsets and forcing under her tweeds.'

Stephen Spender, World Within World, 1951

'March of the Women', the anthem of the suffragettes, was written by the composer Ethel Smyth, a fiery personality who was imprisoned for throwing stones through a cabinet minister's window. While 'doing time' in Holloway Prison, she was often seen conducting her popular battle tune with the wave of her toothbrush. Fifty-four years later, at the age of seventy-one, she fell in love with Virginia Woolf.

But Virginia, despite having written three feminist classics – *A Room of One's Own* (1929), 'Professions for Women' (1931) and *Three Guineas* (1938) – was not a suffragette. She had mixed feelings about the movement and preferred to use words, rather than stones, in her fight for gender equality.

Virginia Woolf and Dame Ethel Smyth, unknown date. At the age of seventy-one, Ethel, a convicted suffragette, fell in love with Virginia.

This recipe is from *The Suffrage Cookbook* (1915).

11 EGGS [ROOM TEMPERATURE] • 1 CUP SWANSDOWN [PLAIN WHITE] FLOUR
1½ CUPS GRANULATED SUGAR • 1 HEAPING TSP CREAM OF TARTAR
2 TSP VANILLA • 1 PINCH OF SALT

Beat the eggs until light – not stiff; sift sugar 7 times, add to eggs, beating as little as possible. Sift flour 9 times, using only the cupful, discarding the extra flour; then put in the flour the cream of tartar; add this to the eggs and sugar; now the vanilla. Put in an angel cake pan with feet. Put in the oven with very little heat [120°C]. Great care must be used in baking this cake to insure success. Light the oven when you commence preparing material. After the first 10 minutes in oven, increase heat and continue to do so every 5 minutes until the last 4 or 5 minutes, when strong heat [205°C] must be used. At 30 minutes remove cake and invert pan allowing it to stand thus until cold.

Chocolate and Tea with Freud

'I only once met Freud in person. The Nazis invaded Austria on March 11, 1938, and it took three months to get Freud out of their clutches. He arrived in London in the first week in June and three months later moved into a house in Maresfield Gardens which was to be his permanent home. When he and his family had had time to settle down there, I made discreet enquiries to see whether he would like Virginia and me to come and see him. The answer was yes, and in the afternoon of Saturday, January 28,

1939, we went and had tea with him. I feel no call to praise the famous men whom I have known. Nearly all famous men are disappointing or bores, or both. Freud was neither; he had an aura, not of fame, but of greatness.… He was extraordinarily courteous in a formal, old-fashioned way – for instance, almost ceremoniously he presented Virginia with a flower. There was something about him as of a half-extinct volcano, something sombre, suppressed, reserved. He gave me the feeling … of great gentleness, but behind the gentleness, great strength.'

Leonard Woolf, *Downhill All the Way*, 1967

The Bloomsbury Group played a significant role in the development of psycho-analysis in the early part of the twentieth century. From 1927 onwards Virginia's brother Adrian Stephen and his wife, Karin, practised as qualified analysts; they were among the first people in Britain to do so. Lytton Strachey's younger brother James and his wife, Alix, were also greatly influenced by Sigmund Freud and travelled to Vienna to be psychoanalysed by him. When they returned to London they opened their own practice, operating out of their flat at 41 Gordon Square. Later, when Freud asked them to translate his work, they agreed, and devoted their lives to making his writings available in English. The Woolfs also hopped on the Freudian bandwagon: in 1924 the Hogarth Press published the Stracheys' translations of Freud's *Collected Papers* in four volumes and, later, all twenty-four volumes of *The Standard Edition of the Complete Psychological Works of Sigmund Freud* (1953–74).

Why, one wonders, if Bloomsbury had such a profound interest in psycho-analysis, did Virginia not seek treatment for her own mental instability? There were two reasons: first, psychoanalysis was deemed to be dangerous for those with suicidal tendencies; second, both Leonard and Virginia believed that her genius was linked to her madness, and that a cure might kill her ability to write.

Alix and James Strachey undoubtedly had their own 'complexes'. It is said that when Alix first fell in love with James, she sat for two days and nights at the door of the Strachey parents' house nourishing herself entirely on chocolate, until James gave in. They eventually married and later Gerald Brenan noted the couple's 'spare, nutritious, calorie-calculated meals, which were taken without wine or beer because alcohol clouds the mind'. Alix was incapable of using a hotel lavatory unless it was directly connected to her bedroom. Alix and James also suffered from a 'neurotic dread of cold'. Surely when he analysed Alix and James in Vienna, Freud must have had much to say to them, especially about the chocolate.

Summer Party at Charleston

'The scene was set in Charleston, in fact on the very spot where it was acted; but the time was about forty years hence, in fact what we now call "the present". The characters were a group of visitors to Charleston and a uniformed guide. Christopher Strachey was the guide, Mlle Jane Simone Bussy (Janie played a major role in most of these theatricals) was a tyrannical French mother, Miss Eve Younger was her hapless daughter, I was a very large American lady…. The guide did most of the talking. He talked about the furniture, and the furniture was the audience. Maynard Keynes was, of course, a safe, Leonard and Virginia Woolf were twin bookcases labelled Fact and Fiction, my father was an eighteenth-century *escritoire*, and so on….

'I was sufficiently imprudent to show the script to a friend, one of those girls who tell you things "for your own good". Her comment was that it was a very bad sketch and that it was based upon an absurdity. The absurdity being that anyone should ever want to preserve Charleston.

'No doubt it was a pretty bad play; but it does allow me to say that, on one occasion at least, I have been a prophet.'

Quentin Bell in 1986, recalling 'Charleston Revisited', performed on 30 August 1939

For Quentin Bell's nineteenth birthday in August 1929, the tradition of a summer party was begun at Charleston. All local Bloomsbury members – the Bells, the Woolfs, the Keyneses and Duncan Grant – assembled for tea and birthday cake and stayed until late. Glasses of audit ale (a strong homemade beer brewed at Oxford and Cambridge) were liberally passed around, while quantities of grouse were prepared by Grace Higgens in the kitchen. There were fireworks. Reds, blues and yellows lit up the night sky and, as gunpowder mixed with cigar smoke, the occasional whistle and bang punctuated the quick-witted banter.

The last summer party took place on 30 August 1939, just before the outbreak of the Second World War. Vanessa Bell organized a buffet of cold pies, puddings and jellied soup, and everyone casually helped themselves. Cold bottles of Harveys Brown, the local beer from Lewes, were available to drink and afterwards a play, 'Charleston Revisited', written by Janie Bussy and Quentin, was performed in Duncan's studio. It was a satirical portrait of the Bloomsbury Group at Charleston, 'forty years hence'.

In his memoir *Elders and Betters,* Quentin admitted that within the family circle he occupied the position of 'pig in the middle'. From this vantage point, however, he was ideally situated to observe the remarkable people with whom he lived (and played). 'It was Quentin', Angelica Bell recalled, 'who brought a leavening of objectivity ... thoughts that had occurred to no one else went deeper,

'Damon and Phyllis', a play by Angelica Bell, performed in the walled garden at Charleston, 1935. Original plays were often part of the entertainment at the Charleston summer parties.

further back, made connections, suave, considered, intellectual and just as erudite as Clive's. Delighted, everyone leant back and sipped their wine while Vanessa carved the bird or helped [serve] the syllabub.' He was sensitive, creative and witty and drew inspiration from his unique milieu. In 1923, aged only thirteen, he produced the *Charleston Bulletin* with his brother Julian; and in 1972 he published the first ever biography of his aunt, Virginia Woolf, which he followed with other personal accounts of his extraordinary family. Quentin became the most prolific, insightful and highly esteemed chronicler of the Bloomsbury Group.

When it came to food preparation, however, 'Quentin was not much of a cook,' recalled his daughter Virginia, 'but was occasionally drafted in to make his "specialities".' His recipe for Beurre d'Escargots 'was one – not to be served with snails, but with grilled steak' – ideal for a summer party. 'He was very insistent that the parsley had to be pulverized with salt first, before the garlic and butter were added, because this released its juices, turning the butter an overall green. He always pulverized the salt and parsley in a large marble mortar using a pestle, and then used a supple artists' palette knife to blend in the softened butter. It was almost like watching a potter at work with his clay.'

Beurre d'Escargots

Pulverize a quantity of parsley leaves with salt in a mortar to release the green juices. Add peeled garlic cloves, then butter.

Grouse season in the United Kingdom begins on the 'Glorious Twelfth' – exactly one week before Quentin's birthday. The young birds, generally the ones that are shot early in the season, can take as little as twenty minutes to cook, the older ones, twice as long.

Roast Grouse

[SEE RECIPE FOR CHARLESTON GROUSE ON P. 274]

This traditional English summer dessert is from *Mrs Beeton's Everyday Cookery*, published in 1936.

Syllabub Pudding

10 MACAROONS • 1 PT [WHIPPING] CREAM • 4 OZ CASTOR SUGAR
JUICE OF 1 LEMON • FINELY GRATED RIND OF ½ A LEMON
1 SMALL WINEGLASSFUL OF SHERRY OR MADEIRA
PINCH OF GROUND CINNAMON • ESSENCE OF RATAFIA [ALMOND EXTRACT]

Mix the sugar, lemon juice and rind, cinnamon and wine together in a large basin, add a few drops of essence of ratafia, stir until the sugar is dissolved, then add the cream and whip to a froth. Arrange the macaroons compactly on

the bottom of a deep dish, and as the froth is formed on the syllabub skim it off and place it on the biscuits. When the whole of the preparation has been reduced to a froth, stand the dish in a cold place, and let it remain for at least 12 hours before serving. Sufficient for 7 or 8 persons.

Bloomsbury's Final Celebration

'The house was packed and of course there were guests such as our neighbours, the Woolfs at Rodmell and the Keyneses at Tilton. A number of my sister's friends provided an element of youth and beauty. The war had not yet touched us so severely that we could not provide an abundance of food and drink. The party continued for several days. There was music and dancing. Maynard told us the story of how he was mistaken for Duncan, and Duncan for him, to the vast annoyance of Mr Bernard Berenson. Marjorie Strachey provided one of her libidinous performances. Lydia Lopokova danced for the last time. Altogether it made a good end.'

Quentin Bell on Christmas 1939, in *Elders and Betters*, 1995

On 3 September 1939, Britain and France declared war on Germany. The cost of the war and the price of victory would leave Britain battered, bruised and broke. The empire was crumbling and the land of privilege and civilization was unceremoniously coming to an end. Britain's golden age – and Bloomsbury's – was nearly over.

But at Charleston, on Christmas Day 1939, Angelica Bell's birthday celebrations went on as before. A splendid cake with twenty-one candles was presented to her at teatime, and in the evening Christmas was celebrated with food, drink and witty speeches. 'We had wonderful turkey, wonderful champagne, wonderful conversation…. Virginia got absolutely drunk in about five minutes, and shrieked and waved her arms. Everyone made speeches – Leonard's and Duncan's were the funniest', Angelica wrote to David 'Bunny' Garnett that night. The merrymaking overflowed into January as youthful singing, dancing and 'good' states of mind continued to reverberate well into the New Year.

Although Bloomsbury's heyday was drawing to a close, its members could celebrate with the satisfaction of having transformed the world on so many different fronts. Their contributions to literature, economics, biography, politics, psychology, art and women's rights were outstanding, and their determination to live as independent thinkers, writers and artists has inspired, and will continue to inspire, all who live in pursuit of truth, honesty and social freedom.

Wartime Stew, Again

> '"We have need of all our courage" are the words that come to the surface this morning: on hearing that all our windows are broken, ceilings down, and most of our china smashed at Mecklenburgh Square.'
>
> Virginia Woolf's diary, 18 September 1940

On 22 June 1940, Leonard and Virginia Woolf were enjoying a literary supper with T. S. Eliot, William Plomer and John Lehmann* at their flat in Mecklenburgh Square, Bloomsbury, when they heard that France had just surrendered to Germany and that an attack on England was imminent. Leonard 'suddenly fell very silent, looking utterly overwhelmed, and we had to break off our discussion about the French collapse, for fear he should collapse himself,' recalled Lehmann. For the second time in less than a generation, Britain would be at war. Civilization, Leonard thought, would never be able to withstand another such war.

Three months later, on 18 September, Leonard and Virginia were blitzed out of Mecklenburgh Square. They had already moved from London to Monk's House, but in Sussex there was no respite from the Germans either. Leonard wrote that 'there was a tremendous roar and we were just in time to see two planes fly a few feet above the church spire, over the garden, and over our roof, and looking up as they passed above the window we saw the swastika on them.'

Out at sea, German submarines torpedoed and sank so many supply ships that British food stores began to dwindle. The government introduced rationing and handed out books with coupons for meat, sugar, preserves, fats, bacon, cheese and eggs. People went hungry. The Woolfs were relatively well off: they had land to grow fruit, vegetables and berries. They kept hens and honey bees and Virginia made her own jams and preserves.

Leonard and Virginia loaned some of their land to the people of Rodmell, so that they too could grow vegetables to eat. They tried to focus on their literary work, but the thud of exploding bombs, the drone of the Luftwaffe and the rumours of Jewish concentration camps (Leonard was of course Jewish) made it difficult. In early 1941, however, Virginia finally completed her novel *Between the Acts*. It was published posthumously that year, shortly after her suicide.

In *The Stork Wartime Cookery Book*, published in the 1940s, there are numerous suggestions for preparing food in wartime: how to make puddings without sugar, how to create appetizing dishes from odd scraps of food, how to economize on

---

* The Woolfs became friends with many of the authors they published, including T. S. Eliot and William Plomer. John Lehmann was managing director of the Hogarth Press from 1938 to 1946.

Heinkel He 111 bomber over London, 7 September 1940. On 18 September 1940, the Luftwaffe continued its massive air raid offensive on London. Leonard and Virginia's flat at Mecklenburgh Square was destroyed and Churchill warned the British public that a German invasion was likely.

meat and how to prepare dishes using canned food. Offal was frequently eaten during the war (since, unlike most other meats, it was generally not rationed, except between 1942 and 1944) and this resourceful recipe for tripe stew from the book is typical of the period.

2 LB TRIPE • 1 SPANISH ONION, CHOPPED
1 HEAD OF CELERY, CUT IN SMALL PIECES • 1 OZ STORK MARGARINE
1 OZ FLOUR • 1 PT MILK AND WATER • SALT AND PEPPER

Cut the tripe in strips or square pieces. Put it into a saucepan with the Stork and chopped onion. Put the lid on the pan and cook the contents for 10 minutes over a gentle heat, shaking the pan from time to time. Add the milk and water and the pieces of celery, bring to the boil, and simmer gently for three quarters of an hour. With a little cold milk, mix the flour to a thin cream. Add a little hot milk and water from the saucepan, then pour into the saucepan and bring to the boil. Cook quickly for 3 minutes. Season with salt and pepper and serve hot. Serves 4–6.

Haddock and Sausage

Dearest,

I feel certain I am going mad again. I feel we can't go through another of those terrible times. And I shan't recover this time. I begin to hear voices, and I can't concentrate. So I am doing what seems the best thing to do. You have given me the greatest possible happiness. You have been in every way all that anyone could be. I don't think two people could have been happier till this terrible disease came. I can't fight any longer. I know that I am spoiling your life, that without me you could work. And you will I know. You see I can't even write properly. I can't read. What I want to say is I owe all the happiness of my life to you. You have been entirely patient with me and incredibly good. I want to say that – everybody knows it. If anybody could have saved me it would have been you. Everything has gone from me but the certainty of your goodness. I can't go on spoiling your life any longer.

I don't think two people could have been happier than we have been.

V.

Virginia Woolf's last letter to Leonard Woolf, 28 March 1941

Virginia Woolf's last journal entry, written on 8 March 1941, reads: 'Occupation is essential. And now with some pleasure I find that it's seven; and must cook dinner. Haddock and sausage meat. I think it is true that one gains a certain hold on sausage and haddock by writing them down.'

Today, haddock and sausage is easy enough to prepare. But in 1941 oil and butter were scarce. Fish was not rationed, but only those who lived near to market towns or the coast were able to obtain sufficient quantities of it. This is how I like to prepare this simple dish.

2 FILLETS HADDOCK • 2 TBS OLIVE OIL

2 TBS BUTTER • ¼ LB SAUSAGE MEAT

SALT • 2 TBS FRESH LEMON JUICE

1 TBS PARSLEY, CHOPPED

Rub the fish fillets all over with with olive oil and a little salt and leave to rest for five minutes. Heat a frying pan until fairly hot and melt the butter into it. Place the fish, skin side down, in the pan and cook for three minutes, then flip the fish over and cook for two or three more minutes. Remove to a serving dish, drizzle with lemon juice and a little parsley and serve immediately. Delicious with mashed potatoes and, using a separate pan, fried sausage meat.

Roger Fry, *Virginia Woolf*, 1912.

Louie's Mutton Roast

'It was done; it was finished. Yes, she thought, laying down her brush in extreme fatigue, I have had my vision.'

Virginia Woolf, *To the Lighthouse*, 1927

Many of Virginia Woolf's novels explore the theme of finding meaning in life despite its inexorable progression towards death. Characters such as Septimus Warren Smith, Rachel Vinrace, Clarissa Dalloway and, indeed, all of us, make irrevocable decisions and choose individual paths. In Virginia's fiction, suicide was portrayed as an emphatic and dramatic ending, a way of avoiding an otherwise uncontrollable fate: madness. It is therefore tragic, yet fitting, that she chose to conclude her own story by taking her life. Depressed by the war, and beset with headaches, inner voices and the certainty of a further bout of madness, Virginia filled her pockets with stones and waded into the River Ouse for one final voyage out.

There was no lunch at Monk's House on 28 March 1941. The meal – leg of mutton with mint sauce – was dutifully prepared by Louie Mayer, but never served.

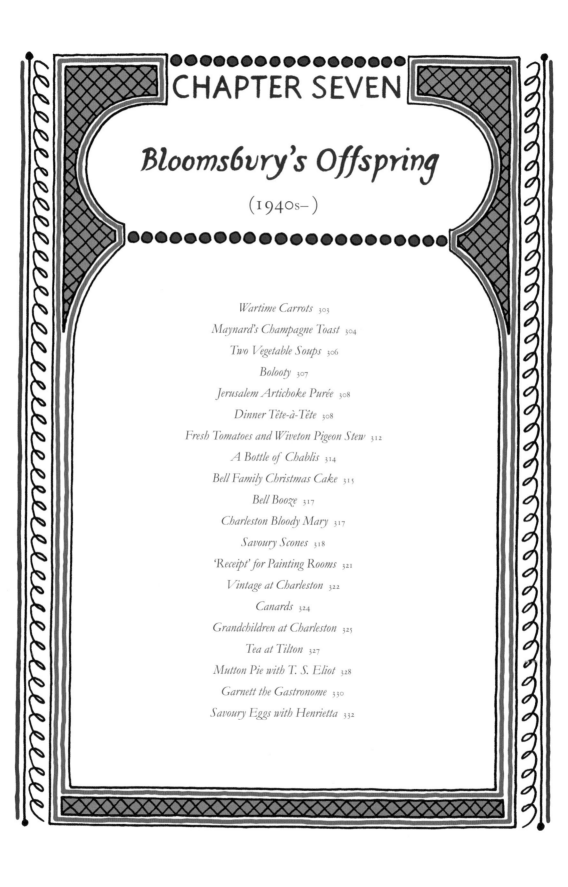

CHAPTER SEVEN

Bloomsbury's Offspring

(1940s–)

Duncan Grant, *Still Life with Carrots*, 1921. In the early 1940s, Britons were encouraged to eat carrots to improve their eyesight during wartime blackouts.

~~~~~~

Wartime Carrots

~~~~~~

'Henceforward, we are to be a permanent body independent in constitution, free from red tape, but financed by the Treasury and ultimately responsible to Parliament…. Our name is to be the Arts Council of Great Britain…. State patronage of the arts has crept in and it's happened in a very English, informal, unostentatious way: "half-baked", if you like…. At last, the public exchequer has recognized the support and encouragement to the civilizing arts of life as part of their duty.'

John Maynard Keynes BBC interview on the formation of the
Arts Council of Great Britain, 12 June 1945

Bloomsbury members had always believed that 'the arts' were an essential ingredient of any civilized society. As the first chairman of the Council for the Encouragement of Music and the Arts (CEMA) and as a high-ranking official in the Treasury, John Maynard Keynes negotiated significant government funding for the arts and, as a result, the Arts Council of Great Britain was born in 1946. Today, partly due to the British government's approach to arts patronage during and after the Second World War, the United Kingdom now has many of the finest art collections, museums, galleries and theatres in the world, as well as one of the most well-organized national systems for the development and support of the arts.

Many of CEMA's early meetings and the negotiations for the Arts Council were held in Maynard and Lydia's drawing room at 46 Gordon Square under wartime conditions. According to Lydia's biographer, Judith Mackrell, Lydia passed around tea and carrots 'to sharpen their eyesight during blackouts'. During the Second World War the British were encouraged to eat carrots because of the vegetable's high vitamin A content, which was known to improve eyesight. This drive, known as the 'Dr Carrot' campaign, allegedly fooled the Germans into believing that the British had superior eyesight, which, in turn, concealed from the Nazis the RAF's use of radar – a new technology that could detect enemy aircraft – even at night. Carrots were one of the few items not rationed during the Second World War, which helps to explain why Lydia was so keen for everyone to have one.

Maynard's Champagne Toast

'I give you the toast of the Royal Economic Society, of economics and economists, who are the trustees, not of civilization, but of the possibility of civilization.'

1st Baron [John Maynard] Keynes, 21 June 1945

'It was a golden hour; our hearts had been touched; we had drunk champagne. We had in fact each had one modest glass of champagne, but had arranged that Maynard should have champagne only, from the soup onwards through the evening.'

Sir Roy Harrod, *The Life of John Maynard Keynes*, 1951

John Maynard Keynes very frequently dined out, but it was not hunger or social pleasure that brought him to the round table over and over again – it was work. He spent long hours arguing about economic theories, negotiating loans and breaking bread with the world's foremost politicians, economists and businessmen. In 1941 he attended over thirty-three official dinners in Washington DC alone, one of which was a sixteen course Chinese dinner to celebrate his fifty-eighth birthday. The routine of endless meetings and late-night dinners played havoc with his health, but still he did not stop. In 1944 he was back in North America visiting Ottawa, Washington DC and Bretton Woods, NH, where plans for the formation of the International Monetary Fund (IMF) and the International Bank for Reconstruction and Development (now part of the World Bank) were gaining momentum. Keeping one's cool was not easy that summer, especially as the eastern United States was suffering one of its worst heat waves on record, but Lydia, Maynard's wife, found a way:

she removed every stitch of clothing and crawled into the refrigerator (presumably leaving the door ajar to prevent suffocation), much 'like Alice in Wonderland disappearing down the White Rabbit's tunnel', in her husband's words.

Sadly, less than a year after Maynard gave his toast to the Royal Economic Society, he lay dying on his bed at Tilton: 'My only regret in life', he is rumoured to have quipped, 'is that I did not drink more Champagne.' Soon afterwards, he passed away.

Duncan Grant, *Empty Champagne Bottle*, 1955. John Maynard Keynes was a devoted champagne drinker, preferring it to wine.

Leonard Woolf in
the greenhouse,
1966. Leonard was an
enthusiastic gardener
and at Monk's House
grew an abundance of
vegetables and fruit in
his garden beds, orchard
and greenhouse. From
the Monk's House
photograph album.

Two Vegetable Soups

'"Musing among the vegetables?" – was that it? – "I prefer men to cauliflowers" – was that it? He must have said it at breakfast one morning when she had gone out on to the terrace'.

Virginia Woolf, *Mrs Dalloway*, 1925

Leonard Woolf, Ralph Partridge and David 'Bunny' Garnett were Bloomsbury's most enthusiastic vegetable gardeners. At the right time of year (summer or autumn, depending on when the seeds were sown), they would have been able to make soup with the fresh produce from their own gardens. This recipe for Cauliflower Soup is from the Frances Partridge archive and the recipe for Salad Soup is by Bunny, from his and Angelica Garnett's recipe book.

Cauliflower Soup
Suggested ingredients

I LARGE HEAD OF CAULIFLOWER • I OZ BUTTER • I MEDIUM ONION, SLICED
½ TBS DRIED THYME, OR I TBS FRESH THYME
SALT AND PEPPER • [2 PT] CREAMY MILK OR CHICKEN STOCK
I BOILED POTATO (OPTIONAL)

Break up a cauliflower, remove stalk & leaves, soften in butter with sliced onion & boil in salted water for about 10 mins. Drain & put through the mixer with about 1 oz butter, ½ tb dried thyme or 1 of fresh, some salt & pepper & chicken stock/milk. (boiled potato optional). Heat [purée] and serve. A few bits may be kept back, chopped and added to the very smooth purée. [Serves 6.]

Salad Soup

After many dinner parties one finds a lot of uneaten salads – lettuce, tomato, peppers, beetroot & potatoes, few of which are fit to reappear the next day. Add them to the chicken bones, or bones of chops etc or fish & put them through the mouli next day.

Bolooty

'Much later during the Second World War Ralph carried the production of food even further, and Ham Spray retained much of its earlier flavour. Sometimes there were surprises of a startling sort. On one visit I was told not to use the best bathroom. It had a specially long bath, in which Lytton could lie at full length, and the walls were lined with tiles that Carrington had painted with shells and starfish and sea anenomes before having them fired. I was to use the other bathroom down the passage. But I forgot the injunction, and on stepping into the best bathroom, I was appalled to see a corpse lying at full length, half submerged in the bath. For the tenth of a second I thought that a murder was being concealed…. Who was the victim? Then I saw that the white skin was not human … the carcase of a large white pig was being cured in brine.'

David Garnett, *Great Friends*, 1979

How did the thoroughly practical Ralph Partridge fit into Bloomsbury?

His physical strength and beauty – qualities Lytton Strachey found irresistible – made him a necessary 'leg' of the Strachey–Carrington–Partridge triangle. At the Mill House and Ham Spray House, his indefatigable prowess in the vegetable garden rendered him essential in the provision of food for the ménage. 'Ralph had more knowledge of housekeeping and cooking than I had, nor can I boast of being quick to learn', his future wife, Frances Marshall, recollected in her memoirs. 'It was he who instructed Mabel, the frightened middle-aged spinster who came to "do for us", making breakfast and even returning to cook excellent but very English meals in the evenings, so that we were able to ask our friends to dinner.' At the Hogarth Press, working with the Woolfs, Ralph again proved himself a key catalyst. He was clever and reliable, and while he was working at the press its output per annum more than doubled. Later, Ralph worked with Frances in researching and editing the unexpurgated eight-volume *Greville Memoirs* project begun by Lytton.*

This Bolooty (Indian meatloaf) recipe from the Frances Partridge collection comes from Ralph's mother, Jessie Partridge (née Sherring), who was the wife of an Indian civil servant.

> To use up cold meat:- Mince it & soak an equal amount of bread in warm water, squeeze it dry, & mix mince & bread, also half an onion chopped fine & fried: season, & add curry powder, a piece of butter & some stock or gravy.
>
> Put it in a buttered dish & pour a well-beaten egg over the top. Bake for about ½ hour & serve with a border of mashed potato or boiled rice.

Jerusalem Artichoke Purée

In August 2002, a commemorative edition of *Eminent Victorians* (illustrated opposite) was published to celebrate the seventieth anniversary of Lytton Strachey's death. Frances Partridge, then aged 102, wrote the foreword, and the food writer Paul Levy, a literary executor of the Strachey estate, wrote the introduction. The two had collaborated earlier, for this recipe by Levy was found in the food-splattered pages of Frances's recipe book. It is quick and simple and eminently delicious.

> Peel & chop coarsely & boil with equal amount of potato. Puréz [*sic*] with milk, butter & a little cream.

Dinner Tête-à-Tête

'*November 19th* [1927]. Ham Spray, with Raymond [Mortimer] and Roger Senhouse. Soaking rain fell all Sunday and we couldn't stir outside. Lytton and Roger were each reading a copy of my Hume, and there was none left for me; as they discussed it I felt tantalized and thwarted. Chess, paper games. At dinner an absurd conversation as to what point must be reached for a woman to be obliged to go to bed with a man, or else give him a perfect right to be furious. Ralph said a hand on the private parts; Carrington a hand on the knee; Lytton "No, no, a kiss – no – a dinner tête-à-tête!"'

Frances Partridge, Memories, 1981

---

* *The journals of Charles Greville (1794–1895) spanned the reigns of three monarchs – George IV, William IV and Queen Victoria – and contained sensitive (often scandalous) social and political information. Lytton Strachey began the project in 1928 and Roger Fulford completed it in 1938.*

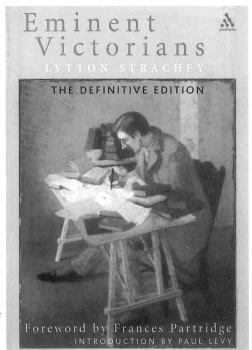

Cover of a commemorative
edition of *Eminent Victorians*
published on the seventieth
anniversary of Lytton
Strachey's death in 2002.

'And what can I say about Ham Spray – my own much loved home for nearly thirty years? When Lytton and Ralph bought the house jointly in 1924 I was still working at Birrell and Garnett's bookshop, but I used to go down to Wiltshire at weekends and help paint the inside of the house, while Carrington covered doors, furniture and tiles with her delicate decorations, very different in style from the bolder ones at Charleston. Meanwhile Lytton would be lovingly arranging his books in the library shelves made by the village carpenter, over which, for purposes of reference, Carrington had mysteriously but characteristically painted the letters of the alphabet from Z to A. Ralph would be at work clearing away the "vulgar" round flowerbeds and the superfluous trees from the lawn – they were mostly conifers, abhorred by Lytton – so that a perfectly clear view could be got from the pink Jane Austen front of the house and its verandah to the Downs half a mile away, leaving nothing between that wasn't green – the lawn, the fields and the ilex drooping gracefully over the ha-ha. Everywhere inside the house were piles of catalogues – Lytton's from antiquarian booksellers and Carrington's from seedsmen. There was always at least one cat in residence.'

Frances Partridge, quoted in *A Cézanne in the Hedge*, 1985

Clive Bell, an aesthete in every respect, once commented on Frances Marshall's natural beauty, and declared that she had the best legs in Bloomsbury. Fortunately, she was also clever, which helped to seduce the hearts and minds of all Bloomsbury members – not just the heterosexual men.

In 1978 Frances Partridge (née Marshall) published her diaries for the first time, shedding new light on life within Bloomsbury's inner circle. She was there: eating from their tables; dancing at their parties; dining with them at The Ivy, Claridges and Boulestin and, on occasion, cooking for them. She shared their gossip, drank their wine, smoked their cigars and joined in their clever conversation. Her position, which was at first tenuous, became increasingly central through her connections with Bunny Garnett and her subsequent marriage to Ralph Partridge. Years later, her son, Lytton Burgo Partridge,* married Bunny and Angelica's daughter, Henrietta; not long afterwards, Frances became a grandmother and the torchbearer for Bloomsbury's third generation. Her later diaries chronicle many of Bloomsbury's meatiest adventures, and divulge her fascinating life among an illustrious and exceptionally talented group of individuals.

In 2010, her collection of intimate papers, private correspondence and family photograph albums in the library of King's College Cambridge was opened to the public. One item was of particular significance to this volume: her cookbook. In preparing and sampling her recipes, one does not just simply taste Bloomsbury; one *digests* it. The intimacy of handling the same ingredients, sharing the same smells, tastes and textures as they did, is the closest one can come to a dinner tête-à-tête with Bloomsbury. These four recipes are from her collection.

Aubergines Provençales

Peel and slice aubergines [thinly] and sautéz in butter with an equal no. of peeled chopped tomatoes & 1 chopped clove of garlic. Season. Put in fireproof dish, sprinkle with breadcrumbs & small pieces of butter (at least 3 oz) chopped parsley & bake in hot oven for about 15 minutes.

Celery, Stir-Fried (by Paul Levy)

1 OR 2 HEADS CELERY • 3 TBS VEGETABLE OIL • ¼ CUP WATER

Scrub celery & cut on the cross, into strips ¼ or ½ inch wide. Heat oil in pan (high heat). Add celery & toss & turn for about 2 mins until translucent; add salt & toss half a minute more. Add water, reduce heat, cover & steam. Then take off lid & turn up heat till liquid has evaporated.

Fondue

TAKE EGGS ACCORDING TO NO. OF PEOPLE

⅓ WEIGHT OF EGGS IN GRUYÈRE CHEESE • ⅙ WEIGHT OF EGGS IN BUTTER

---

* *Lytton Burgo Partridge died suddenly of heart failure on 7 September 1963, three weeks after the birth of his daughter, Sophie Vanessa.*

Grate the cheese. Beat up eggs in a saucepan & add butter & cheese. Turn with a wooden spoon till the mixture is smooth & creamy but not too set. Add little or no salt, pepper. Serve with snippets of fried bread.

Fruit Mousse (Raspberry, Bilberry, Blackberry)
I LB FRUIT • I OZ POWDERED GELATINE • 3 OZ CASTER SUGAR
JUICE OF I LEMON • ½ PT THICK CREAM

Put fruit through mixer. Dissolve the gelatine in a little hot milk, strain into purée, add sugar & lemon. Whisk the cream till thick, stir lightly into the mixture & leave in fridge.

Three recipes, including Fruit Mousse, from Frances Partridge's recipe book.

Fresh Tomatoes and Wiveton Pigeon Stew

'He [Desmond MacCarthy] lived, he said, like a camel off its hump, nourished by literary food garnered in an earlier era; and though he praised where he could, writers such as Herbert Read, Auden and Spender were irritated by his lack of understanding. He shared neither the hopes of the younger generation nor the disillusion and *angst* they saw articulated in T. S. Eliot's *Waste Land.*'

Hugh and Mirabel Cecil, *Clever Hearts*, 1990

Born in 1877, Desmond MacCarthy was sandwiched between two very different periods of social history: a hierarchical Victorian one in which everyone and everything had its place, and a modern one in which religion was no longer the dominant moral force and individual freedoms and social justice were considered radical ideologies worth fighting for. Desmond bridged the two periods as a drama critic, literary critic, columnist, editor and broadcaster, but his real sympathy and expertise lay in his profound understanding of the older generation. 'His ability to bring the reader into intimate contact with the personalities and minds of past authors was always his outstanding gift,' wrote Desmond's grandson Hugh Cecil and his wife Mirabel. 'Indeed he seemed as close to some of these as if they had been personal friends.' The 'Affable Hawk' (Desmond's pen name) was a fair judge: he would praise when he could, but was equally ready to 'swoop down on the shoddy or perfunctory', recalled his publisher James MacGibbon.

When Desmond was not at his table reading or writing, he could usually be found at the dining table of a friend or colleague, or at a fashionable restaurant or at a private member's club nearby. On occasion, he entertained at home and, in 1940, Cyril Connolly, fellow writer, critic and editor, enthused about the ambience at Garrick's Villa, Desmond and Molly's home in Richmond,* and the delicious 'fresh tomatoes and the stew'.

These two recipes are from the Wiveton Hall Café, the restaurant started by Desmond's grandson (also called Desmond MacCarthy) in Norfolk. All ingredients are meticulously home grown and/or locally sourced, which underlies the restaurant's stellar reputation. (Delia Smith once noted that the food served at Wiveton is 'Britain's best'). The food there is, indeed, exquisite.

Fresh Tomatoes

We use for best results either Black Russian (they have dark green streaks on the skin and we grow them here in poly-tunnels) – or other beef tomatoes. It is a meal in itself.

---

* *Desmond and Molly MacCarthy lived at 25 Wellington Square, Chelsea, for most of their married life and it was only in old age that they moved to 2 Garrick's Villa, Richmond.*

A page from Desmond MacCarthy's wife Molly's cookery book, 1952: 'Your husband is not a glutton; but he does like very good food well cooked, & very light, & well served.'

Core and cut in half the tomatoes, sprinkle chopped garlic, basil and extra virgin olive oil, season with salt and pepper, and roast for fifteen to twenty minutes in the oven at 180°C.

Serve on toasted sourdough.

Wiveton Pigeon Stew

8 WHOLE PIGEONS • 500 G PANCETTA OR SMOKED STREAKY BACON
2 LARGE ONIONS • 3 MEDIUM LEEKS
6 LARGE CLOVES (3 WHOLE, 3 CRUSHED) GARLIC
1 MEDIUM HOT RED CHILLI • ¾ BOTTLE RED WINE
1 KG CHOPPED TOMATOES • HANDFUL OF CARROTS
THYME • ROSEMARY • OREGANO

Fry up the bacon, onions, leeks, garlic and chilli. Brown off birds in a separate pan and deglaze the pan with wine. Put the juice and the tomatoes into a large casserole dish. Add the bacon mix, and then add the carrots and herbs. Finally add the pigeons breast-side down. Cook in the oven for two and a half hours at 180°C.

This dish, like any stew, can be reheated the next day and is even better the second time – or save the juice and serve with pasta.

A Bottle of Chablis

'Conversation was his art, and for him the tragedy was that he should have chosen so ephemeral a medium. For Virginia there was an inconvenience of another kind; he would turn up at Richmond for dinner, uninvited very probably, and probably committed to a dinner elsewhere, charm his way out of his social crimes on the telephone, talk enchantingly until the small hours, insist that he be called early so that he might attend to urgent business on the morrow, wake up a trifle late, dawdle somewhat over breakfast, find a passage in *The Times* to excite his ridicule, enter into a lively discussion of Ibsen, declare he must be off, pick up a book which reminded him of something which, in short, would keep him talking until about 12.45, when he would have to ring up and charm the person who had been waiting in an office for him since 10, and at the same time deal with the complications arising from the fact that he had engaged himself to two different hostesses for lunch, and that it was now 1 o'clock, and it would take forty minutes to get from Richmond to the West End. In all this Desmond had been practising his art – the art of conversation.'

Quentin Bell, *Elders and Betters*, 1995

E. M. Forster once said that Desmond MacCarthy 'knew exactly what he wanted to say and, in the end, how to say it'. In May 1921, his friends made an attempt to capture his brilliance on paper. Roger Fry brought a bottle of Chablis and Leonard and Virginia Woolf provided a scribe and a venue, Hogarth House, in Richmond. Desmond, who knew nothing of their plan to document his words, did not suspect, and did not disappoint. He captivated, enraptured and bewitched his listeners. But his words did not scintillate in the same way on paper.

Desmond's grandson Jonathan Cecil was also blessed with the gift of being able to deliver a perfectly timed line. He was a comic actor, known for his portrayal of Bertie Wooster, P. G. Wodehouse's foolish but endearing fictional toff, in the 1981 BBC television film *Thank You, P. G. Wodehouse*. One cannot help but wonder whether he was taking Bloomsbury's critical disparagement of the English upper classes to a new level.

Desmond loved France, enjoyed his wine and was a brilliant raconteur. Why not share his enthusiasm for the good life and crack open a bottle of Chablis – 2010 was an especially fine year.

Duncan Grant, *Quentin Bell as a Boy*, 1919. Quentin matured into a talented writer, potter, sculptor and painter. In 1971, at the age of sixty-one, he published *Virginia Woolf: A Biography*, and in 1995 wrote *Elders and Betters*, a personal memoir of his life growing up in the Bloomsbury Group.

Bell Family Christmas Cake

'The overflow of his imaginative energy in his private life led to the devising of plays and treasure hunts, and to such vigorous ornamentation of Christmas cakes, baked in later years by his daughters* that not a scrap of icing sugar could be seen beneath the crystallized fruit, angelica and silver balls.'

Frances Spalding, obituary of Quentin Bell, 1996

* *Virginia Nicholson notes that the family Christmas cake was in fact usually baked by her mother, Olivier, and only occasionally by herself.*

Virginia Woolf once said to her nephew Quentin Bell: 'You will always be igno-rant and illiterate'. A throwaway comment, perhaps, but she could not have been more mistaken. Quentin may not have been as precocious as his older brother, Julian, or as pretty as his little half-sister, Angelica, but he was clever and creative and blessed with outstanding powers of observation. It was only a matter of time before he found his voice and métier.

Quentin wrote and lectured widely on art, and held professorships at the uni-versities of Leeds and Sussex. He became an accomplished potter, sculptor and painter, but his highest accolade came in the field of literature, for his two-volume biography of Virginia Woolf, which was awarded the James Tait Black Memorial Prize and the Duff Cooper Memorial Book Prize for nonfiction in 1972. If Virginia could only have known of her 'ignorant and illiterate' nephew's vigorous artistic and scholarly achievements, she would no doubt have eaten her words!

Cressida Bell, Quentin's younger daughter, is an artist and designer who is also well-known for her cakes (in 2013 she published *Cressida Bell's Cake Design: Fifty Fabulous Cakes*). She still decorates the family Christmas cake each year. This recipe from *The Times Cookery Book* (1978) by Katie Stewart is the one the Bell family used to follow each Christmas.

10 OZ (275 G) PLAIN FLOUR • 1 LEVEL TSP MIXED SPICE
1 LEVEL TSP SALT • 8 OZ (225 G) BUTTER
8 OZ (225 G) SOFT BROWN SUGAR • 4 LARGE EGGS
1 TBS BLACK TREACLE • ½ TSP VANILLA ESSENCE
4 OZ (100 G) GLACÉ CHERRIES • 8 OZ (225 G) CURRANTS
8 OZ (225 G) SULTANAS • 8 OZ (225 G) SEEDLESS RAISINS
4 OZ (100 G) CHOPPED CANDIED PEEL
2 OZ (50 G) BLANCHED CHOPPED ALMONDS
2 TBS BRANDY OR MILK

Sieve together the flour, spice and salt and set aside. Cream together the butter and sugar until very soft and light. Lightly mix the eggs, treacle and vanilla essence together, then gradually beat into the creamed mixture a little at a time. Add some of the flour along with the last few additions of egg.

Rinse the cherries in warm water to remove the outer sugary coating. Pat dry and cut into quarters. Place in a basin with the currants, sultanas, seed-less raisins, chopped candied peel and chopped almonds. Add 1–2 spoonfuls of the sieved flour to the fruit and mix well. Using a metal spoon, fold in the remaining sieved flour, then the fruit mixture and brandy or milk.

Spoon the mixture into a greased and lined, 8-inch [20 cm], round, deep cake tin, and hollow out the centre slightly. Place on the shelf below centre of a preheated slow oven (300°F, 150°C or Gas No. 2) and bake for 1½ hours. Then lower the heat to slow (275°F, 140°C or Gas No. 1) and bake for a further 2½ hours. Cool the baked cake in the tin before wrapping and storing. Makes one 8-inch (20-cm) cake.

Quentin and
Anne Olivier Bell
in Rome, 1951.

Bell Booze

Most evenings Quentin and Anne Olivier Bell enjoyed a well-made cocktail they named *Bell Booze*. This is how Virginia Nicholson remembers her parents making their favourite tipple.

I LARGE SHOT OF GIN • A DASH OF LIME JUICE
GOOD-QUALITY GINGER BEER

Combine all ingredients in a highball glass with ice.

Charleston Bloody Mary

At eighty-eight, Duncan Grant went to Turkey with his young friend Paul Roche. 'Like all their expeditions, it was fuelled by a liberal supply of alcohol,' noted Frances Spalding, 'for Roche's lethal Bloody Marys took the edge off any disaster.' This Bloody Mary recipe is basic, like the ones Duncan enjoyed at Charleston, but in his honour I have made the drink exceptionally strong!

2½ SHOTS VODKA • 4–5 OZ TOMATO JUICE • ICE • WORCESTERSHIRE SAUCE

Fill three quarters of a highball glass with ice (beaten with a mallet, but not crushed). Add the vodka and the tomato juice and spice up the cocktail by adding three dashes Worcestershire sauce.

Savoury Scones

'Tea was at five o'clock, and at about half past four, the kettle was set to boil on the Aga…. Sometimes, Vanessa would make scones to go with Grace's seed cake. Standing at the table in the poorly lit kitchen with its concrete floor, she would hook her rings onto a convenient nail by the sink and slowly, carefully, sieve flour into a bowl, rubbing in the minimum of butter. Her scones were plain, unglazed and surprisingly good, like the perfect cottage loaves that her sister Virginia, impractical as she too was, taught her young cook Louie Mayer to make.'

John and Diana Higgens's recollections of the kitchen at Charleston, 1990s.

When Vanessa Bell first came to Charleston in the winter of 1916, the kitchen was so cold that the water tap froze. Only after Grace Germany arrived in 1920 was some semblance of domestic order at last achieved. Vanessa was now able to focus on her art and could devote even more time to painting and decorating the house (although much decoration was achieved before 1920). She and Duncan eventually transformed the furniture, walls, door panels, window embrasures and fire surrounds – almost every surface – into a fiesta of original artwork and colour. The kitchen did not escape their notice, though decorations and improvements to this room came later. In the 1950s Vanessa painted still lifes – vases of flowers and bowls of fruit – onto the kitchen cupboards. During the restoration of Charleston (1981–86), Quentin's handmade mugs and painted tiles contributed even more colour, and his friend and assistant Victoria Walton made ceramic lampshades designed to splash delicious speckles of coloured light onto the plain, bare kitchen ceiling.

Every day after breakfast Vanessa went into the kitchen to discuss the order book with Grace. Once menus were sorted out and other domestic matters discussed, Vanessa would join Duncan in the studio for a morning's painting session. Sometimes she would return to the kitchen in the afternoon to bake scones for tea, a relaxing pursuit with a delicious outcome. This is Vanessa's daughter's recipe for savoury drop scones.

¼ LB FLOUR • I TSP BAKING POWDER • SALT • PEPPER
1½ OZ MARGARINE OR BUTTER • JUST UNDER ½ GILL WATER
4 OZ GRATED PARMEZAN [*sic*] • [LARD, FOR FRYING]

Duncan Grant, *Vanessa Bell*, 1917. Vanessa enjoyed baking scones for afternoon tea.

Melt marg & water in a saucepan. Sieve flour & baking powder together. Add [pinch of] salt & pepper. Stir in marg & water & cheese. Fry in spoonfuls in hot lard. Serve hot. [Makes 16–18.]

Duncan Grant, *The Kitchen*, 1902. This work was painted at Duncan's
parents' house in Streatley-on-Thames, Berkshire, when he was seventeen.

Duncan Grant, *Portrait
of Elizabeth Raper*, from
*The Receipt Book of
Elizabeth Raper*, 1924

'Receipt' for Painting Rooms

Duncan Grant's father, Major Bartle Grant, was a great lover of food. He distinguished himself not by his military career but by publishing his great-grandmother's cookery book in 1924, as *The Receipt Book of Elizabeth Raper*. The book covers the period 1756–70 and provides an amusing collection of anecdotes and 'receipts' (recipes). Apart from delicious marinades, roasts and daubes, there are also interesting techniques for successful distillation and recipes contributed by Elizabeth's husband, Dr William Grant, MD, for 'a simple vomit' and 'a purging ptisan [*tisane*]'. The illustrations in the book were by the author's great-great-grandson, Duncan, who shared her interest in interior decoration. Angelica Garnett, Duncan's daughter, also shared this passion.

The following two recipes, Receipt for Painting Rooms and To Die Linnen Yellow, are from *The Receipt Book of Elizabeth Raper*. Duncan and Angelica's modern recipe for French grey is taken from the documentary film *A Painter's Paradise: The Restoration of Charleston Farmhouse* (1989).

Receipt for Painting Rooms

For painting your Rooms lay them over with white Lead and oil, tinctured with a little blue Blake and see that it be thin laid over so that it may drown the Knots, afterwards mix your white Lead with turpentine Varnish half of each, when it is fully dryed and lay it over, and you may depend on't you'll have a clear gloss. Blue Blake is one penny per ounce, Buy one quarter of a pound, when I speak of the first colouring lay it thin over, is meant the colour must be mixed thin with the oil for the first painting. Buy one quarter of an ounce of Prussian blue which will be two shill: sterl. which will serve all your rooms. Brushes, one at one shilling sterl. one at 8ds. and another at 6ds. which is all.

Make your white Lead the thickness of cream for the painting, and mix it with Blue blake.

2nd. Painting, mix your colour of the same thickness above mentioned, but put one half of turpentine Varnish with the Colour after it is grinded and tincture it with a little Prussian Blue.

To Die Linnen Yellow

Boil 4 gallons of water, peel into ½ ounce of ornetto, with the quantity of an egg of flemish ashes, let them boil together 8 minutes, and stand an hour then pour the clear on the linnen, let it lie an hour, then stir it, and rince it in cold water. You may use Japan earth instead of ornetto which will die salmon Color.

Duncan and Angelica's Recipe for French Grey

Combine your water-based pigments: ultramarine, raw umber and a touch of ochre, together with whiting chalk and rabbit-skin glue. It is important that the glue has no acid content and is free of impurities. Mix the colours and the glue with roughly half a bucket of water. Visually, the mixture should resemble a runny paste. To test the colour, paint a swatch and wait for it to dry. Once the paint is dry chalk will appear on the surface adding warm texture to the colour. If the desired colour has been achieved, you can begin painting. Quantities should be sufficient to cover an entire room.

Vintage at Charleston

'Drink was preferably wine, usually red of which everyone except Vanessa drank a good deal, though I don't remember anyone's being drunk. Occasionally there was cider, and at lunch, Harveys beer. For certain guests such as Roger Fry, Vanessa would provide Vichy water.'

Angelica Garnett to Anna Fewster, 5 October 2009

Barrels of Château de Fontcreuse were purchased from France, stored in the cellar at Charleston, and bottled later by Quentin Bell and Duncan Grant. Every day after lunch Duncan and Clive would ask Vanessa what was for dinner, whereupon they would disappear into the depths of the cellar and return with the most appropriate bottle for the occasion. If the bottle was white, it was put in the refrigerator to chill, and if it was red, it was placed on the shelf above the Aga in the kitchen for later.

'After dinner', recalled Anne Olivier Bell, 'Clive would produce some brandy or on very rare occasions he would produce port, which had been through quite a large process of being drained through a linen handkerchief and decanted into a decanter'.

Angelica Garnett, *The Hock Bottle*, 1958. Wine was brought in barrels from
France and later bottled at Charleston.

Before the traditional passing of the port to the left can begin, it is important
first to decant it properly. The port bottle must remain upright for a minimum of
twenty minutes before decanting, allowing sufficient time for the sediment to sink
to the bottom. The cork must then be removed gently and the port filtered carefully through a muslin cloth into a port decanter.

Duncan Grant, *Vanessa Bell at David Garnett's house, Hilton Hall*, unknown date. Once grandchildren started to arrive, the rift between the Garnetts of Hilton and the Bell-Grants of Charleston began to heal.

Canards

'Its beauty is the remarkable thing about it. I think of marrying it; when she is twenty I shall be 46 – will it be scandalous?'

David Garnett to Lytton Strachey on the birth of Angelica, 25 December 1918

Neither Vanessa Bell nor Duncan Grant was invited to Angelica Bell's wedding on 8 May 1942. Their disapproval of the relationship between their twenty-three-year-old daughter and David 'Bunny' Garnett, a contemporary and ex-lover of Duncan, was obvious. Since Bunny had been living with them at the time of Angelica's birth and had even weighed her on the kitchen scales moments after she was born, Vanessa and Duncan thought the affair bordered on the incestuous. For a time, there was a painful, silent separation and it was not until Angelica started to have children of her own (Amaryllis Virginia was born in 1943) that the rift began to heal.

Vanessa enjoyed the company of her grandchildren (Garnetts: Amaryllis, Henrietta, Nerissa and Frances; and Bells: Julian, Virginia and Cressida) and she and Duncan spent many happy hours painting their portraits in the studio at

Charleston. Henrietta recalled that at the end of lunch: 'The duck, a lump of white sugar, would be sent for a sail in a silver teaspoon boat across the dark waters of the black coffee within her painted blue cup, and then, very gently, the silver boat capsized. The snow-white duck became stained with the brown liquid and then Vanessa would lift the spoon as far as she could reach to our gaping mouths and we swiftly gobbled up the ducks.'

Grandchildren at Charleston

'My brother Julian had one goal to fulfil each summer, and that was to complete a circuit of the pond. Every year the brambles covered our pathway, and Julian would return and methodically set about to clip and hack his way back to the far side. It was like exploring the Amazon jungle. I would follow him. When we finally got to the far side, beyond the statue, we made a nest in the roots of a willow tree full of fascinating woodlice, damp and reedy. Triumphantly we held a tea party in this spot (supplied with Grace's rock buns) for the entire household. For Duncan, Clive and Nessa it can't have been a very comfortable celebration.'

Virginia Nicholson, quoted in *A Cézanne in the Hedge*, 1987

above left: **Virginia Nicholson, aged five, at Charleston, 1960;** *above right:* **Vanessa Bell,** *Julian Bell,* **1956. To Vanessa's seven grandchildren, Charleston was an enchanted world of sugar lumps, hand-painted crockery, bushwhacking, oil painting and Grace Higgens's homemade teatime cakes and buns.**

For the seven grandchildren of the Bells and Duncan Grant, Charleston was an enchanted place. Henrietta Garnett recalls that as a child she would often sit for Vanessa and Duncan and, while they painted, she would listen to their stories of the past, to Mozart, and to Duncan's famous non sequiturs. It was not long before the urge to create was upon her, too, and having selected a paintbrush and colour, she would sit with a canvas before her and compose her vision. Later she would swap her brush for a pen, for she discovered that an ability to paint with words also ran through her veins. Indeed, all the grandchildren seem to have been born with this talent; all the wonderful books and marvellous paintings they produce today attest to it.

In recalling childhood food at Charleston, Virginia Nicholson remembers delicious sausages, freshly baked cakes, buns, melba toast and the aforementioned coffee-soaked sugar lumps. 'The kitchen was very much the centre of the Charleston universe,' Cressida Bell recalls. 'Everyone would end up in it. There was always a cup of tea and a "Grace cake".' But she confesses to remembering 'things like the plates we ate off more than the food'. Henrietta writes of the details of Vanessa's scones and also of Grace Higgens's delicious melba toast. Vanessa, Clive and Duncan did not eat with the younger children (who took their meals in what is now the 'Tea Room' at Charleston), but Vanessa and Duncan did occasionally celebrate afternoon tea with them and, every now and then, joined in their rollicking adventures.

Virginia remembers 'helping' Grace in the kitchen, 'which meant scraping out and licking the bowl when she was cooking buns or cakes'. This recipe for Rock Cakes from Mrs Beeton's cookbook is how Virginia remembers Grace making them.

Rock Cakes

4 EGGS • ¾ LB CASTER SUGAR • 1¼ LB FLOUR • ¼ LB CURRANTS
[½ CUP] MILK

Break the eggs into a basin, beat well till light, add sugar, flour and currants. Mix well adding milk if necessary. Put the dough on a baking sheet in heaps, making them look as 'rocky' as possible. Bake 20–30 minutes [at 190°C. Makes 12].

These little nursery cakes from the Grace Higgens archive are perfect for baking with children. Be careful not to over-mix the batter.

Nursery Cakes

¼ [CUP] BUTTER • 2 OZ SUGAR • 4 OZ GROUND ALMONDS
2 OZ SELF RIZING [sic] FLOUR • [½ TSP ALMOND ESSENCE] • [1 EGG]

[Cream butter and sugar and add almond essence and egg]. Sift the almonds and the flour and mix with butter mixture. Place in greased muffin tins and] Bake in a moderate oven from 10 to 15 minutes [or 180°C for 20 mins. Makes 6].

Grace's Currant Buns

Mix together 6 oz of margarine, 6 oz of sugar, 3 eggs, 8 oz self-raising flour, 4 oz currants and a teaspoon of mixed spice. [Spoon into greased muffin tins.] Cook for thirty minutes at 200°C. [Makes 10.]

Grace's Melba Toast

'The great object of dinner was Toast. Melba toast. Nobody bothers nowadays, but I made some last week and the entire house reeked of lost days from long ago. You toast the slices of bread and then, when cool, slit them. Put them into a baking dish in the oven. They will curl up into wafers and *nothing* can beat this humble recipe for stale bread to go with an excellent consommé or indeed a roast grouse.'

Henrietta Garnett to Anna Fewster, 14 September 2009

Tea at Tilton

In 1955 Vanessa Bell's ten-year-old granddaughter, Henrietta Garnett, wandered over from Charleston and knocked on Lydia Keynes's front door at Tilton. The curious child and the elderly Russian got along famously, exchanging stories and enjoying sweet French wine and confectionery.

Vanessa Bell, *Henrietta Garnett, c.* 1955. On her first visit to Tilton, aged ten, Henrietta was offered a glass of wine and a marron glacé by Lydia Keynes.

Later, Henrietta Garnett recalled of Lydia: 'She was tiny. Although I was only ten (and, even now, am not a tall person) I was taller than her. She was wearing a surprising amount of clothes for such a warm day, and around her head were bound a great quantity of scarves. She looked rather like an old tea-cosy, except for her feet, which were delicate and beautiful, and for her hands which were very graceful.... We took to one another like ducks to water. I dare say it seems strange that a little English girl and an old Russian woman should strike up such a friendship. But we did … Lydia had a very engaging, child-like streak in her; I was far from being grown-up. She loved to chatter; I adored to listen and ask her questions…. On this first visit, she offered me a glass of sweet Sauterne[s] and a marron glacé.'

This is a traditional recipe for marrons glacés from *Four Hundred Prize Recipes For Practical Cookery* (1934). Chestnuts crumble easily, so try to use large ones if possible.

4 LB SPANISH CHESTNUTS (LARGE) • 1 QT WATER
3 LB CASTOR SUGAR • 1 TSP VANILLA ESSENCE

Remove outer skins of chestnuts with a small pointed knife, put the chestnuts in a saucepan containing boiling water, bring to the boil, and let simmer for ½ hour.

Make a syrup of the sugar, water, and vanilla essence. Place both saucepans on the kitchen table, lift out the chestnuts, three or four at a time with a perforated spoon, carefully remove the second skin, and place the chestnuts in the syrup. Then place the saucepan with the chestnuts on the fire, bring to the boil, and let simmer very slowly for 1 hour. Then place the saucepan in a cool place.

The next day bring the chestnuts to the boil, and lift them out on to a cake rack to dry. Place them in petits-fours paper cases.

Mutton Pie with T. S. Eliot

'That strange figure Eliot dined here last night.'

Virginia Woolf to Roger Fry, 18 May 1923

On 23 June 1922, after dining with Leonard and Virginia Woolf at Hogarth House in Richmond, T. S. Eliot read aloud his epic poem *The Waste Land*. In 1923 the Hogarth Press published the poem, a haunting work of unprecedented form, style and content that established him as one of the leading poets of his generation. Virginia wrote to Barbara Bagenal: 'I have just finished setting up the whole of Mr Eliots poem with my own hands: You see how my hand trembles.'

Tom, Virginia and Leonard were friends for over twenty years. Tom was not a member of Bloomsbury, as such, but was a part of the Woolfs' literary circle. Even after Virginia's death in 1941, Tom and Leonard continued to meet up for lunch or dinner – usually over mutton pie. In *Leonard Woolf: A Life* (2007) Victoria Glendinning claims that Leonard's delicious mutton pies were probably made by his friend Trekkie Parsons. 'The joke among Leonard's friends was that in London he lived entirely on Lyons meat pies. But since "mutton pie" features in so many of his invitations, and Trekkie was famous for her mutton pies, it seems likely that she was his supplier. (Her mutton pies were a cross between pork pies and pasties, made with flaky pastry.)'

Not even Tom, who famously wrote to a friend in 1915, 'I do not think that I should ever come to like England – a people which is satisfied with such disgusting food *is not* civilized,' complained of Leonard's (or Trekkie's) pies – they were *that* good.

This traditional recipe is from the edition of *Mrs Beeton's Cookery and Household Management* published in 1960. Any leftover pastry may be frozen.

Flaky Pastry
I LB PLAIN FLOUR • COLD WATER TO MIX • PINCH OF SALT
½ TSP LEMON JUICE • 10 OZ BUTTER OR BUTTER AND LARD

Sift the flour and salt into a basin. Divide the butter into 4 equal portions and lightly rub ¼ of the butter into the flour. (If a mixture of butter and lard is used, blend them together with a round-bladed knife to get an even consistency, before dividing into 4.) Mix to a soft dough with cold water and lemon juice. The dough should be of the same consistency as the butter.

Roll out into an oblong strip, keeping the ends square and place a quarter of the butter in small pieces on the top ⅔ of the pastry. Dredge lightly with flour, fold up the bottom third of pastry on to the fat and fold down the top third. Using the rolling-pin, press the edges lightly together to prevent the air escaping. Half-turn the pastry so that the folded edges are left and right when rolling. With the rolling-pin press ridges in the pastry to distribute the air evenly. Roll out as before. Always roll carefully, do not allow the butter to break through the dough. If possible, allow the pastry to relax in a cool place.

Repeat the process with the other two portions of butter and again allow the pastry to relax. Roll out once more and use as required.

Flaky pastry should be put into a very hot oven (450°F) until set, then the heat should be reduced to fairly hot (375°F).

For the pies [adapted for flaky pastry]
12 OZ MINCED MUTTON • FLAKY PASTRY • 1 ONION • [1 TBS OIL]
4 OZ MUSHROOMS • 1 DSP CHOPPED PARSLEY • A PINCH OF THYME
SALT AND PEPPER • A LITTLE GOOD STOCK • EGG OR MILK

Chop and lightly fry the onion [in the oil]. Line twelve small round tins or small saucers with half of the pastry. [Set the pastry in hot oven as directed above.] Mix together the minced mutton, chopped onion, chopped mushrooms, parsley, thyme and seasoning. Divide the mixture between the tins. Add to each a little stock to moisten. Cover with lids made from the rest of the pastry. Brush with egg or milk and bake in a moderate oven (350°F) for about 30–45 minutes. 6 helpings.

Garnett the Gastronome

'For honey and bees occupy my thoughts more than literature.'

David Garnett to Sylvia Townsend Warner, 5 August 1966

David 'Bunny' Garnett was one of Bloomsbury's most prolific and celebrated writers. In his eighty-eight years he wrote and published over twenty works of fiction and over thirteen works of nonfiction, including two collections of letters, three autobiographies and three memoirs. His first major novel, *Lady into Fox* (1922), won him the James Tait Black Memorial Prize and the Hawthornden Prize for imaginative literature. His novel *The Sailor's Return* (1925), about bigotry and an interracial marriage, was made into a feature-length film. *Aspects of Love* (1955) was later adapted into a hit musical production by Andrew Lloyd Webber.

But equal to his enthusiasm and talent for literature was Bunny's passion for nature, including all aspects of gastronomy. He farmed pigs and poultry, kept bees, foraged for mushrooms, grew his own fruit and vegetables and became an accomplished fly-fisherman and cook. In his letters to Sylvia Townsend Warner he recounts such epicurean adventures as identifying (poorly) and eating (hopefully) wild toadstools.* He tells her of exciting visits to the open market in Cahors with its vibrant throng of 'ducks, geese, fowls, guinea-fowls, rabbits, all dead and alive, every known vegetable and fruit with wood mushrooms of every size and shape, cheese, cow, goat and sheep, butter, eggs, fish – tunny, fresh sardines, loup, baby cuttlefish.' He wrote to her of the time he collected so much honey that his bees swarmed and the kitchen table ran 'with pools of thick golden honey.' On another occasion, at a friend's celebration feast, the 'tables … [groaned] with food and every delicacy. But no knives or forks.' He warns her that 'London eggs aren't safe to boil'; '"a dog's nose" is a double gin with half a pint of beer'; and the best way to cook squid or cuttlefish is 'stewed with aubergines and tomato in red wine'.

* Bunny was an expert when it came to mushrooms and in 1914 he identified a new species of fungus, Discinella minutissima Ramsbottom et Garnett, while he was studying fungi at Imperial College London – it was named after him.

Vanessa Bell, *David Garnett*, 1915. Bunny's talents extended beyond the literary: he was an ardent naturalist with interests in mushroom foraging, beekeeping and gastronomy.

Even in his old age, Bunny celebrated dining off fresh boiled country eggs, shopping for 'little melons ... and sacks of gleaming chestnuts' and making meals and preserving fruits. He waged war against asparagus beetles, won prizes at honey-making competitions and enclosed in his letters heart-rending poems and open invitations to lunches and to dinners. He tempted, he lured, and promised sumptuous 'grilled sole' and other delicious dishes aboard his London houseboat *Moby Dick*. He took note of his culinary successes and shared his best recipes. Here are three such triumphs.

David 'Bunny' Garnett, drawing of skewers with liver and onions, 1967.

Lamb's Liver

'24 October 1967: I have just cooked an evening meal of lamb's liver, and eaten it. Prepared like this: Alternate lumps of liver with sage leaves plastered against and between them and onion – transfixed by *two* skewers. Thus [sketch reproduced above]:

You use two skewers because if you use one the bits of liver slide round when you try to turn them over and cook the other side. The result is beyond the dreams of the greediest gastronome. The onion is half-raw. *That makes it infinitely better.* The flavour of sage is wonderful. (You have to pick the sage leaves off the liver before you eat it.)'

Sloe Cheese

'18 September 1976: As there was the largest crop of sloes ever known I picked 2 kilos of them, boiled with 2 kilos of windfall apples, and rubbed it through a sieve for hours on end. Then boiled it and then added 1¾ kilos of sugar, and it has turned out a delicious sloe cheese.'

Orgy of Squid

'22 October 1977: I have just indulged in an orgy of squid or calamari. In Italy they serve these delicious denizens of the sea – I can't call them fish – as little rings of wash-leather. The way to cook them is to fry them gently and then stew them in wine (chopped up) with tomatoes and aubergines for three hours in a gentle oven – garlic and herbs, of course.'

Savoury Eggs with Henrietta

'I arrived for lunch with a couple of bottles of red, a plate of fruit and a loaf of my rugged brown homemade bread. I opened a bottle and we chatted, relaxed. Henrietta had become a friend. She lit the stove (perhaps she has given up entirely on her oven?) and into sizzling oil threw a couple of handfuls of small green Spanish peppers (the kind where one in ten will send you running desperately for a glass of water). Next, pâté, a slice of my (now toasted) bread, devilled eggs (absolutely delicious with a hint of something I couldn't quite place) and a spinach salad. Afterwards, we ate her homemade red and white plums stewed in sweet wine.'

Jans Ondaatje Rolls's diary, 6 February 2013

Henrietta Garnett is not only a connoisseur of nineteenth-century literature, Pre-Raphaelite art, French wine and rare epicurean delights, but she also knows a thing or two about eggs. 'I am very fond of eggs other than hens' eggs too, of tiny cold quails' eggs, of ducks' eggs with their extraordinarily beautiful colour combination of pale green shell and curious orange yolk, of bantams' eggs and of gulls' eggs dipped in salt and washed down with a glass or two of Chablis.' In an article for *Harpers & Queen* in 1976 she wrote, 'I found this recipe of my great-grandmother's [Mrs Herbert Duckworth, Bryanston Square, 1874] the other day when I was looking through *Lady Clark of Tillypronie's Cookery Book*, published in 1909. She is quite right about taking care not to overcook the eggs.' This is Henrietta's retelling of her great-great grandmother's recipe.

4 EGGS • FRESH THYME AND PARSLEY • 4 SHALLOTS • SALT AND PEPPER
I TBS DOUBLE CREAM • I TBS STALE WHITE BREADCRUMBS

Boil the eggs for 6* minutes. Put them in a basin of cold water to prevent them cooking any further and shell them carefully while they are still warm. Cut them lengthways. Scoop out the yolks and pound them, chop herbs (Mrs Duckworth used mint, too. I presume that Lady Clark did not, as she put a couple of exclamation marks beside this in the ingredients) and shallots finely and add, with salt and pepper. Heat the cream in a small pan and stir in the egg mixture until it is hot. Fill the whites with the mixture and scatter a few stale white breadcrumbs on the top sparingly. Put under the grill for just a few moments to toast the breadcrumbs, but be sure the whites do not get too brown to be good to eat. If people leave the whites on their plates, it shows they are overcooked. These are very good eaten with crisply fried bacon.

* Henrietta has since changed the cooking time to 5 minutes.

APPENDIX: ADDITIONAL RECIPES FROM THE BLOOMSBURY ARCHIVES

The following recipes are taken from the unpublished collections of Helen Anrep, Grace Higgens, Frances Partridge and Angelica and David 'Bunny' Garnett, with the addition of two published recipes by Lydia Keynes (née Lopokova).

1. Eggs, Breads and Breakfasts

From Helen Anrep's scrapbook:

Soda Scones

To four pounds of flour add two large teaspoonfuls of salt, half an ounce of soda, and a quart of milk, in which half an ounce of cream of tartar has been well stirred. Mix the whole well, but lightly. Cut into round cakes and bake in a quick oven, or on an iron frying pan over a clear fire. About fifteen minutes are sufficient. The scones should rise well; they need to be turned once. Wheaten meal cakes can be made in the same way, and make an excellent breakfast bread, both delicious and nutritious.

From the Frances Partridge archive:

Cold Eggs in Aspic

Lightly poach eggs & cover them with aspic with tarragon or other herbs, asparagus tips, artichoke fonds, tomatoes, pimentoes or almonds or anything else in it. Leave in fridge.

Croque Monsieur
(Sophie)

Toast one side of a piece of bread. Put a slice of ham on the other (or cooked rashers) and grill until cooked enough. Take it out from under the grill and cover with salted cheese. Toast under the grill until melted and slightly browned.

Eggs à la Tripe

About 2 onions to every 3 eggs. Slice onions fine & cook in butter till tender but not brown. Sprinkle with flour & add hot milk so as to make a thick Béchamel. Season with salt, pepper & nutmeg. In this sauce heat halved (not very) hard-boiled eggs.

Garnish with fried croutons & add a little butter & a spoonful of cream before serving.

Eggs and Spinach in Cheese Sauce

Soft boil one egg per person & shell. Cook creamed spinach & pour into fire-proof dish. Lay the eggs in halves in this. Pour over a thick cheese sauce & brown under grill.

Pain Perdu

Cut crusts off some slices of white bread (& soak in milk for several hours). Then fry in butter till light golden brown, pour golden syrup over & serve.

Quails' Eggs

Put in hot water bring to boil simmer for 2–3 mins.

Eggs en Cocotte
(Boris and ?)

Cook eggs in usual way [fried or poached], but pour over them butter cooked till quite brown, with a teaspoon (about) of tarragon vinegar & some chopped parsley before serving.

From the cookery book of Angelica and David 'Bunny' Garnett:

Humpty-Dumpty
(Angelica Garnett)

If economy is an object one egg only between two people may be used.

Cut a round of bread to each person and fry it gently. Take it out of the pan and soak it for a minute in the beaten egg which you have previously mixed with a little milk, grated cheese, parsley & pepper and salt. Put back in the frying pan and fry quickly till done.

This recipe can be varied by the omission of cheese or the addition of spring onions, tomato pulp, finely chopped mushrooms etc.

Leeks & Eggs au Gratin
(David 'Bunny' Garnett)

Clean 6 leeks & cut into 2 inch lengths. Boil them till cooked. Boil 2 or 3 eggs for 7 minutes. Make a white sauce & embed lengths of leeks in it with shelled eggs cut into 2 or 3 pieces. Pepper & salt added in making sauce. Grate cheese fairly thinly over this & put in oven for 30 or 40 minutes.

2. Sauces and Condiments

From the Grace Higgens archive:

White Sauce

SMALL LUMP [1 OZ] BUTTER
1 HEAPED UP WOODEN SPOONFUL FLOUR
½ PT MILK

Melt butter in sauce-pan, then stir in the flour into butter; pour in milk & stir until thick.

Pimento and Cheese Fritters

TINNED [WHOLE] RED PEPPERS OR PIMENTOS
CHEDDAR CHEESE • FLOUR
SALT AND PEPPER • BUTTER • PARSLEY

Drain pimentos from liquid & dry in cloth. Prepare some slices of Chedar [*sic*], cut about ⅛ of an inch in thickness & a little smaller than Peppers. Season the pieces with pepper & salt & slip one inside each of the red peppers. Coat lightly in flour cook them in a little hot butter slowly until cheese has melted turning them once. Place on rounds of toast … & serve very hot. Garnish with parsley.

Pâté de Foie

1 LB PIGS LIVER
½ LB [COMBINED WEIGHT] SAUSAGE MEAT &
BACON RASHERS • 1 SMALL TIN TRUFFLES
1 TBS COGNAC • ¼ PT STOCK
½ OZ CRUSHED GARLIC • 2 EGGS
1 OZ BUTTER • 2 BAY LEAVES
½ OZ FLOUR • SALT AND PEPPER

Melt butter on low heat, stir in flour and add the stock, stir till it thickens, remove from heat, add the rest of the ingredients, except rashers and bay leaves. Put 4 rashers (& a bay leaf) in bottom of 2 pt terrine, add the mixture, cover with remaining Rashers and Bayleaf, seal hole in lid. Place in container of water cook for 1½ hours, leave to stand for at least 24 hours before eating.

From the Frances Partridge archive:

Ajo Blanco
(Janetta) – 4 people

2 cloves garlic, 2 tbs olive oil, 6 oz skinned almonds, 1 tb. vinegar, salt, water, peeled white grapes. Put the garlic in the mixer first & give it a whizz, then add almonds, salt, oil & enough water to cover them. Put the mixer on maximum speed, till almonds are fine-ground to desired thickness. Put in refrigerator. Before serving add vinegar, lumps of ice, peeled white grapes at the last moment – or nearly (they can be bought in tins).

Avocado Mousse

¼ pt cold water & stock cube, 1 rounded tab. gelatine, 2 teasp. Worcester sauce, ½ pt stock, ¼ pt mayonnaise, ¼ pt double cream, 2 large avocados or 3 small. Melt gelatine in cold water & warm gently till melted (don't boil). Stir in stock & set aside to cool. Mash avocados, season, add Worcester sauce. Slowly pour in liquid & stir till it thickens. Fold in mayonnaise and highly whipped cream. Pour into a mould & chill in fridge.

Cucumber Elisha

Peel & slice cucumber in sticks about ½ in. thick, halved or whole. Salt for ½ hour, then wash under tap. Seethe a small onion, a sprig of mint, bay-leaf, parsley or fennel in milk. Cook the cucumber in water till tender. Drain & cover it in a béchamel sauce. Make from this milk and cream and chopped parsley.

Gelatine

1 oz will stiffen 1 pint of fluid. ½ oz will stiffen mayonnaise or thick sauce. 1 oz is a shade more than the measure gives for sugar.

Guacamole
(Janetta)

For 4. 2 very ripe avocados. lemon juice, small quantity of raw onion chopped fine & or garlic, pepper & salt. Mash together with fork (& add cream?). Not long before wanted sprinkle with plenty of coriander. Leave stones until ready to serve to prevent browning.

Haddock Mousse

1 lb haddock, 2 eggs, nearly ¾ pint cream, nearly ¾ pint béchamel sauce, 1¼ oz gelatine (1 rounded tabs), parsley. Cook the haddock in milk, put through mixer (with some parsley). Make béchamel sauce with the milk, mix fish, sauce & cream in a bowl, add the gelatine melted in cold water (or milk) & gradually warm. Butter a soufflé dish, put the eggs (sliced & hardboiled) over the bottom, pour in the mixture & let it set.

Mornay Sauce

Add (off the heat) to sauce Béchamel – 1 egg-yolk & 2 table-spoons of grated Gruyère cheese. Mix well.

From the cookery book of Angelica and David 'Bunny' Garnett:

Sauce Piquante

(Angelica Garnett)

This sauce goes very well with mackerel.

Take your fish and cook it gently in vinegar and water in equal proportions. Add pepper and salt, chopped spring onions, parsley, and a chopped gherkin or two, together with a bay leaf and a little thyme.

When the fish is done take it out and keep it hot. Make a thin white roux and add to it the liquid in which the fish was cooked, having first removed the bay leaf. Serve with the fish.

Tarama Salata

(David 'Bunny' Garnett, 25 May 1970)

Cods Roe, cream cheese, chives, garlic, yoghourt

Skin cods roe. Pound with equal quantities of cream cheese & thick yoghourt, with chives & garlic with a little olive oil in a mortar.

This is excellent with buttered rye biscuits or/and:

Flesh of ripe Avocado with 3 tablespoons of above, a spoonful of oil & vinegar dressing well mixed up. A real discovery. 25.5.70.

Green Tomato Chutney

(Squadron Leader Bill Hilch's – David 'Bunny' Garnett, 29 October 1969)

4 LBS GREEN & JUST COLOURING TOMATOES

A LARGE HEAD OF GARLIC

1 LB DARK BROWN SUGAR

A HANDFUL OF SEEDLESS RAISINS

1/3 LB SHALLOTS • PEPPERCORNS

CUMMIN SEEDS • A LITTLE GINGER GRATED

2 MEDIUM RED CHILLIES CUT UP

1 PINT VINEGAR

[Combine all ingredients in a blender.]

Repeated 28. Nov. 69 but with ground cumin as no seeds left.

Repeated 15.10.71 at Charry with pale brown sugar, ground cumin, little chilli powder.

Repeated Sept 19 1977.

Repeated with pale sandy sugar 17.9.72 (with Rose Jackson). More sultanas & powdered cumin.

Repeated 29.9.72 using chiefly white sugar & adding a little wine. - + using powdered cumin.

Repeated 4.11.73. Very few shallots so used an onion as well. Guesswork in weights.

Repeated 26 Oct. 1978. Used very dark moist sugar. Half quantities – except for pimonts [chillies] – one piquante & one green not piquant & special vinegar given me – Ch. [Chateau] Loudenne.

Small-Holders Cheese

(Angelica Garnett)

Take 5 gallons of milk – the mornings and the evenings mixed. It is better not to cool the evenings.

Place all in a large open pan and bring to a temperature of 86°[F] on the stove. Add a souplade of starter (or if the starter is old 1½ souplades) and stir gently so that all is well mixed. Then add 2 teaspoons of cheese Rennet mixed with 6 teaspoons of water. Deep stir for 5 minutes or more, then flick it with the thermometer until there are bubbles which stay on the surface, which show that it is setting. When that happens don't deep stir again. When set cover over and leave for 20 mins to half an hour.

Take a long carving knife and cut it in long strips ½"–1" wide from end to end holding the knife straight up and drawing it cleanly out each time. Then cut it across in the same way and then diagonally. Stir it up with your hand and mix it thoroughly. Leave for 20 mins. Continue to stir and mix for an hour or more and during that time put it back on the stove and bring to 100°[F].

The pieces of curd should feel rubbery and solid. When the whey forms into solid lumps and falls to the bottom cover it up and leave for 20 mins or more until you are certain the curd is really hard and rubbery.

Line the cheese mould with muslin. Pour off the whey and mix the curd with 2 oz of salt. Mix well. Put it in the mould and press it down as you put it in. Slight pressure is first put on, increased after 1 hr. Increase each day until in 3 days it is full on. Turn each day. On the 4th day take it out & put on a shelf. Turn each day. Ready to eat in 6–12 weeks.

Preserved Cèpes

(David 'Bunny' Garnett, 14 September 1972)
The fungus used was Boletus Erythropus. Removed gills & cut in slices. Dried in oven with a little olive oil to prevent burning or sticking. Then packed with oil into airproof jar.

First used some on 12 October chopped up mixed with boiled rice & parsley to stuff a green pepper – split in half & baked in a little oil in a covered earthenware dish. Delicious.

3. Vegetarian Dishes, Soups and Salads

From Helen Anrep's scrapbook:

Boiled Lettuce

If the lettuce is not delicate enough for salad, cut it in pieces and boil it soft in water slightly salted; when cooked, drain every drop of water from the leaves. Put some flour in a pan with some butter on the fire, and let it cook until it is yellow; turn the lettuce in it, and let it boil once or twice. Pour some stock over the lettuce; let it boil once again, and just before serving pour in a little cream. A little nutmeg is sometimes liked.

Stuffed Tomatoes

Get them as large and as firm as possible; cut a round place on the top and scrape out most of the inside and mix it with fine bread crumbs, parsley, onion, pepper and salt. Chop all fine and stuff the tomatoes carefully. Put a good lump of butter in the pan and baste while baking. Cook until brown and well done.

From a recipe by Lydia Keynes (Lopokova) published in the *Evening News*, 18 May 1927:

A Really Good Cabbage Dish

Slice and fry an onion to a light brown in a tablespoon of butter. Then add two tablespoons of flour, two cups of water and season with pepper and salt. Cut up the cabbage, pour the sauce over it, and cook slowly for an hour. Then put into a baking dish, add half a teaspoon of Worcester sauce, sprinkle the top with breadcrumbs and small lumps of butter, and put into a hot oven until the breadcrumbs are brown.

From the Frances Partridge archive:

Aubergines with Paprika

1 aubergine for 2 people, 1 small onion, 1 heaped teasp. paprika, 4 tablesp. olive oil. Glass white wine. Parsley. Cut aubergine (unpeeled) in slices ¼ in thick. Brown gently in oil; keep hot & cook onion finely sliced. Add paprika & wine, & add to aubergines; sprinkle with parsley. [Serve with] snippets of fried bread.

Garlic Soup with Eggs

(Lucila)
Allow 2 cloves of garlic per person. Less than 2 tablesp. olive oil per person, bread, stock (Knorr), 1 egg per person. Fry the cloves of garlic whole in the oil until black – then remove them. Break some pieces of bread roughly & fry lightly. Set aside. Add stock & poach eggs in liquid. Serve bread & eggs in soup plates.

Gravy. Leave about 1 tbsp. of fat in which whatever it has been frying. Add 1 level tablesp. of seasoned flour. Stir until it is dark brown. Gradually stir in ½ pint stock & bring to the boil.

Lettuce Soup

Take outer leaves of a lettuce (when the heart is to be salad). Cook gently in butter, add water, cream or milk, thyme & finely chopped onion. Season & put through blender.

Vichyssoise

Cut up 1 whole pint of leeks & pots [potatoes] (raw) & cook with lid on in oil & butter mixer for about 15 mins on gentle heat. Add milk (or milk & water), put through mixer. Add seasoning, cream & parsley.

Parsley Soup

Chop a lot of parsley & fry lightly in butter. Add a stock cube, & milk & cream. [Gently bring to the boil.] Season. Put through liquidizer.

Tomato Salad

Dip into near boiling water for 1 minute exactly & skin. Let cool & slice. Sprinkle with *sweet* basil, mint & chopped garlic & dress.

Tunny Fish Salad

Cut a tin of tunny-fish [tuna] in chunks, add chicken, parsley, chives or other herbs, black pitted olives & salad dressing.

From the cookery book of Angelica and David 'Bunny' Garnett:

Potage Saint-Germain

(Angelica Garnett)

I PT DRIED PEAS • 2½ PT WATER
HAM BONE OR BEEF BONE
2 ONIONS • 2 CARROTS
CREAM & BUTTER IN SMALL AMOUNTS

Soak peas for 12 hours in water. Put them in the saucepan with the bones, sliced vegetables & water adding seasoning & herbs. Bring to the boil, remove scum, simmer for 3 hours. Drain, keep the liquid but remove bones & herbs.

Rub peas & vegetables to a purée. Return this to liquid, add dash of cayenne. Stir in cream & butter & serve with croutons.

Blewits

(David 'Bunny' Garnett)

Blewits are in season at Hilton in late autumn & early winter and can survive frost. They are found in pastures.

Remove pieces of grass & cut off stalks. Fry in margarine until tender. Put in covered casserole with chopped clove of garlic, bay leaf, chopped parsley, a sprig of thyme & chopped [onion?]. Add salt and pepper and cream. Bake in hot oven for 5 minutes then transfer to lower oven & simmer for 2 hours or so.

Dandylions or Pissenlit

(David 'Bunny' Garnett)

An excellent spring salad when one longs for raw green things. Dandylions may be blanched. Found in flowerpots or just cut out of the lawn.

Wash & chop your dandylion including the very young flower buds. Spread on a plate. On this put 3 or 4 rashers of bacon and one or two fried eggs & all the fat they have been fried in.

Cèps Montcuq

(David 'Bunny' Garnett)

In this case Boletus Erythropus.*

Cut up cap & stalk finely (after removing & throwing away gills).

When you have a heaped saucer full, with a chopped up clove of garlic & one small sliced tomato put in small frying pan or cocotte & cook gently in oil. When the ceps are tender but not before, break

an egg into centre of the pan & leave to cook gently until white […] set. Season with salt & pepper.

* 'I am a bit doubtful about this cep. I have eaten dozens & then suddenly one made me sick in the night – or I was sick.'

Cèpes (Boletus Fungi)

(David 'Bunny' Garnett, gathered at Charry early September 1972)

Boletus Luridus & Boletus Erythropus. Rather old species.

1. With Eggs. Removed Gills. Sliced caps. Stewed gently in oil (walnut oil added once) with garlic until thoroughly cooked. Sprinkle with parsley & salt. Pour off any extra oil. Add two beaten up eggs.

2. Soup. Make vegetable soup of tomatoes, garlic, onions, leeks, etc. and caps of cèps sliced. Add bones if available or Knorr chicken cube or bits of pork belly. Put through a moulis.

1974 July. I found a few Boletus Badius which has a sticky top when damp and turns blue rapidly or instantly, when cut. Cooked it in oil with garlic & added tomato.

4. Fish

From Helen Anrep's scrapbook:

Creamed Lobster

Carefully cut freshly boiled lobster into halves with a sharp knife, remove the meat, rub the coral and the soft green meat together, put these latter into a saucepan with a lump of butter, well rolled in corn-flour, a tablespoon of anchovy sauce, season with a dash of cayenne pepper and salt to taste, then let it warm slowly. When smoking hot, stir in a cup of cream and [heat again, but do not boil. Pour over the lobster meat and serve immediately].

From a newspaper clipping in the Grace Higgens archive:

Fish Scallops

4 OZ WHITE FISH PER PERSON • BÉCHAMEL SAUCE
BREADCRUMBS • BUTTER • [SCALLOP SHELLS]

Mix some cooked flaked white fish with some white sauce, put into buttered scallop shells, cover with buttered crumbs and bake.

Duncan Grant, *Helen Anrep in the Dining Room at Charleston, c.* 1945.

From the Frances Partridge archive:

Cold Salmon (Scotch way)

Any size. Fill fish kettle with lightly salted water, 1 tb. vinegar (if liked).

Bring to the boil, put in salmon. When it reboils, boil it hard for 2 mins exactly. Draw off the heat, & leave covered for 12 hrs if poss. Then: dish up.

Fillets of Fish with Bananas

For 2. About 4 small fillets, 2 bans [bananas], 2 oz mushrooms, ½ glass white wine, seasoning and butter. Cut bananas lengthwise & lay in greased baking dish. Slice mushrooms & put over bananas; next the fillets (or mixed). Season & pour on wine. Cook in hot oven for 5 or 10 mins, covered in foil. Add a little cream & lots of butter & brown under grill.

Herring in Oatmeal

1 herring per person, heads removed. Wash herrings well & dry. Brush with melted butter, roll them in fine oatmeal, brush again & score on both sides. Season & grill (or fry, or both) quickly both sides.

Serve with béchamel sauce to which a teaspoon of mustard is added.

Fish Fillets

(Julia)

Put fillets in flat fireproof dish. Pour over them ¼ lb butter, pepper, salt, chopped parsley & juice of one lemon. Brown in the oven for about 20 mins.

Kedgeree (of Haddock or Salmon)

(Mary Henderson)

For 4 or 3

1 LB HADDOCK OR SALMON

MILK • BUTTER • SEASONING

1 CUP RICE PER 2 PEOPLE

1 HARD BOILED EGG EACH

Poach the fish in milk. (Haddock – pour boiling water over & leave for 2 mins. Drain & poach in milk for 10 mins on a low heat, covered.) Flake the fish into a dish & keep warm. Cook rice in boiling salted water for 18(?) mins. Strain & put in earthenware dish with hard boiled eggs cut in quarters, about

1 oz melted butter, pepper & parsley. (Make a rich béchamel & add curry.)

Haddock Soufflée

Make a béchamel with 1 oz butter, 1 tablesp. flour & ¼ pint milk. Add about half a large cooked flaked haddock. Put through electric mixer. Stir in yolks of 2 eggs & 2 oz grated cheese (Gruyère if possible), pepper. When cool fold in whites of 4 eggs stiffly beaten. Cook for 20 to 25 mins. Enough for 3.

Scallops

Chop & put in their own shells (buttered) with breadcrumbs, parsley & lots of butter & cook for about 20 minutes.

Sole Filets

Butter a fireproof dish & sprinkle 1 onion finely chopped over it. Lay the fillets on top. Skin one lb. tomatoes & chop up; lay over the fillet with chopped parsley & seasoning. Pour over a glass of white wine & ½ a cup of water. Bake in the oven. Remove fish, reduce the liquid & add cream. Pour sauce over the fish. Serve hot or cold.

Truite aux Amandes

Melt butter in serving-dish, lay trout in it basting, and pricking, add salt & pepper & a glass of dry white wine. Cook fairly gently for 20 mins or more. Fry flaked almonds in butter & sprinkle thickly over.

Fish Soufflée

Take about ¾ lb of cold turbot or other cooked fish – i.e. salmon. Put it through mixer, season with salt, pepper & paprika; add yolks of 2 eggs, a glass of cream, then the whites stiffly beaten. Mix well, put in buttered soufflé dish & bake for 15 to 20 mins.

From the cookery book of
Angelica and David 'Bunny' Garnett:

Fillet of Sturgeon

(Angelica Garnett, 12 June 1942)

1 Fillet of Sturgeon about 2 lbs. laid in earthenware dish. Pepper and salt, 2 oz of mutton fat or dripping or butter, 3 or 4 sliced shallots or onion, rosemary & bay. Bake slowly, basting every ten minutes allowing ¾ hour for a fillet of 2½ lbs. Turn after twenty-five minutes. Ten minutes before it is done, sprinkle with chopped parsley. Serve with new peas and new potatoes.

Lobster Salad

(Angelica Garnett – Recipe from Antica Trattoria, citta di Milano, S. Marco 599, Venezia)

Dress the lobster with salt, pepper, oil & vinegar & chopped chervil before adding the mayonnaise.

5. Meats

From Helen Anrep's scrapbook:

Kidneys à la Maître d'Hôtel

Plunge some mutton kidneys in boiling water; open them down the centre, but do not separate them; peel and pass a skewer across them to keep them open; pepper, salt, and dip them into melted butter; broil them over a clear fire on both sides, cooking the cut side first; remove the skewers, have ready some maître d'hôtel butter, viz., butter beaten up with chopped parsley, salt, pepper, and a little lemon juice – put a small piece into the hollow of each kidney, and serve very hot.

From a recipe by Lydia Keynes (Lopokova) published in the *Evening News*, 30 March 1927:

Black Game

The black game [grouse], I am told, is put into a sack and buried for a fortnight to make it tender. Then it is dug up, plucked, drawn, stuffed with a mixture of chestnuts and apples, and gently braised for a long while, not roasted. It is served with little savoury dumplings and young carrots, fried parsley, and green peas.

From the Frances Partridge archive:

Braised Veal

Take a piece of boned & rolled veal & put in a casserole with some butter & brown it both sides. Add onions & brown them. Then turn heat very low, add salt & mushrooms. Turn from time to time & be sure it doesn't brown. Add plenty of cream before serving. A piece of about 4 lbs will take about 1½ hours on very slow heat.

Calves Liver, Sauté with Cream

Dip fairly thin slices of calves liver in flour & put in smoking butter in a frying-pan. Cook 3 mins one side, 4 the other. Season & add a few drops of vinegar, a piece of butter & a tablespoon or more of thick cream. Pour sauce over liver.

Beef, Cold Fillet

(Mary)

For supper. 2 lbs fillet of beef. Roast for 10 mins in hot oven. Turn off oven & leave 10 mins more. Let it cool. Surround with cooked carrots & peas & pour over a tin of Campbells consommée [*sic*] with a tablespoon of sherry in it. Leave in fridge.

Chicken with Honey Lemon

(Mrs D. Glyn)

Cold roast chicken. Cut in quarters. Cover with lemon juice, plenty of thick honey, parsley and pats of butter. Heat through in moderate oven of about 20 min.

Kidneys with Mushrooms and Cream Sauce

2 kidneys per person, mushrooms, 1 sliced onion. Cut the kidneys in slices with scissors, & slice the mushrooms. Heat 2 oz butter in a frying pan, add the kidneys & mushrooms, seasoning & a small glass of white wine,* and simmer for 5 minutes or so. Add cream & chopped parsley before serving.

* 'or a dessert-spoon of brandy, flambé'.

Lamb & Mushroom Casserole

For 4. 4 loin lamb chops, flour, 1 oz butter, ½ pt. stock, 1 sliced onion, ½ lb mushrooms, potatoes, chopped parsley. Trim, flour & brown chops both sides in butter, lay at bottom of casserole – into 1 tb. of hot butter put 1 level tb. seasoned flour & stir till dark brown, gradually stir in stock & reboil to make a good gravy. Add sliced onions, mushrooms & gravy to chops & a layer of thinly sliced potatoes. Cook 1½ hrs in 355° oven, with lid off for last 10 mins. NB – Can keep in fridge until this last operation.

Dublin Steak

Cut 2 lbs chuck steak into convenient pieces & brown them in butter & oil. Remove them to casserole & soften 4 onions in the fat. Sprinkle with salt, pepper & a heaped tablesp. of flour, stirring well. Add these to casserole, with a bayleaf, ½ pint of Guinness & teasp. brown sugar & a few sultanas.

Cover & cook fairly slowly for 2 to 3 hours or till tender. Reheats well. For 4 people.

Goulash

For 5. 2 lbs rump steak cut into cubes (about 1 inch), 1 large Spanish onion, ½ tin tomato purée, ditto tinned pimento, 1 tabs. paprika, 1 clove garlic, crushed; 2 glasses red wine, ¼ pint sour cream, parsley. Chop onion, fry in oil & butter in casserole & very gently till transparent. Stir in paprika & add red pepper, tomato purée, & garlic. Brown meat & add to the rest, plus wine, cover & cook on asbestos mat as slowly as possible for 1½ hours. Remove & let cool. Reheat 1½ hrs before wanted. Stir in sour cream & chopped parsley just before serving.

Partridge au Choux
(suggested ingredients)

I HEAD WHITE CABBAGE
½ TSP SALT • BUTTER
2 PARTRIDGES
2 RASHERS BACON, CUT INTO SMALL PIECES
I CARROT, SLICED • I BOUQUET GARNI
SALT AND PEPPER

Cut a white cabbage in pieces removing hard parts & boil in salted water. Drain well. Cut partridges in half, toss them in butter for 2 or 3 minutes. Put in a casserole a little butter, 2 rashers of bacon cut in pieces, 1 sliced carrot, a bouquet, a little water & the partridges. Cook gently for 20 minutes. Add the cabbage, season well & cook slowly in oven for another 20 mins. or until done.

From the cookery book of
Angelica and David 'Bunny' Garnett:

Rabbit Pudding with Mushrooms

(Angelica Garnett, August 1941)

Line a good size basin with a suet crust, put in a layer of rabbit, chopped sage and onion, then a layer of peeled mushrooms, and continue until the basin is filled. Sprinkle plenty of flour between each layer, as that makes good thick gravy. The slices of bacon should be cut up in thin strips and put in each layer. Nearly fill the basin with water, cover with suet crust, and steam for about 3 hours. This is a very tasty and nourishing dish.

Ceps du Montcuq,

in this case Boletus Erythropus *

.Cut up cap & stalk finely (after removing + throwing away gills)

When you have a heaped saucer full, with a chopped up clove of garlic + one small strip tomato put in small frying pan or cocotte & cook gently in oil,

When the ceps are tender but not before, break an egg into centre of the pan + leave to cook gently until white has set. Season with salt & pepper.

* I am a bit doubtful about this Cep. I have eaten dozens — + then suddenly one made me sick in the night — or I was sick.

Barbecued Lamb

(Angelica Garnett)

Barbecued lamb is shoulder of lamb roast with garlic inserted, dredged with flour & dry mustard. When three parts cooked pour over sauce & leave until ready to eat in oven, basting frequently.

Sauce – 4 tablespoons Worcester Sauce, 4 tablespoons mushroom ketchup, 4 tablespoons tomato ketchup (not purée), 1 onion sliced, 1 dessertspoon sugar brown, salt, pepper, 1 tablespoon butter, 1 small cup broth, 2 bay leaves.

Simmer together until onion is tender.

Lamb's Testicles or Sweetbreads

(David Garnett)

Stew very gently in a court-bouillon of wine with a bouquet garni, garlic, tomato & onion. Pour some melted butter over before serving and a squeeze of lemon. OR With cream sauce to which some capers are added. Or a cream sauce with mushrooms. Difficulty is to cook mushrooms without overcooking the lamb's balls. Perhaps use fried mushrooms chopped up. Lamb's balls are on sale in many French butchers and charcuteries. OR Fry a small onion chopped up, a tomato & ½ clove garlic. Add stock & herbs (I used a little rosemary as well as parsley etc.) & stew them gently in this sauce which is much what one has with spaghetti.

6. Puddings, Cakes and Tea Parties

From Helen Anrep's scrapbook:

Baked Apple Pudding

1 LB APPLES • ½ LB SUGAR
1 LEMON • 6 EGGS
¼ LB BUTTER • PUFF PASTE

Pare and core the apples, stew until they will pulp, add pounded sugar, rind of lemon, grated, and the eggs well beaten. Stir well together and just before putting into oven melt the butter and stir into other ingredients. Put a puff paste round a pie dish, pour in the pudding and bake.

opposite: David 'Bunny' Garnett's recipe for Cèps Montcuq, from his and Angelica Garnett's cookery book.

Blackberry Shortcake

Sift half a pound of flour with two teaspoonfuls of baking powder, a heaping teaspoonful of sugar and the same quantity of salt. Mix this with a quarter of a pound of butter, which should be as firm as possible, adding, little by little, half a pint of cold boiled milk. The mixing should be done with a knife, rapidly. Place the paste on a floured pastry board, turning it about until it is covered with the flour. Roll it out to the thickness of half an inch, and cut it in round pieces the size of a breakfast plate. This may be done by inverting a plate on the paste and cutting around it. Lay the pieces on a greased pan and bake. When done, cut around the edge and pull them apart. Lay the blackberries on each half piece, sprinkling them well with sugar. The berries [on the top] layer should be placed upright.

Dried Peach Pie

An excellent pie can be made of dried peaches. Let the peaches soak in cold water all night, stew them in the same water until so soft that you can mash them fine; add for one pie two tablespoonfuls of sweet cream and a little more than half a cup of sugar – too much sugar destroys the flavour of the fruit. Butter may be used in place of cream, but if possible use cream, it gives such smoothness to the filling.

Fig Sauce

A nice sauce for tea can be made of figs. Let them soak in cold water, or better still, in a little sour cider, all night. Then let them boil gently until they are tender. Just before taking them from the fire add sugar to your taste. If you do not use cider, the juice of one or two lemons should be used to prevent the sauce from tasting insipid.

Ginger Pudding

¼ LB FLOUR • 6 OZ SUET
2 TSP GROUND GINGER • 1 EGG
½ LB BREADCRUMBS (LESS CRUMBS AND MORE
FLOUR COULD BE USED)
1 TSP BAKING POWDER
1 GILL MILK • PINCH OF SALT
4 OZ DEMERARA SUGAR
1 GILL GOLDEN SYRUP OR TREACLE

The flour, B[aking] powder [and] ginger should be sieved into a basin, mix in b[read] crumbs [and] suet. Put the syrup [and] milk and sugar into a pan and stir over low heat until the sugar is melted, then stir these into mixture [then] beat eggs [and] add. Put the mixture into a greased basin [and] cover with greased paper and steam for 3 hours, served with melted butter or treacle sauce.

Golden Pudding

4 OZ FLOUR • 4 OZ B[READ] CRUMBS
4 OZ SUET • 4 OZ SUGAR
4 OZ MARMALADE • 1 EGG

Mix all ingredients together. Stir in marmalade then fold in beaten egg. Put mixture in greased basin and boil or steam for 2½ to 3 hours, serve with marmalade sauce.

From the Grace Higgens archive:

Caramel of Orange

Cut oranges into thick slices, taking all pips, pith, & skin away, arange [sic] in a glass dish. cover with sugar. Make a caramel with 4 lb. sugar and ½ tumbler water. Chop up caramel coarsely and cover oranges with it. Then whip some cream up stiffly and cover over. 3 oranges sufficient for three people.

Italian Cream

Take 4 Ratafia Biscuits 8 yolks of eggs 1 glass Curascoa 1 bruised stick of cinnamon, a little orange rind, 1 pint milk 6 oz sugar. & Boil all together stir till it thickens; then rub through a sieve add 2 oz. gelatine ½ pint cream whipped, 22 oz preserved ginger & cherries (each) cut small, mix well & fill a mould.

Norwegian Soufflé

3 EGGS
2 OZ B[ROWN] SUGAR
5 LEAVES GELATINE
1 GLASS SHERRY

Melt Gel[atine] in sherry beat yolks of eggs with sugar. & add to sherry and Gel: then beat White very stiff & add to other ingredients. Pour in soufflé dish & when set cover with layer of Raspberry Jam, serve with cream.

Vanilla Cream

¾ PT MILK • 1 OZ. B[ROWN] SUGAR
½ TSP VANILLA • 1 EGG
½ OZ GELATINE • ORANGES

Melt gela[tine] in milk, when soft add sugar & stir over gentle heat till gela[tine] is dissolved, whisk yolk of egg and stir in cook until it boils & add the Vanilla Remove from fire & add stiffly whipped white of egg. Fold in gently. Leave until nearly cold, turn into wet mould, turn out when set and serve with fruit, or Real orange slice & arrange round mould & pour orange juice over.

Coffee Pudding

2 oz butter, cream with 2 oz sugar add 2 eggs, 3 oz flour 1 teaspoonful baking powder + 1 tablespoonful of coffee essence. Steam one hour.

Mandarin (or Pineapple) Meringue

2 OZ PUDDING (CAROLINA) RICE
1 PT MILK
1 OZ GRANULATED SUGAR
½ OZ BUTTER
2 LGE EGGS, SEPERATED [sic]
11 OZ CAN OF MANDARIN ORANGES
4 OZ CASTER SUGAR
1¾ PT OVENPROOF DISH

Melt butter in a pan, add the milk & bring it to the boil. Stir in the rice and granulated sugar & simmer the mixture, uncovered for 25 minutes, or until it is a creamy consistency & the rice cooked.

Stir the egg yolks into the rice. Drain the fruit & reserve some for decoration. Stir the rest into the rice. With the pan over a medium heat, & stirring all the time, bring the mixture almost back to the boil, so that it thickens slightly. Turn the rice into the dish. Whisk the egg whites, until they are stiff, & stand in peaks, add 2 level teaspoons of caster sugar from the measured amount, then re-whisk the mixture until it regains (P.T.O.) its original stiffness. Using a metal spoon, fold in the rest of the sugar, then carefully spread it over the creamy rice. Arrange the reserved fruit on top, then place the dish under a pre-heated grill and cook it for a few minutes until it is tinged light brown. Serve the pudding hot or cold. [Serves 4–6.] DELICIOUS

Chocolate Sponge

1½ OZ CHOCOLATE • ¼ CUP SUGAR
4 YOLKS EGGS • 1¾ CUPS MILK SCOLDED [SIC]
1 PKT CHIVERS STRAWBERRY JELLY
1 SHAKE SALT
1 SHAKE POWDERED CINNAMON
1 TSP VANILLA • 4 EGG WHITES

[C]ut the chocolate in pieces add half the sugar & melt over hot water, stir until smooth. Beat yolks slightly & mix rest of sugar. Pour boiling milk over this, stirring while pouring.

Cook in a double saucepan till the mixture is smooth and creamy, stirring constantly add a little at a time the choc mixture & stir. Pour at once over the jelly, place in a pan of hot water until dissolved. When cold and slightly thick add salt cinnamon & vanilla. Beat with an egg whisk till it is of a consistency of whipped cream. Beat egg whites till stiff & fold in mixture turn into mould.

Dundee Cake

5 OZ BUTTER, CREAMED • 5 [OZ] SUGAR
3 EGGS, ADD A LITTLE AT A TIME
3 OZ PLAIN FLOUR
1 TSP BAKING POWDER
6 OZ CURRANTS
6 OZ SULTANAS • 2 OZ CHERRIES
GRATED ORANGE AND LEMON PEEL
2 OZ PEEL • ALMONDS

[Preheat oven. Cream butter, add sugar, then eggs. Sieve flour and baking powder together and add to butter mixture. Mix in the dried fruit. Line baking tin with parchment.] Put almonds on top. [Cook.] Gas Mark No. 3 [170°C], for 2½ hours.

From the Frances Partridge archive:

Baked Bananas

Butter a dish. Cut the bananas in half (or smaller); add lemon juice & rum and cinnamon (or white wine or sherry) & brown sugar to cover the bananas. Bake in the oven ¼ to ½ hour. Or add two tbs. rum flambé, but must be served at once.

Brazilian Bananas

4 BANANAS
2 LEVEL TBS DARK SOFT BROWN SUGAR
1 TBS RUM • (2 TSP INSTANT COFFEE)
½ PT DOUBLE CREAM

Dissolve coffee in 1 tsp. boiling water & let cool. Whip cream (not too stiff). Peel & slice bananas & lay in a bowl or dish. Sprinkle them with the sugar & rum. Add ½ the cream mixed with coffee. Mix. Spread a layer of plain whipped cream on top & chill – slightly only.

Ginger & Banana Cream

Slice stem ginger & bananas, sprinkle with sugar & mix with cream (about twice as much banana as ginger).

From the cookery book of
Angelica and David 'Bunny' Garnett:

Chocolat Angelique

(Angelica Garnett, 27 February 1942)
Take 2–3 oz margarine or preferably butter & melt in a small saucepan. When sizzling add 4 tablespoons of sugar and ¾ pint of milk. Stir with wooden spoon and soon add 2 oz of grated chocolate or if not available 3 oz of cocoa. Leave it to boil, occasionally stirring. When it has reduced itself and become a thick cream add 3 tablespoons of Rum. Stir vigorously and pour into small glass cups. Decorate with a sweet white almond sticking out from a circle of Angelica. Serve when cold.

Highland Flummery

(David 'Bunny' Garnett – Linda Garnett's recipe)
Whip 1½ gills of cream until really stiff. Add 3 tablespoons of heather honey, melted but not hot, gradually, then 3 tablespoons of whisky and a few squeezes of lemon. Whisk again to restore stiffness. Sprinkle some medium oatmeal toasted for 2 or 3 minutes on top. Enough for 3.

CHRONOLOGY OF BLOOMSBURY

1885 Roger Fry enters King's College, Cambridge

1887 Roger Fry elected to Cambridge Apostles

1894 Desmond MacCarthy enters Trinity College, Cambridge

1895 Death of Julia Prinsep Stephen; Virginia Stephen has her
first breakdown

Desmond MacCarthy elected to Apostles

1897 E. M. Forster enters King's College, Cambridge

1899 Clive Bell, Thoby Stephen, Lytton Strachey, Saxon Sydney-
Turner and Leonard Woolf enter Trinity College,
Cambridge

1900 Midnight Society founded at Cambridge

1901 E. M. Forster elected to Apostles

1902 Saxon Sydney-Turner, Lytton Strachey and Leonard Woolf
elected to Apostles

Adrian Stephen enters Trinity College, Cambridge

John Maynard Keynes enters King's College, Cambridge

1903 John Maynard Keynes elected to Apostles

Roger Fry establishes *Burlington Magazine* with Herbert
Horne, Bernard Berenson and Charles Holmes

G. E. Moore publishes *Principia Ethica*

1904 Sir Leslie Stephen dies; Virginia Stephen has second
breakdown

Vanessa, Thoby, Virginia and Adrian Stephen move to
46 Gordon Square

Saxon Sydney-Turner joins Treasury

Leonard Woolf joins the Colonial Civil Service in Ceylon

1905 Thoby Stephen invites his friends to attend Thursday
evenings in Bloomsbury

Vanessa Stephen starts Friday Club

E. M. Forster publishes *Where Angels Fear to Tread*

1906 Roger Fry becomes curator at Metropolitan Museum of
Art, New York

Duncan Grant studies art in Paris

John Maynard Keynes becomes clerk in the India Office

Desmond MacCarthy marries Mary (Molly) Warre-Cornish

The Stephens visit Greece

Thoby Stephen dies of typhoid

1907 Vanessa Stephen marries Clive Bell

Virginia and Adrian Stephen move to 29 Fitzroy Square

'Thursday evenings' resume at 29 Fitzroy Square

E. M. Forster publishes *The Longest Journey*

1908 Birth of Julian Bell

E. M. Forster publishes *A Room with a View*

John Maynard Keynes researches probability theory at
Cambridge

1910 Roger Fry meets the Bells on chance railway journey
from Cambridge to London

HMS *Dreadnought* hoax by various members of
Bloomsbury

Birth of Quentin Bell

E. M. Forster publishes *Howards End*

Lydia Lopokova joins Sergei Diaghilev's Ballets Russes

Roger Fry curates 'Manet and the Post-Impressionists' at
Grafton Galleries

1911 Roger Fry and Vanessa Bell begin affair

Leonard Woolf returns from Ceylon

John Maynard Keynes appointed editor of *Economic Journal*

Lydia Lopokova dances in the United States

Virginia Stephen, Adrian Stephen, John Maynard Keynes,
Duncan Grant and Leonard Woolf move to 38
Brunswick Square, Bloomsbury

1912 Leonard Woolf marries Virginia Stephen

Second Post-Impressionist Exhibition in London

1913 Omega Workshops opened by Roger Fry

Virginia Woolf has third breakdown; attempts suicide

Leonard Woolf publishes *A Village in the Jungle*

1914 Vanessa Bell and Duncan Grant begin intimate relationship

Clive Bell publishes *Art*

Leonard Woolf publishes *The Wise Virgins*

(First World War begins)

Leonard and Virginia Woolf move to Richmond, Surrey

1915 John Maynard Keynes joins Treasury

Virginia Woolf publishes *The Voyage Out*

1916 Vanessa Bell moves to Wissett Lodge and then to
Charleston with Duncan Grant, David Garnett and
Julian and Quentin Bell

Clive Bell, a conscientious objector, works at Garsington
Manor, house of Ottoline and Philip Morrell near
Oxford

Lydia Lopokova rejoins Ballets Russes; dances with
Nijinsky

John Maynard Keynes takes over 46 Gordon Square

Lytton Strachey and Leonard Woolf exempted from
military service on medical grounds

1917 Leonard and Virginia found the Hogarth Press

The Hogarth Press publishes *Two Stories*

Leonard Woolf appointed secretary to Labour Party's
advisory committee

Desmond MacCarthy joins *New Statesman* as drama critic

Lytton Strachey and Dora Carrington move to Mill House,
Tidmarsh

1918 Lytton Strachey publishes *Eminent Victorians*

Molly MacCarthy publishes *A Pier and a Band*

Clive Bell publishes *Pot-Boilers*

Lydia Lopokova dances in London and partners Leonide
Massine

John Maynard Keynes purchases works of art for nation in
Paris with Treasury funds

(First World War ends)

Birth of Angelica Bell at Charleston

(Representation of the People Act – Fourth Reform Act:
women over age thirty granted right to vote)

1919 Leonard and Virginia Woolf purchase Monk's House,
Rodmell

Virginia Woolf publishes *Night and Day*

The Hogarth Press publishes *Kew Gardens* and T. S. Eliot's
Poems

John Maynard Keynes resigns from Treasury and writes
The Economic Consequences of the Peace

Omega Workshops close

1920 Roger Fry publishes *Vision and Design*
Leonard Woolf publishes *Economic Imperialism*
Omega Workshops liquidated
Desmond MacCarthy becomes literary critic at *New Statesman*
Memoir Club meets for the first time
Duncan Grant holds first solo exhibition at the Carfax Gallery, London
1921 Lytton Strachey publishes *Queen Victoria*
John Maynard Keynes publishes *A Treatise on Probability*
Lydia Lopokova dances in *The Sleeping Princess*
Virginia Woolf has fourth breakdown; lasts four months
Dora Carrington and Ralph Partridge marry
1922 Virginia Woolf publishes *Jacob's Room*
Vanessa Bell solo exhibition at the Independent Gallery, London
David Garnett publishes *Lady into Fox*
Clive Bell publishes *Since Cézanne*
1923 The Hogarth Press publishes T. S. Eliot's *The Waste Land*
John Maynard Keynes becomes chairman of the *Nation and Athenaeum* and Leonard Woolf appointed its literary editor
1924 E. M. Forster publishes *A Passage to India*
The Hogarth Press publishes Sigmund Freud's *Complete Psychological Works* (translated by James and Alix Strachey)
Lytton Strachey, Dora Carrington and Ralph Partridge move to Ham Spray House
Leonard and Virginia Woolf move to 52 Tavistock Square, Bloomsbury
Roger Fry and Helen Anrep begin a long love affair
1925 Virginia Woolf publishes *The Common Reader* and *Mrs Dalloway*
John Maynard Keynes and Lydia Lopokova marry
Roger Fry publishes *Transformations*
Virginia Woolf has fifth breakdown; lasts three months
Virginia Woolf and Vita Sackville-West begin an intermittent three-year love affair
1927 Virginia Woolf publishes *To the Lighthouse*
Roger Fry publishes *Cézanne*
Clive Bell publishes *Landmarks in Nineteenth-Century Painting*
Leonard Woolf publishes *Essays on Literature, History and Politics*
1928 Virginia Woolf publishes *Orlando: A Biography*
Lytton Strachey publishes *Elizabeth and Essex*
Clive Bell publishes *Civilization* and *Proust*
1929 Virginia Woolf publishes *A Room of One's Own*
Duncan Grant holds retrospective exhibition at Paul Guillaume Brandon Davis Ltd in Grosvenor Street
Roger Fry lectures at Royal Academy
1930 Roger Fry publishes *Henri Matisse*
Vanessa Bell solo exhibition at Cooling Galleries, London
John Maynard Keynes publishes *A Treatise on Money*
1931 Virginia Woolf publishes *The Waves*
Desmond MacCarthy publishes *Portraits*
Clive Bell publishes *An Account of French Painting*
Leonard Woolf publishes *After the Deluge (Principia Politica)*
Roger Fry holds retrospective exhibition at Cooling Galleries
1932 Virginia Woolf publishes *The Common Reader, Second Series*
Death of Lytton Strachey

Death of Dora Carrington, by suicide
1933 Roger Fry appointed to Slade Professorship at University of Cambridge
Lydia Lopokova gives final dance performance
Clive Bell becomes art critic for *New Statesman and Nation*, until 1943
David Garnett publishes *Pocahontas*
1934 Death of Roger Fry
1936 (Outbreak of Spanish Civil War)
Virginia Woolf has sixth breakdown; lasts two months
John Maynard Keynes publishes *The General Theory on Employment, Interest and Money*
John Maynard Keynes, Lydia Lopokova and George Rylands found Cambridge Arts Theatre
1937 Julian Bell killed in Spanish Civil War
1938 Virginia Woolf publishes *Three Guineas*
1939 Leonard and Virginia Woolf move to 37 Mecklenburgh Square, Bloomsbury
(Britain declares war on Germany)
Angelica Bell's twenty-first birthday party – Bloomsbury's final party at Charleston
1940 Virginia Woolf publishes *Roger Fry: A Biography*
John Maynard Keynes publishes *How to Pay for the War*
London Blitz; Woolfs' house in Bloomsbury destroyed by bombs
1941 Virginia Woolf completes *Between the Acts*
Death of Virginia Woolf, by suicide
1942 Angelica Bell and David Garnett marry
1943 Amaryllis Garnett born
1945 Henrietta Garnett born
(Second World War ends)
1946 John Maynard Keynes founding chairman of the Arts Council of Great Britain
Nerissa and Frances Garnett born
Death of John Maynard Keynes
1948 Death of Adrian Stephen
1952 Julian Bell born
Death of Desmond MacCarthy
1953 Death of Molly MacCarthy
1955 Virginia Bell born
David Garnett publishes *Aspects of Love*
1956 Final Memoir Club meeting
Clive Bell publishes *Old Friends*
1959 Cressida Bell born
1960 Leonard Woolf publishes *Sowing*, first volume of his autobiography (completed in 1969)
1961 Death of Vanessa Bell
1962 Death of Saxon Sydney-Turner
1964 Death of Clive Bell
1969 Death of Leonard Woolf
1970 Death of E. M. Forster
1972 Quentin Bell publishes *Virginia Woolf: A Biography*
1973 Death of Amaryllis Garnett
1978 Death of Duncan Grant
1984 Angelica Garnett publishes *Deceived with Kindness*
1994 Frances Partridge interviewed on *Desert Island Discs*
1996 Death of Quentin Bell
2004 Death of Frances Partridge
Death of Nerissa Garnett
2012 Death of Angelica Garnett

NOTE ON IMPERIAL AND
METRIC MEASURES IN RECIPES

Cooking Measurements				
	LIQUID		DRY	
	Imperial	Metric	Imperial	Metric
1 dash	6 drops		1 oz	25 g
1 teaspoon		5 ml	2 oz	50 g
1 dessertspoon		13 ml	3 oz	75 g
1 tablespoon		15 ml	¼ lb	125 g
2 tablespoons	1 fl oz	30 ml	5 oz	150 g
	2 fl oz	60 ml	6 oz	175 g
	4 fl oz	125 ml	7 oz	200 g
	1 gill (¼ pint)	142 ml	½ lb	225 g
	6 fl oz	175 ml	9 oz	250 g
	9 fl oz	237 ml	10 oz	275 g
	10 fl oz (½ pint)	284 ml/1 cup	11 oz	300 g
	16 fl oz	475 ml	12 oz	350 g
	4 gills (1 pint)	568 ml/2 cups	13 oz	375 g
1 breakfastcup	½ pint	284 ml/1 cup	14 oz	400 g
1 teacup	¼ pint	½ cup	15 oz	425 g
1 wineglass	60 ml	¼ cup	1 lb	450 g
1 quart	2 pints	4 cups	1.5 lb	675 g
			2.2 lb	1 kg
			2.5 lb	1.1 kg
			3 lb	1.3 kg
			4 lb	1.8 kg
			5 lb	2.25 kg

Oven Temperatures			Temperature Equivalents	
	°F	°C	°F	°C
Cool Oven	250–300	130–150	265	129
Moderate Oven	325–375	170–190	270	132
Hot Oven	400–500	200–250	280	138
			290	143
			300	149
			320	160
			340	170
			350	177
			400	205
			500	260

SOURCES OF RECIPES

'Suggested ingredients' lists have occasionally been added by the author to clarify original prose recipes. Other author's insertions are enclosed in square brackets. Otherwise, recipes are printed as originally written, with minor corrections to punctuation where essential for clarity. Credits for published recipes in copyright are listed in the Acknowledgments.

1. BEFORE BLOOMSBURY

p. 25 Talland House Crème Brûlée: unpublished recipe for Crème Brûlée by Frances Partridge, in the Frances Partridge archive at King's College, Cambridge, ref. no. FCP/8/3.

p. 27 Gingernut Biscuits: unpublished recipe by Angelica Garnett, from the cookery book of Angelica and David Garnett.

pp. 28–30 Recipe for Bread: from a newspaper clipping in Helen Anrep's scrapbook, in the Anrep/Fry archive collection, Tate Archive, London (TGA 200611).

pp. 31–32 Thoby Stephen's Monolithic Birthday Cake: from Isabella Beeton, *The Book of Household Management*, London: Ward, Lock and Bowden, 1895, pp. 1127–28.

p. 36 Strachey Rice Pudding: from Ibid., pp. 873–74.

p. 39 Mushrooms with Anchovy Cream: from Florence White, *Good Things in England*, London: Jonathan Cape, 1932, p. 264.

p. 40 Cambridge Zwieback Biscuits: by Norah Warn Hinkins, from *Cambridge Cuisine: In Aid of Save the Children Fund*, London, unknown date, p. 88.

p. 41 Whales: unpublished recipe for Sardine Savoury by Frances Partridge, in the Frances Partridge archive at King's College, Cambridge, ref. no. FCP/8/3.

2. OLD BLOOMSBURY

p. 46 Apples: 46 Gordon Square: from the author.

p. 49 Thoby's Cocoa and Biscuits: cocoa from *Fry's Chocolate Recipes: Economical and Simple*, Bristol and Somerdale (UK): J. S. Fry and Sons, unknown date, unpaginated; biscuits from a newspaper clipping in Helen Anrep's scrapbook, in the Anrep/Fry archive collection, Tate Archive, London (TGA 200611).

p. 50 Vanessa's Loving Cup: from Isabella Beeton, *All About Cookery*, London: Ward, Lock, 1909, p. 527.

pp. 52–53 Freedom Pie: recipe for Fig or Fag Pie from White, *Good Things in England*, p. 336.

p. 54 Raie au Beurre Noir: from Auguste Escoffier, *2,000 Favourite French Recipes*, London: Treasure Press, 1992, p. 199.

p. 57 Studio Omelette: from Diana Higgens, *Grace at Charleston*, Brighton (UK): Lockholt and Co. [Charleston Trust], 1994, p. 20.

pp. 59–60 Clive's Chocolate Layer Cake: from *Fry's Chocolate Recipes*.

p. 64 Ottoline's Plum Pudding: from a newspaper clipping in Helen Anrep's scrapbook, in the Anrep/Fry archive collection, Tate Archive, London (TGA 200611).

p. 65 Peppard Bones: from Herman Senn, *War Time Cooking Guide*, London: Food and Cookery Publishing Co., p. 7.

p. 69 Recipe for Marmalade: handwritten recipe by Vanessa Bell in the Grace Higgens archive, British Library.

pp. 73–74 Post-Impressionist Barbeque Beef: from the author.

pp. 74–75 Post-Impressionist Centenary Orange Cake: from a newspaper clipping in Helen Anrep's scrapbook, in the Anrep/Fry archive collection, Tate Archive, London (TGA 200611).

pp. 76–80 Omega's Alpha Feast: Potage Alpha Saumon from Catherine Frances Frere, *The Cookery Book of Lady Clark of Tillypronie*, London: Constable, 1909, p. 372; Crème de Volaille aux Petits Pois from Allison Wright, *The Wright Cookery Book*, London: Gay and Hancock, 1911, p. 137; Espagnole sauce from Ibid. p. 26; Cotelettes d'Agneau from from Ibid., p. 127; David Garnett's Cumberland Sauce from an unpublished recipe 'Cumberland Sauce' by David Garnett in the cookery book of Angelica and David Garnett; Frances Partridge's Haricots Verts from an unpublished recipe 'Beans, Haricot Salad. Napoleon on St Helena' by Frances Partridge, in the Frances Partridge archive at King's College, Cambridge, ref. no. FCP/8/3; Galantine from Wright, *The Wright Cookery Book*, p. 171; *chaudfroid* sauce from Ibid., p. 25; aspic jelly from Ibid., p. 55; rice stand from from Ibid., p. 54; mayonnaise from from Ibid., p. 43; Salade Russe from from Ibid., p. 267; Glaces à l'Omega from from Ibid., pp. 317–18.

p. 82 Brandon Camp Poulet Provençal: from Georgiana, countess of Dudley, *The Dudley Book of Cookery and Household Recipes*, London: Edward Arnold, 1913, pp. 63–64.

p. 84 Tunisian Citrus Fruits with Pork Chops and Crushed Sage: from the author.

p. 88 Meat Bobbity: from *English-Tamil Cookery Book* [A Friend in Need Society, Women's Workshop Ladies Committee], Madras: Diocesan Press, 1937, p. 82. This recipe is from my great-aunt Zillah Gratiaen.

p. 91 Brunswick Square Cold Apple Sweet: from an unpublished recipe for 'Cold Apple Sweet' by Frances Partridge, in the Frances Partridge archive, King's College, Cambridge, ref. no. FCP/8/3.

p. 92 Melymbrosia: from the author.

p. 93 Ye Olde Cock Steak Pie: from Edith Clarke, *The Official Handbook of the National Training School of Cookery*, London: William Clowes, 1915, pp. 123–24.

3. BLOOMSBURY IN WARTIME

p. 97 Plain Suet Pudding: from an unpublished recipe by Helen Anrep in her scrapbook, in the Anrep/Fry archive collection, Tate Archive, London (TGA 200611).

p. 99 Leonard's Fish and Chips: from a recipe by cookery writer Helen Burke in *Handy Hints by Famous Broadcasters and Writers: A Family Reference Book and Household Guide*, Slough (UK): Aspro Ltd, 1954, p. 22.

pp. 100–1 Nellie's 'Good Soup': from Senn, *War Time Cooking Guide*, p. 7.

p. 102 War Rations: from Ibid., p. 22.

p. 105 Asheham Rum Punch: from Isabella Beeton, *Mrs Beeton's Cookery Book*, London: Ward, Lock, 1915, p. 292.

p. 111 Teatime in Tidmarsh: Jam Roly Poly from an unpublished recipe by Helen Anrep, and Johnny Cake from a newspaper clipping, both in Helen Anrep's scrapbook, in the Anrep/Fry archive collection, Tate Archive, London (TGA 200611).

pp. 111–12 Pickled Pears: from Isabella Beeton, *Book of Household Management*, London: Ward, Lock and Bowden, 1915, p. 1152.

p. 112 Bloomsbury Jam: from May Byron, *May Byron's Jam Book*, London: Hodder and Stoughton, 1923, p. 117.

pp. 114–15 Cowslip Wine and Sloe Gin: Cowslip Wine from Georgiana, countess of Dudley, *The Dudley Book of Cookery and Household Recipes*, p. 206; Sloe Gin from Beeton, *All About Cookery*, p. 525.

p. 115 Tipsy Chicken: from an unpublished recipe for 'Spanish Chicken' by Helen Anrep, in the Frances Partridge archive, King's College, Cambridge, ref. no. FCP/8/3.

p. 117 Hunter Chicken: unpublished recipe by Frances Partridge, in the Frances Partridge archive, King's College, Cambridge, ref. no. FCP/8/3.

p. 120 Savoury Loin of Pork: from a newspaper clipping in the Anrep/Fry archive collection, Tate Archive, London (TGA 200611).

p. 120 Garsington Pickled Cabbage: from a newspaper clipping in Helen Anrep's scrapbook, in the Anrep/Fry archive collection, Tate Archive, London (TGA 200611).

p. 121 Chicken Pancakes: from an unpublished recipe by Frances Partridge, in the Frances Partridge archive, King's College, Cambridge, ref. no. FCP/8/3.

p. 123 Little Henry's Honey Cake: adapted from Beeton, *Mrs Beeton's Book of Household Management*, p. 1594.

p. 124–25 Charleston Coffee Pot: from Igor Anrep, *Food for My Daughter, Cubus Delectabilis*, 1988, unpublished book, private collection, p. 47.

p. 128 Marrow and Ginger Jam: from Diana Higgens, *Grace at Charleston*, p. 42.

p. 133 Lytton Soup: adapted from Florence A. George, *King Edward's Cookery* Book, London: Edward Arnold, 1920, p. 12.

p. 134 Armistice Chocolate Creams: from *McDougall's Cookery Book*, London: McDougalls, *c.* 1930, p. 29.

p. 136 Poulet en Casserole: unpublished recipe for 'Chicken a l'Estragon' by Frances Partridge, in the Frances Partridge archive, King's College, Cambridge, ref. no. FCP/8/3.

p. 137–38 Mill House Christmas Chicken: from Senn, *War Time Cooking Guide*, p. 15.

p. 141 Economical Fish Dish: from the Grace Higgens archive, British Library.

4. AN APPETITE FOR BLOOMSBURY

p. 144 Hasty Pudding: from an unpublished recipe by Helen Anrep, in her scrapbook, in the Anrep/Fry archive collection, Tate Archive, London (TGA 200611).

p. 145–47 Picasso Dines with Bohemia: from Ruth Lowinsky, *Lovely Food*, London: Nonesuch Press, 1931, pp. 54–57.

p. 148 A Bloomsbury Stew: from Tanaquil Le Clerq, ed., *The Ballet Cook Book*, New York: Stein and Day, 1966, p. 244.

p. 148 New Year's Oyster Feast: adapted from *Success: 1500 New Economy Cookery and Household Recipes*, London: Success Publishing Co., 1933, p. 19.

p. 158 Butter: from the author.

p. 164 Kedgeree: from the Grace Higgens archive, British Library.

p. 160 Cockerel for Virginia: unpublished recipe for 'Chicken with Honey Lemon (Mrs D. Glyn)' by Frances Partridge, in the Frances Partridge archive, King's College, Cambridge, ref. no. FCP/8/3.

pp. 160–61 Ham Spray Triangles: from an unpublished recipe for 'Ham and Soft Roes' by Raymond (Mortimer?) in the Frances Partridge archive, King's College, Cambridge, ref. no. FCP/8/3.

pp. 162–63 Ham Spray Breakfast Rolls: from William Cobbett, *Cottage Economy*, London: Douglas Pepler, 1916, pp. 66–69. (First published 1821.)

p. 167 Dodo's Quince Marmalade: from an unpublished letter by Dorelia John to Helen Anrep, in the Anrep/Fry archive collection, Tate Archive, London (TGA 200611).

p. 170 Clive Bell's Significant Form: from the Grace Higgens archive, British Library.

pp. 174–75 Grace's Algerian Omelette: from Diana Higgens, *Grace at Charleston*, p. 20.

p. 176 Mrs Harland's Fruit Fool: from an unpublished recipe by Mrs Harland in the Frances Partridge archive, King's College, Cambridge, ref. no. FCP/8/3.

p. 178 Afternoon Tea in the Garden at Charleston: all from Diana Higgens, *Grace at Charleston*, pp. 40–41.

p. 182 Monk's House Tea: Tea recipe from G. F. Scotson-Clark, *Kitchenette Cookery*, London: Jonathan Cape, 1926, p. 32; Banana Loaf Cake from the Grace Higgens archive, British Library.

p. 184 Hogarth Eccles Cakes: from *The Golden Book of Confectioners' Recipes*, Bolton: Pendlebury and Sons, *c.* 1920, p. 7.

p. 186 Veal Schnitzel with Mushrooms: from an unpublished recipe for 'Veal Scallops' by Frances Partridge, in the Frances Partridge archive, King's College, Cambridge, ref. no. FCP/8/3.

pp. 187–88 A Welcome Night In: Ham and Eggs from Lucy H. Yates, *Cooking for 2*, London: Country Life, 1930, pp. 134–35; Canary Pudding from an unpublished recipe by Helen Anrep, in her scrapbook, in the Anrep/Fry archive collection, Tate Archive, London (TGA 200611).

pp. 188–90 A Bloomsbury Tea Party: Chocolate Tea Biscuits from *Fry's Chocolate Recipes*; Lady Fingers from a newspaper clipping in Helen Anrep's scrapbook, in the Anrep/Fry archive collection, Tate Archive, London (TGA 200611); Cucumber Sandwiches from Florence A. Cowlen, *Five Hundred Sandwiches*, London: Chatto & Windus, 1929, p. 91.

p. 193 L'Etoile Fish Cakes: original recipe by Kevin Hopgood, from Elena Salvoni, *Eating Famously*, London: Walnut West One Ltd, 2007, p. 116.

p. 194 Boulestin's Summer Luncheon: Omelette à la Crème from Marcel Boulestin, *What Shall We Have To-day?*, London: William Heinemann, 1931, p. 83; Salade Parisienne, from Ibid., p. 87; Crème de Framboises from Ibid., pp. 145–46.

p. 196 German Ragout: from Lydia Keynes (Lopokova), 'Food in other lands: two banquets in Germany', *Evening News*, 30 March 1927.

p. 197 Pâté Maison: from a recipe by Stephen Spender in Renee Hellman, *Celebrity Cooking for You*, London: Hamlyn, 1967, p. 20.

pp. 199–200 Mrs Dalloway's Dinner: Cucumber Vichyssoise from an unpublished recipe co-written by Henrietta and David Garnett, from the cookery book of Angelica and David Garnett; Mayonnaise of Cold Salmon from Chester, ed., *French Cooking for English Homes*, London: Thornton Butterworth, 1923, p. 120; Chicken in Aspic from George, *King Edward's Cookery Book*, p. 102; Chocolate Ice Cream from Frere, *The Cookery Book of Lady Clark of Tillypronie*, pp. 418–19; Homemade Gateau de Pommes from Ibid., p. 388.

pp. 202–3 Lady Millicent Bruton's Lunch: Turbot en Aspic from a recipe by Marcel Boulestin, *A Second Helping*, London: William Heinemann, 1925, p. 38; Chicken 'en Casserole' from Frere, *The Cookery Book of Lady Clark of Tillypronie*, p. 261; Small Soufflés from Ibid., p. 444.

p. 205 Augustus Soup: from White, *Good Things in England*, p. 107.

pp. 205–7 Mildred's Masterpiece: from the author.

p. 208 Neptune's Fruit Banquet: from the author.

pp. 210–12 Menu 1: Dinner at a Women's College: Consommé from A. H. Adair, *Dinners Long and Short*, London: Gollancz, 1928, p. 105; Beef Loaf from the Grace Higgens archive, British Library; Sprouts from Scotson-Clark, *Kitchenette Cookery*, p. 130; Prunes from the Grace Higgens archive, British Library; Custard from *Simple Home Cookery by the Check Apron Girl*, London: Brown & Polson, *c.* 1930, p. 20; Savoury Biscuits and Sour Milk Cheese from Maud Baines and Edgar J. Saxon, *Complete Guide to Sound, Successful and Attractive Food Reform,* London: C. W. Daniel, 1929, pp. 143 and 54.

pp. 213–14 Menu 2: Lunch at a Men's College: all from Adair, *Dinners*: Fillets de Sole à la Crème, p. 141; Perdrix en Cocotte, p. 182; Salade de Haricots Verts, p. 232; Pommes Sautées, p. 191; Gateau de Riz en Moule, pp. 227–28; Polite Wine Drinking, pp. 45–46.

pp. 215–16 A Picnic in the Old Umbrella: all from from Lady Jekyll, *Kitchen Essays with Recipes and Their Occasions*, London: Thomas Nelson and Sons, *c.* 1921, pp. 119–21.

pp. 218–19 A Bohemian Picnic: Boris Anrep's Frankfurt Sausages from a recipe by Boris (Anrep?) in the Frances Partridge archive, King's College, Cambridge, ref. no. FCP/8/3; Virginia Nicholson's Stuffed Charleston Vine Leaves from an unpublished letter from Virginia Nicholson to Jans Ondaatje Rolls, 26 February 2013; Igor Anrep's Marinade of Mushrooms from Igor Anrep, *Food for My Daughter, Cubus Delectabilis*, p. 9; Helen Anrep's Lemon Jelly Cake from a newspaper clipping in Helen Anrep's scrapbook, in the Anrep/Fry archive collection, Tate Archive, London (TGA 200611); Angelica Garnett's Cherry Tart from an unpublished recipe by Angelica Garnett (8 July 1942) from the cookery book of Angelica and David Garnett.

5. BLOOMSBURY AND ABROAD

pp. 224–25 La Bergère Beignets: from Lady Gage, *Food from Firle*, Tisbury (UK): Compton Press, 1978, p. 12.

p. 227 Charleston Boeuf à la Mode: from unpublished recipes 'Boeuf Bourguignon (Bistro book)' and 'Beouf Braisé Creole' by Frances Partridge, in the Frances Partridge archive, King's College, Cambridge, ref. no. FCP/8/3.

p. 230 Soupe au Poisson: from an unpublished recipe by Helen Anrep (originally written in French), in her scrapbook, in the Anrep/Fry archive collection, Tate Archive, London (TGA 200611).

pp. 234–35 Burgundy Pears Ad Lib: from the author.

pp. 238–39 Broeto Ciozoto: from 'The Traditional Recipes in Venetian Languages of Some Specialities of the Islands of Lagoon', <www.ristorantegiorgione.it/eng/recipes.htm#broetociozoto> (accessed August 2012). Translated by Jayne Walker.

pp. 239–40 Italian Spaghetti Sauce: from Maria Luisa Taglienti, *The Italian Cookbook*, London: Spring Books, 1955, pp. 48–49.

p. 242 Andalusian Vegetable Paella: from the author.

p. 244 Avocado Soup for Four: from an unpublished recipe by Frances Partridge, in the Frances Partridge archive, King's College, Cambridge, ref. no. FCP/8/3.

p. 246 Ballet and Sole: from Lydia Keynes (Lopokova), 'Food in other lands: snails in Spain', *Evening News*, 11 May 1927.

p. 247 Lydia's Sorrel Soup: from Lydia Keynes (Lopokova), 'Food in other lands: the Polish count and the pheasant', *Evening News*, 13 April 1927.

pp. 247–48 Lydia's Piroshki Pies: from Ibid.

p. 248 Blinies: from Lydia Keynes (Lopokova), 'Food in other lands: your English food is so dignified', *Evening News*, 20 April 1927; Angelica Garnett's 'Extra Good Pancakes' from an unpublished recipe by Angelica Garnett from the cookery book of Angelica and David Garnett.

p. 249 Two Russian Soups: both from Lydia Lopokova, 'Food in other lands: some soups we like in Russia', *Evening News*, 6 April 1927.

p. 250 Southern American Chicken: both from Lydia Lopokova, 'Food in other lands: how America makes a joy of chicken', *Evening News*, 27 April 1927.

p. 251 Russian Tea and Talk: from the author.

pp. 251–53 Borscht: from an unpublished recipe by Helen Anrep, in her scrapbook, in the Anrep/Fry archive collection, Tate Archive, London (TGA 200611); from an unpublished recipe by Frances Partridge, in the Frances Partridge archive, King's College, Cambridge, ref. no. FCP/8/3.

pp. 253–54 Pashka: from the author.

6. BLOOMSBURY IN ECLIPSE

p. 260 Gin Sling: from W. J. Tarling, *Café Royal Cocktail Book*, Cheltenham: Mixellany Books, 2008, p. 237. (First published 1937.)

pp. 260–61 Blue and Green Cocktails: Green Dragon from Giovanni Quaglino, *The Complete Hostess*, London: Hamish Hamilton, 1935, p. 19; Blue Devil Cocktail from Harry Craddock, *The Savoy Cocktail Book*, London: Constable, 1930, p. 31; Charleson Cocktail from Ibid., p. 44; London Cocktail from Ibid., p. 97.

p. 264 Artichoke Fonds with Saxon: Artichoke Fonds from an unpublished recipe by Frances Partridge, in the Frances Partridge archive, King's College, Cambridge, ref. no. FCP/8/3; *Pâté truffe* from the author.

pp. 266–67 Onions au Gratin: recipe by Sophie MacCarthy, from a letter to Jennie Condell, 16 January 2013.

pp. 269–70 Duncan's Blanquette and Fricassée à l'Amegeville: Blanquette from an unpublished recipe copied by Duncan

Grant, in the Grace Higgens archive, British Library; Fricassée à l'Amegeville by Duncan Grant, in the Grace Higgens archive, British Library.

p. 271 Breakfast at Charleston: from an unpublished recipe by Angelica Garnett from the cookery book of Angelica and David Garnett.

pp. 273–74 Lunch at Charleston: Corned Mutton from a newspaper clipping in Helen Anrep's scrapbook, in the Anrep/Fry archive collection, Tate Archive, London (TGA 200611); Queen of Pudding from Diana Higgens, *Grace at Charleston*, p. 34.

pp. 274–75 Charleston Grouse: from Mabel Wijey, *Warne's Everyday Cookery*, London and New York: Frederick Warne, 1929, p. 202.

p. 276 Two Charleston Meat Recipes: both from the Grace Higgens archive, British Library.

p. 277 Salmon at Charleston: both from the Grace Higgens archive, British Library.

p. 280 Glyndebourne Gammon: from Diana Higgens, *Grace at Charleston*, p. 26.

p. 282 Angelica's Birthday Roast: from Olive Humphries, *Cook with Ease*, Birmingham (UK): Cornish Bros, 1935, p. 49.

p. 283 Plovers' Eggs with Clive: adapted from an unpublished recipe for 'Eggs en Cocotte Pascal' by Frances Partridge, in the Frances Partridge archive, King's College, Cambridge, ref. no. FCP/8/3.

p. 288 Chicken Strut: from an unpublished recipe for 'Chicken in Milk' by Frances Partridge, in the Frances Partridge archive, King's College, Cambridge, ref. no. FCP/8/3.

p. 289 Rest and Rice Pudding for Leonard (and Flush): from *The Recipe Book of 'Atora', the Good Beef Suet*, Manchester (UK): Hugon & Co., *c.* 1925, p. 42.

p. 290 Vita's Magnificent Strasbourg Pie: from Anne Chotzinoff Grossman and Lisa Grossman Thomas, *Lobscouse & Spotted Dog*, New York: W. W. Norton & Company, 1997, p. 23.

p. 292 Suffrage Angel Cake: from a recipe by Eliza Kennedy in L. O. Kleber, ed., *The Suffrage Cookbook*, Pittsburgh (PA): The Equal Franchise Federation of Western Pennsylvania, 1915, p. 122.

pp. 296–97 Summer Party at Charleston: Beurre d'Escargots from an unpublished letter from Virginia Nicholson to Jans Ondaatje Rolls, 26 February 2013; Syllabub Pudding from Isabella Beeton, *Mrs. Beeton's Everyday Cookery*, London: Ward, Lock, 1936, p. 479.

p. 299 Wartime Stew, Again: from Susan Croft, *The Stork Wartime Cookery Book*, London: Stork Margarine Company, 1946, p. 42.

p. 300 Haddock and Sausage: from the author.

7. BLOOMSBURY'S OFFSPRING

pp. 306–7 Two Vegetable Soups: Cauliflower Soup from an unpublished recipe by Frances Partridge, in the Frances Partridge archive, King's College, Cambridge, ref. no. FCP/8/3; Salad Soup from an unpublished recipe by David Garnett from the cookery book of Angelica and David Garnett.

p. 308 Bolooty: from an unpublished recipe by Jessie Partridge in the Frances Partridge archive, King's College, Cambridge, ref. no. FCP/8/3.

p. 308 Jerusalem Artichoke Purée: from an unpublished recipe 'Artichokes (Jerusalem) Puree of' by Paul Levy in the

Frances Partridge archive, King's College, Cambridge, ref. no. FCP/8/3.

pp. 310–11 Dinner Tête-à-Tête: from unpublished recipes 'Aubergines Provençales' and 'Celery (Stir-Fried)' by Paul Levy; 'Fondue' and 'Fruit Mousse' in the Frances Partridge archive, King's College, Cambridge, ref. no. FCP/8/3.

pp. 312–14 Fresh Tomatoes and Wiveton Pigeon Stew: unpublished recipe from Wiveton Hall Café, Norfolk.

p. 316 Bell Family Christmas Cake: from Katie Stewart, *The Times Cookery Book*, Glasgow and London: Collins, 1978, p. 183.

p. 317 Bell Booze: from a recipe by Virginia Nicholson.

pp. 317–18 Charleston Bloody Mary: from the author.

pp. 318–19 Savoury Scones: from an unpublished recipe for 'Drop Scones' by Angelica Garnett from the cookery book of Angelica and David Garnett.

pp. 321–22 'Receipt' for Painting Rooms: from *The Receipt Book of Elizabeth Raper And a portion of her Cipher Journal. Edited by her great-grandson the late Bartle Grant with a portrait and decorations by Duncan Grant*, London: Nonesuch Books, 1924, pp. 81 and 71; transcribed from a DVD of the documentary film *A Painter's Paradise: The Restoration of Charleston Farmhouse*, Spilsby (UK): Malachite Productions in association with Channel Four Television, 1989.

pp. 326–27 Grandchildren at Charleston: Rock Cakes from Mrs Beeton, in an unpublished letter from Virginia Nicholson to Jans Ondaatje Rolls, 26 February 2013; Nursery Cakes from the Grace Higgens archive, British Library; Grace's Currant Buns from Diana Higgens, *Grace at Charleston*, p. 38.

p. 328 Tea at Tilton: from *Four Hundred Prize Recipes for Practical Cookery: Reprinted from the Daily Telegraph,* Andover (UK): Chapel River Press, 1934, p. 141.

pp. 329–30 Mutton Pie with T. S. Eliot: both from Isabella Beeton, *Mrs Beeton's Cookery and Household Management*, London: Ward, Lock, 1960: Flaky Pastry, p. 956; Mutton Pies, p. 612.

p. 332 Garnett the Gastronome: all from Sylvia Townsend Warner and David Garnett, *Sylvia and David: The Townsend Warner/Garnett Letters* (Richard Garnett, ed.), London: Sinclair-Stevenson, 1994: Lamb's Liver, pp. 127–28; Orgy of Squid, p. 232; Sloe Cheese, p. 218.

p. 333 Savoury Eggs with Henrietta: from Henrietta Partridge, 'Good Eggs', *Harpers & Queen*, March 1976, pp. 120–21.

APPENDIX: ADDITIONAL RECIPES FROM THE BLOOMSBURY ARCHIVES

Recipes by Helen Anrep are from her scrapbook in the Anrep/ Fry archive collection, Tate Archive, London (TGA 200611). All are newspaper clippings, except the following: Baked Apple Pudding, Ginger Pudding, Golden Pudding.

Recipes by Angelica and David Garnett are from the cookery book of Angelica and David Garnett.

Recipes by Grace Higgens are from the Grace Higgens archive, British Library.

Recipes by Lydia Keynes (Lopokova) were originally published in the *Evening News*.

Recipes by Frances Partridge are from the Frances Partridge archive at King's College, Cambridge, ref. no. FCP/8/3.

SOURCES OF QUOTATIONS

Credits for published material in copyright are listed in the Acknowledgments.

INTRODUCTION

p. 12 'Theirs was an England' – Pamela Todd, *Bloomsbury at Home*, New York: Abrams, 1999, p. 22.

pp. 12–15 'Where they seem to me' – Virginia Woolf quoted in William Pryor, ed., *Virginia Woolf and the Raverats: A Different Sort of Friendship*, Bath: Clear Press, 2003, p. 182.

p. 15 'Are you changing' – Vanessa Bell, 9 August 1911, quoted in Frances Spalding, *Vanessa Bell*, London: Weidenfeld & Nicolson, 1983, p. 98.

p. 16 'a good dinner is of great' – Virginia Woolf, *A Room of One's Own and Three Guineas,* London: Penguin, 1993, p. 16.

p. 18 'Who bought the bacon' – Frances Partridge, *Memories*, London: Gollancz, 1981, p. 128.

p. 19 'dedicated to the preservation' – Details of the Charleston Trust can be found at: <http://www.charleston.org.uk/about-us/the-charleston-trust> (accessed 18 November 2013).

1. BEFORE BLOOMSBURY

Talland House Crème Brûlée

p. 23 'The kitchen, Sophie's kitchen' – Virginia Woolf, *Moments of Being* (Jeanne Schulkind, ed.), London: Pimlico, 2002, p. 137.

p. 24 '[I]n retrospect nothing' – Virginia Woolf, *Moments of Being*, p. 133.

p. 25 'favourite pudding' – Nellie Boxall, 'Portrait of Virginia Woolf', BBC interview, 1956. Transcribed from the audio CD *The Spoken Word: The Bloomsbury Group*, London: British Library, 2009, disc 2, track 22.

Gingernut Biscuits

pp. 25–26 'I remember one evening' – Vanessa Bell, 'Portrait of Virginia Woolf', BBC interview, 1956. Transcribed from the audio CD *The Spoken Word: The Bloomsbury Group*, London: British Library, 2009, disc 1, track 9.

p. 26 'I could hear her voice' – Virginia Woolf, *Moments of Being*, p. 92.

p. 27 'She should not waste it' – Virginia Woolf, *To the Lighthouse*, London: Hogarth Press, 1927, p. 315.

p. 27 'just as I rubbed out' – Virginia Woolf, *Moments of Being*, p. 116.

Recipe for Bread

p. 27 'My Billy' – Vanessa Bell, *Selected Letters of Vanessa Bell* (Regina Marler, ed.), London: Bloomsbury, 1993, p. 207.

p. 28 'purple with rage' – Vanessa Bell, quoted in J. H. Stape, ed., *Virginia Woolf: Interviews and Recollections*, Iowa City (IA): University of Iowa Press, 1995, p. 3.

p. 28 'Nessa and I' – Virginia Woolf quoted in Hugh Lee, ed., *A Cézanne in the Hedge, and Other Memories of Charleston and Bloomsbury*, London: Collins & Brown, 1992, p. 71.

Thoby Stephen's Monolithic Birthday Cake

pp. 30–31 'Mr Thoby Stephen's birthday' – Virginia Stephen, et al., *Hyde Park Gate News: The Stephen Family Newspaper*, London: Hesperus, 2005., 12 September 1892, p. 107.

p. 31 'In his monolithic character' – Leonard Woolf, *Sowing: An Autobiography of the Years 1880–1904*, London: Hogarth Press, 1962, p. 104.

Strachey Family Mealtime Reading Menu

p. 32 'My first dinner' – Bertrand Russell, *Autobiography,* London: Routledge, 2008, p. 69. (First published 1967–69.)

p. 33 'inelasticity' – David Garnett quoted Keith Hale's introduction to Rupert Brooke and James Strachey, *Friends and Apostles: The Correspondence of Rupert Brooke and James Strachey, 1905–1914* (Keith Hale, ed.), New Haven (CT): Yale University Press, 1999, p. 3.

p. 33 'rigid adherence' – David Garnett, *The Golden Echo*, London: Chatto & Windus, 1953, p. 257.

p. 33 'The level of intelligence' – Leonard Woolf, *Sowing*, pp. 165–66.

Strachey Rice Pudding

p. 34 'For much of his life' – David Garnett, *Great Friends: Portraits of Seventeen Writers*, New York: Atheneum, 1980, p. 152. (First published 1979.)

p. 34 'Here comes a glass' – Lytton Strachey quoted in Michael Holroyd, *Lytton Strachey: A Critical Biography*, vol. 1, London: William Heinemann, 1967, p. 327.

p. 34 'Every Strachey' – Quentin Bell quoted in Lee, ed., *A Cézanne in the Hedge*, p. 132.

Trinity Cream

p. 36 'The real enchantment' – Lytton Strachey, 'Cambridge', *The Spectator* 99 (2 November 1907), pp. 668–69, quoted in Charles Richard Sanders, *Lytton Strachey: His Mind and Art* , Oxford: Oxford University Press, 1957, pp. 52–53.

p. 37 'If, therefore, I altogether ignore' – John Maynard Keynes quoted in S. P. Rosenbaum, ed., *The Bloomsbury Group: A Collection of Memoirs, Commentary and Criticism,* Toronto: University of Toronto Press, 1975, p. 64.

p. 37 'I am calm' – Lytton Strachey quoted in Michael Holroyd, *Lytton Strachey: The New Biography*, London: Vintage, 1995, p. 71.

p. 37 'whisky or punch' – Lytton Strachey quoted in Ibid., p. 58.

Mushrooms with Anchovy Cream

pp. 37–38 'George Moore was a great man' – Leonard Woolf, *Sowing*, p. 111.

p. 38 'personal affections' – G. E. Moore, *Principia Ethica*, Cambridge: Cambridge University Press, 1903, p. 189.

p. 38 'Good' – Ibid., p. 9.

Cambridge Zwieback Biscuits

p. 39 'The fire was dancing' – E. M. Forster, *The Longest Journey*, London: Penguin, 2001, p. 5. (First published 1907.)

Midnight Society Dates

pp. 40–41 'There was a sofa' – Virginia Woolf, *Jacob's Room*, London: Hogarth Press, 1929, pp. 68–69. (First published 1922.)

Whales

p. 41 'I spoke whales' – Leonard Woolf quoted in Victoria Glendinning, *Leonard Woolf: A Life*, London: Pocket Books, 2007, p. 242.

Cambridge, Bohemianism and Bloomsbury

p. 43 'We were full of experiments' – Virginia Woolf, *Moments of Being*, pp. 46–47.

p. 43 'I first saw them' – Leonard Woolf, *Sowing*, p. 158.

p. 43 'disinfectants and curatives' – Diamond Mills Paper Company's 'Bromo Paper' printed advertisement, *c.* 1905.

2. OLD BLOOMSBURY

Apples: 46 Gordon Square

p. 46 '46 Gordon Square could never' – Virginia Woolf, *Moments of Being*, p. 44.

Thoby's Cocoa and Biscuits

p. 47 'It seemed to him' – Vanessa Bell, *Sketches in Pen and Ink: A Bloomsbury Notebook*, London: Pimlico, 1998, pp. 99–100.

p. 47 'When it is said that' – Ibid., p. 105.

p. 47 'very addicted to cocoa' – Dame Janet Vaughan quoted in Stape, ed., *Virginia Woolf*, p. 10.

Freedom Pie

p. 50 '[Our] freedom was' – Vanessa Bell, *Sketches in Pen and Ink*, p. 106.

p. 52 'With that one word' – Virginia Woolf, *Moments of Being*, p. 56.

Raie au Beurre Noir

p. 53 'You must go out' – Duncan Grant quoted in Frances Spalding, *Duncan Grant: A Biography*, London: Pimlico, 1998, p. 22.

p. 54 'I seem to like them all' – Duncan Grant quoted in Ibid., p. 62.

Studio Omelette

pp. 54–56 'Duncan was still creating' – Quentin Bell, *Elders and Betters*, London: John Murray, 1995, p. 61.

p. 56 'the most entertaining companion' – David Garnett quoted in Spalding, *Duncan Grant*, p. 198.

p. 56 'his lively mind' – David Garnett quoted in Ibid., p. 198.

p. 56 'as a congeries of men' – Claude Summers, ed., *The Gay & Lesbian Literary Heritage*, rev. edn, New York: Routledge, 2002, p. 102.

p. 56 '[He] seemed unaware of the fact' – Vanessa Bell, *Sketches in Pen and Ink*, p. 107.

p. 56 'He made me an omelette' – Lytton Strachey quoted in Holroyd, *Lytton Strachey: The New Biography*, p. 126.

Clive's Chocolate Layer Cake

p. 58 'he never did a lick' – Dorothy Brett, quoted in Sean Hignett, *Brett, From Bloomsbury to New Mexico: A Biography*, London: Hodder and Stoughton, 1984.

p. 58 'his character has several' – Lytton Strachey quoted in Holroyd, *Lytton Strachey: A Critical Biography*, vol. 1, p. 105.

Drinks from the Sideboard

p. 60 'There was little to eat' – Duncan Grant, BBC interview for 'Omnibus' programme, 1970. Transcribed from the audio CD *The Spoken Word: The Bloomsbury Group*, London: British Library, 2009, disc 1, track 12.

p. 61 'We dined alone together' – Adrian Stephen quoted in Quentin Bell, *Virginia Woolf: A Biography*, vol. 1, New York: Harcourt Brace Jovanovich, 1972, p. 146.

Ottoline's Plum Pudding

p. 61 'One Thursday' – David Garnett, *Great Friends*, p. 85

p. 61 'We have just got to know' – Virginia Woolf to Madge Vaughan, May 1909, in Virginia Woolf, *The Letters of Virginia Woolf*: vol. 1, 'The Flight of the Mind', 1888–1912 (Nigel Nicolson, ed., with Joanne Trautmann), London: Hogarth Press, 1975, p. 395.

p. 62 'It existed in four forms' – Leonard Woolf, *Downhill All the Way: An Autobiography of the Years 1919–1939*, New York: Hogarth Press, 1968, p. 101.

p. 62 'danced madly together' – Barbara Bagenal quoted in Joan Russell Noble, ed., *Recollections of Virginia Woolf*, London: Penguin, 1975, p. 176. (First published in 1972.)

Peppard Bones

p. 64 'She had a small house' – Russell, *Autobiography*, pp. 214–15.

p. 64 'Fearing that' – Ottoline Morrell, *The Early Memoirs of Lady Ottoline Morrell* (Robert Gathorne-Hardy, ed.), London: Faber, 1963, p. 163.

Bunga Bunga

p. 66 'I hadnt realized till that moment' – Virginia Woolf, *The Platform of Time: Memoirs of Family and Friends* (S. P. Rosenbaum, ed.), London: Hesperus, 2008, p. 195.

p. 67 'As one might have expected' – Adrian Stephen, *The Dreadnought Hoax*, London: Hogarth Press, 1936, p. 30.

Recipe for Marmalade

p. 69 'Add to these gifts' – Clive Bell, *Old Friends*, London: Chatto & Windus, 1956, p. 90.

p. 69 'the flesh and blood' – Virginia Woolf, *Moments of Being*, p. 57.

Post-Impressionist Paris Feast

p. 70 'I enjoyed choosing the pictures' – Desmond MacCarthy quoted in Hugh and Mirabel Cecil, *Clever Hearts, Desmond and Molly MacCarthy: A Biography*, London: Gollancz, 1990, p. 107.

Post-Impressionist Barbeque Beef

pp. 72–73 'It was some time during that winter' – Vanessa Bell, *Sketches in Pen and Ink*, pp. 133–34.

p. 73 'every now and then' – Leonard Woolf, *Beginning Again: An Autobiography of the Years 1911–1918*, London: Hogarth Press, 1965, p. 94.

p. 73 'here was a sudden' – Vanessa Bell, *Sketches in Pen and Ink*, p. 130.

p. 73 'not to imitate life' – Roger Fry, *Second Post-Impressionist Exhibition* (exhibition catalogue), London: Grafton Galleries, 1912, 'The French Group', p. 26.

p. 73 'to arouse the conviction of a new and definite reality' – Ibid.

p. 73 'All art depends' – Ibid., p. 28.

Post-Impressionist Centenary Orange Cake

p. 74 'The public in 1910' – Virginia Woolf, *Roger Fry: A Biography*, London: Vintage, 2003, pp. 153–54. (First published 1940.)

p. 74 'form' – Roger Fry, 'Retrospect', in his *Vision and Design*, London: Chatto & Windus, 1920, p. 194.

p. 74 'the direct outcome' – Ibid.

p. 74 'self-centred' – Fry, 'Claude', in his *Vision and Design*, p. 152.

p. 74 'only to the eye' – Heinrich Wölfflin, *Principles of Art History: The Problem of the Development of Style in Later Art* (M. D. Hottinger, trans.), New York: Dover Publications, 1950, p. 21.

p. 74 'not concerned with' – Roger Fry, preface to *Manet and The Post-Impressionists* (exhibition catalogue), London: Grafton Galleries, 1910–11, p. 8.

p. 74 'peculiar quality of' – Fry, 'Retrospect', in his *Vision and Design*, p. 199.

p. 74 'the objects themselves' – Fry, preface to *Manet and The Post-Impressionists*, p. 8.

Omega's Alpha Feast

p. 75 'With Post-Impressionism' – *Pall Mall Gazette*, 11 April 1913.

Brandon Camp Poulet Provençale

p. 81 'I am sitting over the fire' – Vanessa Bell, *Selected Letters*, p. 140.

p. 82 'That autumn of 1910' – Vanessa Bell, *Sketches in Pen and Ink*, p. 126.

Tunisian Citrus Fruits with Pork Chops and Crushed Sage

p. 82 'Your basket of oranges' – Vanessa Bell, *Selected Letters*, p. 160.

p. 84 'stoical warmth' – Angelica Garnett quoted in Rosenbaum, ed., *The Bloomsbury Group*, p. 175.

p. 84 'She sat and sewed' – Angelica Garnett quoted in Ibid.

Tender Cutlets with Aphrodisiac Sauce

p. 84 'I see nothing of Nessa' – Clive Bell, 30 December 1908, quoted in Spalding, *Vanessa Bell*, p. 77.

p. 85 'You know only rich soft natures' – Virginia Woolf, 1 December 1906, in *Letters*, vol. 1, p. 255.

pp. 85–86 'Clive came in late' – Virginia Woolf quoted in Pryor, *Virginia Woolf and the Raverats*, p. 146.

p. 86 'I must love' – Mary Hutchinson, 7 September 1934, quoted in Hermione Lee, *Virginia Woolf*, London: Vintage, 1997, p. 383.

Meat Bobbity

p. 86 'Walked to Buttawa' – Leonard Woolf, *Diaries in Ceylon and Stories from the East*, London: Hogarth Press, 1963, p. 235.

p. 87 'Colombo was' – Leonard Woolf, *Growing: An Autobiography of the Years 1904–1911*, London: Hogarth Press, 1967, p. 21.

p. 87 'eternal aged stringy curried chicken' – Ibid., p. 200.

p. 87 'Every particle of food' – Ibid., p. 90.

Supper at 46 Gordon Square

p. 88 'There had certainly been' – Leonard Woolf, *Beginning Again*, pp. 26–27. (First published 1964.)

p. 88 '[I]t would be worth the risk' – Leonard Woolf, 12 January 1912, *Letters of Leonard Woolf* (Frederic Spotts, ed.), London: Bloomsbury, 1992, p. 169.

Brunswick Square Tray Food

p. 89 'Brunswick would come' – Vanessa Bell quoted in Rosenbaum, ed., *The Bloomsbury Group*, p. 81.

p. 90 'To be intimate with' – Duncan Grant quoted in Noble, ed., *Recollections of Virginia Woolf*, pp. 29–30.

Melymbrosia

p. 91 'Meanwhile Helen herself' – Virginia Woolf, *The Voyage Out*, London: Hogarth Press, 1971, pp. 20–21. (First published 1915.)

p. 92 'it might have been intended' – Louise DeSalvo's introduction to Virginia Woolf, *Melymbrosia* (Louise DeSalvo, ed.), San Francisco (CA): Cleis Press, 1982, p. xxv.

Ye Olde Cock Steak Pie

p. 92 'And then? Go on looking' – Virginia Woolf, *The Common Reader* (Andrew McNeillie, ed.), New York and London: Harvest-Harcourt, 1984, p. 109. (First published 1925.)

3. BLOOMSBURY IN WARTIME

Plain Suet Pudding

p. 97 'She liked good talk' – William Plomer quoted in Noble, ed., *Recollections of Virginia Woolf*, p. 130. (First published in *Horizon* magazine, 1941.)

p. 97 'distinguished myself by cooking' – Virginia Woolf, 10 December 1914, in *The Letters of Virginia Woolf* (Nigel Nicolson, ed., with Joanne Trautmann): vol. 2, 'The Question of Things Happening', 1912–1922, London: Hogarth Press, 1976, p. 55.

Leonard's Fish and Chips

p. 98 'Every morning, therefore' – Leonard Woolf, *Downhill All the Way: An Autobiography of the Years 1911–1918*, London: Hogarth Press, 1965, pp. 156–57. (First published 1967.)

p. 98 'first of many plates' – Leonard Woolf quoted in Glendinning, *Leonard Woolf*, p. 170.

p. 98 'Of all public events' – Leonard Woolf, *Downhill All the Way*, p. 217.

p. 98 'drank quantities of tea' – Leonard Woolf, *Beginning Again*, p. 113.

Nellie's 'Good Soup'

pp. 99–100 'I particularly remember' – Barbara Bagenal quoted in Noble, ed., *Recollections of Virginia Woolf*, p. 182.

p. 100 'a season ticket to Richmond' – Barbara Bagenal quoted in Ibid., p. 179.

p. 100 'We don't dine' – Virginia Woolf, 3 January 1923, in *The Letters of Virginia Woolf* (Nigel Nicolson, ed., with Joanne Trautmann): vol. 3, 'A Change of Perspective', 1923–1928, London: Hogarth Press, 1977, p. 2.

p. 100 'good soups' – Nellie Boxall, 'Portrait of Virginia Woolf', transcribed from the audio CD *The Bloomsbury Group*, disc 2, track 22.

War Rations

p. 101 'My steak was admirable' – Lytton Strachey, *The Letters of Lytton Strachey* (Paul Levy, ed.), London: Viking, 2005, pp. 391–92.

p. 101 'cheap dishes' – Virginia Woolf, 11 February 1917, *Letters*, vol. 2, p. 144.

p. 101 'Last week we ran out' – Ibid.

p. 101 'impossible to get any milk' – Virginia Woolf, 22 March 1918, Ibid., p. 225.

p. 101 'I think if you want meat' – Virginia Woolf, 24 March 1918, Ibid., p. 227.

p. 102 'You wicked, wicked' – Vanessa Bell, *Selected Letters*, p. 217.

Asheham Scrambled Eggs

p. 102 'One week-end' – Barbara Bagenal quoted in Noble, ed., *Recollections of Virginia Woolf*, p. 185.

p. 103 'the lower division' – Quentin Bell, *Virginia Woolf: A Biography*, vol. 1, p. 20.

Asheham Rum Punch

p. 102 'I have just come back' – Dora Carrington, December 1915, in Carrington, *Carrington: Letters and Extracts from Her Diaries* (David Garnett, ed.), New York: Rinehart and Winston, 1971, p. 21.

Carrington's Virgin Salad

pp. 105–6 'I spent a wretched time' – Ibid., p. 33.

p. 106 'The family and their' – Virginia Nicholson, *Among the Bohemians: Experiments in Living, 1900–1939*, London: Viking, 2002, p. 170.

Fruition in Wales

p. 107 'Oh! I am feeling' – Lytton Strachey, *Letters*, p. 321.

p. 107 '[E]verything was perfectly civilized' – Lytton Strachey quoted in David Garnett, *Great Friends*, p. 152.

p. 107 'A great deal of many kinds of love' – Lytton Strachey to Dora Carrington, 23 March 1917, quoted in Gretchen Gerzina, *Carrington: A Life of Dora Carrington, 1893–1932*, Oxford: Oxford University Press, 1990, p. 107.

Sugar

p. 107 '[I am going] to make' – Dora Carrington–Mark Gertler correspondence quoted in Gerzina, *Carrington*, pp. 60–61.

p. 108 'I read Marlowe again' – Carrington, December 1916, in *Carrington: Letters*, p. 50.

p. 108 'After the first course' – Mark Gertler, quoted in Virginia Nicholson, *Among the Bohemians*, p. 178.

Teatime in Tidmarsh

p. 108 'Tea was served' – Gerald Brenan, *Personal Record, 1920–1972*, London: Jonathan Cape, 1974, p. 23.

p. 109 'Everything is packed' – Dora Carrington, 20 November 1917, in *Carrington: Letters*, p. 92.

p. 110 'indescribably grand' – Carrington, 26 September 1925, Ibid., p. 328.

p. 110 'after tea Lytton and Carrington' – Virginia Woolf, 17 January 1918, in Virginia Woolf, *Letters*, vol. 2, p. 212.

Pickled Pears

p. 111 'But beside the rooms' – David Garnett, *Great Friends*, p. 156.

Cowslip Wine and Sloe Gin

p. 112 'nectar' and 'unequalled' – Ibid.

Tipsy Chicken

p. 115 'I've just picked some peas' – Lytton Strachey, *Letters*, p. 407.

Hunter Chicken

p. 117 'Of course your grandfather'– John Higgens in conversation with Virginia Nicholson, *c.* 2000, from the unpublished papers of Virginia Nicholson.

p. 117 'Bunny always had' – Henrietta Garnett in an email to Jans Ondaatje Rolls, 8 March 2014.

Savoury Loin of Pork

p. 117 '[G]ather here' – Ottoline Morrell quoted in Miranda Seymour, *Ottoline Morrell: Life on the Grand Scale*, London: Hodder and Stoughton, 1992, p. 370.

p. 118 'The war has done' – Virginia Woolf to Molly MacCarthy, 26 August 1916, in Virginia Woolf, *Letters*, vol. 2, p. 113.

p. 118 '[Clive] sits in a farmhouse' – Virginia Woolf to Clive Bell, 24 July 1917, in Ibid., p. 167.

p. 119 'stingy with the food' – Lytton Strachey, quoted by Paul Levy in Lytton Strachey, *Letters*, p. 336.

p. 119 'the story of a peacock' – Quentin Bell, *Elders and Betters*, p. 164.

p. 119 'breakfast in bed' – Lytton Strachey, 4 January 1917, in Strachey, *Letters*, p. 337.

p. 120 'The rest continued to starve' – Ibid.

p. 120 'the simple excellence' – Gathorne-Hardy, ed., *The Early Memoirs*, p. 25.

Garsington Pickled Cabbage

p. 120 'Only is the sunlight' – Virginia Woolf quoted in Clive Bell, *Old Friends*, p. 104.

Chicken Pancakes

p. 120 'Philip is fairly contented' – Vanessa Bell, *Selected Letters*, p. 191.

Little Henry's Honey Cake

p. 122 'He races swiftly' – Quentin Bell, *Elders and Betters*, p. 71.

Charleston Coffee Pot

p. 124 'It has a charming garden' – Virginia Woolf, *Letters*, vol. 2, p. 95.

p. 124 'The English generally make' – Igor Anrep, *Food for My Daughter, Cubus Delectabilis*, unpublished book, private collection, p. 47.

Bunny's Honey

p. 126 'If [Bunny] had been edible' – Quentin Bell, *Elders and Betters*, p. 71.

p. 126 'One evening he went' – David Garnett, *Lady into Fox* London: Hesperus Press, 2009, p. 70. (First published 1922.)

p. 126 'Its beauty is' – David Garnett, 25 December 1918, quoted in Spalding, *Duncan Grant*, p. 215.

Marrow and Ginger Jam

p. 127 'Art is significant deformity' – Roger Fry quoted in Virginia Woolf, *Roger Fry*, p. 195.

p. 128 'a confection called … vegetable marrows' – Quentin Bell, in Quentin Bell and Virginia Nicholson, *Charleston: A Bloomsbury House & Garden*, London: Frances Lincoln, 1997, p. 24. (First published 1989.)

A Forsterian Salad with Quentin Bell's Chapon Seasoning

p. 128 'A pageant requires' – E. M. Forster, *Abinger Harvest and England's Pleasant Land*, London: Andre Deutsch, 1996, p. 52. (First published 1936.)

p. 128 'Lytton nicknamed him' – Leonard Woolf, *Sowing*, p. 148.

pp. 129–30 'They always insisted' – Virginia Nicholson in a letter to Jans Ondaatje Rolls, 22 April 2013.

Asheham – 'Such a Dinner'

p. 130 'Saxon is now' – Dora Carrington, 4 February 1917, in *Carrington: Letters*, p. 57.

p. 131 'ate the most tremendous tea' – Carrington, 29 January 1917, Ibid., p. 55.

p. 131 'Such a dinner' – Carrington, 4 February 1917, Ibid., p. 57.

Lytton Soup

p. 132 'Lytton, had written a book' – Quentin Bell, *Elders and Betters*, p. 149.

p. 133 'Je n'impose rien' – Lytton Strachey quoted in Holroyd, *Lytton Strachey: The New Biography*, p. 420.

p. 133 'Discretion is not' – Lytton Strachey quoted in Ibid., p. xvi.

p. 133 'The ill-cooked hunks' – Lytton Strachey, *Eminent Victorians*, Oxford: Oxford University Press, 2003, p. 108. (First published 1918.)

Armistice Chocolate Creams

p. 134 'I'm glad you are fat' – Virginia Woolf quoted in Pryor, ed., *Virginia Woolf and the Raverats*, p. 52.

p. 134 'she rolls along' – Lytton Strachey, 23 April 1916, quoted in Glendinning, *Leonard Woolf*, p. 201.

Pot-Boilers

p. 135 'Obliged by hunger' – Clive Bell, *Pot-Boilers*, p. 2.

p. 135 'an odd lot' – Ibid., p. 15.

Poulet en Casserole

p. 136 'Have you ever tasted' – Mary [Molly] MacCarthy, *A Pier and a Band: A Novel of the Nineties*, London: Martin Secker, 1931, p. 198. (First published 1918.)

p. 136 'a very good fellow' – Ibid., p. 219.

p. 136 'Perdita sometimes felt' – Ibid.

Mill House Christmas Chicken

p. 136 'We had quite a' – Lytton Strachey, *Letters*, p. 380.

p. 137 'We eat large chickens' – Lytton Strachey, 27 December 1918, quoted in Todd, *Bloomsbury at Home*, p. 133.

Unusual Oysters

p. 138 'He appeared, I seem' – Virginia Woolf, *Moments of Being*, p. 57.

p. 138 'What unusual oysters' – Osbert Sitwell, *Laughter in the Next Room*, London: Macmillan, 1949, pp. 40–41.

The Omega Wine Cup

p. 139 'He cooked; he washed up' – Virginia Woolf, *Roger Fry*, p. 213.

p. 140 'But some of the things' – Ibid., p. 218.

Economical Fish Dish

p. 140 'The danger confronting' – John Maynard Keynes, *The Economic Consequences of the Peace*, London: Macmillan, 1919, p. 213.

4. AN APPETITE FOR BLOOMSBURY

Hasty Pudding

p. 143 'The clock cannot' – Keynes, *The Economic Consequences of the Peace*, p. 33.

p. 143 'The servants rebelled' – Robert Skidelsky quoted in Hugh Lee, ed., *A Cézanne in the Hedge*, p. 142.

Picasso Dines with Bohemia

p. 144 'As it happened, continental' – Clive Bell, *Old Friends*, pp. 170–71.

p. 144 'Civilization requires' – Clive Bell, *Civilization: An Essay*. West Drayton (PA): Penguin, 1947, p. 127.

p. 144 'in the end it turns out' – quoted in Quentin Bell, *Virginia Woolf: A Biography*, vol. 2, New York: Harcourt Brace Jovanovich, 1972, p. 137.

pp. 144–45 'Maynard, Duncan Grant' – Clive Bell, *Old Friends*, p. 172.

p. 145 'a dream party' – Ruth Lowinsky, *Lovely Food*, London: Nonesuch Press, 1931, pp. 54–55.

A Bloomsbury Stew

p. 147 'I again fell' – quoted in D. E. Moggridge, *Maynard Keynes: An Economist's Biography*, London: Routledge, 1992, p. 395.

p. 147 'grace, pathos' – Sitwell, *Laughter in the Next Room*, p. 14.

p. 147 'a symphony' – Clive Bell, 'The New Ballet', *New Republic*, 30 July 1919.

Maynard's Parties at No. 46

pp. 148–49 '[A]fter the end of the first war' – George Rylands quoted in Noble, ed., *Recollections of Virginia Woolf*, p. 171. (Adapted from an interview for the BBC documentary 'A Night's Darkness, A Day's Sail', 1970.)

pp. 149–50 'of Civilization' – Clive Bell, *Old Friends*, p. 56.

p. 150 'the grandest' – quoted in Moggridge, *Maynard Keynes*, p. 404.

pp. 150–51 'Let the scene open' – Virginia Woolf, diary entry for first week in January 1923, quoted in Leonard Woolf, *Downhill All the Way*, pp. 115–16.

Sunday Lunch at Cambridge

p. 151 'Keynes's intellect' – Russell, *Autobiography*, p. 69.

p. 151 'In a few minutes I have' – Lydia Lopokova, *Lydia and Maynard: Letters between Lydia Lopokova and John Maynard Keynes* (Polly Hill and Richard Keynes, eds), London: Andre Deutsch, 1989, p. 124.

Teetotalism at Tilton

p. 152 'But when Maynard, having invited' – Clive Bell, *Old Friends*, p. 45.

p. 152 'Would you believe it?' – Lytton Strachey quoted in Moggridge, *Maynard Keynes*, p. 402.

p. 152 'I had an enormous Sunday lunch' – Duncan Grant, 18 April 1926, quoted in Ibid.

Tilton Grouse

p. 152 'It was the common opinion' – quoted in Lee, ed., *A Cézanne in the Hedge*, p. 147.

p. 153 'the bargain-hunter' – Clive Bell, *Old Friends*, p. 53.

p. 153 'Last night, at Tilton' – Virginia Woolf, 3 September 1927, in Virginia Woolf, *Letters*, vol. 3, p. 418.

p. 154 'The French have a way' – from a newspaper clipping in Helen Anrep's scrapbook, in the Anrep collection, Tate Archive, London.

Lytton's 'Victoria'

p. 154 'Lytton's "Victoria" has been' – Dora Carrington, 15 April 1921, in *Carrington: Letters*, pp. 173–74.

Tidmarsh Triptych

pp. 155–56 'I seem to see Lytton' – Brenan, *Personal Record*, p. 24.

p. 156 'everything at sixes and sevens' – Lytton Strachey to Dora Carrington, 11 July 1919, in Strachey, *Letters*, p. 444.

Butter

p. 156 'Carrington introduced me' – Brenan, *Personal Record*, p. 23.

p. 158 'I discover that there are' – Ibid., p. 57.

Cockerel for Virginia

p. 158 'I will kill our one' – Dora Carrington, October 1918, in *Carrington: Letters*, p. 107.

p. 158 'so that you will have no fault' – Carrington, 29 January 1915, quoted in Gerzina, *Carrington*, p. 61.

p. 158 'vast quantities' – Carrington, 10 December 1916, in *Carrington: Letters*, p. 49.

p. 158 'strawberry ices' – Carrington, 28 June 1921, quoted in Gerzina, *Carrington*, p. 173.

Ham Spray Triangles

p. 160 'Ralph Partridge took over' – David Garnett, *Great Friends*, p. 156.

Ham Spray Breakfast Rolls

p. 161 'Breakfast was lavish.' – David Garnett, *Great Friends*, p. 157.

p. 162 'arches in the' – Frances Partridge, *Memories*, p. 99.

p. 162 'the letters of the' – Frances Partridge quoted in Lee, ed., *A Cézanne in the Hedge*, p. 134.

p. 162 'a continual stream' – David Garnett, *Great Friends*, p. 157.

Kedgeree

p. 163 'Ralph has become' – Dora Carrington, 18 December 1921, in *Carrington: Letters*, pp. 200–1.

Epoch-Making Dinners at Ham Spray

p. 165 'The dinner was indescribably grand' – Dora Carrington, 26 September 1925, in Ibid., p. 328.

p. 166 'lugubrious' – Lytton Strachey quoted in Holroyd, *Lytton Strachey: The New Biography*, p. 556.

Dodo's Quince Marmalade

p. 166 'John is encamped' – John Maynard Keynes quoted in Holroyd, *Augustus John*, p. 286.

p. 167 'Peel quinces as thin' – from an uncatalogued letter from Dorelia John to Helen Anrep, *c.* 1960s, in the Anrep collection, Tate Archive, London.

'Males'

p. 167 'There was a dish' – Frances Partridge, *Memories*, p. 125.

Breakfast with Clive

p. 169 'Every morning, a gong' – Quentin Bell, *Elders and Betters*, p. 24.

p. 169 'A bad sleeper' – Angelica Garnett, *Deceived with Kindness: A Bloomsbury Childhood*, London: Chatto & Windus, 1984, p. 92.

Clive Bell's Significant Form

p. 170 'Clive, who has nothing' – Virginia Woolf quoted in Clive Bell, *Old Friends*, p. 106.

p. 170 'What quality is common' – Clive Bell, *Art*, London: Chatto & Windus, 1914 (repr. 1916), p. 8.

The Bloomsbury Pot

p. 171 'When the door was opened' – David Garnett quoted in Rosenbaum, ed., *The Bloomsbury Group*, p. 196.

p. 171 'there is no state of mind' – Clive Bell, *Art*, p. 114.

p. 171 'the secret of which' – Frances Partridge quoted in Lee, ed., *A Cézanne in the Hedge*, p. 130.

Grace Cakes

p. 171 'By the grace of God' – David Garnett in a letter to Richard Shone, unknown date, quoted in Todd, *Bloomsbury at Home*, p. 110.

p. 172 'Our French cook' – Vanessa Bell, 23 October 1921, quoted in Spalding, *Vanessa Bell*, p. 192.

p. 173 'When I was' – Virginia Nicholson in a note to Jans Ondaatje Rolls, 26 February 2013.

Grace's Algerian Omelette

p. 173 'Lydia, like everyone' – Quentin Bell, foreword to Diana Higgens, *Grace at Charleston*, Brighton (UK): Lockholt and Co. [Charleston Trust], *c.* 1994, p. 5.

p. 174 'stories of old Russia' – Ibid.

p. 174 'never lost' – Quentin Bell, *Elders and Betters*, p. 100.

p. 174 'I have a passion' – Lydia Lopokova, 24 June 1922, in Lopokova, *Lydia and Maynard*, p. 46.

Mrs Harland's Fruit Fool

p. 175 'What shall we do' – Lydia Lopokova quoted in Judith Mackrell, *Bloomsbury Ballerina: Lydia Lopokova, Imperial Dancer and Mrs John Maynard Keynes*, London: Weidenfeld & Nicolson, 2008, p. 285.

p. 176 'obliged to work in the garden' – Frances Spalding, *Duncan Grant*, p. 246.

p. 176 'the food was so prominent' – Lydia Lopokova, 14 November 1930, quoted in Mackrell, *Bloomsbury Ballerina*, p. 314.

Afternoon Tea in the Garden at Charleston

p. 176 'Charleston is as usual' – Virginia Woolf, *The Diary of Virginia Woolf* (Anne Olivier Bell, ed., with Andrew McNeillie): vol. 2, 1920–1924, New York: Harcourt Brace Jovanovich, 1978, p. 195.

p. 177 'they looked absolute freaks' – quoted in Anthony Gardner, 'What the housemaid saw', *Sunday Times*, 18 February 2007.

p. 177 'She might be divinely witty' – Clive Bell, *Old Friends*, pp. 102–3.

Tea Party Fooling

p. 178 'Was she the bewitched' – Christopher Isherwood quoted in Noble, ed., *Recollections of Virginia Woolf*, p. 218.

p. 178 'could cook, and bottle fruit' – Angelica Bell quoted in Ibid., p. 104.

p. 179 'It's such a pity' – Virginia Woolf quoted by Elizabeth Bowen in Ibid., p. 65.

Monk's House Tea

p. 180 'Tea was set out' – G. E. Easdale quoted in Stape, ed., *Virginia Woolf*, p. 18.

p. 180 'like a sea-shell' – Angelica Garnett quoted in Rosenbaum, ed., *The Bloomsbury Group*, p. 177.

p. 181 'Virginia leant, listening magically' – Enid Bagnold, *Adam International Review*, 364–66 (1972), p. 15, quoted in Stape, ed., *Virginia Woolf*, p. 21.

p. 181 'Virginia has gone to talk' – Vita Sackville-West, 18 February 1941, quoted in Stape, ed., *Virginia Woolf*, p. 80.

pp. 181–82 'Yet Byron never' – Virginia Woolf, *The Waves*, London, Hogarth Press, 1950, pp. 62–63.

p. 182 'there were biscuits' – Angelica Garnett, *Deceived with Kindness*, p. 110.

Hogarth Eccles Cakes

p. 183 'Nearly all the implements' – Leonard Woolf, *Beginning Again*, p. 234.

p. 183 'When the printing machine' – Leonard Woolf, *Downhill All the Way*, pp. 72–73.

p. 184 'printed in the larder' – Leonard Woolf, *Downhill All the Way*, p. 77.

Veal Schnitzel with Mushrooms

p. 184 'All human relations' – Virginia Woolf, *Mr Bennett and Mrs Brown*, London: Hogarth Press, 1924, p. 5.

pp. 184–85 'I am sick of' – Virginia Woolf quoted in Alison Light, *Mrs Woolf and the Servants*, London: Penguin, 2007, p. 173.

p. 185 'She doesn't care for me' – Virginia Woolf quoted in Ibid., p. 164.

p. 186 'she liked veal schnitzels' – Nellie Boxall, 'Portrait of Virginia Woolf', transcribed from the audio CD *The Bloomsbury Group*, disc 2, track 22.

A Welcome Night In

p. 186 'I was thinking' – Virginia Woolf, *A Writer's Diary: Being Extracts from the Diary of Virginia Woolf* (Leonard Woolf, ed.), New York: Harvest-Harcourt, 1982, p. 339.

p. 187 'He completely arranged' – Alix Strachey quoted in Noble, ed., *Recollections of Virginia Woolf*, p. 139.

p. 187 'an omelette with good coffee' – Virginia Woolf to Vita Sackville-West, 17 February 1926, in Virginia Woolf, *Letters*, vol. 3, p. 241.

p. 187 'grilled herring' – Virginia Woolf to Ethel Smyth, 22 April 1930, in Virginia Woolf, *Letters*, vol. 4, p. 160.

p. 187 'roast mutton' – Virginia Woolf to Pernel Strachey, 24 August 1924, in Virginia Woolf, *Letters*, vol. 3, p. 126.

p. 187 'ham and eggs and an odious pudding' – Virginia Woolf to Pernel Strachey, 3 August 1923, Ibid., p. 62.

p. 187 'dishing up' and '2 chops, broiled in gravy' – Virginia Woolf to Vita Sackville-West, 9 August 1930, in Virginia Woolf, *Letters*, vol. 4, p. 197.

A Bloomsbury Tea Party

p. 188 'Straight lines' – René Crevel, *The As Stable Pamphlets* (Keith Waldrop, trans.), no. 3, Englewood (NJ): Elysium Press, 1996, first page.

p. 188 'The whole thing' – Logan Pearsall Smith quoted in Cecil and Cecil, *Clever Hearts*, p. 218.

Dining Out

p. 190 'In the evening we had' – Dora Carrington, 29 October 1929, in *Carrington: Letters*, p. 429.

p. 191 'Here one sat … poured over them' – Brenan, *Personal Record*, p. 153.

L'Etoile Fish Cakes

p. 191 'I was woken' – Lytton Strachey quoted in Rosenbaum, ed., *The Bloomsbury Group*, p. 5.

p. 192 'I delighted in him' – Desmond MacCarthy quoted in Ibid., p. 29.

p. 192 'Perched away' – E. M. Forster, from 'Tributes to Sir Desmond MacCarthy, II', *Listener*, 26 June 1952 quoted in Rosenbaum, ed., *The Bloomsbury Group*, p. 157.

pp. 192–93 'After all *we*' – Desmond MacCarthy, quoted in Cecil and Cecil, *Clever Hearts*, p. 265.

p. 193 'If everyone at this table' – Clive Bell, *Old Friends*, p. 52.

Boulestin's Summer Luncheon

p. 193 'Ah, what better luncheon' – Marcel Boulestin, *What Shall We Have To-day?*, London: William Heinemann, 1931, p. 34.

German Ragout

p. 194 'We both learnt the rules' – Virginia Woolf, *Moments of Being*, p. 152.

p. 195 'to do without' – Ibid, pp. 46–47.

p. 195 'perfect manners' – Ibid., p. 63.

pp. 195–96 'It was true' – Quentin Bell, *Elders and Betters*, p. 97.

p. 196 'Maynard would help himself' – David Garnett quoted in Rosenbaum, ed., *The Bloomsbury Group*, p. 225.

Pâté Maison

p. 196 'She seemed to hate' – Stephen Spender, *World Within World: The Autobiography of Stephen Spender*, London: Hamish Hamilton, 1951, p. 156.

pp. 196–97 'looking at all the glories' – Virginia Woolf to Jacques Raverat, 8 March 1924, in Virginia Woolf, *Congenial Spirits: The Selected Letters of Virginia Woolf* (Joanne Trautmann Banks, ed.), London: Hogarth Press, 1989, p. 186.

p. 197 'the crèmes, soufflés' – Light, *Mrs Woolf and the Servants*, London, p. 236.

Mrs Dalloway's Dinner

p. 197 'It made no difference' – Virginia Woolf, *Mrs Dalloway*, p. 146.

p. 198 'salmon on an iceblock' – Ibid., p. 8.

p. 199 'nothing … not even Clarissa' – Ibid.

Lady Millicent Bruton's Luncheon

p. 201 'And so there began' – Ibid., pp. 91–92.

The Lighthouse Dinner Menu

p. 203 'It is always helpful' – E. M. Forster's Rede lecture, 1941, quoted in Rosenbaum, ed., *The Bloomsbury Group*, p. 212.

p. 203 'We drank an immense' – Virginia Woolf, 4 October 1908, in Virginia Woolf, *Letters*, vol. 1, p. 369.

p. 203 'It was rich' – Virginia Woolf, *To the Lighthouse*, p. 156.

p. 203 'But how do you make' – Virginia Woolf, 11 May 1927, in Vanessa Bell, *Selected Letters*, p. 318.

Augustus Soup

p. 204 'Ellen, please' – Virginia Woolf, *To the Lighthouse*, p. 149.

Mildred's Masterpiece (Boeuf en Daube)

p. 205 '[A]n exquisite scent' – Ibid., pp. 155–56.

p. 205 'on the moment' – Virginia Woolf, 11 May 1927, in Vanessa Bell, *Selected Letters*, p. 318.

Neptune's Fruit Banquet

p. 207 'Rose's arrangement' – Virginia Woolf, *To the Lighthouse*, pp. 150–51.

A Room of One's Own: Two Menus

p. 208 'It is part of the novelist's' – Virginia Woolf, *A Room of One's Own*, p. 9.

p. 208 'The visit of Miss Strachey's' – E. E. Duncan-Jones and U. K. Stevenson quoted in Stape, ed., *Virginia Woolf*, p. 14.

p. 209 'intellectual freedom' – Virginia Woolf, *A Room of One's Own*, p. 97.

p. 209 'a woman must have' – Ibid., p. 3.

p. 209 'One cannot think well' – Ibid., p. 16.

Menu 1: Dinner at a Women's College

pp. 209–10 'Here was the soup' – Ibid., p. 15.

Menu 2: Lunch at a Men's College

pp. 212–13 '[L]unch on this occasion began' – Ibid., pp. 9–10.

A Picnic in the Old Umbrella

p. 214 'Did Leonard tell you how' – Virginia Woolf, 24 August 1927, *Letters*, vol. 3, p. 413.

p. 214 'The Singer runs so fast' – Virginia Woolf, 7 April 1928, Ibid., p. 482.

A Bohemian Picnic

pp. 216–17 'Boris Anrep had completed' – Quentin Bell, *Elders and Betters*, pp. 89–90.

p. 218 'A vine grew' – Virginia Nicholson in a letter to Jans Ondaatje Rolls, 26 February 2013.

5. BLOOMSBURY AND ABROAD

Cézanne's Pommes

p. 221 'I've got a Cézanne' – John Maynard Keynes quoted in Rosenbaum, ed., *The Bloomsbury Group*, p. 222.

The Food Hamper

p. 222 'The children are as happy' – Duncan Grant quoted in Spalding, *Duncan Grant*, p. 238.

p. 222 'The food hamper arrived' – Ibid., p. 239.

La Bergère Beignets

pp. 222–23 'She was an excellent cook' – Angelica Garnett, *Deceived with Kindness*, pp. 69–70.

p. 223, caption, 'she would establish "Charleston in France"' – Glendinning, *Leonard Woolf*, p. 272.

p. 224 'I admire that woman' – Duncan Grant, 2 June 1929, quoted in Spalding, *Duncan Grant*, p. 289.

Still Life

pp. 225–26 'Oh why do I admire you?' – Roger Fry quoted in Spalding, *Vanessa Bell*, p. 165.

Charleston Boeuf à la Mode

p. 227 'And the food which is partly' – Vanessa Bell, undated letter from the Grace Higgens archive, British Library.

Roger's Boeuf en Daube

p. 228 'As for the cooking' – Virginia Woolf, *Roger Fry*, p. 283.

p. 228 'museum appetite' – Ibid., p. 99.

p. 228 'he tried unsuccessfully' – Ibid., p. 36.

p. 228 'ventured into the kitchen' – Ibid., p. 170.

p. 228 'an arrangement of flowers' – Ibid., p. 201.

p. 228 'a trifle tough' – Ibid., p. 270.

p. 228 'a dream' – Ibid., p. 283.

Soupe au Poisson

p. 230 'It was now, in these last' – Clive Bell, *Old Friends*, pp. 83–84.

p. 230 'clasping in his arms' – Virginia Woolf, *Roger Fry*, p. 282.

Proustian Madeleines

p. 231 'She sent out for' – Marcel Proust, *Remembrance of Things Past* (C. K. Scott Moncrieff, trans.) Harmondsworth (UK): Penguin, 1957, pp. 55–59. (First published in French in 1913.)

p. 231 'Everyone is reading Proust' – Virginia Woolf, 21 January 1922, in Virginia Woolf, *Letters*, vol. 2, p. 499.

p. 232 'Proust so titillates' – Virginia Woolf, 6 May 1922, Ibid., p. 525.

p. 233 'tedious' – Clive Bell, *Proust*, London: Hogarth Press, 1928, p. 11.

p. 233 'clumsy' – Ibid., p. 19.

p. 233 'From the unsurveyed mines' – Ibid., p. 89.

Burgundy Pears Ad Lib

p. 233 'We had breakfast' – Vita Sackville-West quoted in Stape, ed., *Virginia Woolf*, p. 35.

p. 233 'Dear Vita has the body' – Virginia Woolf, 23 January 1924, in Virginia Woolf, *Letters*, vol. 3, p. 85.

p. 233 'elaborate love-letter' – Nigel Nicolson's introduction to Ibid., p. xxii.

p. 234 'For it would seem' – Virginia Woolf, *Orlando: A Biography*, London: Penguin, 1993, p. 167.

p. 234 'vastest most delicious meal' – Vita Sackville-West, 25 September 1928, in Virginia Woolf, *Letters*, vol. 3, p. 534.

Roquebrune Salad

p. 235 'I had last seen' – Angelica Garnett, *Deceived with Kindness*, p. 169.

p. 235 'instinctive power' – Cecil and Cecil, *Clever Hearts*, p. 14.

I Tatti Pranzo

pp. 235–36 'I was hardly halfway' – Duncan Grant, *Charleston Magazine* 10 (autumn/winter 1994), p. 9.

p. 236 'gaze in an ecstasy' – Desmond MacCarthy quoted in Cecil and Cecil, *Clever Hearts*, p. 253.

Broeto Ciozoto

p. 236 '[Duncan's] *Doorway* is brilliant' – Gwen Raverat, from *Time and Tide* magazine, quoted in Pryor, ed., *Virginia Woolf and the Raverats*, p. 192.

p. 238 'to the family of "fish soups"' – Ristorante Giorgione website, <http://www.ristorantegiorgione.it/eng/recipes.htm> (Accessed August 2012.) Translated by Jayne Walker.

Italian Spaghetti Sauce

p. 239 'For the youth was hungry' – E. M. Forster, *Where Angels Fear to Tread*, London: Penguin, 2001, p. 23. (First published 1905.)

p. 239 'bullety bottled peas' – E. M. Forster, *A Passage to India*, London: Penguin, 2005, p. 43. (First published 1924.)

p. 239 'in pallid, grey lumps … scented jelly' – E. M. Forster quoted in John Burnett, *England Eats Out, 1830–Present*, Harlow (UK): Pearson Longman, 2004, p. 207.

Andalusian Vegetable Paella

p. 240 'Nowhere have I seen wheat' – Brenan, *Personal Record*, p. 14.

p. 240 'It was "death"' – Gerald Brenan, *South From Granada*, London: Penguin, 2008, p. 54.

p. 240 'that anyone who could not see' – Brenan, *Personal Record*, p. 41.

p. 242 'I don't want to come back' – Virginia Woolf, 22 April 1923, in Virginia Woolf, *Letters*, vol. 3, p. 30.

The Table at Segovia

p. 242 'I was really rather surprised' – comment from Roger Fry quoted in Virginia Woolf's letter to Barbara Bagenal, 24 June 1923, Ibid., p. 50.

p. 242 'He seemed to glide' – Leonard Woolf, *Sowing*, p. 87.

pp. 242–43 'was extremely spasmodic' – Ibid., p. 88.

p. 243 'make him almost voluble' – Barbara Bagenal quoted in Noble, ed., *Recollections of Virginia Woolf*, p. 177.

p. 243 'ate very little' – Leonard Woolf, *Sowing*, p. 88.

Asparagus for Angelica

p. 244 'When I was very small' – Angelica Garnett, *Deceived with Kindness*, pp. 103–4.

p. 244 'a grandfather' – Ibid., p. 101.

p. 244 'limp rods … enough' – Ibid., p. 103.

p. 245 'He loved it steamed' – Virginia Nicholson in a note to Jans Ondaatje Rolls, 26 February 2013.

Ballet and Sole

p. 245 'Living in Spain' – Lydia Keynes [Lopokova], 'Snails in Spain', *Evening News*, 11 May 1927.

p. 246 'I, too, watched' – Ibid.

Lydia's Sorrel Soup

p. 247 'It was delightful' – David Garnett, *Great Friends*, pp. 142–43.

Blinies

p. 248 'Your English food' – Lydia Keynes [Lopokova], 'Your English food is so dignified', *Evening News*, 20 April 1927.

Two Russian Soups

pp. 248–49 'But I do not think' – Lydia Keynes [Lopokova], 'Some soups we like in Russia', *Evening News*, 6 April 1927.

Southern American Chicken

pp. 249–50 '[Water] tastes' – Lydia Keynes [Lopokova], 'How America makes a joy of chicken', *Evening News*, 27 April 1927.

Russian Tea and Talk

p. 250 'The Russians love' – draft of a newspaper article written between 1921 and 1934 in the Lydia Lopokova Keynes archive at King's College, Cambridge, ref. LLK 4/1.

p. 250 'destroyed all conversation' – Clive Bell, 15 May 1922, quoted in Moggridge, *Maynard Keynes*, p. 398.

p. 251 'It will be no good' – Lydia Keynes [Lopokova], 'Tea-Drinking All Day Long!', *Evening News*, 4 May 1927.

Pashka

p. 253 'It is said that when Lytton' – Quentin Bell, *Elders and Betters*, p. 166.

Morgan's Indian Curry

p. 254 'It is odd that' – E. M. Forster, *The Hill of Devi*, London: Penguin, 1965, pp. 20–21. (First published 1953.)

pp. 254–56 '1. A mound of delicious rice' – Ibid., pp. 18–19.

Heavenly Peking Duck

p. 256 'My cook tried' – Julian Bell, 31 October 1935, in his *Essays, Poems and Letters*, London: Hogarth Press, 1938, p. 52.

pp. 256–57 'The nicest dish in the world' – Julian Bell, January 1936, Ibid., p. 78.

6. BLOOMSBURY IN ECLIPSE

Gin Sling

p. 259 'Henry [Lamb] was entertained' – Ralph Partridge quoted in Frances Partridge, *Memories*, p. 194.

p. 259 'was a favourite resort of poets' – Augustus John quoted in Richard Cork, *Art Beyond the Gallery: In Early Twentieth-Century England*, New Haven and London: Yale University Press, 1985, p. 214.

Blue and Green Cocktails

p. 260 '[Y]oung men in white' – Spalding, *Duncan Grant*, p. 324.

A Glass of Sherry

p. 262 'Carrington … was the dominating' – Paul Nash, *Outline: An Autobiography and Other Writings*, London: Faber and Faber, 1949, pp. 104–5.

p. 262 'We found her propped on rugs' – Frances Partridge, *Memories*, p. 210.

Artichoke Fonds with Saxon

p. 263 'Saxon arrived' – Frances Partridge, *Diaries, 1939–1972*, London: Phoenix, 2001, p. 33.

Onions au Gratin

p. 265 'For all the "war depression"' – Cecil and Cecil, *Clever Hearts*, p. 173.

p. 266 'has become fascinated' – Roger Fry to N. Wedd, 2 June 1918, quoted in Ibid, p. 114.

p. 266 'I am silent with pleasure' – Desmond MacCarthy, 20 March 1950, quoted in Ibid, p. 294.

p. 266 'I never knew my grandfather' – Sophie MacCarthy in a letter to Jennie Condell, 16 January 2013.

Still Life Transformation

p. 267 'When at last the apple' – Virginia Woolf, *Roger Fry*, p. 285.

Breakfast at Charleston

p. 270 'Vanessa presided' – Angelica Garnett, *Deceived with Kindness*, pp. 90–93.

pp. 270–71 'scrambled eggs, or boiled' – Anne Olivier Bell, 'A Day in the Life of Charleston', 14 October 2004, tape-recorded interview held in the archives at Charleston.

Lunch at Charleston

p. 272 'the round table came' – Quentin Bell and Virginia Nicholson, *Charleston: A Bloomsbury House & Garden*, pp. 32–34.

p. 272 'lunch on the whole' – Anne Olivier Bell, 'A Day in the Life of Charleston'.

pp. 272–73 'a letter from Angelica Garnett' – refers to an unpublished letter to Dr Anna Fewster, 5 October 2009.

Charleston Grouse

p. 274 'Dinner was at eight' – Angelica Garnett, from an unpublished letter to Dr Anna Fewster, 5 October 2009.

Glyndebourne Gammon

pp. 278–79 'Vanessa herself, as they sat' – Spalding, *Vanessa Bell*, p. 282.

p. 279 'and I had to pull' – Vanessa Bell to Julian Bell, 5 July 1936, quoted in Ibid., p. 282.

Angelica's Birthday Roast

p. 280 'Here we are spending' – Vanessa Bell quoted in Angelica Garnett, *Deceived with Kindness*, p. 40.

p. 280 'They didn't wish to' – Anne Olivier Bell, 'A Day in the Life of Charleston'.

Plovers' Eggs with Clive

p. 282 'If Clive had ever suffered' – Angelica Garnett, *Deceived with Kindness*, pp. 138–39.

p. 282 'no one seemed capable' – Ibid., p. 136.

p. 282 'the lie' – Ibid., p. 134.

p. 282 'It haunted her' – Virginia Nicholson in a letter to Jans Ondaatje Rolls, 22 April 2013.

Pudding for Julian

p. 283 'And one, my best' – Julian Bell, *Essays*, pp. 228–29.

p. 283 'I longed for her' – Angelica Garnett, *Deceived with Kindness*, pp. 42–43.

pp. 283–84 'While his plans were' – Quentin Bell, *Elders and Betters*, p. 56.

Nonsense

p. 284 'He was a wilful child' – David Garnett, quoted in Julian Bell, *Essays*, p. 3.

p. 285 'Sing a song of sixpence' – Julian Bell, 'Nonsense', from *Work from the Winter and Other Poems*, 1936, repr. in his *Essays, Poems and Letters*, p. 226.

p. 285 'fundamentally political in thought' – Julian Bell, *Times Literary Supplement*, 29 February 1936.

p. 285 'Well, I always wanted' – Julian Bell quoted in Peter Stansky and William Abrahams, *Julian Bell: From Bloomsbury to the Spanish Civil War*, Stanford (CA): Stanford University Press, 2012, p. 279.

Monk's House Cottage Loaf

p. 286 'there was one thing' – Louie Mayer quoted in Noble, ed., *Recollections of Virginia Woolf*, p. 191.

p. 287 'did not want to give' – Louie Mayer quoted in Ibid.

p. 287 'she used every dish' – Nellie Boxall, 'Portrait of Virginia Woolf', transcribed from the audio CD *The Bloomsbury Group*, disc 2, track 22.

Chicken Strut

p. 287 'I am free for tea on Wednesday' – T. S. Eliot quoted in Lee, *Virginia Woolf*, p. 453.

p. 287 'I shall walk across' – Virginia Woolf, *Letters*, vol. 3, p. 66.

Rest and Rice Pudding for Leonard (and Flush)

p. 289 'And then she looked up' – Virginia Woolf, *Flush: A Biography*, London: Vintage, 2002, p. 68. (First published 1933.)

Vita's Magnificent Strasbourg Pie

p. 289 'Oh an English Christmas!' – Virginia Woolf quoted in Pryor, ed., *Virginia Woolf and the Raverats*, p. 129.

p. 289 'Heaven above us' – Virginia Woolf to Vita Sackville-West, 26? December 1937, in Vita Sackville-West, *The Letters of Vita Sackville-West to Virginia Woolf* (Louise DeSalvo and Mitchell A. Leaska, eds), London: Papermac, 1985, p. 432.

Suffrage Angel Cake

pp. 290–91 'Dame Ethel was' – Spender, *World Within World*, p. 157.

Chocolate and Tea with Freud

pp. 292–93 'I only once met Freud' – Leonard Woolf, *Downhill All the Way*, pp. 168–69.

p. 293 'spare, nutritious' – Brenan, *Personal Record*, p. 92.

p. 293 'neurotic dread of' – Ibid.

Summer Party at Charleston

p. 294 'The scene was set' – Quentin Bell, 'Charleston Revisited', *Charleston Newsletter*, 17 (December 1986), pp. 7–8.

p. 294 'pig in the middle' – Quentin Bell, *Elders and Betters*, p. 1.

p. 296 'It was Quentin who' – Angelica Garnett quoted in Lee, ed., *A Cézanne in the Hedge*, p. 160.

p. 296 'was not much … work at his clay' – Virginia Nicholson in a letter to Jans Ondaatje Rolls, 26 February 2013.

Bloomsbury's Final Celebration

p. 297 'The house was packed' – Quentin Bell, *Elders and Betters*, p. 21.

p. 297 'We had wonderful turkey' – Angelica Garnett quoted in Spalding, *Duncan Grant*, p. 370.

Wartime Stew, Again

p. 298 'We have need' – Virginia Woolf, *A Writer's Diary*, p. 338.

p. 298 'suddenly fell very silent' – John Lehmann, *Thrown to the Woolfs*, London: Weidenfeld & Nicolson, 1978, p. 90.

p. 298 'there was a tremendous roar' – Leonard Woolf, *The Journey Not the Arrival Matters: An Autobiography of the Years 1939–1969*, New York: Harcourt Brace Jovanovich, 1975, p. 32.

Haddock and Sausage

p. 300 'I feel certain that' – Virginia Woolf quoted in Phyllis Rose, *Woman of Letters: A Life of Virginia Woolf*, London: Routledge & Kegan Paul, 1986, p. 243. (First published 1978.)

p. 300 'Occupation is essential' – Virginia Woolf, *A Writer's Diary*, p. 351.

Louie's Mutton Roast

p. 301 'It was done' – Virginia Woolf, *To the Lighthouse*, p. 320.

7. BLOOMSBURY'S OFFSPRING

Wartime Carrots

p. 303 'Henceforward, we are' – John Maynard Keynes, 'The Arts Council of Great Britain', BBC interview, 12 June 1945. Transcribed from the audio CD *The Spoken Word: The Bloomsbury Group*, London: British Library, 2009, disc 1, track 11.

p. 304 'to sharpen their eyesight' – Mackrell, *Bloomsbury Ballerina*, p. 382.

Maynard's Champagne Toast

p. 304 'I give you the toast' – John Maynard Keynes, quoted in R. F. Harrod, *The Life of John Maynard Keynes*, New York: W. W. Norton & Company, 1982, pp. 193–94. (First published 1951.)

p. 304 'It was a golden hour' – Ibid., pp. 193–94.

p. 305 'like Alice in Wonderland' – John Maynard Keynes, quoted in Mackrell, *Bloomsbury Ballerina*, p. 390.

p. 305 'My only regret in life' – John Maynard Keynes, quoted in Terry Breverton, *Immortal Last Words*, London: Quercus Publishing, 2010, p. 281.

Two Vegetable Soups

p. 306 'Musing among the vegetables?' – Virginia Woolf, *Mrs Dalloway*, p. 1.

Bolooty

p. 307 'Much later during' – David Garnett, *Great Friends*, p. 156.

p. 307 'Ralph had more knowledge' – Frances Partridge, *Memories*, p. 116.

Dinner Tête-à-Tête

p. 308 'November 19th' – Frances Partridge, *Memories*, p. 133.

p. 309 'And what can I say' – quoted in Lee, ed., *A Cézanne in the Hedge*, p. 134.

Fresh Tomatoes and Wiveton Pigeon Stew

p. 312 'He lived, he said' – Cecil and Cecil, *Clever Hearts*, p. 258.

p. 312 'His ability to bring the reader' – Ibid., p. 259.

p. 312 'swoop down' – James MacGibbon quoted in Lee, ed., *A Cézanne in the Hedge*, p. 115.

p. 312 'fresh tomatoes and the stew' – Cyril Connolly to Molly MacCarthy, c. 1940, quoted in Cecil and Cecil, *Clever Hearts*, p. 293.

p. 312 'Britain's best' – Delia Smith quoted in Matthew Bell, 'World's top eatery? A tiny café in Norfolk', *The Independent*, 17 July 2011.

A Bottle of Chablis

p. 314 'Conversation was his art' – Quentin Bell, *Elders and Betters*, pp. 129–30.

p. 314 'knew exactly what he wanted to say' – E. M. Forster, 'Talk on Desmond MacCarthy', BBC interview, 1952. Transcribed from the audio CD *The Spoken Word: The Bloomsbury Group*, London: British Library, 2009, disc 1, track 3.

Bell Family Christmas Cake

p. 315 'The overflow of' – Frances Spalding, 'Quentin Bell', *The Independent*, 18 December 1996.

p. 316 'You will always be' – Virginia Woolf quoted in Mel Gussow, 'Quentin Bell', *New York Times*, 19 December 1996.

Charleston Bloody Mary

p. 317 'Like all their expeditions' – Frances Spalding, 'Paul Roche', *The Independent*, 8 November 2007.

Savoury Scones

p. 318 'Tea was at five o'clock' – John and Diana Higgens, from the Grace Higgens archive, British Library, BL MS 83249, *c*. 1990s.

Vintage at Charleston

p. 322 'Drink was preferably wine' – Angelica Garnett, from an unpublished letter to Dr Anna Fewster, 5 October 2009.

p. 322 'After dinner' – Anne Olivier Bell, 'A Day in the Life of Charleston'.

Canards

p. 324 'Its beauty is' – David Garnett quoted in Spalding, *Duncan Grant*, p. 215.

p. 325 'The duck, a lump of white sugar' – Henrietta Garnett quoted in Todd, *Bloomsbury at Home*, p. 125.

Grandchildren at Charleston

p. 325 'My brother Julian' – Virginia Nicholson quoted in Lee, ed., *A Cézanne in the Hedge*, p. 163.

p. 326 'The kitchen was' – Cressida Bell, in an e-mail to Dr Anna Fewster, 14 September 2009.

p. 326 'helping, which meant' – Virginia Nicholson in a letter to Jans Ondaatje Rolls, 26 February 2013.

p. 327 'The great object of dinner' – Henrietta Garnett, in an e-mail to Dr Anna Fewster, 14 September 2009.

Tea at Tilton

p. 328 'She was tiny' – Henrietta Garnett quoted in Lee, ed., *A Cézanne in the Hedge*, p. 149.

Mutton Pie with T. S. Eliot

p. 328 'That strange figure' – Virginia Woolf, 18 May 1923, *Letters*, vol. 3, p. 38.

p. 328 'I have just finished' – Virginia Woolf, 8 July 1923, Ibid., p. 56.

p. 329 'The joke among' – Glendinning, *Leonard Woolf*, p. 397.

p. 329 'I do not think' – T. S. Eliot to Conrad Aiken, 25 February 1915, in T. S. Eliot, *The Letters of T. S. Eliot* (Valerie Eliot and Hugh Haughton): vol. 1: 1898–1922, London: Faber and Faber, 2009, p. 95.

Garnett the Gastronome

p. 330 'For honey and bees' – David Garnett, 5 August 1966, in Sylvia Townsend Warner and David Garnett, *Sylvia and David: The Townsend Warner/Garnett Letters* (Richard Garnett, ed.), London: Sinclair-Stevenson, 1994, p. 107.

p. 330 'ducks, geese' – Ibid., 29 September 1965, p. 89.

p. 330 'with pools of' – Ibid., 5 August 1966, p. 107.

p. 330 'tables…[groaned]' – Ibid., 9 August 1976, p. 215.

p. 330 'London eggs' – Ibid., 5 May 1972, p. 168.

p. 330 'a dog's nose' – Ibid., 5 May 1972, p. 167.

p. 330 'stewed with aubergines' – Ibid., 28 March 1974, p. 191.

p. 331 'little melons … and sacks' – Ibid., 22 October 1977, p. 233.

Savoury Eggs with Henrietta

p. 333 'I am very fond' – Henrietta Partridge [Garnett], 'Good Eggs', *Harpers & Queen*, March 1976.

p. 333 'I found this recipe' – Henrietta Partridge [Garnett], 'Good Eggs'.

BIBLIOGRAPHY

This general bibliography is followed by a list of books on food and cookery, p. 367.

Anscombe, Isabelle, *Omega and After: Bloomsbury and the Decorative Arts*, London: Thames & Hudson, 1981.

A Painter's Paradise: The Restoration of Charleston Farmhouse, Spilsby (UK): Malachite Productions in association with Channel Four Television, 1989 (DVD).

Arts Council of Great Britain, *Vision and Design: The Life, Work and Influence of Roger Fry 1866–1934*, London: Arts Council of Great Britain, 1966.

Baron, Wendy, *The Camden Town Group*, London: Scolar Press, 1979.

Beauman, Nicola, *Morgan: A Biography of E. M. Forster*, London: Hodder and Stoughton, 1993.

Behlmer, George K., and Fred M. Leventhal, eds, *Singular Continuities: Tradition, Nostalgia, and Identity in Modern British Culture*, Stanford (CA): Stanford University Press, 2000.

Bell, Clive, *Art*, London: Chatto & Windus, 1916.

——, *Civilization: An Essay*, West Drayton: Penguin, 1947.

——, *Old Friends*, London: Chatto & Windus, 1956.

——, 'The new ballet', *New Republic*, 30 July 1919.

——, *Pot-Boilers*, London: Chatto & Windus, 1918.

——, *Proust*, London: Hogarth Press, 1928.

——, *War Mongers*, London: The Peace Pledge Union, 1938.

Bell, Cressida, *Cressida Bell's Cake Design*, London: Double-Barrelled Books, 2013.

Bell, Julian, *Essays, Poems and Letters*, London: Hogarth Press, 1938.

Bell, Quentin, 'Charleston Revisited', *Charleston Newsletter*, 17 (December 1986).

——, *Elders and Betters*, London: John Murray, 1995. (Published in the USA as *Bloomsbury Recalled*.)

——, *Virginia Woolf: A Biography*, 2 vols, New York: Harcourt Brace Jovanovich, 1972.

Bell, Quentin, and Virginia Nicholson, *Charleston: A Bloomsbury House & Garden*, London: Frances Lincoln, 1997.

Bell, Vanessa, *Sketches in Pen and Ink: A Bloomsbury Notebook*, London: Pimlico, 1998.

——, *Selected Letters of Vanessa Bell* (Regina Marler, ed.), London: Bloomsbury, 1993.

Blythe, Ronald, *First Friends: Paul and Bunty, John and Christine – and Carrington*, London: Viking, 1999.

Bradshaw, David, ed., *The Cambridge Companion to E. M. Forster*, Cambridge: Cambridge University Press, 2007.

Bradshaw, Tony, *The Bloomsbury Artists: Prints and Book Design*, Aldershot (UK): Scolar Press, 1999.

——, ed., *A Bloomsbury Canvas: Reflections on the Bloomsbury Group*, London: Lund Humphries, 2001.

Brenan, Gerald, *A Life of One's Own: Childhood and Youth*, London: Hamish Hamilton, 1962.

——, *Personal Record, 1920–1972*, London: Jonathan Cape, 1974.

——, *South From Granada*, London: Penguin, 2008. (First published 1957.)

Brenan, Gerald, and Ralph Partridge, *Best of Friends: The Brenan-Partridge Letters* (Xan Fielding, ed.), London: Chatto & Windus, 1986.

Brooke, Rupert and James Strachey, *Friends and Apostles: The Correspondence of Rupert Brooke and James Strachey, 1905–1914* (Keith Hale, ed.), New Haven (CT): Yale University Press, 1999.

Caine, Barbara, *Bombay to Bloomsbury: A Biography of the Strachey Family*, Oxford: Oxford University Press, 2005.

Carrington, Dora, *Carrington: Letters and Extracts from Her Diaries* (David Garnett, ed.), New York: Rinehart and Winston, 1971.

Caws, Mary Ann and Sarah Bird Wright, *Bloomsbury and France: Art and Friends,* Oxford: Oxford University Press, 2000.

Cecil, Hugh and Mirabel, *Clever Hearts, Desmond and Molly MacCarthy: A Biography*, London: Gollancz, 1990.

Chisholm, Anne, *Frances Partridge: The Biography*, London: Weidenfeld & Nicolson, 2009.

Christie, George, *Glyndebourne: A Visual History*, London: Quercus, 2009.

Coss, Melinda, *Bloomsbury Needlepoint: From the Tapestries at Charleston Farmhouse*, London: Ebury, 1992.

Cork, Richard, *Art Beyond the Gallery: In Early Twentieth-Century England*, New Haven and London: Yale University Press, 1985.

Crevel, René, *The As Stable Pamphlets* (Keith Waldrop, trans.), no. 3, Englewood (NJ): Elysium Press, 1996.

Croft, Peter, and David Scrase, *Maynard Keynes, Collector of Pictures, Books and Manuscripts: Catalogue of an Exhibition Held at the Fitzwilliam Museum, Cambridge, 5 July–29 August 1983*, Cambridge: Provost and Scholars of King's College, Cambridge, 1983.

Curtis, Anthony, *Virginia Woolf: Bloomsbury and Beyond*, London: Haus, 2006.

Curtis, Vanessa, *The Hidden Houses of Virginia Woolf and Vanessa Bell*, London: Robert Hale, 2005.

Edel, Leon, *Bloomsbury: A House of Lions*, London: Hogarth Press, 1979.

Eliot, T. S., *The Letters of T. S. Eliot* (Valerie Eliot and Hugh Haughton): vol. 1: 1898–1922, London: Faber and Faber, 2009.

——, *The Letters of T. S. Eliot* (Valerie Eliot and Hugh Haughton): vol. 111: 1926–1927, London: Faber and Faber, 2012.

Forster, E. M., *Abinger Harvest and England's Pleasant Land*, London: Andre Deutsch, 1996. (First published 1936.)

——, *The Hill of Devi*, London: Penguin, 1965. (First published 1953.)

——, *Howards End*, London: Penguin, 2000. (First published 1910.)

——, *The Longest Journey*, London: Penguin, 2001. (First published 1907.)

——, *A Passage to India*, London: Penguin, 2005. (First published 1924.)

——, *A Room with a View*, New York: Penguin, 2000. (First published 1908.)

——, *Two Cheers for Democracy*, Harmondsworth (UK): Penguin, 1970. (First published 1951.)

——, *Where Angels Fear to Tread*, London: Penguin, 2001. (First published 1905.)

Fry, Roger, *Cézanne: A Study of his Development*, London: Hogarth Press, 1927.

——, *Last Lectures*, Cambridge: Cambridge University Press, 1939.

——, *Letters of Roger Fry* (Denys Sutton, ed.), 2 vols, London: Chatto & Windus, 1972.

——, *Second Post-Impressionist Exhibition*, exhibition catalogue, London: Grafton Galleries, 1912.

——, *Manet and The Post-Impressionists*, exhibition catalogue, London: Grafton Galleries, 1910–11.

——, *Vision and Design*, London: Chatto & Windus, 1920.

Garnett, Angelica, *Deceived with Kindness: A Bloomsbury Childhood*, London: Chatto & Windus, 1984.

Garnett, David, *The Familiar Faces*, New York: Harcourt, Brace and World, 1962.

——, *The Golden Echo*, London: Chatto & Windus, 1953.

——, *Great Friends: Portraits of Seventeen Writers*, New York: Atheneum, 1980.

——, *Lady into Fox*, London: Chatto & Windus, 1922.

Gathorne-Hardy, Jonathan, *The Interior Castle: A Life of Gerald Brenan*, London: Sinclair-Stevenson, *c.* 1992.

Gerstein, Alexandra, *Beyond Bloomsbury: Designs of the Omega Workshops 1913–19*, London: Courtauld Gallery, 2009.

Gertler, Mark, *Selected Letters* (Noel Carrington, ed.), London: Rupert Hart-Davis, 1965.

Gerzina, Gretchen, *Carrington: A Life of Dora Carrington, 1893–1932*, Oxford: Oxford University Press, 1990.

Gide, André, and Dorothy Bussy, *Selected Letters of André Gide and Dorothy Bussy* (Richard Tedeschi, ed.), Oxford: Oxford University Press, 1983.

Glenavy, Beatrice Lady, *Today We Will Only Gossip*, London: Constable, 1964.

Glendinning, Victoria, *Leonard Woolf: A Life*, London: Pocket Books, 2007.

Grant, Duncan, 'I Tatti: a question of labels: a paper written for the Memoir Club and delivered *c.* 1950', *Charleston Magazine*, 10 (autumn/winter 1994), pp. 5–12.

Hall, Sarah M., *The Bedside, Bathtub and Armchair Companion to Virginia Woolf and Bloomsbury*, New York: Continuum, 2007.

Harris, Alexandra, *Romantic Moderns: English Writers, Artists and the Imagination from Virginia Woolf to John Piper*, London and New York: Thames & Hudson, 2010.

Harrod, R. F., *The Life of John Maynard Keynes*, New York: W. W. Norton & Company, 1982.

Hignett, Sean, *Brett, From Bloomsbury to New Mexico: A Biography*, London: Hodder and Stoughton, 1984.

Hill, Jane, *The Art of Dora Carrington*, London: Herbert Press, 1994.

Holroyd, Michael, *Augustus John: The New Biography*, London: Vintage, 1997.

——, *Lytton Strachey: A Critical Biography*, 2 vols, London: William Heinemann, 1967 (vol. 1) and 1968 (vol. 2).

——, *Lytton Strachey: The New Biography*, London: Vintage, 1995.

Humm, Maggie, *Modernist Women and Visual Cultures: Virginia Woolf, Vanessa Bell, Photography and Cinema*, Edinburgh: Edinburgh University Press; and New Brunswick (NJ): Rutgers University Press, 2002.

——, *Snapshots of Bloomsbury: The Private Lives of Virginia Woolf and Vanessa Bell*, London: Tate Publications; and New Brunswick (NJ): Rutgers University Press, 2006.

Huxley, Aldous, *Crome Yellow*, London: Flamingo, 1977. (First published 1921.)

Kennedy, Richard, *A Boy at the Hogarth Press*, London: Hesperus, 2011. (First published 1972.)

Keynes, John Maynard, *The Economic Consequences of the Peace*, London: Macmillan, 1919.

King, Francis, *E. M. Forster*, London: Thames & Hudson, 1987.

Lee, Hermione, *Virginia Woolf*, London: Vintage, 1997.

Lee, Hugh, ed., *A Cézanne in the Hedge, and Other Memories of Charleston and Bloomsbury*, London: Collins & Brown, 1992.

Lehmann, John, *Thrown to the Woolfs*, London: Weidenfeld & Nicolson, 1978.

Light, Alison, *Mrs Woolf and the Servants*, London: Penguin, 2007.

Lopokova, Lydia, *Lydia and Maynard: Letters between Lydia Lopokova and John Maynard Keynes* (Polly Hill and Richard Keynes, eds), London: Andre Deutsch, 1989.

MacCarthy, Desmond, *Memories*, London: MacGibbon & Kee, 1953.

MacCarthy, Mary, *A Pier and a Band: A Novel of the Nineties*, London: Martin Secker, 1931. (First published 1918.)

Mackrell, Judith, *Bloomsbury Ballerina: Lydia Lopokova, Imperial Dancer and Mrs John Maynard Keynes*, London: Weidenfeld & Nicolson, 2008.

Marler, Regina, *Bloomsbury Pie: The Making of the Bloomsbury Boom*, New York: Henry Holt, 1997.

Moggridge, D. E., *Maynard Keynes: An Economist's Biography*, London: Routledge, 1992.

Morrell, Ottoline, *The Early Memoirs of Lady Ottoline Morrell* (Robert Gathorne-Hardy, ed.), London: Faber and Faber, 1963.

Moore, G. E., *Principia Ethica*, Cambridge: Cambridge University Press, 1903.

Mortimer, Raymond, *Duncan Grant*, London: Penguin, 1944.

Nash, Paul, *Outline: An Autobiography and Other Writings*, London: Faber and Faber, 1949.

Naylor, Gillian, ed., *Bloomsbury: The Artists, Authors and Designers by Themselves*, London: Pyramid Books, 1990.

Nicolson, Adam, *Sissinghurst: An Unfinished Story*, London: Harper Press, 2008.

Nicolson, Nigel, *Sissinghurst Castle Garden*, Swindon (UK): National Trust, 1995.

Nicholson, Virginia, *Among the Bohemians: Experiments in Living, 1900–1939*, London: Viking, 2002.

Noble, Joan Russell, ed., *Recollections of Virginia Woolf*, London: Penguin, 1975.

Nunez, Sigrid, *Mitz: Marmoset of Bloomsbury*, New York: Soft Skull Press, 2007.

Ondaatje, Christopher, *Woolf in Ceylon: An Imperial Journey in the Shadow of Leonard Woolf*, Toronto: HarperCollins, 2005.

Partridge, Frances, *Diaries, 1939–1972*, London: Phoenix, 2001.

——, *Memories*, London: Gollancz, 1981.

——, *A Pacifist's War*, London: Hogarth Press, 1978.

Proust, Marcel, *Remembrance of Things Past* (C. K. Scott Moncrieff, trans.), 7 vols, Harmondsworth (UK): Penguin, 1957. (First published 1922–30.)

Pryor, William, ed., *Virginia Woolf and the Raverats: A Different Sort of Friendship*, Bath (UK): Clear Press, 2003.

Rhein, Donna E., *The Handprinted Books of Leonard and Virginia Woolf at the Hogarth Press, 1917–1932*, Ann Arbor (MI): UMI Research Press, 1985.

Richardson, Elizabeth P., *A Bloomsbury Iconography*, Winchester (UK): St Pauls Bibliographies, 1989.

Rose, Phyllis, *Woman of Letters: A Life of Virginia Woolf*, London: Routledge & Kegan Paul, 1986. (First published 1978.)

Rosenbaum, S. P., ed., *The Bloomsbury Group: A Collection of Memoirs, Commentary and Criticism*, Toronto: University of Toronto Press, 1975.

Russell, Bertrand, *Autobiography*, London: Routledge, 2008. (First published 1967–69.)

Sackville-West, V., *The Edwardians*, London: Virago, 1978. (First published 1930.)

——, *The Letters of Vita Sackville-West to Virginia Woolf* (Louise DeSalvo and Mitchell A. Leaska, eds), London: Papermac, 1985.

Sanders, Charles Richard, *Lytton Strachey: His Mind and Art*, New Haven (CT): Yale University Press, 1957.

Seymour, Miranda, *Ottoline Morrell: Life on the Grand Scale*, London: Hodder and Stoughton, 1992.

Shone, Richard, *The Art of Bloomsbury: Roger Fry, Vanessa Bell and Duncan Grant*, Princeton: Princeton University Press, 2002.

——, *Bloomsbury Portraits: Vanessa Bell, Duncan Grant, and Their Circle*, Oxford: Phaidon, 1976.

Sitwell, Osbert, *Laughter in the Next Room*, London: Macmillan, 1949.

Skidelsky, Robert, *Keynes: The Return of the Master*, London: Allen Lane, 2009.

Southworth, Helen, *The Intersecting Realities and Fictions of Virginia Woolf and Colette*, Columbus (OH): Ohio State University Press, 2004.

Spalding, Frances, *Duncan Grant: A Biography*, London: Pimlico, 1998.

——, *Vanessa Bell*, London: Weidenfeld & Nicolson, 1983.

Spender, Stephen, *World Within World: The Autobiography of Stephen Spender*, London: Hamish Hamilton, 1951.

The Spoken Word: The Bloomsbury Group, London: British Library, 2009 (2 audio CDs).

Stansky, Peter, and William Abrahams, *Julian Bell: From Bloomsbury to the Spanish Civil War*, Stanford (CA): Stanford University Press, 2012.

Stape, J. H., ed., *Virginia Woolf: Interviews and Recollections*, Iowa City (IA): University of Iowa Press, 1995.

Stephen, Adrian, *The Dreadnought Hoax*, London: Hogarth Press, 1936.

Strachey, Lytton, *Eminent Victorians*, Oxford: Oxford University Press, 2003. (First published 1918.)

——, *The Letters of Lytton Strachey* (Paul Levy, ed.), London: Viking, 2005.

Summers, Claude J., ed., *The Gay & Lesbian Literary Heritage*, rev. edn, New York: Routledge, 2002.

Todd, Pamela, *Bloomsbury at Home*, New York: Abrams, 1999.

Warner, Sylvia Townsend, and David Garnett, *Sylvia and David: The Townsend Warner/Garnett Letters* (Richard Garnett, ed.), London: Sinclair-Stevenson, 1994.

Watney, Simon, *Bloomsbury in Sussex*, Alfriston (UK): Snake River Press, 2007.

Winterson, Jeanette, 'Back from the lighthouse', *Charleston Magazine*, 20 (autumn/winter 1999), pp. 5–9.

Wölfflin, Heinrich, *Principles of Art History: The Problem of the Development of Style in Later Art* (M. D. Hottinger, trans.), New York: Dover Publications, 1950. (First published in English 1932.)

Woolf, Leonard, *Beginning Again: An Autobiography of the Years 1911–1918*, London: Hogarth Press, 1965.

——, *Diaries in Ceylon and Stories from the East*, London: Hogarth Press, 1963.

——, *Downhill All the Way: An Autobiography of the Years 1919–1939*, New York: Hogarth Press, 1968.

——, *Growing: An Autobiography of the Years 1904–1911*, London: Hogarth Press, 1967.

——, *The Journey Not the Arrival Matters: An Autobiography of the Years 1939–1969*, New York: Harcourt Brace Jovanovich, 1975.

——, *Letters of Leonard Woolf* (Frederic Spotts, ed.), London: Bloomsbury, 1992.

——, *Sowing: An Autobiography of the Years 1880–1904*, London: Hogarth Press, 1962.

——, *Stories of the East*, London: Hogarth Press, 1921.

——, *The Village in the Jungle*, London: Eland, 2005. (First published 1913.)

Woolf, Leonard, and Trekkie Ritchie Parsons, *Love Letters: Leonard Woolf and Trekkie Ritchie Parsons (1941–1968)* (Judith Adamson, ed.), London: Pimlico, 2002.

Woolf, Virginia:

Fiction, essays, drama, biography:

——, *The Common Reader* (Andrew McNeillie, ed.), New York and London: Harvest-Harcourt, 1984. (First published 1925.)

——, *Flush: A Biography*, London: Vintage, 2002. (First published 1933.)

——, *Jacob's Room*, London: Hogarth Press, 1929. (First published 1922.)

——, *Kew Gardens*, London: Hogarth Press, 1927. (First published 1919.)

——, *Melymbrosia* (Louise DeSalvo, ed.), San Francisco (CA): Cleis Press, 1982.

——, *Moments of Being* (Jeanne Schulkind, ed.), London: Pimlico, 2002. (First published 1976.)

——, *Mr Bennett and Mrs Brown*, London: Hogarth Press, 1924.

——, *Mrs Dalloway*, London: Vintage, 2004. (First published 1925.)

——, *Orlando: A Biography*, London: Penguin, 1993. (First published 1928.)

——, *Roger Fry: A Biography*, London: Vintage, 2003. (First published 1940.)

——, *A Room of One's Own and Three Guineas*, London: Penguin, 1993. (First published 1928 and 1930.)

——, *To the Lighthouse*, London: Hogarth Press, 1927.

——, *The Voyage Out*, London: Hogarth Press, 1971. (First published 1915.)

——, *Walter Sickert: A Conversation*, London: Hogarth Press, 1934.

——, *The Waves*, London: Hogarth Press, 1950. (First published 1931.)

——, *The Years*, London: Vintage, 2004. (First published 1937.)

Diaries and letters:

——, *The Diary of Virginia Woolf* (Anne Olivier Bell, ed., with Andrew McNeillie), 5 vols: vol. 1, 1915–1919, London: Hogarth Press, 1977; vol. 2, 1920–1924, New York, Harcourt Brace Jovanovich, 1978; vol. 3, 1925–1930, London: Hogarth Press, 1980; vol. 4, 1931–1935, London: Hogarth Press, 1982; vol. 5, 1936–1941, London: Hogarth Press, 1984.

——, *A Writer's Diary: Being Extracts from the Diary of Virginia Woolf* (Leonard Woolf, ed.), New York: Harvest-Harcourt, 1982.

——, *The Letters of Virginia Woolf* (Nigel Nicolson, ed., with Joanne Trautmann), 6 vols: vol. 1, 'The Flight of the Mind', 1888–1912, London: Hogarth Press, 1975; vol. 2, 'The Question of Things Happening', 1912–1922, London: Hogarth Press, 1976; vol. 3, 'A Change of Perspective', 1923–1928, London: Hogarth Press, 1977; vol. 4, 'A Reflection of the Other Person', 1929–1931, London: Hogarth Press, 1978; vol. 5, 'The Sickle Side of the Moon', 1932–1935, London: Hogarth Press, 1979; vol. 6, 'Leave the Letters Till We're Dead', 1936–1941, London: Hogarth Press, 1980.

——, *Congenial Spirits: The Selected Letters of Virginia Woolf* (Joanne Trautmann Banks, ed.), London: Hogarth Press, 1989.

Other works:

——, *The Platform of Time: Memoirs of Family and Friends* (S. P. Rosenbaum, ed.), London: Hesperus, 2008.

——, with Vanessa Bell, and Thoby Stephen, *Hyde Park Gate News: The Stephen Family Newspaper*, London: Hesperus, 2005.

Food and Cookery

Adair, A. H., *Dinners Long and Short,* London: Gollancz, 1928.

Baines, Maud, and Edgar J. Saxon, *Complete Guide to Sound, Successful and Attractive Food Reform,* London: C. W. Daniel, 1929.

Beeton, Isabella, *All About Cookery*, London: Ward, Lock, 1909.

——, *The Book of Household Management*, London: Ward, Lock and Bowden, 1895.

——, *Mrs Beeton's Book of Household Management*, London: Ward, Lock, 1915.

——, *Mrs Beeton's Cookery Book*, London: Ward, Lock, 1915.

——, *Mrs Beeton's Cookery and Household Management*, London: Ward, Lock, 1960.

——, *Mrs Beeton's Everyday Cookery*, London: Ward, Lock. 1936.

Boulestin, X. M., *The Finer Cooking*, London: Cassell, 1937.

——, *A Second Helping*, London: William Heinemann, 1925.

——, *Simple French Cooking for English Homes*, London: Quadrille, 2011. (First published 1923.)

——, *What Shall We Have To-day?*, London: William Heinemann, 1931.

Boxer, Arabella, *Book of English Food*, London: Penguin, 1991.

Burnett, John, *England Eats Out, 1830–Present*, Harlow (UK): Pearson Longman, 2004.

Byron, May, *May Byron's Jam Book*, London: Hodder and Stoughton, 1923.

Cambridge Cuisine: In Aid of Save the Children Fund, Save the Children Fund, London, unknown date.

Chester, ed., *French Cooking for English Homes*, London: Thornton Butterworth, 1923.

Chotzinoff Grossman, Anne, and Lisa Thomas Grossman, *Lobscouse and Spotted Dog*, New York: W. W. Norton & Company, 1997.

Cobbett, William, *Cottage Economy*, London: Douglas Pepler, 1916. (First published 1821.)

Cowles, Florence A., *Five Hundred Sandwiches*, London: Chatto & Windus, 1929.

Croft, Susan, *The Stork Wartime Cookery Book*, London: Stork Margarine Company, 1946.

Craddock, Harry, *The Savoy Cocktail Book*, London: Constable, 1930.

Dallas, E. S., *Kettner's Book of the Table*, London: Centaur Press, 1968. (First published 1877.)

Dudley, Georgiana, Countess of, *The Dudley Book of Cookery and Household Recipes,* London: Edward Arnold, 1913.

Edden, Helen, *Cooking by Gas*, London: British Commercial Gas Association, 1910.

English-Tamil Cookery Book, A Friend in Need Society, Women's Workshop Ladies Committee, Madras: Diocesan Press, 1937.

Escoffier, Auguste, *The Escoffier Cookbook: A Guide to the Fine Art of French Cuisine*, New York: Crown, 1989. (First published as *Le Guide Culinaire*, 1903.)

——, *2,000 Favourite French Recipes*, (Marion Howells, ed. and trans.) London: Treasure Press, 1992.

Four Hundred Prize Recipes for Practical Cookery: Reprinted from the Daily Telegraph, Andover (UK): Chapel River Press, 1934.

de la Falaise, Maxime, *Seven Centuries of English Cooking*, New York: Grove Press, 1992.

Frere, Catherine Frances, *The Cookery Book of Lady Clark of Tillypronie*, London: Constable, 1909.

Fry's Chocolate Recipes: Economical and Simple, Bristol and Somerdale (UK): J. S. Fry & Sons, unknown date.

Gage, Lady, *Food from Firle*, Tisbury (UK): Compton Press, 1978.

George, Florence A., *King Edward's Cookery Book*, London: Edward Arnold, unknown date.

The Golden Book of Confectioners' Recipes, Bolton: Pendlebury and Sons, unknown date.

Grigson, Jane, *English Food*, London: Penguin, 1992.

Handy Hints by Famous Broadcasters and Writers: A Family Reference Book and Household Guide, Slough (UK): Aspro Ltd, 1954.

Hellman, Renee, *Celebrity Cooking for You*, London: Hamlyn, 1967.

Higgens, Diana, *Grace at Charleston*, Brighton (UK): Lockholt and Co. [Charleston Trust], 1994.

Humphries, Olive L., *Cook with Ease*, Birmingham (UK): Cornish Bros, 1935.

Jack, Florence B., *Good Housekeeping Cookery Book*, London: Good Housekeeping Magazine, 1925.

Jekyll, Lady, *Kitchen Essays with Recipes and Their Occasions*, London: Thomas Nelson and Sons, *c.* 1921.

Keynes [Lopokova], Lydia, 'Food in other lands', *Evening News*, 30 March – 18 May 1927 (series of eight articles).

Kleber, L. O., *The Suffrage Cookbook*, Pittsburgh (PA): The Equal Franchise Federation of Western Pennsylvania, 1915.

Le Clercq, Tanaquil, *The Ballet Cook Book*, New York: Stein and Day, 1966.

Lowinsky, Ruth, *Lovely Food*, London: Nonesuch Press, 1931.

McDougall's Cookery Book, London: McDougalls, *c.* 1930.

Naudin, Jean-Bernard, *Cézanne and the Provençal Table*, New York: Clarkson Potter, 1995.

Official Handbook of the National Training School of Cookery, London: William Clowes, 1915.

Purvis, Ester, *The Electric Cooker and How To Use It*, London: Odhams, 1936.

Quaglino, Giovanni, *The Complete Hostess*, London: Hamish Hamilton, 1935.

Raper, Elizabeth, *The Receipt Book of Elizabeth Raper. And a portion of her Cipher Journal. Edited by her great-grandson the late Bartle Grant with a portrait and decorations by Duncan Grant*, London: Nonesuch Press, 1924.

The Recipe Book of 'Atora', Manchester (UK): Hugon & Co., *c.* 1925.

Salvoni, Elena, *Eating Famously*, London: Walnut West One Ltd, 2007.

Scotson-Clark, G. F., *Kitchenette Cookery*, London: Jonathan Cape, 1926.

Senn, Herman, *War Time Cooking Guide*, London: Food and Cookery Publishing Co., 1915.

Simple Home Cookery by the Check Apron Girl, London: Brown & Polson, *c.* 1930.

Stewart, Katie, *The Times Cookery Book*, Glasgow and London: Collins, 1978.

Success: 1500 New Economy Cookery and Household Recipes, London: Success Publishing Co., 1933.

Taglienti, Maria Luisa, *The Italian Cookbook*, London: Spring Books, 1955.

Tarling, W. J., *Café Royal Cocktail Book*, Cheltenham: Mixellany Books, 2008. (First published 1937.)

White, Florence, *Good Things in England*, London: Jonathan Cape, 1932.

Wijey, Mabel, *Warne's Everyday Cookery*, London and New York: Frederick Warne, 1929.

Wright, Allison, *The Wright Cookery Book*, London: Gay and Hancock, 1911.

Yates, Lucy H., *Cooking for 2*, London: Country Life, 1930.

LIST OF ILLUSTRATIONS

Dimensions of artworks are given in centimetres and inches, height before width.

Illustrated chapter openers on pp. 22, 44, 94, 142, 220, 258 and 302 by Cressida Bell.

All works by Vanessa Bell © Estate of Vanessa Bell, courtesy-Henrietta Garnett, except where indicated by *.

All works by Duncan Grant © Estate of Duncan Grant. All rights reserved, DACS 2014, except where indicated by **.

All works by Frances Partridge © Frances Partridge. Reproduced by permission of the Estate of Frances Partridge, c/o Rogers, Coleridge & White Ltd, 20 Powis Mews, London W11 1JN.

p. 75 – Letter from Roger Fry to Duncan Grant, written on Omega Workshops headed paper, 1913–19. Tate, London 2014.

p. 77 – Omega Workshops invitation card, probably designed by Duncan Grant with lettering by Roger Fry, 1913. Watercolour on paper; 19 × 14 (7½ × 5½). Private Collection. Photo Peter Nahum at The Leicester Galleries/Bridgeman Art Library.

p. 78 – Menu card for the opening of the Omega Workshops, by either Duncan Grant or Vanessa Bell, 12 June 1913. © reserved, 2014. Tate, London 2014.

p. 81 – Vanessa Bell, *Summer Camp*, 1913. Oil on board; 78.7 × 83.8 (31 × 33). Collection Bryan Ferry.

p. 83 – Vanessa Bell, *Oranges and Lemons*, 1914. Oil on cardboard; 73 × 51.5 (28¾ × 5 1¼). Private Collection.

p. 85 – Virginia Stephen (later Woolf) and Clive Bell on the beach at Studland Bay, Dorset, by Vanessa Bell, 1910. Black and white negative. © Tate, London, 2014.*

p. 87 – Recipe for Meat Bobbity in Tamil. From *Friend in Need: English-Tamil Cookery Book*, Madras: Diocesan Press, 1938.

p. 89 – Vanessa Bell, *Virginia Woolf (née Stephen)*, 1912. Oil on board; 40 × 34 (15¾ × 13⅜). © National Portrait Gallery, London.*

p. 90 – Virginia Stephen's (later Woolf) handwritten instructions to Leonard Woolf about 'meals on trays' at 38 Brunswick Square, 2 December 1911. From the Monk's House Papers, University of Sussex Library (reference number: SxMs18/1/A/2/1). Letter reprinted in *The Flight of the Mind: The Letters of Virginia Woolf: Volume 1, 1888–1912*, edited by Nigel Nicolson and Joanne Trautmann, published by The Hogarth Press. Reprinted by permission of The Random House Group Limited. Letter from *The Letters of Virginia Woolf*, Volume I, edited by Nigel Nicolson and Joanne Trautmann. Letters © 1975 by Quentin Bell and Angelica Garnett. Reprinted by permission of Houghton Mifflin Harcourt Publishing Company. All rights reserved.

p. 95 – Vanessa Bell, *Leonard Sidney Woolf*, 1940. Oil on canvas; 81.3 × 64.8 (32 × 25½). © National Portrait Gallery, London.*

p. 96 – Recipe for Plain Suet Pudding from Helen Anrep's scrapbook. © 2014 The Estate of Helen Anrep. Reproduced with their kind permission. From the Anrep/Fry archive collection housed in Tate Archive, London (TGA 200611). Tate, London 2014.

p. 99 – Dora Carrington, *The Servant Girl*, from *Two Stories*, written and printed by Virginia and Leonard Woolf. London: Hogarth Press, 1917. Woodcut on paper. Victoria University, E. J. Pratt Library.

p. 103 – Vanessa Bell, *Still Life with Milk Jug and Eggs, Asheham*, 1917. Oil on board; 31.1 × 36.6 (12¼ × 14½). Courtesy Sotheby's Picture Library.

p. 104 – Dora Carrington, sketch of a dining table in a letter to Julia Strachey, February 1929. Whereabouts of original letter unknown, despite much research.

p. 105 – Garsington Manor, 2012. Photo Jans Ondaatje Rolls.

p. 106 – Lady Ottoline Morrell with friends, possibly by Philip Edward Morrell, 1916. Vintage snapshot print. National Portrait Gallery, London.

p. 109 – Mark Gertler, *Portrait of a Girl Wearing a Blue Jersey*, 1912. Tempera and gouache on board; 47.5 × 38.75 (18¾ × 38¼). Reproduced with permission of Luke Gertler. Image courtesy Piano Nobile (Robert Travers Works of Art Ltd).

p. 110 – Dora Carrington, sketch of Tidmarsh Mill in a letter to Lytton Strachey, 20 October 1917. Whereabouts of original letter unknown, despite much research.

p. 113 – Mark Gertler, *Still Life with Apples and a Mixing Bowl*, 1913. Oil on board; 39.5 × 29.5 (15⅝ × 11⅝). Reproduced with permission of Luke Gertler. Hatton Gallery, University of Newcastle Upon Tyne/Tyne and Wear Archives & Museums/ Bridgeman Art Library.

p. 114 – Dora Carrington, by unknown photographer, 1920s. Bromide snapshot print. National Portrait Gallery, London.

p. 116 (above) – Recipe for Hunter Chicken from Frances Partridge's recipe book. By kind permission of the Provost and Fellows of King's College, Cambridge. King's College Cambridge, FCP/8/4/3.

p. 116 (left) – Dora Carrington, sketch of Ralph Partridge shooting a pheasant in a letter to Poppet John, *c.* 1928. The British Library Board. MS Egerton 3867.

p. 118 – Mark Gertler, *Merry-Go-Round*, 1916. Oil on canvas; 189.2 × 142.2 (74½ ×56). Reproduced with permission of Luke Gertler. Photo Tate, London 2014.

p. 119 – Clive Bell and two farm workers at Garsington, by Lady Ottoline Morrell, 1917. Vintage snapshot print. National Portrait Gallery, London.

p. 121 – Dora Carrington, *Picking Vegetables*, 1912. Fresco panel at Ashridge House, Berkhamsted; 183 × 152 (72 × 59⅞). Photo permission of Ashridge Business School.

p. 122 – Duncan Grant, *Henry the Lurcher*, *c.* 1916–17. Window decoration, panel. Oil on board; 62 × 145 (24½ × 57). Photograph © Penelope Fewster. Courtesy the Charleston Trust.

p. 125 – Duncan Grant, *The Coffee Pot*, *c.* 1918. Oil on canvas; 61 × 50.8 (24 × 20). Image The Metropolitan Museum of Art/Art Resource/Scala, Florence.

p. 126 – Dora Carrington, honey label for David Garnett, 1917. Woodcut. Collection of Bannon and Barnabas McHenry. Image courtesy the Herbert F. Johnson Museum of Art, Cornell University.

p. 127 – The hearth in Clive Bell's study, Charleston. Photograph Alen MacWeeney.

p. 129 – Dora Carrington, *E. M. Forster*, 1920. Oil on canvas; 50.8 × 40.6 (20 × 16). National Portrait Gallery, London.

p. 130 – Duncan Grant, *Asheham, Still Life*, 1912. Oil on canvas; 54.2 × 78.7 (21½ × 31). The Collection of Craufurd and Nancy Goodwin. Photo The Bloomsbury Workshop.

p. 131 – Rachel Pearsall Conn 'Ray' Strachey (née Costelloe), *Barbara Bagenal (née Hiles)*, late 1920s or early 1930s. Oil on board; 48.3 × 30.5 (19 × 12). National Portrait Gallery, London.

p. 132 – Dora Carrington, sketch of Lytton Strachey in a soup bowl, in a letter to Strachey, December 1920. Whereabouts of original letter unknown, despite much research.

p. 133 – Dora Carrington, sketch of Lytton Strachey in bed receiving a letter from Dora, in a letter to Strachey, 7 November 1918. Whereabouts of original letter unknown, despite much research.

p. 135 – Roger Fry, *Clive Bell*, *c.* 1924. Oil on canvas; 73.4 × 60 (28⅞ × 23⅝). National Portrait Gallery, London.

p. 137 (left) – Vanessa Bell, *Nude*, from *Original Woodcuts by Various Artists*. London: Omega Workshops, printed by Richard Medley, 1918. Woodcut on paper; 18.5 × 10.9 (7¼ × 4¼). E. J. Pratt Library, Victoria University, Toronto.

p. 137 (right) – Roger Fry, *The Cup*, from *Original Woodcuts by Various Artists*. London: Omega Workshops, printed by Richard Medley, 1918. Woodcut on paper. E. J. Pratt Library, Victoria University, Toronto.

p. 139 – Duncan Grant, *The Blue China Plate*, 1949. Oil on canvas; 52 × 51 (20½ × 20⅛). Courtesy the Government Art Collection (UK).

p. 141 – Duncan Grant, *John Maynard Keynes*, 1908. Oil on canvas; 80 × 59.5 (31½ × 23½). By kind permission of the Provost and Fellows of King's College, Cambridge. King's College Cambridge, KCAR/3/5/15/1 P/109.

p. 143 – Duncan Grant, *Portrait of John Maynard Keynes*, 1917. Oil on canvas; 56.5 × 46.3 (22¼ × 18¼). Courtesy the Charleston Trust.

p. 145 – Olga and Picasso in his London workshop where he made the curtain for *Le Tricorne*, unknown photographer, 1919. © Succession Picasso/DACS, London 2014. Photo © RMN-Grand Palais/Droits réservés. Collection: Picasso Museum, Paris.

p. 146 – Duncan Grant, *Ballet Decoration*, unknown date. Oil on paper laid on board; 81 × 56 (31⅞ × 22). Whereabouts of original work unknown.

p. 149 – Dora Carrington, *Lytton Strachey Reading*, 1916. Oil on panel; 50.8 × 60.9 (20 × 24). National Portrait Gallery, London.

p. 150 – Vanessa Bell, *The Keynes-Keynes*, c. 1927. Oil, gouache and charcoal on paper laid down on board; 153 × 111 (60¼ × 43¾). Reproduced by the kind permission of the Master and Fellows of King's College, Cambridge. Image supplied by The Fitzwilliam Museum, Cambridge.

p. 153 – Vanessa Bell, *Snow at Tilton*, 1941. Oil on canvas; 36.5 × 29.2 (14⅜ × 11½). Arts Council Collection, Southbank Centre, London.

p. 155 – Vanessa Bell, *Lytton Strachey*, c. 1912. Oil on cardboard, 35.6 × 25.4 (14 × 10). Photo Anthony d'Offay, London.

p. 157 – Dora Carrington, *Eggs on a Table, Tidmarsh Mill*, c. 1924. Oil on board; 53.3 × 76.8 (21 × 30). Private Collection. Photo The Bloomsbury Workshop.

p. 159 – Dora Carrington, sketch of hens feeding, in a letter to Gerald Brenan, June 1922. Harry Ransom Center. The University of Texas at Austin.

p. 161 – Ralph Partridge, Dora Carrington, Lytton Strachey and Saxon Sydney-Turner having breakfast on the lawn at Ham Spray House, Wiltshire, by Frances Partridge, 1927. Photo Frances Partridge/Getty Images.

p. 163 – Dora Carrington, sketch of food and glass, in a letter to Lytton Strachey, 4 February 1917. Whereabouts of original letter unknown.

p. 164 – Dora Carrington, *Annie Stiles*, 1921. Oil on canvas; 51.4 × 41.3 (20¼ × 16¼). Private Collection. Photo Christie's Images/Bridgeman Art Library.

p. 165 – Christine Kühlenthal, *Dora Carrington Cooking*, c. 1915. Ink; 20.4 × 16.4 (8 × 6½). Private Collection. Reproduced by kind permission of the Estate of Christine Kühlenthal.

p. 167 – Dorelia McNeill (Dorelia John), by Charles F. Slade, 1909. Snapshot enlargement. © reserved; collection National Portrait Gallery, London.

p. 168 (left) – Henrietta Bingham and Stephen Tomlin, possibly by Dora Carrington, 1920s. Vintage snapshot print. National Portrait Gallery, London.

p. 168 (right) – Lytton Strachey and Ralph Partridge, probably by Dora Carrington, 1920. Vintage snapshot print. National Portrait Gallery, London.

p. 172 – Handwritten notes in French by Grace Germany. Reproduced by kind permission of John and Diana Higgens. The British Library Board. MS Add. 83247.

p. 173 – Vanessa Bell, *The Kitchen*, 1943. Oil on canvas; 87.3 × 119.5 (34⅜ × 47⅛). Courtesy the Charleston Trust.

p. 174 – Duncan Grant, *Still Life with Jug, Knife and Onion*, 1920. Watercolour; 43.18 × 58.42 (17 × 23). The Court Gallery, Somerset.

p. 175 – Vanessa Bell, linocut of a basket of fruit, 1950. 17 × 11 (6¾ × 4⅜). The Bloomsbury Workshop.

p. 177 – Vanessa Bell, *Tea Things*, 1919. Oil on board; 39 × 94.7 (15⅜ × 37¼). Private Collection. Photo Christie's Images/Bridgeman Art Library.

p. 179 – Virginia Woolf with Angelica Bell, by Ramsey & Muspratt, 1932. Bromide print. © Peter Lofts Photography/National Portrait Gallery, London.

p. 180 – Virginia Woolf's thank-you card to Grace Higgens, 1936. The Society of Authors as the Literary Representative of the Estate of Virginia Woolf. Reproduced by kind permission of John and Diana Higgens. The British Library Board. MS Add. 83198.

p. 181 – Duncan Grant, Quentin Bell and Angelica Bell bowling on the lawn. Monk's House, Sussex, unknown date. Gelatin silver print. Virginia Woolf Monk's House Photograph Album (MH-5), [MS Thr 562], Harvard Theatre Collection, Houghton Library, Harvard University, Cambridge (MA).

p. 183 (left) – Plan of the Hogarth Press sketched by Richard Kennedy, 1920s. The Estate of Olive M. M. Kennedy.

p. 183 (right) – The Hogarth Press colophon, designed by Vanessa Bell, 1925. E. J. Pratt Library, Victoria University, Toronto.

p. 185 – Vanessa Bell, *Interior with Housemaid*, 1939. Oil on canvas; 74 × 54 (29⅛ × 21¼). The Williamson Art Gallery & Museum, Birkenhead.

p. 189 – Photograph of Molly MacCarthy by Lady Ottoline Morrell, 1923. Vintage snapshot print. National Portrait Gallery, London.

p. 195 – Duncan Grant, *Still Life (Table with Fruit and Vegetables)*, 1930. Oil on canvas; 60.9 × 50.8 (24 × 20). Leeds Museums and Galleries (Leeds Art Gallery)/Bridgeman Art Library.

p. 198 – Jacket design by Vanessa Bell for *Mrs Dalloway* by Virginia Woolf. London: Hogarth Press, 1925. E. J. Pratt Library, Victoria University, Toronto.

p. 201 – Vanessa Bell, *Apples and Vinegar Bottle*, 1937. Oil on canvas; 37 × 44 (14⅝ × 17⅜). Private Collection. Photo The Bloomsbury Workshop.

p. 204 – Jacket design by Vanessa Bell for *To the Lighthouse* by Virginia Woolf. London: Hogarth Press, 1927. Victoria University, E. J. Pratt Library.

p. 206 – Vanessa Bell, *Door in the Spare Room, Charleston*, 1936; Oil on wood; 188 × 83 (74 × 32⅝). Photograph © Penelope Fewster. Courtesy the Charleston Trust.

p. 209 – Jacket design by Vanessa Bell for *A Room of One's Own* by Virginia Woolf. London: Hogarth Press, 1929. E. J. Pratt Library, Victoria University, Toronto.

p. 215 – Vanessa Bell, Leonard and Virginia Woolf and Singer car at Cassis, 1928. Black and white print. © Tate, London 2014.*

p. 277 – Vanessa Bell, *The Cook*, 1948. Oil on canvas; 100.3 × 74.7 (39½ × 29⅜). Arts Council Collection, Southbank Centre, London.

p. 278 – Green Room lawn, Glyndebourne, by Bill Brandt, 1936. © Bill Brandt Archive. Photo Glyndebourne Archive.

p. 279 – Roger Fry, *Omega Virginal*, 1917–18. Private Collection, on long-term loan to The Courtauld Gallery, London.

p. 281 – Vanessa Bell, *Angelica Bell, c.* 1930. Oil on canvas; 62.5 × 55 (24½ × 21⅝). Courtesy the Charleston Trust.

p. 284 – Julian and Vanessa Bell, by unknown photographer, 1909. Black and white print. © Tate, London 2014.

p. 286 – Virginia Woolf, by Lady Ottoline Morrell, *c.* 1917. Vintage snapshot print. National Portrait Gallery, London.

p. 287 – Virginia Woolf at Monk's House, 1931. Gelatin silver print. Virginia Woolf Monk's House Photograph Album (MH-3), [MS Thr 560], Harvard Theatre Collection, Houghton Library, Harvard University, Cambridge (MA).

p. 288 – Leonard Woolf and his dog Pinka in Monk's House garden, by unknown photographer, 1931. Frederic Spotts Collection of Papers on the Letters of Leonard Woolf, Mortimer Rare Book Room, Smith College, Northampton (MA).

p. 291 – Exterior view of a snow-covered Monk's House, Sussex, 1938. Gelatin silver print. Virginia Woolf Monk's House Photograph Album (MH-5), [MS Thr 562], Harvard Theatre Collection, Houghton Library, Harvard University, Cambridge (MA).

p. 292 – Virginia Woolf and Dame Ethel Smyth, by unknown photographer, unknown date. Gelatin silver print. Henry W. and Albert A. Berg Collection of English and American Literature, The New York Public Library, Astor, Lenox and Tilden Foundations.

p. 295 – 'Damon and Phyllis', a play by Angelica Bell performed in the walled garden at Charleston, by Vanessa Bell, 1935. Black and white negative. © Tate, London 2014.*

p. 299 – Heinkel He 111 bomber over London, 7 September 1940. Imperial War Museum (C 5422).

p. 301 – Roger Fry, *Virginia Woolf*, 1912. Oil on board; 40.2 × 31 (15⅞ × 12¼). On Loan to Leeds Museums and Galleries (City Art Gallery)/Bridgeman Art Library.

p. 303 – Duncan Grant, *Still Life with Carrots*, 1921. Oil on canvas; 50.8 × 68.6 (20 × 27). Tate, London 2014.

p. 305 – Duncan Grant, *Empty Champagne Bottle*, 1955. Oil on canvas; 75.3 × 60 (29⅝ × 24). Kirklees Collection, Huddersfield Art Gallery.

p. 306 – Leonard Woolf in the greenhouse, by unknown photographer, 1966. Frederic Spotts Collection of Papers on the Letters of Leonard Woolf, Mortimer Rare Book Room, Smith College, Northampton (MA).

p. 309 – Front cover of *Eminent Victorians* by Lytton Strachey, showing Simon Bussy, *Lytton Strachey*, 1904; pastel; 53.3 ×

43.2 (21 × 17 in). © reserved; collection National Portrait Gallery, London. © Lytton Strachey, 2002, *Eminent Victorians*, Continuum Publishers, an imprint of Bloomsbury Publishing Plc.

p. 311 – Recipe for Fruit Mousse from Frances Partridge's recipe book. By kind permission of the Provost and Fellows of King's College, Cambridge. King's College Cambridge, FCP/8/4/3.

p. 313 – Page from Molly MacCarthy's personal cookbook, 1952. Courtesy Mrs Michael MacCarthy and Desmond MacCarthy.

p. 315 – Duncan Grant, *Quentin Bell as a Boy*, 1919. Oil on board; 52.4 × 57 (20⅝ × 22½). Courtesy the Charleston Trust.

p. 317 – Quentin Bell and Anne Popham in Rome, by unknown photographer, 1951. Courtesy Anne Olivier Bell.

p. 319 – Duncan Grant, *Vanessa Bell (née Stephen)*, 1917. Oil on canvas; 127 × 102.2 (50 × 40¼). Photo National Portrait Gallery, London.

p. 320 – Duncan Grant, *The Kitchen*, 1902. Oil on canvas; 50.8 × 40.6 (20 × 16). Tate, London 2014.

p. 321 – Duncan Grant, portrait of Elizabeth Raper, unknown date. From *The Receipt Book of Elizabeth Raper. And a portion of her Cipher Journal. Edited by her great-grandson the late Bartle Grant with a portrait and decorations by Duncan Grant*, London: The Nonesuch Press, 1924.

p. 323 – Angelica Garnett, *The Hock Bottle*, 1958. Oil on canvas; 79.5 × 58.5 (31⅜ × 23). Courtesy the Charleston Trust.

p. 324 – Duncan Grant, *Vanessa Bell at David Garnett's house, Hilton Hall*, unknown date. Oil on canvas; 61.6 × 50.8 (24¼ × 20). Private Collection. Photo Christie's Images/Bridgeman Art Library.

p. 325 (left) – Virginia Nicholson, aged five, at Charleston, 1960. Courtesy Anne Olivier Bell.

p. 325 (right) – Vanessa Bell, *Julian Bell, the Artist's Grandson*, 1956. Gouache on paper mounted on hardboard; 47.7 × 36.2 (18½ × 14¼). Courtesy the Charleston Trust.

p. 327 – Vanessa Bell, *Henrietta Garnett, c.* 1955. Oil on canvas; 54.5 × 39 (21½ × 15⅜). Courtesy the Charleston Trust.

p. 331 – Vanessa Bell, *David Garnett*, 1915. Oil and gouache on cardboard; 76.4 × 52.6 (30⅛ × 20¾). © National Portrait Gallery, London.*

p. 332 – David Garnett, drawing of skewers with liver and onions, 24 October 1967. © The Estate of David Garnett.

p. 339 – Duncan Grant, *Helen Anrep in the Dining Room at Charleston, c.* 1945. Oil on canvas; 56.5 × 88 (22¼ × 34⅝). Courtesy the Charleston Trust.

p. 342 – Recipe for Cèps Montcuq, an unpublished recipe by David Garnett, from the cookery book of Angelica and David Garnett. © 2014 The David Garnett Estate and The Angelica Garnett Estate, courtesy Henrietta Garnett.

ACKNOWLEDGMENTS

I am very grateful to Frances Spalding, Michael Holroyd, Judith Mackrell, Alison Light, Miranda Seymour, Robert Skidelsky, Gretchen Gerzina, Anne Chisholm, Victoria Glendinning, S. P. Rosenbaum, Pamela Todd, Hermione Lee, Paul Levy, Richard Shone, Ronald Blythe, Robert Gathorne-Hardy, Hugh and Mirabel Cecil whose books helped me enormously with my initial research. I owe a huge debt of gratitude to Jamie Camplin who was enthusiastic about my book from the word 'go'; Andrew Robinson for his brilliant first edit; Jennie Condell for obtaining all text permissions and for incorporating all pre-proof manuscript revisions; Flora Spiegel and Karin Fremer who consolidated narrative with artwork and led me through final proof stage to completion; Lucy Macmillan for obtaining all picture permissions; and Tony Bradshaw whose introductions and assistance in locating 'lost' Bloomsbury artworks was a tremendous help. I am also extremely grateful to Johanna Neurath, Amanda Vinnicombe, Niki Medlik, Rachel Heley and the rest of the Thames & Hudson team who were unbelievably helpful at each stage of production. Very special thanks to Colin Mckenzie for that inspirational first cup of tea at Charleston in 2009, Anna Fewster for helping me source many original Bloomsbury recipes, Wendy Hitchmough for answering my endless list of questions and for checking my facts; Darren Clarke and the archivists at Charleston; Patricia McGuire, archivist at King's College, Cambridge; Adrian Glew at the Tate Archive; the archivists at the Hyman Kreitman Reading Rooms at Tate Britain; Sussex University Special Collections; the Archives and Manuscripts department at the British Library; DACS; the National Portrait Gallery; the Harry Ransom Centre; the British Library; the New York Public Library; the Virginia Woolf Society; Sarah Burton, Society of Authors; Annabel Cole; Save the Children; Pallant House Gallery; Jo Emery at Premier Foods; and Gill Coleridge at Rogers, Coleridge & White. I am grateful to Deborah Alun-Jones for her ongoing helpful advice, Caroline Rolls for her early editorial support, Jayne Walker for her translations and Barbara MacMillan for testing many of the recipes. I am also grateful to Michael Berry, Wendy Partridge, Nicolette Allen, Dr Kate Sealey Rahman, David Haycock, Mahtab Hussain, Sue Fox, Sarah Le Fort and Christopher Phipps for their assistance with photography, indexing and/or help with research enquiries. I am extremely fortunate for the significant input I received from Anne Olivier Bell, Virginia Nicholson, Henrietta Garnett, Cressida Bell, Sophie MacCarthy, Desmond MacCarthy, Mrs Michael MacCarthy, Olivia Isherwood, Benjamin Anrep, Diana Higgens and her late husband John Higgens and the late Angelica Garnett. Their editorial feedback, illustrations, personal recollections and private family recipes were generously contributed, shared and entrusted and for their assistance and support I am truly grateful. I owe an enormous debt of gratitude to my parents without whose inspiration and encouragement this book would never have been begun - or completed. I am also enormously grateful to Charlie, Sam, Alexa, George and Katie: this has been a long haul, sorry for my absences, thank you for your support, your patience, and for keeping me social. Finally, this book would not have been possible without the many inspirational diaries, letters, books and artworks that 'the Bloomsberries' themselves produced. I am indebted to them and thankful to everyone who gave their time, assistance and permission to use copyright material.

The author and publishers would like to thank all of the individuals and organizations who have kindly granted permission to reproduce copyright material.

Thanks to Anne Olivier Bell, Cressida Bell, Henrietta Garnett, Paul Levy, Virginia Nicholson, Desmond MacCarthy and Sophie MacCarthy, who have kindly granted permission to reproduce their recipes and quotations. © the authors.

Recipes from A. H. Adair, *Dinners Long and Short*, originally published by the Orion Publishing Group. All attempts at tracing the copyright holder have been unsuccessful.

Recipe by Boris Anrep from the Frances Partridge archive © 2014 The Estate of Boris Anrep. Reproduced with their kind permission.

Recipes from Helen Anrep's scrapbook © 2014 The Estate of Helen Anrep. Reproduced with their kind permission.

Recipes from *Food for My Daughter, Cubus Delectabilis* by Igor Anrep © 2014 The Estate of Igor Anrep. Reproduced with their kind permission.

Excerpts by Barbara Bagenal reproduced by kind permission of The Estate of Barbara Bagenal.

Excerpts by Clive Bell reproduced courtesy of The Society of Authors as the Literary Representative of the Estate of Clive Bell.

Excerpts by Julian Bell reproduced courtesy of The Society of Authors as the Literary Representative of the Estate of Julian Bell.

Excerpts by Quentin Bell reproduced courtesy of The Society of Authors as the Literary Representative of the Estate of Quentin Bell.

Excerpts from *Charleston: A Bloomsbury House and Garden* by Quentin Bell and Virginia Nicholson. © 1987 Frances Lincoln Ltd. Reproduced by permission of Frances Lincoln Ltd.

Excerpts by Vanessa Bell © The Vanessa Bell Estate, courtesy Henrietta Garnett.

Excerpts from *Sketches in Pen and Ink: A Bloomsbury Notebook* by Vanessa Bell, published by The Hogarth Press. Reprinted by permission of The Random House Group Limited.

Excerpts by Gerald Brenan reproduced courtesy of The Hanbury Agency.

Recipe from *Cambridge Cuisine* reproduced courtesy of Save the Children.

Excerpts from Hugh and Mirabel Cecil, *Clever Hearts*, reproduced courtesy of The Orion Publishing Group, London © 1990 by Hugh and Mirabel Cecil, and Sheil Land Associates Ltd.

Excerpt by René Crevel, *As Stable Pamphlets*, translated by Keith Waldrop, reproduced by kind permission of Elysium Books.

Excerpts from T. S. Eliot., *The Letters of T. S. Eliot* (ed. Valerie Eliot and Hugh Haughton): vol. 1: 1898–1922, London: Faber and Faber, 2009, and vol. 111: 1926–1927, London: Faber and Faber, 2012, reproduced courtesy of Faber and Faber. In the United States excerpts from *The Letters of T. S. Eliot* (ed. Valerie Eliot and Hugh Haughton): vol. 1: 1898–1922, New Haven: Yale University Press, 2009, and vol. 111: 1926–1927, New Haven: Yale University Press, 2012, reproduced courtesy of Yale University Press.

Excerpts by E. M. Forster reproduced courtesy of The Provost and Scholars of King's College, Cambridge and The Society of Authors as the E. M. Forster estate. In Canada: excerpt from *The Longest Journey* by E. M. Forster used by permission

Levy, © 2005 by The Strachey Trust. Reprinted by permission of Farrar, Straus and Giroux, LLC.

Worldwide, excluding the UK: recipe from *The Italian Cookbook* by Maria Luisa Taglienti, © 1955 by Maria Luisa Taglienti, renewed 1983 by Maria Luisa Taglienti and Random House LLC. Used by permission of Random House, an imprint of Random House Publishing Group, a division of Random House LLC. All rights reserved. All attempts at tracing the UK copyright holder have been unsuccessful.

Recipe by William J. Tarling, *Café Royal Cocktail Book*, reproduced by kind permission of the UK Bartenders' Guild.

Bloomsbury at Home by Pamela Todd, © 1999 by Pamela Todd. Used by permission of Harry N. Abrams, Inc., New York. All rights reserved.

Recipes from Wiveton Hall Café reproduced courtesy of Desmond MacCarthy.

Excerpts by Leonard Woolf reproduced courtesy of The University of Sussex and The Society of Authors as the Literary Representative of the Estate of Leonard Woolf.

Excerpts by Virginia Woolf reproduced courtesy of The Society of Authors as the Literary Representative of the Estate of Virginia Woolf.

Excerpts from *Moments of Being* by Virginia Woolf, published by Chatto & Windus. Reprinted by permission of The Random House Group Limited.

Excerpts from *The Letters of Virginia Woolf*, edited by Nigel Nicolson and Joanne Trautmann, published by The Hogarth Press. Reprinted by permission of The Random House Group Limited.

Excerpts from *The Diary of Virginia Woolf*, edited by Anne Olivier Bell, published by The Hogarth Press. Reprinted by permission of The Random House Group Limited.

Excerpts from *Congenial Spirits: The Selected Letters of Virginia Woolf*, edited by Nigel Nicolson and Joanne Trautmann, published by Chatto & Windus. Reprinted by permission of The Random House Group Limited.

In the United States:

Excerpts from *Orlando: A Biography* by Virginia Woolf. © 1928 by Houghton Mifflin Harcourt Publishing Company. © renewed 1956 by Leonard Woolf. Reprinted by permission of Houghton Mifflin Harcourt Publishing Company. All rights reserved.

Excerpts from *The Waves* by Virginia Woolf. © 1931 by Houghton Mifflin Harcourt Publishing Company. © renewed 1959 by Leonard Woolf. Reprinted by permission of Houghton Mifflin Harcourt Publishing Company. All rights reserved.

Excerpts from *Flush: A Biography* by Virginia Woolf. © 1933 by Houghton Mifflin Harcourt Publishing Company. © renewed 1961 by Leonard Woolf. Reprinted by permission of Houghton Mifflin Harcourt Publishing Company. All rights reserved.

Excerpts from *Roger Fry: A Biography* by Virginia Woolf. © 1940 by Houghton Mifflin Harcourt Publishing Company. © renewed 1968 by Leonard Woolf. Reprinted by permission of Houghton Mifflin Harcourt Publishing Company. All rights reserved.

Excerpts from *Mrs Dalloway* by Virginia Woolf. © 1925 by Houghton Mifflin Harcourt Publishing Company. © renewed 1953 by Leonard Woolf. Reprinted by permission of Houghton Mifflin Harcourt Publishing Company. All rights reserved.

Excerpts from *Congenial Spirits: The Selected Letters of Virginia Woolf*. © 1989 by Quentin Bell and Angelica Garnett. Reprinted by permission of Houghton Mifflin Harcourt Publishing Company. All rights reserved.

Excerpts from *A Writer's Diary* by Virginia Woolf. © 1954 by Leonard Woolf. © Renewed 1982 by Quentin Bell and Angelica Garnett. Reprinted by permission of Houghton Mifflin Harcourt Publishing Company. All rights reserved.

Excerpt from 'Mr. Bennett and Mrs. Brown' from *The Captain's Death Bed and Other Essays* by Virginia Woolf. © 1950, renewed 1978 by Houghton Mifflin Harcourt Publishing Company. Reprinted by permission of Houghton Mifflin Harcourt Publishing Company. All rights reserved.

Excerpts from *The Diary of Virginia Woolf*, Volume II, edited by Anne Olivier Bell. Diary © 1978 by Quentin Bell and Angelica Garnett. Reprinted by permission of Houghton Mifflin Harcourt Publishing Company. All rights reserved.

Excerpts from *The Common Reader* by Virginia Woolf. 1925 by Houghton Mifflin Harcourt Publishing Company. © renewed 1953 by Leonard Woolf. Reprinted by permission of Houghton Mifflin Harcourt Publishing Company. All rights reserved.

Excerpts from *The Voyage Out* by Virginia Woolf. © 1920 by Houghton Mifflin Harcourt Publishing Company, renewed 1948 by Leonard Woolf. Reprinted by permission of Houghton Mifflin Harcourt Publishing Company. All rights reserved.

Excerpts from *The Letters of Virginia Woolf*, Volume I, edited by Nigel Nicolson and Joanne Trautmann. Letters © 1975 by Quentin Bell and Angelica Garnett. Reprinted by permission of Houghton Mifflin Harcourt Publishing Company. All rights reserved.

Excerpts from *The Letters of Virginia Woolf*, Volume II, edited by Nigel Nicolson and Joanne Trautmann. Letters © 1976 by Quentin Bell and Angelica Garnett. Reprinted by permission of Houghton Mifflin Harcourt Publishing Company. All rights reserved.

Excerpts from *The Letters of Virginia Woolf*, Volume III, edited by Nigel Nicolson and Joanne Trautmann. Letters © 1977 by Quentin Bell and Angelica Garnett. Reprinted by permission of Houghton Mifflin Harcourt Publishing Company. All rights reserved.

Excerpts from *The Letters of Virginia Woolf*, Volume IV, edited by Nigel Nicolson and Joanne Trautmann. Letters © 1980 by Quentin Bell and Angelica Garnett. Reprinted by permission of Houghton Mifflin Harcourt Publishing Company. All rights reserved.

Excerpts from *Moments of Being* by Virginia Woolf. © 1985, 1976 by Quentin Bell and Angelica Garnett. Reprinted by permission of Houghton Mifflin Harcourt Publishing Company. All rights reserved.

Excerpts from *Jacob's Room* by Virginia Woolf. © 1922 by Houghton Mifflin Harcourt Publishing Company. © renewed 1950 by Leonard Woolf. Reprinted by permission of Houghton Mifflin Harcourt Publishing Company. All rights reserved.

Excerpts from *To the Lighthouse* by Virginia Woolf. © 1927 by Houghton Mifflin Harcourt Publishing Company. © renewed 1954 by Leonard Woolf. Reprinted by permission of Houghton Mifflin Harcourt Publishing Company. All rights reserved.

Excerpts from *A Room of One's Own* by Virginia Woolf. © 1929 by Houghton Mifflin Harcourt Publishing Company. © renewed 1957 by Leonard Woolf. Reprinted by permission of Houghton Mifflin Harcourt Publishing Company. All rights reserved.

Extracts from Lucy Yates, *Cooking for 2*, reproduced courtesy of Country Life.

INDEX OF RECIPES

INDEX